ILLUSTRATED HISTORY
OF THE
NEW YORK GIANTS

Richard Whittingham

TRIUMPH
B O O K S
CHICAGO

Library of Congress Control Number: 2005927669

This book is available in quantity at special discounts for your group or organization. For further information,
contact:

Triumph Books
542 South Dearborn Street
Suite 750
Chicago, Illinois 60605
(312) 939-3330
Fax (312) 663-3557

Printed in U.S.A.
ISBN-13: 978-1-57243-641-1
ISBN-10: 1-57243-641-7
Design by Jill Donovan, Wagner/Donovan Design

Photos for *Illustrated History of the New York Giants* are from the author's collection, used with permission,
except where indicated otherwise.

CONTENTS

FOREWORD

My earliest recollection of the Giants was on a Sunday morning in the autumn of 1925; I was about nine years old. We were coming out of mass, and I remember my father saying to one of his friends, "I'm gonna try to put pro football over in New York today." Then I recall going to the game. I don't think my father had ever seen a football game before.

During the game—and I've told the story many times—we were sitting on the Giants' side of the field, and it was a little chilly. My mother complained to my father that we were sitting in the shade. Why couldn't we go over and sit in the sun where we'd be nice and warm? So, the next game, and from then on, the Giants' sideline in the Polo Grounds was in the sun.

Another thing I remember from those first days was that I wanted to sit on the bench, and I got to. I remember our coach, Bob Folwell, a former Navy coach, turning to one of the players on the bench—his name was Paul Jappe—and saying, "Jappe, get in there and give 'em hell!" I thought, boy, this is really a rough game.

My father came to own the Giants in a kind of roundabout way. He was a bookmaker in New York, and he was very friendly with Billy Gibson, who was the manager of Gene Tunney, the boxer. My father had actually been instrumental in Tunney's early career. He also had been very friendly from boyhood with Al Smith, and

through him with the political organization in New York City and New York state, and boxing at that time was very politically oriented. My father helped Tunney to get some fights that he otherwise might not have been able to get.

Billy Gibson came into my father's office one day and brought with him a gentleman named Harry A. March, who was a retired army doctor. Dr. March had been interested in pro football and its origins out in Ohio—the Canton area. There had not been a pro football team in New York before that time, although I've heard that Jimmy Jemail, a columnist back then for the *New York Daily News*—he wrote "The Inquiring Reporter"—claimed that he had a team in New York in 1924 and that my father took over that franchise.

From what I heard later, there was talk about buying an NFL franchise. I heard that my father simply said, "How much will it cost?" and that was it. There are two versions of the answer to that question: one was that it was $500, the other that it was $2,500. I know my father did say something to the effect that an empty store in New York City was worth that, whichever figure it was, and that's how he got into pro football.

Pro football in New York was very unsuccessful at first. My father's friends all told him that he was foolish to stay with it. I remember Governor Al Smith in our house one day after the team had just lost rather badly to Green Bay. Al Smith said to my father, "Your team will never amount to anything. Why don't you give it up?" My father looked at Jack and me and said, "The boys would run me right out of the house if I did."

Money was very tight in the thirties. However, according to my father, compared to other areas of the entertainment business, sports somewhat prospered during the Depression because they really offered the best entertainment for the money. A football game or a baseball game was great entertainment, and a man could afford to bring his whole family. Still, the Giants were just barely breaking even in the midthirties.

Of course, football was a very different game back then. I recall the days when you didn't have hash marks at all, and a little later when you did, but to get the ball placed on one of them you actually had to go out of bounds. If you were tackled one yard from the sideline, that was where the ball was put in play. I remember teams having special plays for that. Along those lines, I remember Tony Plansky, a tailback from Georgetown, who had been a great decathlon athlete, drop-kicking a field goal for us from around the 40-yard line that won a game. The thing was, however, that he was way over to the left side of the field. He was ambidextrous and kicked it with his left foot, where ordinarily he did his kicking right-footed.

It was also a one-platoon game then. As Steve Owen used to say, men were men in those days. He was our great coach for so many years, and he saw a lot of truly sturdy, talented 60-minute men who played for and against us. Stamina played a big role in those days, and the players had to pace themselves. They couldn't go all out on every play—you just couldn't do that for 60 minutes of football-playing time. The players against you were under the same handicap, but it still was grueling.

The war came along and took the great majority of the athletes out of the NFL. It threatened to close down pro football altogether. George Halas was going back into the navy, and since he was going to be gone from football, he kind of led a drive to cancel the season, call the whole thing off. George Marshall, owner of the Redskins, Bert Bell, owner of the Steelers, and my father crusaded to keep it going at any cost, even if we had to play 4-Fs

and high school players, which we in fact did. It may very well be that playing under those circumstances helped to save the NFL, because when the war was over Arch Ward started the All-America Football Conference. It started at a terrible disadvantage because we were already established. I think if we had suspended operations for three or four years and then tried to start it up again, the AAFC would have started on more equal terms with us, and the league might be a very different one from what it is today.

The game changed considerably after the war. The offenses became more sophisticated, there was a lot more passing, and the players were getting bigger and faster all the time.

We had some of our most noteworthy and memorable teams in the fifties and early sixties. Jim Lee Howell, our head coach for much of that time, had the best pair of assistants ever under one roof: Vince Lombardi handling the offense and Tom Landry the defense. With Charlie Conerly and later Y. A. Tittle quarterbacking, backs like Frank Gifford and Alex Webster, and pass catchers of the caliber of Kyle Rote and Del Shofner, we provided a lot of exciting offense. And the defense! It was simply one of the best of all time: Andy Robustelli, Sam Huff, Rosey Grier, Em Tunnell, Dick Modzelewski, Jim Katcavage, Dick Lynch, Jimmy Patton, and others.

Certainly the game was less rewarding financially in those early days. Most of the players and coaches had to get other jobs to survive. Vince Lombardi had an off-season job with a bank when he was with us in the late fifties. The game was still great fun, though, and the men who played it were very memorable.

Nothing, however, has been more gratifying than watching the Giants of 1986 march through the season and the playoffs to the Super Bowl and triumph there in the Rose Bowl Stadium [39–20 over Denver], and the Giants of 1990 repeating this victory down in Tampa [20–19 over Buffalo], giving us two world championships in five years.

We've been around for quite some time now, and many great players have come and gone. They've given us a wonderful store of memories. They really were Giants, in all senses of the word.

—Wellington Mara

ILLUSTRATED HISTORY
OF THE
NEW YORK GIANTS

Tim Mara, a New York book-maker and renowned man about Manhattan, bought an NFL franchise for his hometown for $500. Some claim the team went for $2,500. Whatever the figure, he launched the Giants in 1925, saw them through the tough times, and passed the team ownership on to the able hands of his two sons, Jack and Wellington. He was honored in 1963 as one of 17 charter members of the Pro Football Hall of Fame.

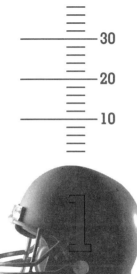

"I'M GONNA TRY TO PUT PRO FOOTBALL OVER IN NEW YORK TODAY"

It was Sunday morning in New York, a clear, sunny October day in 1925. Mass was just letting out at Our Lady of Esperanza Roman Catholic Church up on 156th Street, between Broadway and Riverside Drive. Among the congregation milling about on the sidewalk was a tall, handsome Irishman named Timothy J. Mara. He stood there with his wife and one of his two sons, nine-year-old Wellington, and talked with a friend. The boy listened idly to the conversation, but looked up suddenly and curiously when he heard his father say to the man, "I'm gonna try to put pro football over in New York today."

And indeed he was. That afternoon the newly enfranchised New York Giants of the National Football League were to take on the Frankford Yellow Jackets at the Polo Grounds in their very first home game. Tim Mara, a 38-year-old bookmaker (a legal occupation in those days), was to unveil the team he owned and launch what was to become a football institution in New York. Wellington and his older brother Jack would be there on the sideline to begin a lifelong association with the club.

Tim Mara was successful in business and a colorful promoter, who could claim among his closer friends Governor Al Smith of New York and at that time the soon-to-be mayor of New York City, Jimmy Walker. Another associate of Mara's was Billy Gibson, who managed boxer Gene Tunney, among other interests. As the story goes, Mara wanted to invest in Tunney, but on the day of the meeting to discuss that particular deal, Gibson was sidetracked by another potential investment. Harry March, a retired army doctor from Ohio who wanted to see an NFL franchise opened in New York, and Joe Carr, the league commissioner, were trying to entice Gibson into putting up the money to found a team. Gibson, who had been burned before in an attempt to bring pro football to the city, was apprehensive. Into the midst of the discussion appeared Mara, which prompted Gibson to suggest that perhaps the franchise would be better off in the bookmaker's hands. Mara asked, "How much will the franchise cost?" Some say the price tag was $500, others that it was $2,500, and no one really knows for certain. Mara knew it was a risky venture, but that kind of thing had never fazed him before. So he took the chance, and the Giants football team became a reality in New York City.

Dr. March, with the title of club secretary, quickly assumed the duties of putting the team together. Mara came up with the approximately $25,000 necessary to provide players, a coach, a stadium lease, equipment, transportation, and other sundry business expenses. First to be hired was Bob Folwell as

Dr. Harry March, a retired army doctor and erstwhile advocate of "postgraduate football," as he called the pro game in 1925, was instrumental in convincing Tim Mara of the efficacy of bringing the sport to New York City. After Mara bought the franchise, March was appointed secretary and contributed much to the development of the team and the organization, eventually succeeding to the club presidency.

head coach. Folwell had been a college coach for a number of years, most recently at Navy. Together March and Folwell set about building a team.

Mara knew that for the venture to succeed in New York, the team had to be a good one and the players had to be at least fairly well known. So he and March decided to try to sign the biggest football name around, Jim Thorpe, who the year before had played for the Rock Island (Illinois) Independents.

He would not be difficult to sign, Mara told March, because there was a kind of mutual disenchantment between the new coach at Rock Island and Thorpe, who was considered elderly for football and was a reputed imbiber. March got in touch with Thorpe and asked him to come to New York to talk over the possibility of playing for the new franchise. Thorpe was delighted at the prospect of coming to New York, and in Mara's office in Manhattan, he quickly came to terms with the club.

The only problem was that Thorpe was 37 years old and not in very good shape, but Mara wanted him for his presence on the team, not necessarily for his performance. He was signed to a unique contract in pro football history: Thorpe was to be paid $200 "per half game" because it was clear he would not be able to go a full 60 minutes.

At the same time, the Giants lined up some first-rate talent that was both young and in good condition. Century Milstead had been a consensus All-American tackle at Yale in 1923. The 5'10", 165-pound tailback Henry "Hinkey" Haines from Penn State and fullback Jack McBride of Syracuse were considered

Before the 1925 regular season got under way up in Providence, Rhode Island, this was the projected starting lineup, pictured here at the Polo Grounds. Top row, left to right: the backfield—wingback Oscar "Dutch" Hendrian, tailback Hinkey Haines, halfback Jim Thorpe, fullback Jack McBride. Bottom row, left to right: the line—end Lynn Bomar, tackle Century Milstead, tackle Ed McGinley, center Doc Alexander, guard Joe Williams, guard Art Carney, end Paul Jappe. There were some changes by the time the team debuted in New York City, and the fabled Thorpe only made it through three games with the Giants.

to be two of the best backs coming from the college ranks. Joe Alexander, who was also a physician and called "Doc" by his fellow players, had been an All-American guard at Syracuse in 1918 and 1919, then played several years in the pros with the Rochester Jeffersons, signed on to play center for the Giants.

Life in the six-year-old NFL in 1925 was obviously quite different from what it is today. An average player earned somewhere between $50 and $150 per game, the bigger name stars perhaps as much as $400 per game. They all worked at regular jobs during the week; therefore practices had to be scheduled after ordinary working hours. The top price for a ticket at the Polo Grounds that year was $2.75, the cheapest seat in the stadium a mere half-dollar. The NFL itself claimed 20 franchises in 1925, with teams from such towns as Pottsville, Pennsylvania; Canton, Ohio; Hammond, Indiana; and Duluth, Minnesota. And one team, the Milwaukee Badgers, was fined $500 for using four high school players in a game against the Chicago Bears.

The brand-new New York Giants made their debut in early October at their only preseason game, a match staged in New Britain, Connecticut, with a team known as Ducky Pond's All-Stars, which was not a member of the NFL. (Pond had been a standout on the Yale teams of 1922–1924, but he never played in the NFL. He would, however, return to his alma mater as head coach from 1934 through 1940.) To get the franchise off on the proverbial right foot, the Giants demolished Ducky Pond's All-Stars that afternoon, 26–0.

The regular-season schedule called for the Giants to play two road games then to host nine straight games at the Polo Grounds. The first was against the Providence Steam Roller up in Rhode Island, another newcomer to the NFL that year. The Giants flopped in their regular-season football debut, losing 14–0. Six days later the Giants appeared in Philadelphia to take on the Frankford Yellow Jackets, a team led on the field and coached by Berlin "Guy" Chamberlain, one of the greatest of the early players. Frankford won that one, 5–3, the winning margin coming from a safety.

That game was held on a Saturday. Afterward both teams entrained for New York to meet again the next day at the Polo Grounds. Mara brought his wife and two sons to the stadium for the next game, joining about twenty-five thousand other fans for the home opener. Jack Mara, who was 17 at the time, got to sit on the sideline; Wellington, eight years younger, sat with his mother in the stands but managed to talk his way into a seat on the bench just before the second half got under way.

Perhaps Tim Mara hadn't prayed hard enough that morning in church, or maybe the Giants were a little nervous on their formal introduction to New York; whatever the reason, they lost, 14–0, and garnered a record of 0–3. Jim Thorpe, slowed by age and an injured knee, was ineffective. He did not play a full half but still collected his $200. It was his last game as a New York Giant. He was released by Mara, whereupon he returned to Rock Island to finish out the season with the Independents, who decided they still wanted him despite his condition. After that, the Giants pulled together, especially the defense, and treated New Yorkers to four straight shutouts: 19–0 over the Cleveland Bulldogs, 7–0 over the Buffalo Bisons, 19–0 over the

Henry "Hinkey" Haines, a 5'10", 165-pound tailback from Penn State, proved to be one of the best rookies the Giants acquired during their maiden season and was a mainstay in the backfield through the 1928 season.

Columbus Tigers, and 13–0 over the Rochester Jeffersons. Three more wins over the Providence Steam Roller, Kansas City Cowboys, and the Dayton Triangles brought the Giants' record to 7–3–0.

The Giants had become successful on the field, but they were not as successful at the gate—at least in terms of those who actually paid to get into the Polo Grounds. The home opener had been a big draw, but more than half of the twenty-five thousand spectators had been admitted free of charge.

By the time the Chicago Bears came out to New York in early December, the Giants were deep in debt—estimated at about $40,000—and Mara's friends and colleagues, almost to a man, urged him to forget altogether what they felt was the ill-fated business of professional football. Wellington Mara remembered one evening at the Mara home around that time when Governor Al Smith, a frequent visitor, said to Tim Mara, "Pro football will never amount to anything. Why don't you give it up?" Mara paused for a moment, looked at his two sons, and said, "The boys would run me right out of the house if I did."

Financial resurrection was at hand, however. The Chicago Bears were

THE FIRST CAPTAIN

Bob Nash, born in Ireland and raised in New Jersey, has the distinction of being the first captain of the New York Giants. He was 33 years old in 1925, a sometime end and sometime tackle who had played with the famous black athlete and singer Paul Robeson during their college days. Nash then went on to play with pro teams in Massillon and Akron, Ohio, and Buffalo, New York, before joining the newly enfranchised Giants.

Nash also has the distinction of being the first NFL player involved in a transaction. The Akron Pros sold him for $300 (or $500, depending on who tells the story) to the Buffalo All-Americans. He played with the Giants that charter year and then retired from the game, but was brought back as an honored guest, at the age of 84, to the opening of Giants Stadium in the New Jersey Meadowlands in 1976.

GOING TO GET GRANGE

In the second half of the season, Tim Mara was all too aware that he was doling out much more money than the Giants were bringing in. He felt he had to do something to get paying customers into the Polo Grounds, and he had an idea.

Mara told Dr. Harry March that he was going out to Illinois to sign up the most dazzling star ever to hit college football, Harold "Red" Grange. The great breakaway back who could lure sixty- to seventy thousand fans into college stadiums to see him run with a football was about to play his last college game. Mara's plan was to sign him and get him into a Giants uniform to play against the Chicago Bears at the Polo Grounds. It would save the franchise, Mara told March. Mara then promptly reserved a drawing room aboard the 20th Century Limited.

Wellington Mara remembers that everyone was very excited about the prospect, and after a few days, the family received a telegram:

> **Partially successful STOP**
> **Returning on train tomorrow**
> **STOP**
> **Will explain STOP**
> **Tim Mara**

"We couldn't figure out what 'partially successful' meant," Wellington Mara later explained. They found out on his father's return. "He'll be playing in the Giants-Bears game here," the elder Mara told them, "only he'll be playing for the Bears."

George Halas and "Dutch Sternaman," co-owners of the Chicago Bears, had been dealing with Grange's manager, C. C. Pyle, and had struck an incredible deal to get Grange. Pyle would arrange two postseason tours of the United States, 17 games in all. The tour would take the Bears from New York to Florida to California, with Grange and Pyle splitting profits 50/50 with the Bears. It was a deal that would bring Grange and Pyle approximately $250,000 in gate receipts alone, and one that was impossible for Mara to compete with. Still, Mara had been "partially successful" in getting Red Grange to play at the Polo Grounds in 1925.

on the way to New York with their most recent acquisition, Red Grange—already a fabled football star. Grange had played his last college game the Saturday before Thanksgiving, and his first pro game had been on Thanksgiving Day. The East Coast had been deprived of watching the fabulous halfback zig and zag his way through three years of the best of college defenses. Mara was now hosting the game that would finally allow Easterners the chance to experience the phenomenon.

The Galloping Ghost, as Grange had been dubbed by famed sportswriter Grantland Rice, was still technically a senior in college, but he was as well-known a sports figure in 1925 as Babe Ruth, Jack Dempsey, Bobby Jones, and Bill Tilden. At Illinois, where he had won All-American honors three years in a row, he became the most dazzling runner the game of football had yet seen. His finest day had been against Fielding Yost's top-ranked Michigan team in 1924, when he scored four touchdowns in the first 12 minutes of the game (a 95-yard kickoff return and runs of 67, 55, and 44 yards). He ran for another touchdown later in the game, then passed for still another as he led his team to an upset 39–14 victory over the Wolverines.

The game between the Giants and the Bears was scheduled for December 6, a propitious time because it was the week after the Army-Navy game at the Polo Grounds—always a major attraction. Thousands of extra seats were still in place from that spectacle. Mara, with the help of two employees, manned the ticket

Red Grange, the "Galloping Ghost," on the bench next to Chicago Bears future Hall of Fame center George Trafton, awaits his turn as a pro. Right: out of uniform, resplendent in the style of the twenties, the redheaded Grange poses with his agent, entrepreneur extraordinaire C. C. "Cash and Carry" Pyle. Sought desperately by Tim Mara, Grange played in New York as a visiting Chicago Bear instead of as a Giant, but saved the Giants franchise by attracting more than seventy thousand people to the Polo Grounds to watch him gallop.

Memorabilia from the game that saved the New York franchise: the Giants versus the Chicago Bears and Red Grange, December 6, 1925.

Red Grange was still the feature when the Giants came to Chicago seeking revenge for the 19–7 defeat they suffered at the hands of the Galloping Ghost and his teammates the week prior at the Polo Grounds. They got it, with a 9–0 victory, to end their first season in the NFL.

office in the Knickerbocker Building. And New York responded. By game time more than seventy thousand tickets had been sold and more than one hundred press credentials issued. In the press box were such sportswriting luminaries of the day as Damon Runyon, Rice, Paul Gallico, and Westbrook Pegler.

Runyon later observed, "Seventy thousand men, women, and children were in the stands, blocking the aisles and runways. Twenty thousand more were perched on Coogan's Bluff and the roofs of apartment houses, content with just an occasional glimpse of the whirling mass of players on the field far below and wondering which was Red Grange." Actually *more* than seventy thousand squeezed and squashed their way into the sixty-five thousand–seat capacity Polo Grounds that afternoon, at the time by far the largest crowd ever to attend a professional football game.

All eyes were on Grange after the game began, including those of the Giants defense, who were keying on him. This turned out to be unfortunate because it enabled the Bears' diminutive quarterback, Joey Sternaman, to pull off what had become his favorite play: a fake handoff with Grange going around one end and then a Sternaman bootleg around the other. By the end of the first quarter, "Little" Joey, as he was affectionately known, had scored two touchdowns, and the Bears had a 12–0 lead.

PROFITABLE DAY

Paul Vidmer, writing for *The New York Times,* had this boxed introduction to his article reporting the debut of the Chicago Bears and Red Grange at the Polo Grounds, December 6, 1925:

How Grange Earned $30,000

- played all of one quarter and parts of two others
- gained 53 yards on 11 plays from scrimmage
- ran back two kicks for a total of 12 yards
- threw three forward passes, two of which were completed for a total gain of 32 yards
- received one forward pass for a gain of 23 yards
- intercepted one forward pass and ran 35 yards for a touchdown

The Giants came back in the second quarter with a concerted drive. A touchdown came on a 3-yard plunge by fullback Phil White. The score remained 12–7 well into the fourth quarter, when the Giants decided to take a very risky gamble. With third down and eight yards to go for a first down, deep in their own territory the Giants lined up in punt formation. But it was a fake, and the Giants' kicker tossed a pass to Jack McBride, who was racing along the side-line, only to have Red Grange step in front of him, pick it off, then do what everyone had come to see him do. He raced with it 35 yards, away from pursuing Giants, to add another touchdown for the Bears.

That was the extent of the scoring that historic afternoon in New York: the final score was the Bears 19, the Giants 7. When the tally from the gate was figured, word was that Grange's share alone was $30,000. For the Giants, not only was Mara's $40,000 deficit wiped out, but at season's end he showed a profit of approximately $18,000.

The Giants played the Bears one more time that year, one week later at Cubs Park in Chicago. The game was tacked on to the schedule because of the Grange/Bears barnstorming tour that had been hastily devised to showcase Grange after he turned pro. During that seven-day span, the Bears and Red Grange played exhibition games in Washington, D.C., Providence, Pittsburgh, and Detroit. In fact when they took the field against the Giants that day in Chicago, the Bears had played seven games in 11 days. It was not surprising that the bedraggled and battered Bears fell victim to the New Yorkers, 9–0, that frigid December day. A touchdown from White and a field goal booted by McBride was all that was needed, and the Giants' first season was over with a respectable record of 8–4–0 and a standing of fourth place in the 20-team National Football League.

Red Grange, with his accompanying flood of publicity and his fan following, had done for the Giants, and professional football in general for that matter, just what Mara thought he would. Mara's only regret was that the redhead was not doing it as a Giant.

Where it all began: the Polo Grounds, on the banks of the Harlem River, just beneath Coogan's Bluff. The first Giants home game was played there in early autumn 1925, but the New Yorkers stumbled in their debut and fell to the Frankford Yellow Jackets, 14–0. Jim Thorpe made a fleeting appearance that opening day; Red Grange came later in the year in a Bears uniform to help to fill the stadium and save the franchise. Tim Mara and his sons, Jack and Wellington, were steady dwellers on the sideline. During the 31 years that the Giants claimed the Polo Grounds as their home field, they won three national championships and nine division titles. The last game that the Giants played there was near the end of the 1955 season, a 35–35 tie with the Cleveland Browns.

PRICE **15** CENTS

N. Y. FOOTBALL GIANTS
(National Football League)
VS.
PHILADELPHIA QUAKERS
(American Football League)

Captain JACK McBRIDE
Fullback
New York Football Giants

Sunday
December 12, 1926

Polo Grounds
New York

Fullback Jack McBride, the Giants' second captain and program cover boy in 1926. An alumnus of Syracuse, he was a premier running back for New York during the first four years of the club's existence. After one year with Providence and a three-year sojourn with the Brooklyn Dodgers, he returned to round out his career with the Giants from 1932 through 1934.

HANGING IN THERE

The appearance of Red Grange in a football uniform in New York City, so delightfully redemptive for the Giants in 1925, took on a totally different aspect in 1926. Instead of drawing masses into the Polo Grounds to nourish Tim Mara's pleasure and bank account, the spectral Grange was across the Harlem River enticing potential paying customers of the Giants into Yankee Stadium to watch him perform in the brand-new uniform of the New York Yankees football franchise.

C. C. Pyle, Red Grange's agent and the organizer of the Bears-Grange barnstorming tour the year before, and the co-owners of the Chicago Bears were unable to come to terms on a contract for the 1926 season. Pyle's demand of a third of the ownership of the ballclub was quite a bit more than George Halas and Dutch Sternaman were willing to part with—even for Grange's magisterial presence. So "Cash and Carry" Pyle, as the entrepreneur was known, went to NFL president Joe Carr to formally request a franchise of his own in New York City, where he had already secured a deal to play in Yankee Stadium.

The idea of a competing franchise not a lot farther than a Hail Mary pass away from the Polo Grounds, one showcasing the nation's best-known football player, obviously had little appeal to Mara. Knowing how difficult it was to get people to pay their way into the Polo Grounds on a Sunday afternoon *without* competition, Mara, along with Dr. Harry March, went to the now-annual NFL owners meeting determined to block Pyle's incursion into New York. Pyle went too. The Giants owner pleaded his case as convincingly as Clarence Darrow might have, with the result that the other owners sided with him and voted against granting Pyle a franchise.

Undeterred, Pyle said fine—he would take Grange and launch another league to compete with the entire NFL. The New York City franchise would be his, it would feature Grange, and it would play in Yankee Stadium. Wizard of a promoter that he was, Pyle did indeed organize the first American Football League with franchises in nine cities and an impressive array of players who were lured out of the NFL.

Not only were the Yankees and Grange going to play over in the Bronx, the AFL set up franchises in Brooklyn and Newark as well. Meanwhile the NFL sanctioned still another team, the Brooklyn Lions, who would play at Ebbets Field. Among the changes, the Giants lost their best lineman, Century Milstead, and their coach, Bob Folwell, to the new league.

The Giants passed Folwell's head coaching duties to Joe "Doc" Alexander and acquired a 5'10", 225-pound tackle named Steve Owen, who the year before had played for the Kansas City Cowboys and the Cleveland Bulldogs. The acquisition launched Owen's Giants career as a player, and later as a coach, which would last through the 1953 season. They also added two fine rookie backs: Jack Hagerty of Georgetown and Walt Koppisch from Columbia.

With Hinkey Haines and Jack McBride still leading the attack, the Giants won their first two games, breezing by the Hartford Blues and having to fight the Providence Steam Roller a little harder. But then the Giants took the train to Chicago to face the powerful Bears, now without Grange but led by the best tailback in the game, triple-threat John "Paddy" Driscoll. The ensuing 7–0 loss in the Windy City was the Giants' first of the season and was followed ignominiously by back-to-back shutouts, each 6–0, at the hands of the Frankford Yellow Jackets, who were destined to win the NFL title that year.

After that, however, Doc Alexander's boys pulled together and salvaged a respectable season. They won five of their last six games, ending up with a record of 8–4–1, good enough for seventh place in the now 22-team NFL. McBride was the league's fifth-highest scorer with 48 points, scoring five touchdowns and kicking a field goal and 15 extra points.

With the regular season over, Mara challenged Pyle and his AFL Yankees to an "intracity championship game." Pyle agreed at first, but later backed out. So Mara invited the AFL-champion Philadelphia Quakers, the team that had pirated Folwell and Milstead before the season, to come to the Polo Grounds to face his Giants. They agreed. On December 12 the two teams lined up before five thousand chilled fans on a snow-covered field that, before the afternoon was over, would be churned into a morass of snow, mud, and slop.

The Quakers were confident: some even boasted in the newspapers before the game of the trifling concern they had for the seventh-place Giants of the NFL. Perhaps they should have concerned themselves more.

The game was pure defense in the slush of the first half, but McBride managed a field goal to give the Giants a 3–0 lead at intermission. Then all hell broke loose. McBride burst in for a score early in the third period, and on the Giants' next possession Hagerty skid-

ded in with another. In the final period, McBride picked off a Quaker pass and ran it back for a touchdown; a little later Tillie Voss snatched away another and carried it in for six more points. Besides all that, Hagerty had raced 65 yards for a touchdown, but it was called back because of a penalty. Another penalty nullified a 52-yard touchdown run by McBride. The Giants defense allowed the Quakers only one first down the entire game, and when it was over the seventh-place NFL Giants had outscored the AFL-champion Quakers, 31–0. Babe Parnell, a tackle who played the full 60 minutes for the Giants, said of it much later, "Everyone on the Giants wanted to win that one. The Quakers thought the Giants were pushovers, but we kicked the bleep out of them." And so ended the Giants' 1926 football season.

The bad news for Mara was that his organization had lost $40,000. Better news perhaps was that Pyle's Yankees dropped $100,000, and the rival AFL collapsed.

The Yankees and Pyle, however,

THE WAY IT WAS

Home opener, 1926, against the Frankford Yellow Jackets.

Everyone was ready for the big afternoon. [Tim] Mara had hired baseball comics Nick Altrock and Al Schacht to entertain, 4,000 Frankford rooters were in town with their own band and cheerleaders, and a crowd of more than 35,000 was expected. Then, the rains came. The game was delayed almost an hour to wait for Mayor Jimmy Walker to arrive and officially kick out the first ball, then started without him. He finally did make his appearance, late in the second quarter, minutes after Frankford had scored on a 46-yard pass, stayed until halftime, marched around the field with Tim Mara, waved to the 15,000 fans, and quickly left the ballpark. He didn't miss a thing.

The game ended at 6–0, the Giants' third straight defeat.

Excerpted from The Giants of New York, *Barry Gottehrer, G. P Putnam's Sons, 1963.*

SUNDAY PRO FOOTBALL GAMES HERE ARE DEFENDED BY COURT

"I attend the games myself, and I fail to see any basis for such charges."

With this statement Magistrate James Barrett, in a Washington Heights court, dismissed charges that players of the New York and Cleveland professional football clubs violated Sabbath "blue laws" by playing on Sunday at the Polo Grounds. Summonses had been handed to the captains and to Dr. Harry March, sponsor of the local club, following a game at the Polo Grounds on November 1, 1926. When the case came before him, Magistrate Barrett, on lack of evidence that the game disturbed the peace, dismissed the complaint.

did not go away. The NFL granted them a franchise for the 1927 season, although they had to play all but four of their sixteen games on the road. But they proved to be no competition on the field, despite having Red Grange and Eddie Tryon in their backfield, "Iron" Mike Michalske on the line, and a pair of Hall of Fame–bound ends in Ray Flaherty and Morris "Red" Badgro, because the Giants were the best team in the league that year, with a defense so niggardly that they gave up only 20 points in 13 games. When the Giants did meet up with Pyle's Yankees, they shut them out 14–0 at the Polo Grounds and 13–0 at Yankee Stadium on successive Sundays in December.

The NFL was down from 22 teams to 12 by 1927. At season's start, the class of the league appeared to be the Chicago Bears with Paddy Driscoll and Joey Sternaman, the Green Bay Packers with Earl "Curly" Lambeau and Joseph "Red" Dunn, the Cleveland Bulldogs behind rookie tailback Benny Friedman, and the Providence Steam Roller with George "Wildcat" Wilson and Jimmy Conzelman. And, of course, the Giants.

March had wanted to beef up the Giants' defense, and so he recruited a 6'2", 235-pound All-American tackle, Cal Hubbard from Centenary College in

Shreveport, Louisiana. In addition, March talked Milstead into redonning a Giants uniform. With Owen, Al Nesser, Hec Garvey, Mickey Murtagh, and Chuck Corgan, the Giants had a virtually impregnable front wall. Wingback Bill "Mule" Wilson was acquired to join Haines and McBride in the backfield, as was 34-year-old American Indian Joe Guyon. And Messrs. Mara and March decided to replace coach Doc Alexander, whose medical practice was taking too much of his time, with Earl Potteiger.

The Giants knocked off the Providence Steam Roller up in Rhode Island, 8–0, to open the season. But at Cleveland, the Bulldogs held New York scoreless; fortunately, the awesome defense of the Giants also prevented Friedman and his cohorts from putting a point on the scoreboard. Two weeks later, however, after an easy win over the Pottsville Maroons, the Giants were not so lucky. Hosting Cleveland at their home opener in the Polo Grounds, the Giants again failed to score, but Friedman got the Bulldogs a touchdown that gusty October afternoon, and New York suffered its first loss of the season.

After that, the Giants' running game came to life, most excitingly on the legs of Haines, McBride, and Hagerty. The defense allowed only two touchdowns in the next nine games. With nine straight victories, the Giants easily took the NFL crown that season. Only the Chicago Bears, late in the season, gave them a first-class fight. Still harboring hopes for the title, George Halas brought his Bears to the Polo Grounds with a record of 6–2–2, not an insurmountable stride behind the 8–1–1 Giants with several games still to play in the season.

The field was muddy from an early morning rain that November day. The sky was overcast, and with dropping temperatures, there was the threat of snow, which was probably part of the reason a crowd of only about ten thousand fans showed up. The Bears marched from the outset and ended up in a fourth-down, goal-to-go situation from the Giants' 1-yard line. But when a Bears back hit the line, he ran smack into Giants guard Nesser, who dropped him just short of the goal.

The game remained a battle of the defenses through the first half. Several more times during the period the Bears pounded their way deep into New York territory, but each time the Giants' defense rose up and stopped them. In the third quarter, it was a different story, however. Now it was the Giants' turn to threaten, moving to the Bears' 2-yard line in the third quarter. McBride cut off the tackle and fell into the end zone with the game's first score. Later in the period, the Giants again moved the ball, this time to the 1-yard line, from where McBride again bulled it in. The Bears, trailing 13–0 in the fourth quarter, came back and posted a touchdown of their own on a pass from Laurie Walquist to Joey Sternaman. The remaining 10 minutes were brutal and bloody, especially at the line of scrimmage. At the gun, defense had prevailed, and the score remained the Giants 13, Bears 7.

A few years later, Owen recalled, "That was the roughest, toughest game I ever played. I played 60 minutes at tackle opposite Jim McMillen, who later became a world wrestling champion. When the gun went off, both of us just sat on the ground in the middle of the field. He smiled in

Steve Owen, as both player and coach, was a Giants institution for 28 years. He arrived from the Kansas City Cowboys in 1926, a 5'10", 225-pound tackle, and played through 1933. He then served as coach from 1931 through 1953. Notorious as a brutal tackler when he was a player and famed for his "umbrella defense" as a coach, Owen was enshrined in the Pro Football Hall of Fame in 1966.

NEVER SNEAK UP ON AN INDIAN

In 1927 an aging Joe Guyon (34 years old), an American Indian, was in the backfield for the Giants. As he faded back for a pass, George Halas, the Chicago Bears' right defensive end, burst through. Guyon's back was to Halas, a perfect setup for a blind-side hit, maybe a fumble, but if nothing else a reminder that the game of football was a rough one. At the last second, however, Guyon unloaded the pass and wheeled around to greet the charging Halas with his knee. It broke several of Halas' ribs. Guyon shook his head at the grimacing Chicago Bear on the ground. "Come on, Halas," he said, "you should know better than to try to sneak up on an Indian." And making Halas even more miserable, the referee called him for clipping and marched off 15 yards against the Bears.

Excerpted from The Chicago Bears, *Richard Whittingham, Rand McNally, 1979.*

Cal Hubbard, the only player to be enshrined in both the Pro Football Hall of Fame and major league baseball's Hall of Fame (as an umpire), came to the Giants in 1927. He played tackle for the Giants for two years before going to the Green Bay Packers in one of the Giants' more lamentable trades. The 6'2", 260-pounder proved to be one of the greatest linemen of his time. In 1936, at age 35, he returned to New York to play out the last year of his career. Hubbard was elected a charter member of the Pro Football Hall of Fame in 1963.

BENNY FRIEDMAN

"He was the best quarterback I ever played against," Red Grange said of Benny Friedman. "There was no one his equal in throwing a football in those days." Indeed, and the Giants wanted him so badly that they bought the entire franchise of the faltering Detroit Wolverines in 1929 to get him.

Only 5'10" and approximately 180 pounds, Friedman came from Cleveland, Ohio, but played his college ball at Michigan under the legendary Fielding "Hurry Up" Yost. Friedman led the league in passing, with 20 touchdown passes his first year with the Giants and 13 the following year, throwing to such able receivers as Ray Flaherty and Len Sedbrook.

But passing wasn't all that Friedman could do. Paul Gallico wrote in *Liberty* magazine back in the thirties:

> The things that the perfect football player must do are kick, pass, run the ends, plunge the line, block, tackle, weave his way through broken fields, drop and place kick, interfere, diagnose plays, spot enemy weaknesses, direct an offense, and not get hurt. I have been describing Friedman's repertoire to you.

a tired way, reached over to me, and we shook hands. We didn't say a word. We couldn't. It was fully five minutes before we got up to go to the dressing room."

When the season ended, the Giants were 11–1–1, comfortably ahead of the Green Bay Packers (7–2–1) and the Bears (9–3–2). It was their first NFL championship, which made Mara and March quite happy, although they were still far from putting some profit into their pockets.

If there had been a Most Valuable Player Award in the NFL, it would have to have gone to McBride. He led the league in scoring with 57 points, in touchdowns rushing (6), and in extra points kicked (15). He kicked two field goals and threw seven touchdown passes, the latter exceeded only by Friedman, who was universally acknowledged as the best passer in the game. Haines, along with

Flaherty of the New York Yankees, caught the most touchdown passes (4). And no one doubted that the Giants had far and away the best defense in the league. It had been a year to remember, but that would be the only solace for them during the long, depressing season of 1928.

Mara was talking about a repeat championship before the 1928 season ever got under way. After all, he had virtually the same team back and what looked like a very promising new back in rookie Bruce Caldwell from Yale. Haines had decided to retire at age 29, but Mara and March were in the process of talking him back into uniform.

The schedule called for five road games to start the season, then four at home. They beat Pottsville (12–6) and Green Bay (6–0), but the team had a decidedly lackluster appearance on both playing fields. March told Mara they would never beat the Chicago Bears or the

New York's first NFL championship team, 1927, winner of 11 games. The season's record was marred by only one loss and a tie to the Cleveland Bulldogs. Top row, left to right: Joe "Doc" Alexander, Wilbur "Pete" Henry, Riley Biggs, Al Nesser, Dick Stahlman, Steve Owen, Cal Hubbard, Chuck Corgan, George Murtagh, Arthur Harms, Paul Jappe. Bottom row, left to right: Phil White, Doug Wycoff, Jack Hagerty, Talma "Tut" Imlay, Hinkey Haines, Earl Potteiger (coach), Jack McBride, Joe Guyon, Fay "Mule" Wilson, Cliff Marker. Photo courtesy of the New York Giants.

Detroit Wolverines, their next two opponents, unless they shaped up. He was only too right. The Bears mauled them, 13–0; then the Wolverines chewed them up, 28–0, behind Friedman's passing and running—Detroit had acquired him from Cleveland.

End Ray Flaherty came to the Giants from the New York Yankees in 1928 and starred for them on offense and defense for six seasons thereafter. After his playing days ended, he went on to become head coach of the Redskins in Boston and then Washington. After World War II, he was coach of the New York Yankees in the All-America Football Conference (AAFC). He was inducted into the Pro Football Hall of Fame in 1976.

The players were disgruntled, mostly because the Giants were a no-frills team in 1928. After losing money two years in a row, Mara had appropriately tightened the proverbial purse strings (witness: the team stayed at the YMCA in Chicago). And the word came down from Mara and March that if the players didn't start playing respectable football, they might find themselves even more disgruntled looking for other jobs.

It worked somewhat. The Giants squeaked by their in-town rivals, the Yankees, by a field goal, then held a fine Frankford team to a scoreless tie (the Yellow Jackets would finish second at the end of the year with a record of 11–3–2). Another win over the Pottsville Maroons, and the Giants were ready to face the Detroit Wolverines again, this time in the friendly confines of the Polo Grounds. At least they were ready through the first three quarters. Taking a 19–7 lead into the final period, the Giants felt they were vindicating themselves. Friedman had other ideas, however, and led his Wolverines down the field twice, capping each drive with a touchdown pass. Friedman's only problem was that he failed to kick

FRIEDMAN REMEMBERS . . .

I think one of the highlights along the charity trail was when we played the Notre Dame alumni for Mayor Jimmy Walker's unemployment fund in the depths of the Depression. . . .

There were a couple of funny things that came out of it. Just before the game, Rockne walked into our dressing room with a cane—he wasn't well at the time. I was getting my ankles taped. . . . I looked up at him—he was one of my idols—and said, "Hi, Coach," and he said, "Hello, Benny."

[He asked how I was.] I said, "Fine."

He said, "That's too bad."

I asked, "What can I do for you?"

He started giving me a story about some of these old men that he had, and he told me that one of these guys had taken a big step off a Pullman and got a charley horse. He said, "I think we ought to have free substitution."

I said, "OK, Coach, anything else?"

He said, "Yes, I think we ought to cut the quarters down to 10 minutes—from 15."

I said, "Oh, Lord, we can't do that. There are forty-five thousand people out there who have paid five bucks apiece to see this game. I'll tell you what we'll do—we'll cut it down to 12 minutes and a half, and if it gets bad we'll cut it down some more in the second half." I then said, "Anything else?"

He said, "Yes, for Pete's sake, take it easy."

Excerpted from Pro Football's Rag Days, *Bob Curran, Bonanza Books, 1969.*

either conversion (a mistake he would make only 7 times out of 26 attempts that year), and the Giants escaped with a 19–19 tie.

After that, it was disastrous. The Giants lost their last five games in a row, two of them, in fact, to their hated neighbors, the Yankees. The Giants tumbled from the NFL throne down to sixth place, with a record of 4–7–2, having averaged only six points per game. And the organization lost somewhere in the vicinity of $40,000. The mood was a little gloomy in the front office.

Not surprisingly, coach Earl Potteiger was the first to get the message: he would not be back the following year. Then practically everybody on the team followed him out the door at the request of the management. The only returnees of any note were tackle Owen and backs Hagerty and Wilson (and only Owen would start on the 1929 Giants).

In all, 18 Giants departed as Mara and March carried out one of the most massive slate-cleanings in football history. Mara knew what he wanted for the Giants, or perhaps more precisely *whom* he wanted: Benny Friedman, the tailback he had watched pick apart his Giants the year before. To obtain his exclusive services, Mara had to buy the entire Detroit team—part-owner and coach Roy Andrews included. It was neither difficult nor expensive because the Detroit franchise was in deep financial trouble

Playing in the late twenties and early thirties at the end opposite Ray Flaherty was Morris "Red" Badgro. Winning a post on three of the first four All-Pro teams (1931, 1933–1934), he was, in the words of Red Grange, who often played against him, "one of the best half-dozen ends I ever saw." Badgro played with the Giants from 1928 through 1935, taking a year off in 1929 to play baseball for the St. Louis Browns in the American League. Like Flaherty, he too was elected to the Pro Football Hall of Fame, although the redhead had to wait until 1981 for the honor.

and about to go out of business. In essence, all Mara had to do was to sign up Andrews and then negotiate with the Detroit players that he wanted. Andrews was installed as head coach of the Giants, and the best of the Detroit players were retained. To keep superstar Friedman happy, Mara dug deep and signed him for $10,000 for the season, by far the most ever paid to a pro player up to that time, excluding, of course, the Red Grange deal with the Chicago Bears in 1925.

Among the other standouts the Giants acquired from Detroit were tackle Bill Owen (Steve's brother), wingback Sedbrook, a fine blocking back by the name of Elvin "Tiny" Feather, and center Joe Westoupal. They also added Flaherty, from the newly defunct New York Yankees.

It was a new show at the Polo Grounds, and it paid off, at least on the field. Only two teams were in contention for the NFL crown that season: the Giants and the Green Bay Packers. Like the Giants, the Packers had

The pro game's first great passer, Benny Friedman (right), poses with rookie Cliff Montgomery when both were with the Brooklyn Dodgers. Friedman joined the Giants in 1929, and during his three seasons with the club he was the highest-paid player in the NFL ($10,000 per year). His 19 touchdown passes in 1929—a time when other passers might throw 5 or 6 at best per season— remained the NFL record until Cecil Isbell of the Packers broke it in the much more pass-oriented season of 1942.

made some key acquisitions—one who would come back to haunt the Giants many times over the next five years, the monolithic Cal Hubbard. Many times Mara admitted he rued having let the Hall of Fame–bound tackle get away from the Giants. Two other future Hall of Famers picked up by the Pack were halfback Johnny "Blood" McNally and guard "Iron" Mike Michalske.

The Giants were a little shaky coming out of the starting blocks that season, however. They were held to a scoreless tie by the Orange Tornadoes of New Jersey, a newcomer to the NFL. But that would be the last mishap during the next two months. Behind Friedman's pinpoint passing and the fine running of fullback Tony Plansky (a second-year man who had been injured for most of the preceding season) and an absolutely stalwart defense, the Giants beat and battered their next eight opponents to a collective score of 204–29. Among those triumphs was a 34–0 drubbing of the once-proud Chicago Bears, who, after the Yankees' demise, once again showcased Red Grange. During the same period of time, the Packers also went undefeated in their nine games, allowing their beleaguered opponents a paltry 16 points.

The clash of the two unbeatens took place at the Polo Grounds on November 24, 1929. Lambeau told his team that if they were to beat the Giants, they had to stop Friedman's passing. All week before the game the Green Bay defense worked on rushing the passer. They had probably the biggest and strongest line in the league, but Lambeau said they also had to be fast enough to put great pressure on Friedman.

The Packers defense did its job that day. Friedman's passing game was thwarted in the first half, and when he tried a running attack the Pack shut it down as well. But the Giants defense was no slouch either. They held the Packers during the first half until they lost the ball on a fumble deep in their own territory, which Green Bay took advantage of to score the half's only touchdown.

In the third quarter, Friedman finally escaped the Packers pressure and hit Plansky for a touchdown but missed the extra point, and New York trailed 7–6. Later in the half, however, Green Bay faked a punt, and the pass to McNally brought them well into Giants territory. A sustained march followed, the icing applied when fullback Bo Molenda charged in for the score. McNally added another touchdown before time ran out, and the Packers had the win, 20–6.

It was the Giants' only loss all season, which they ended with an impressive record of 13–1–1. But Green Bay remained on top with a final record of 12–0–1. (Schedules were not uniform in those days, so some teams ended up playing more games than other teams.) Friedman had proved to be the imposing force that Mara and March believed he would be. His 20 touchdown passes were more than three times the 6 thrown by runner-up Ernie Nevers of the Chicago Cardinals. And Friedman's 20 of 32 extra points were well above the next kicker in that column, Dunn, who booted 11 of

22. The top three receivers, at least in terms of touchdowns, that year were all Giants: end Flaherty with eight and backs Sedbrook and Hap Moran with six and five, respectively. Only Nevers, who scored 85 points that year, tallied more than the 66 scored by Sedbrook and the 62 by Plansky.

It was a most pleasant reversal for Mara. And not only that, people were finally coming out to watch his team play ball. More than twenty-five thousand had shown up to watch the fateful game with the Packers, and when the season's final figures were added up, Mara's Giants had earned about $8,500—the first black ink on the register since Red Grange came out with the Bears to top off the 1925 football season.

An action shot from the early thirties shows the great Ernie Nevers downed with the ball in a game against the Giants at the Polo Grounds, surrounded mostly by Chicago Cardinals teammates.

"WHAT, AND LEAVE ME HERE ALL ALONE?"

The bad news for Tim Mara and the Giants staff in 1930—besides the Great Depression—seemed to come from all directions. It began after trying to sign and then losing Ken Strong, the All-American triple threat from New York University, to the Staten Island Stapletons. It was a blow of major proportions. Watching the refurbished Chicago Bears sign rookie fullback Bronko Nagurski was discomforting, to say the least. Noting that the Green Bay Packers, with the addition of an unheralded but quickly impressive all-around back named Arnie Herber, appeared even stronger than they had winning the NFL crown the year previous was not overly encouraging. To top it off, Benny Friedman took an additional job coaching at Yale and was noticeably fatigued by the daily round-trip commute from Brooklyn to New Haven, Connecticut, and back to Brooklyn, which he was forced to make before each Giants practice session.

Outside the world of professional football, Mara had suffered substantial losses in the stock market crash of 1929 and was embroiled in an expensive lawsuit. He was suing world heavyweight champion Gene Tunney and his manager, Billy Gibson. Mara had formerly been associated with Gibson, but was suing him for money that was due him, he claimed, but that had not been paid. With the overriding fear that the financial setbacks of that

dismal time and the litigation in which he was involved might possibly result in the loss of the franchise, Mara turned over total ownership in the ballclub to his sons Jack, 22, and Wellington, 14, certainly the youngest owners in the history of professional football (they were titular owners then, not taking part in management, but later the team would become the life work of both).

Although the Giants hadn't signed Strong, they did make some fine acquisitions that year. End Morris "Red" Badgro, who played football for the New York Yankees for two years then took a year off to play major league baseball for the St. Louis Browns, was lured to the Giants. Through press coverage of college games and word of mouth, the Giants learned about then hired a strong running back named Dale Burnett from Kansas State Teachers College and a spunky guard by the name of Butch Gibson from a school called Grove City College in Pennsylvania. The Giants were certainly considered to be in the running for the NFL title in 1930.

After two easy wins, however, the Giants traveled out to central Wisconsin to take on the Packers and found they were mortal, losing 14–7. It seemed to bring the team closer together, because the New Yorkers sailed through their next eight straight games without another defeat. Along the way they shut out the Chicago Bears

12–0 (despite the Bears' running combo of Red Grange and Nagurski), twice clobbered the Chicago Cardinals and Ernie Nevers, and annihilated the hapless Frankford Yellow Jackets by a score of 53–0.

An especially pleasing victory during that streak involved thwarting Strong and his Staten Island Stapletons. Because Messrs. Mara and Dr. Harry March were under the misapprehension that Strong had snubbed them and their generous salary offer of $10,000 per year (see sidebar), they very much wanted the triple threat to see what he was missing by not playing for the Giants. The game brought out one of the better crowds of the season to the Polo Grounds, approximately eighteen thousand, but it almost didn't turn out as the Giants brass had anticipated. After an overly zealous Giants defense knocked Strong unconscious early in the third quarter, the Stapleton star cleared the fog from his head, came back onto the field, grabbed a short pass, and raced 60 yards for a touchdown. He then booted the extra point to put Staten Island ahead, 7–6. The lead held until late in the fourth quarter. Then Friedman, who was having an uncommonly poor day, moved the Giants to the Staten Island 35-yard line, and on the fourth down with just two minutes to go, he kicked a field goal to give New York a 9–7 win. By November 10, 1930, the Giants boasted a handsome record of 10–1, but the Green Bay Packers remained ahead of them with a mark of 8–0.

The Chicago Bears then came to the Polo Grounds seeking revenge for their earlier loss. They were 4–4–1 at the time and virtually out of the race for the title. The Giants were a predictable favorite at that point in the season. But there were several factors, other than Grange and Nagurski, that would contribute to the New Yorkers' second defeat of the regular season. After just edging the Chicago Cardinals, 13–7, by scoring two touchdowns late in the fourth quarter the previous Sunday, the Giants stopped off in Cincinnati, Ohio, on their way back from the Windy City to play an Armistice Day exhibition game against a local pro team known as the Ironton Tanks. But the Tanks proved not to be the pushover the Giants

Dale Burnett came to the Giants in 1930 from Kansas State Teachers College and earned a starting assignment in the backfield the following year. He proved to be a fine runner and pass catcher during his 10-year career with the Giants.

ON LOSING KEN STRONG

Wellington Mara was only a youngster when Ken Strong entered the NFL, but he remembers the Giants' inability to sign Strong well:

> Ken Strong had been a great back at New York University in the years when my brother Jack was going to Fordham. That made him a hated rival, of course, but we still thought he was the greatest. We wanted him for the Giants very badly. My father had this employee who was instructed to make every effort to sign Ken Strong. But he failed, and we were very upset when Ken signed with the Staten Island Stapletons, who were a key rival of ours. He then came over and beat us a couple of times.
>
> When the Staten Island team disbanded, Strong came to us. My father said, "Well, Ken, you are three years too late. I never understood why you went over there for less money than we offered you."
>
> Ken said, "What do you mean?"
>
> "We offered you $10,000 a year."
>
> "No, you didn't. You offered me $5,000."
>
> Apparently our employee was going to pocket the $5,000 difference, or else he thought he was going to save the club some money and make some points for himself. I don't know which. All I know is that's how we lost Ken Strong.

expected. They were a determined team coached by Earle "Greasy" Neale and guided on the field by tailback Glenn Presnell—both of whom would soon make their names very well known in the NFL. Neale, who also played eight years of baseball with the Cincinnati Reds (he was their leading hitter in the 1919 fixed World Series against the Chicago "Black Sox"), later coached the Philadelphia Eagles throughout the forties and earned his way into the Pro Football Hall of Fame. Presnell later made his mark as an outstanding runner and passer with the Portsmouth Spartans and the Detroit Lions.

The Giants scored first on a pass from Hap Moran to Bill "Mule" Wilson, but Presnell brought the Tanks right back with a 40-yard touchdown pass to Tex Mitchell, and the score at the half was 6–6. After the kickoff to start the second half the Giants marched the length of the field, and Len Sedbrook carried it in from the 1, but the try for an extra point was fumbled away. From that point on, the Tanks totally shut down the New York offense. In the final minutes of the game, Presnell stunned the Giants by running and passing his Ironton team to a last-second touchdown, the garland being a 28-yard toss to Jack Alford, who stepped into the end zone with only seconds remaining. The successful extra point gave Ironton a 13–12 triumph and sent a surprised and morose Giants team back to New York to face the Bears five days later.

With the Giants and the Bears running head to head into the final stretch for the NFL crown and such superstars as Grange and Nagurski performing for the Bears, it would have seemed that the rush for tickets to the game at the Polo Grounds would be substantial. But the rains came Sunday morning and continued into the afternoon, and only about four thousand stalwarts showed up to watch the two teams wallow in several inches of mud.

It was a game the Giants truly needed because arriving the next week would be undefeated Green Bay. Friedman tried to pass his team to victory, but his receivers slipped and slid all over the rain-soaked, windswept field, and he had little control over the slippery ball. Pass after pass fell incomplete (he completed only three all afternoon). At the same time the Bears' vaunted running attack was also stalled in the mire. The two teams merely exchanged possession of the ball through the first three scoreless quarters. But in the fourth quarter Grange found his footing and zig-zagged his way 30 yards to the Giants' 15. Reserve running back Joe Lintzenich then carried it to the 6, and Nagurski blasted through for a touchdown on the next play. With time running out, Friedman passed in desperation, and the Bears picked one off. With only seconds left, Nagurski took a pitchout and stormed around the right end, shaking off Giants tacklers for 20 yards before sloshing into the end zone. The final score was 12–0. The only solace was the announcement in the dressing room that Green Bay had also fallen that day in its encounter with the Chicago Cardinals.

The sports pages heralded the game between the Giants and the Packers as the one that would decide the 1930 national championship. To aid their cause the Giants lured Army's three-time consensus All-American back, Chris "Red" Cagle, up to New York from his coaching job at Mississippi A&M. The breakaway back was signed for $7,500, it was reported—one of the highest salaries in the league.

Cagle made hardly any difference in his professional debut, however. He was injured in the first quarter and contributed very little when he returned in the second half. But, as it turned out, the Giants didn't really need him that cold November afternoon. With approximately forty-five thousand fans shivering at the Polo Grounds, the Giants put the first score on the board in the second quarter on a 22-yard pass from Friedman

Chris "Red" Cagle, an All-American from Army who joined the Giants in 1930, puts a move on a would-be tackler during a Giants scrimmage. The fleet redheaded halfback, at 5'10" and 170 pounds, was a breakaway runner, but also a respected blocker and tackler. He left the Giants after the 1932 season to launch the Brooklyn Dodgers with fellow Giants departee John "Shipwreck" Kelly. Photo courtesy of the New York Giants.

ONE FOR THE CITY

The postseason exhibition game of 1930 was played to benefit the unemployed of New York City.

New York Giants		Notre Dame All-Stars
Red Badgro	LE	Chuck Collins
Bill Owen	LT	Joe Bach
Les Caywood	LG	Hearley "Hunk" Anderson
Mickey Murtagh	C	Adam Walsh
Rudy Comstock	RG	Noble Kizer
Len Grant	RT	Rip Miller
Glenn Campbell	RE	Ed Hunsinger
Benny Friedman	QB	Harry Stuhldreyer
Len Sedbrook	LH	Don Miller
Ossie Wiberg	RH	Jim Crowley
Tiny Feather	FB	Elmer Layden
Benny Friedman	Coach	Knute Rockne

	1	2	3	4	T
New York Giants	2	13	7	0	22
Notre Dame All-Stars	0	0	0	0	0

Touchdowns—Giants: Friedman (2), Campbell.

PATs—Giants: Friedman, Moran.

Safety: Stuhldreyer.

to Badgro. Friedman booted the conversion for a 7–0 lead. In the third quarter, with the Giants deep in their own territory, Moran surprised everyone in the stadium, especially the Packers, by faking a punt and then racing around the end for 84 yards before he was dragged down at the Green Bay 1-yard line. Moments later Friedman carried it in for the touchdown.

Green Bay came back in the last period with Verne Lewellen scoring from the 5 after a concerted drive. The Pack threatened again in the closing minutes of the game, moving down to the Giants' 5-yard line. Three plunges got them to the 1, and on fourth down, substitute

Tim Mara presents his good friend and New York's mayor Jimmy Walker with a check for $115,153—the proceeds of the post-season exhibition game played between the Giants and Knute Rockne's Notre Dame All-Stars. The benefit to aid the New York Unemployment Fund during the Depression-racked time was the brainchild of Mara, and more than fifty-five thousand watched the Giants drub the former Fighting Irish, 22–0, at the Polo Grounds.

ON THE BENCH

In 1931, there weren't a lot of restrictions as to who might sit on the bench along with the team and coaches. Paul Gallico, one of the best sportswriters of the time before he turned his authorial talents to fiction-writing, remembers one incident in an article for *Liberty* magazine that year, which also gives an insight into the talents of Benny Friedman:

> Late this fall I sat on the sidelines at the Polo Grounds in New York with Leroy [Roy] Andrews, coach of the New York Giants, Tim Mara's professional football team. They were playing the Providence Steam Roller pretty even. The score was 0–0. Benny Friedman was on the field as captain and quarterback of the New Yorkers.
>
> Suddenly Andrews dug a huge elbow into my side. "Look at that halfback!" he cried, pointing to the defensive right halfback of the Providence team. I couldn't see anything wrong with him. He looked reasonably alert, and I said so.
>
> "Alert, hell! He's two yards out of position. It's the spot for a pass and a touchdown. Watch Benny now! I wonder . . ."
>
> The ball was snapped while he was still talking and a blue-shirted Giant streaked through the left side of the line and in a second was out and beyond the Providence man. Even then the defender failed to catch the scent of danger because Friedman, who was drifting lazily slantwise to the sideline, was looking down the other side of the field, where decoys were spreading out fanwise. Not until he had pulled his arm back did Friedman suddenly whirl and spiral the ball down to the lone runner. The defensive halfback who had been standing those bare—and to the layman imperceptible—two yards out of position never had a chance. The receiver was beyond him; he turned, raising his right shoulder, and the ball was at his fingertips—touchdown!

fullback Hurdis McCrary bolted through for the score. But offside was called on both teams, and the touchdown was nullified. McCrary tried again on the next play, but the Giants line stopped him short of the goal. The game ended with the Giants on top, 13–6, and in first place with a record of 11–2, three wins better than Green Bay's 8–2 (the Giants had played three additional weeknight games during the season).

It was the acme of their season, as it turned out, because the next week the Giants fell to the Stapletons, the winning touchdown contributed by Strong. The following Sunday they were beaten by the Brooklyn Dodgers, a newcomer to the NFL that year. The loss and its ramifications cost Roy Andrews his head coaching job and the Giants the NFL crown. They ran second (13–4–0) to Green Bay (10–3–1).

Friedman had had a spectacular year, justifying his hefty salary in Mara's eyes. The versatile tailback, as expected, threw the most touchdown passes that year (13), and he was fourth in total points scored (49).

There was, however, a most colorful epilogue to the 1930 season. Mara had approached his friend, Mayor Jimmy Walker, and told him that he would like to do something to help the many unemployed people in his Depression-racked hometown. He suggested that his Giants play a charity game against a Knute Rockne–coached team of former Notre Dame greats, including the fabled Four Horsemen. Charles Stoneham, owner of the baseball Giants and the Polo Grounds, agreed to provide the stadium free of rent, and all income from the contest was turned over to the mayor to be used to help New York's unemployed.

Despite a bitingly cold day, the contest attracted a crowd of more than fifty-five thousand, including Mayor Walker and former New York governor and presidential candidate Al Smith. Rockne knew his former collegians were undersized, less experienced, and had been fashioned into a team in just one week. In the locker room before the game he told them, "Boys, these Giants are big and heavy, but slow. Go out there and score two or three touchdowns on passes right off, and then defend." Then thoughtfully he added, "And don't get hurt."

Out of their league, so to speak, the All-Stars went out and got throttled. The final score was 22–0. The day's

John "Shipwreck" Kelly, one of the more colorful characters both on and off the field in New York, poses with a ball he could run with, catch, and kick with equal talent. His field performances were erratic, but his exploits in New York's café society were legendary. Kelly played for the Giants for only one season (1932), then went over to Brooklyn with Chris Cagle to own and lead the Dodgers.

action was probably best summed up in a story Notre Dame guard Noble Kizer often told later. At the line of scrimmage during the second quarter, Kizer whispered to center Adam Walsh, "I think they're going to pass. I'm going to pull out and take the inside back."

Walsh looked over at him wide-eyed and said, "What, and leave me here all alone?"

On the plus side, Mara was able to hand Mayor Walker a check for the New York Unemployment Fund totaling $115,153—the entire gate receipts. The $15,000 worth of expenses that had been promised to Rockne and his players was paid out of Mara's personal bank account.

The 1931 season was not a memorable one—at least the way the Giants played it. After being a solid contender the year before, the team suffered through a 7–6–1 season in 1931, landing in fifth place in the then 10-team NFL. But there were some significant events that would have very positive effects on the Giants' future. Among them were the appointment of Steve Owen as head coach and the signing of a tall, rangy center from Washington State by the name of Mel Hein. At the start of the season the Giants lost Friedman, who decided to make his coaching job at Yale full time, but after the Giants lost three of their first four games, Mara talked Friedman into coming back. By November 1, he succeeded. The return of Friedman helped at the gate and, at least for the first two games, on the field. With a renewed passing attack, the Giants knocked off the undefeated Portsmouth Spartans (who were 8–0 going into the game) and then the Frankford Yellow Jackets. But success was short-lived. Over the next three weeks, New York was manhandled successively by the Bears, Packers, and Stapletons. The Giants won their last two games of the year, beating Brooklyn and surprising the Chicago Bears, but 1931 proved to be the first of two disappointing seasons. Still, two Giants were selected to the NFL's first All-Pro team: end Badgro and guard Gibson.

Benny Friedman left the Giants for good before the start of the 1932 season. He had asked for a piece of the ballclub as well as his salary, but Mara told him the organization was going to remain a family operation. Friedman signed with the Brooklyn Dodgers, and the Giants went in search of a tailback, one who could

SHIPWRECK, AS IN KELLY

John Kieran, writing for *The New York Times,* described the coming to the Giants in 1932 of John "Shipwreck" Kelly, who would become one of the more colorful figures in pro football, as well as New York's cafe society, over the next four or five years:

> It was in the summer that a big, lanky, redheaded chap came into Tim Mara's office on Twenty-third Street.
>
> "Ah'm Shipwreck Kelly," explained the visitor.
>
> "What?" said Mr. Mara. "The fellow who sits on flagpoles?" [One of the more famous characters of the stunt-filled Roaring Twenties was a flagpole sitter who had dubbed himself Shipwreck Kelly.]
>
> "No, suh," said the visitor. "Ah play football. Played foh Kain-tucky."

Barry Gottehrer later elaborated on the story in his book, *The Giants of New York:*

> Mara, who had been given a list of the top college prospects by his 16-year-old son Wellington, suddenly realized who his visitor was. "Welcome," said the Giants' owner, smiling and offering a chair. "I've heard of you, my boy. Here, look at this." Opening his drawer, Mara pulled out a folder crammed with clippings detailing the exploits of Shipwreck Kelly of Kain-tucky.
>
> "I've seen them all," said Kelly, "and I'd lak to play football this fall with yah Giants. Ah hear it's a right smart team, suh."

Mara and the Giants needed Kelly, but not at his price—a percentage of the gate similar to the deal Red Grange had back in 1925. "I'd love to have you, but I can't afford you," said Mara. "Well, the news about the Depression will get back to the hills of Kentucky sooner or later, and you might as well be the one to carry the word."

The Giants had not heard the last of Shipwreck Kelly.

Totally unannounced, the drawling redheaded halfback reported to the Giants' training camp at Magnetic Springs, Ohio.

"Glad to have you," said [coach Steve] Owen, "but really we weren't expecting you."

"That's why I came," drawled Kelly. "I do the most ah-stonishing things. Nevah know why myself. Now, Coach, there's nothing to do but give me the ball and let me get going."

Shipwreck got the chance to prove himself early in the 1932 season and proved to be an exciting, elusive runner, as well as a fine punter. He quickly became the focus of the fans at the Polo Grounds. But:

> For the Portsmouth game, Kelly's picture was on the cover of the program. . . . Only one thing was missing—Kelly himself. When he didn't show up by game time, the band started playing, "Has Anybody Here Seen Kelly?" but Shipwreck obviously had better things to do for the afternoon. . . .
>
> "What happened to Kelly?" a writer asked Owen after the game.
>
> "Maybe he's sitting on a flagpole," quipped one of the Giants.
>
> "As far as I'm concerned, he can sit on a tack," said Owen. "He's suspended." And colorful John "Shipwreck" Kelly, who never fully explained his mysterious absence, never played another game as a Giant.

Shipwreck Kelly did explain his absence to this author in an interview in 1983: "I played about six or seven games with the Giants that year, but then I quit because the doctor told me I wasn't in shape for it. I had a small touch of rheumatic fever, and I didn't feel very good, and they weren't paying me very much money anyway. I had some money myself, and so I went back to Kentucky."

Mel Hein, whom the Giants were almost too late in signing, was named the NFL's All-Pro center an unprecedented and unequaled eight consecutive times (1933–1940). A Giant of legendary proportions, he holds the club service record of 15 seasons (1931–1945), later equaled by Phil Simms. His Giants jersey No. 7 has been retired. Hein was a charter enshrinee in the Pro Football Hall of Fame in 1963.

pass the ball well. With Friedman at Ebbets Field, the Dodgers no longer needed McBride and released him, so the Giants hired their former tailback to join Cagle, Burnett, and Bo Molenda (acquired from Green Bay that year) in the backfield. New York still had two of the classiest ends in the league, Ray Flaherty and Badgro, and the finest center in the game, Hein. They also took on a swift and cagey running back from the University of Kentucky, John "Shipwreck" Kelly (see sidebar). But the Giants hardly played as a team, and in their first six games could come up with only one win, a 20–12 rout of Friedman and his Dodgers. It got a little better after that, with three wins and a tie in their last four games, the highlight being a 6–0 upset of the defending NFL-champion Green Bay Packers.

A PROVIDENTIAL POSTMASTER IN PROVIDENCE

Mel Hein tells the fateful story of how he became a New York Giant in 1931:

I went from Washington State to the New York Giants, but I almost went with another team. I had a contract offer from the Providence Steam Roller out of New England. I hadn't received anything from the Giants, although I'd heard they were planning to make me an offer. Well, Jimmy Conzelman was the Steam Roller coach, and he was pushing me, so I signed with Providence for $125 a game.

After I signed the contract, I went down to Spokane for a basketball game, another sport I played at Washington State. We were playing Gonzaga, and Ray Flaherty, the Giants' captain, coached them in the off-season. He came down to the dressing room after the game and asked me if I'd received a contract yet from the Giants.

"No, I haven't," I said. "But if one's on the way, it's too late now. I signed one with Providence and mailed it back to them yesterday."

"Oh, no," Ray said. "How much are they paying you?" I told him, and he said, "The Giant contract is a better offer, $150 a game. I know that's the figure, and I know the contract's on its way to you. Damn." A little later he came back to me and said, "Why don't you go down to the postmaster when you get home and see if he won't send a telegram to the postmaster in Providence to see if he would intercept the letter?"

The next morning I did, but the postmaster said he wouldn't do it. He said that I could try myself, but he truly doubted I'd get the letter back. So I sent the telegram myself and, sure enough, the postmaster in Providence sent the letter with the signed contract back. In the meantime, the Giants' contract for $150 a game had arrived. I signed with the Giants and tore up the other contract. I think at that time $150 a game was probably the highest pay of any lineman in the league. It was pretty good money, even though it wouldn't sound that way now… but you could buy a loaf of bread for a nickel and get a full meal for 35¢ in the Automat back then. And you had no income tax!

The Giants of 1931, the first team coached by Steve Owen. They expected to be a title contender, but could only muster a fifth-place, 7–6–1 season. Top row, left to right: Steve Owen, Johnnie Kitzmiller, Len Sedbrook, Hap Moran, Dale Burnett, Tim Mara, Dr. Harry March, Doug Wycoff, Ted Bucklin, Chris Cagle, Benny Friedman. Bottom row, left to right: Sam Stein, Ray Flaherty, Len Grant, Bill Owen, Lester Caywood, Mel Hein, George Murtaugh, Butch Gibson, Laurie Walquist, Corwan Altman, George Munday, Glenn Campbell, Red Badgro. Photo courtesy of the New York Giants.

TEAM POET LAUREATE

On the occasion of "Tim Mara Day" at the Polo Grounds in November 1932, Westbrook Pegler, in his syndicated column "Speaking Out," observed a new Giant in the fold:

> They have hired cheerleaders from time to time and yesterday a poet laureate bobbed up in the literature of the official program (price, 15 cents) with a new alma mater song dedicated to Tim Mara, entitled "My Song." . . .

> The new alma mater song, struck from the lyre of Poet Thomas J. McCarthy, runs about a hundred lines, which is somewhat longer than the formula for such works.

> A few lines will serve to tell you about the new song:

> > Each fall my joy is without bounds,
> > On Sundays at the Polo Grounds.
> > For when our football Giants play,
> > Just try to keep this guy away.

> It is a little better than most college songs, but, then, the college poets are amateurs, like the college players, and cannot be expected to write as well as the pros.

When the season ended, the Giants had a record of 4–6–2 and resided in fifth place, finishing ahead of only the Brooklyn Dodgers, Chicago Cardinals, and the Staten Island Stapletons. Flaherty was the only Giant to earn All-Pro honors. But times were about to change in the Giants' camp.

PRICE **10** CENTS

NEW YORK FOOTBALL GIANTS
vs.
PORTSMOUTH SPARTANS

KEN STRONG (Giant Back)

The Giants finally got Ken Strong into a uniform in 1933 after a recruiting snafu let him get away to the Staten Island Stapletons four years earlier. A great running back and kicker, he was a key force in the divisional champion Giants of 1933, 1934, and 1935. He came back to the Giants as a kicking specialist in 1939 and again from 1944 through 1947, then retired with a host of club scoring and kicking records. Strong was inducted into the Pro Football Hall of Fame in 1967.

POLO GROUNDS   **NOVEMBER 5, 1933**

THREE CHAMPIONSHIP SEASONS

The year 1933 was an important one in the NFL. A variety of rules changes modernized the game and opened up the art of offense considerably. The ball itself, which had gradually been slimming down over the past decade and a half, received a further paring that year, bringing it to the shape it is today. The change made it much easier to pass, but signaled the demise of the drop kick.

Among the rules changes was a provision allowing a back to pass from anywhere behind the line of scrimmage (previously the passer had to be at least five yards back of the scrimmage line). The goal posts were moved from the end lines up to the goal lines, a big help for field-goal kickers and designed to boost the scoring. Hash marks were introduced for the first time, and after any play that ended within 5 yards of a sideline, the ball was placed on the hash mark line, which was set 10 yards in from the sideline.

George Preston Marshall, owner of the Boston Redskins in their second year in the league, lobbied for dividing the 10-team NFL into two divisions then holding a championship game between the two division leaders at the end of the regular season. It was accepted unanimously. The Giants were placed in the Eastern Division along with the Redskins, the Brooklyn Dodgers, and two new franchises, the Philadelphia Eagles, owned by Bert Bell and Lud Wray, and the Pittsburgh Pirates, headed by Art Rooney.

With the passing game revitalized and Benny Friedman lost forever to the Giants, Tim Mara was determined to add someone to pilot an aerial attack. The person he saw in that role was a 5'8", 175-pound All-American quarterback from the University of Michigan named Harry Newman, whom Wellington Mara aptly described later as a "perfect clone of Friedman." But Newman decided not to come out to the East Coast cheaply: he bargained with Mara and Dr. Harry March and finally worked out a deal in which he was guaranteed a percentage of the Giants' gate receipts, one that would prove quite lucrative for him and cause more than a little consternation in the New York front office during the course of the next two years.

Another prize was unearthed when the Staten Island Stapletons went out of business, leaving triple-threat back Ken Strong unemployed. This time Mara did not dispatch an emissary to talk with Strong; he did it himself and signed the great back the same day. The Giants now had the best backfield in the Eastern Division, rivaled in the entire NFL by only the Chicago Bears with Bronko Nagurski and Red Grange.

SOME DON'T COME FROM THE DRAFT

Steve Owen got this letter, postmarked Garden Grove, Iowa, in the early summer of 1933:

> I think I could be a pretty good back. . . . Weight 190. . . . Simpson College last three years. . . . Led Iowa Conference in scoring two years. . . . I'll pay my own expenses east for a tryout. . . . Name is Elvin Richards.

Owen wrote back tersely: "Come on along."

Elvin "Kink" Richards not only made the team, but was a mainstay in the Giants' backfield from 1933 through 1939.

Steve Owen felt confident that, with Newman's passing, Strong's running and kicking, and a defense that he was especially proud of, the Giants had a good shot at being the Eastern Division representative in the NFL's first championship game. After the first four games of the regular season, however, his confidence severely eroded. Losses to the Portsmouth Spartans and the Boston Redskins gave them only a .500 record, with some of their toughest games still to be played, including two with the Chicago Bears, who had handily won their first four games.

Those first four contests were all on the road. Owen pleaded and berated his players to make a good showing at their hometown debut; he wanted the Giants fans convinced that the team was as good as he felt they were. He obviously got through to them: the Giants systematically destroyed the Philadelphia Eagles before eighteen thousand fans at the Polo Grounds by the score of 56–0, then the highest score in the club's history and a standard that would remain until 1972. Newman got the scoring going in the first period with a touchdown pass to Hap Moran, then threw another to him for the extra point. Throughout the game, he marched the Giants up and down the field and made everyone forget Friedman's passing wizardry. When the home opener finally came to an end, fullback Bo Molenda had rushed for two touchdowns, Ken Strong one, Kink Richards one, and Stu Clancy had raced 46

yards for still another. Jack McBride came off the bench and tossed two touchdown passes in the fourth quarter to Richards and to Dale Burnett.

The following week more than thirty thousand fans filed into the Polo Grounds to watch the Giants take on the Brooklyn Dodgers. It was a reunion of sorts: the Dodgers' backfield featured former Giants running backs Red Cagle and John "Shipwreck" Kelly, who were co-owners of the Dodgers franchise, and, of course, Friedman. Newman set the tone on the third play of the game. Dropping back to pass, he couldn't find a receiver, so he legged it himself 25 yards for a touchdown. Later in the half he hit end Glenn Campbell with an 18-yard touchdown strike. On the first play of the second half, Richards zig-zagged his way 70 yards for a third New York touchdown. The Dodgers got one, but that was it for the day, 21–7, and the Giants were on their way to their first divisional title.

The game also contained one of the more unique plays in pro football. With the score 7–0, Strong sent a punt spiraling deep down the field. Kelly trotted back under it and, as the two teams thundered down the field toward him, calmly caught the ball. Instead of running with it, he simply punted it straight back up the field. It was also noted in the next day's sports pages that "Kelly and [Ray] Flaherty, hard workers both, played without headgears. . . . Shipwreck had more hair to protect him though."

The Giants lost only one other game in 1933, a 14–10 squeaker to the Bears out in Chicago. When the Chicagoans came out to the Polo Grounds, Owen's proud defense held them scoreless, and Strong's lone field goal provided the margin of victory. In the Eastern Division, the Giants' record of 11–3–0 was far ahead of second-place Brooklyn (5–4–1). In the Western Division, the Bears did not surprise anyone by taking the title with a record of 10–2–1. And so the stage was set for the NFL's first championship battle.

The scene was Wrigley Field in Chicago, December 17, 1933, a cold, overcast day with a mist that from time to time would turn to a drizzle. The baseball park in which the Chicago Cubs played had a capacity of about forty thousand, and some twenty-six thousand seats were occupied for the premier NFL championship match.

THE POWER OF PRAYER

In 1933, Ken Strong kicked a field goal to defeat the Chicago Bears, 3–0, in a game at the Polo Grounds that eventually enabled the Giants to meet the Bears for the NFL title that year. On his first attempt, however, New York was offside, and the ball was moved back. Strong kicked again, and again it was good.

Steve Owen fumed on the sideline, not because of the offside penalty, but because he had observed his brother Bill, a tackle, on both kicks. Bill had made no attempt to pulverize the Bear across the line from him, guard Joe Kopcha. "Why didn't you destroy that Kopcha?" Steve shouted at Bill on the sideline after the second kick. "He just knelt there at the line of scrimmage, and you didn't do anything."

"I couldn't," Bill said, shaking his head in dismay. "On each kick Kopcha raised his eyes toward the heavens and said, 'Please, God, don't let him make it.' Gosh, Steve, I couldn't belt a guy when he was praying."

The Giants had prepared well. They were not only fired up, but they came with a pocketful of tricks as well. The most memorable was a play devised by Newman and later described by center Mel Hein as the "center-with-ball-hidden-under-shirt-keeper-play." He explained the play this way: "We put all the linemen on my right, except the left end. Then he shifted back a yard, making me end man on the line, while the wingback moved up on the line on the right. Harry Newman came right up under me, like a T-formation quarterback. I handed the ball to him between my legs, and he immediately put it right back in my hands—the shortest forward pass on record." Hein quickly stuffed the ball under his shirt and began strolling downfield while the Bears defense was rushing after Newman, who was fading back as if to pass. About 30 yards downfield Bears safety Keith Molesworth saw Hein begin to run and tackled him, thereby preventing a touchdown.

The Bears were the first to get on the scoreboard in that first championship game, on a 16-yard field goal from "Automatic" Jack Manders. He followed that with a 40-yarder. Meanwhile the Giants offense could not get going until well into the second quarter, not until Richards slashed through the Bears defense for 30 yards, and then Newman hit Red Badgro with a 29-yard touchdown pass. Strong's extra point gave New York a 7–6 lead at the half. The field was muddy, the air raw and damp, and it was hardly a setting for what lay ahead—one of the most exciting halves ever to be played in an NFL title game.

On the opening series of the second half, the Bears marched down to the Giants' 13, where Manders booted another field goal to return the lead to Chicago. The Giants came right back, with Newman throwing five consecutive completions that ate up 61 yards before Max Krause lugged it in from the 1-yard line. Then it was the Bears' turn. At their own 25 with long third-down yardage, reserve halfback George Corbett rolled out and tossed one to Carl Brumbaugh, who shook loose for 67 yards, leaving the ball on the Giants' 8-yard line. The Giants keyed on Bronko Nagurski, expecting him to hammer into the line. He did take the handoff, but suddenly reared back and hoisted a floater into the hands of Bill Karr in the end zone. Manders' extra point put the Bears back on top, 16–14.

In the fourth quarter, Newman continued his deadly passing game: four straight completions to bring the ball to the Bears' 8. Then, with a little razzle-dazzle, albeit unplanned, the Giants regained the lead. Strong described it later. "Newman handed off to me on a reverse to the left, but the line was jammed up. I turned and saw Newman standing there [back at about the 15-yard line], so I threw him the ball. He was quite surprised. He took off to the right, but then he got bottled up. By now I had crossed into the end zone, and the Bears had forgotten me. Newman saw me wildly waving my hands and threw me the ball. I caught it and fell into the first-base dugout." Strong clambered out of the dugout and kicked the extra point to put the Giants ahead, 21–16.

With time running out, the Bears were forced to eschew their powerful running game and go to the pass. Molesworth arched one to Brumbaugh, and suddenly the Bears were on the Giants' 33-yard line. Nagurski got the ball on the next play, started around the end, and then rifled a short pass to end Bill Hewitt over the middle. Hewitt headed for the sideline with two Giants defenders in pursuit, and just as one of them was about to pounce on him, he flipped a lateral to Karr, who was streaking behind him. Karr carried the ball in for the final touchdown of the game.

The Bears won it, 23–21, but they almost didn't. With just a few seconds remaining, the Giants had the ball, and Newman spotted Red Badgro downfield. Newman hit him with his 12th completion of the afternoon. Only Red Grange stood between Badgro and the Bears' goal line. Trailing behind Badgro was Dale Burnett, waiting to take the lateral when Grange tackled Badgro. But Grange was not only one of the most talented defensive backs in the game, he was also one of the shrewdest, so instead of tackling Badgro low, he hit him high in a bear

hug, pinning the ball between them. They both went down in a heap—the lateral thwarted—prompting Mara to say after the game: "Red Grange saved the game for Chicago . . . that quick thinking prevented a score on the last play."

Each of the Giants went back to New York richer by $142.22, their individual shares of the title game gate; the Bears collected $210.34 apiece.

When the statistics were in for 1933, Newman led the NFL in pass completions (53), passing yardage (973), and touchdown passes (11). Richards had the best rushing average in the league (6.2 yards per carry), and Strong kicked the most extra points (14) and the most field goals (5). Newman, Badgro, and Hein won All-Pro recognition.

The Giants earned the opportunity to avenge themselves against the Bears in 1934 in what turned out to be one of the strangest and most storied NFL championship games in history. But it was not nearly as easy getting to

The famous lateral that did in the Giants during the last minute of the 1933 NFL championship game. Helmetless, Bill Hewitt of the Bears, after catching a pass and about to be tackled by Giants defender Ken Strong, wheels and pitches the ball back to Bill Karr (No. 22), who would then carry it for a touchdown to give the Chicagoans a come-from-behind 23–21 victory.

THE FIRST NFL CHAMPIONSHIP GAME, 1933

New York Giants		Chicago Bears
Red Badgro	LE	Bill Hewitt
Len Grant	LT	Link Lyman
Butch Gibson	LG	Zuck Carlson
Mel Hein	C	Ookie Miller
Potsy Jones	RG	Joe Kopcha
Bill Owen	RT	George Musso
Ray Flaherty	RE	Bill Karr
Harry Newman	QB	Carl Brumbaugh
Ken Strong	LH	Keith Molesworth
Dale Burnett	RH	Gene Ronzani
Bo Molenda	FB	Bronko Nagurski

	1	2	3	4		T
Giants	0	7	7	7	—	21
Bears	3	3	10	7	—	23

Touchdowns—*Giants*: Badgro, Krause, Strong; *Bears*: Karr (2).

Field goals—*Bears*: Manders (3).

PATs—*Giants*: Strong (3); *Bears*: Brumbaugh, Manders.

The thus-far disappointing Giants barely got by Pittsburgh, 14–12, but the turn had been made. New York beat down its next four opponents, looking better each game. Then it was out to Chicago to face the unruly Bears, who were undefeated in five games. Unfortunately it was still not time for revenge. The Giants were blown out at Wrigley Field, 27–7.

The next chance came two weeks later at the Polo Grounds, and it was a much more respectable showing for the New Yorkers. A Giants-loyal crowd of approximately fifty-five thousand warmed Mara's heart, as did a Strong touchdown in the second quarter. New York added two points with a safety when the defense smothered Bears halfback Corbett in the end zone on the kickoff to open the second half, enabling the Giants to take a 9–0 lead into the fourth quarter.

It did not come without cost, however. Newman was sacked at one point and had to be helped off the field. He tried to come back a bit later but ended up limping off again. The next day x-rays showed that he suffered two broken bones in his back, and he was out for the remainder of the season. Ed Danowski took over the duties at tailback that afternoon against the Bears and for the rest of the year.

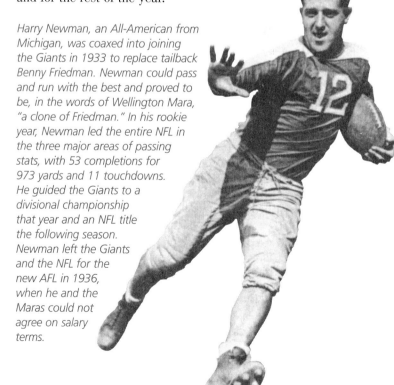

Harry Newman, an All-American from Michigan, was coaxed into joining the Giants in 1933 to replace tailback Benny Friedman. Newman could pass and run with the best and proved to be, in the words of Wellington Mara, "a clone of Friedman." In his rookie year, Newman led the entire NFL in the three major areas of passing stats, with 53 completions for 973 yards and 11 touchdowns. He guided the Giants to a divisional championship that year and an NFL title the following season. Newman left the Giants and the NFL for the new AFL in 1936, when he and the Maras could not agree on salary terms.

the title game, the first ever held at the Polo Grounds, as everyone in the organization might have liked.

To improve his team's chances in 1934, Mara snared two Fordham graduates who would launch fine Giants careers that year. They were tailback Ed Danowski and guard/center Johnny Dell Isola. Already powerful, the team was favored to take the Eastern Division title, and only the Boston Redskins were considered to have a chance at unseating them.

The Giants, however, got off to a dismal start, posting only six points in losses to Detroit and Green Bay in the first two games of the season. Coach Owen railed at them all week before they traveled to Pittsburgh to take on the team then known as the Pirates, whose only real claim to distinction that year was speedster Johnny "Blood" McNally, whom Rooney had acquired from the Packers. Fortunately for the Giants, Blood was sidelined that week with an injury.

It was still not time for the Giants to reap their revenge—so the fates and a few Bears decreed. In the fourth quarter, with Nagurski both carrying the ball and, on other plays, leading the blocking for the swift Beattie Feathers, the Bears marched down the field and scored. Manders' extra point put them within two points of the Giants.

The Giants had the ball with less than two minutes to play, but disaster struck when Krause fumbled on his own 33-yard line and the Bears recovered. Chicago powered to the 16, where, with only a few seconds left, Manders booted a game-winning field goal.

The Giants won two of their last three games, posting a record of 8–5–0, good enough to earn the divisional crown, comfortably ahead of the runner-up Boston Redskins, who were 6–6–0.

No one had come close to the 13–0–0 Bears in the NFL West, and so the stage was set for the Giants' third confrontation that year with their everlasting nemesis from Chicago. The site for the NFL's second champion-

Johnny Dell Isola, initially a center on offense, was switched by Steve Owen to a guard because of Mel Hein's monopoly of the position and played linebacker on defense. He joined forces with the Giants in 1934, after a fine college career at Fordham, and became an important figure in the Giants' offensive and defensive alignments for seven seasons. Dell Isola made All-Pro in 1939 and returned to the team as an assistant coach from 1957 through 1959.

ship game was the Polo Grounds, and the day, December 9, 1934, was bitterly cold (nine degrees above zero at game time). The field was frozen hard and coated with a treacherous veneer of ice.

The conditions prompted Flaherty to come up with a brainchild that would be forever remembered in the annals of pro football. "Why don't we wear sneakers?" he suggested to coach Owen before the game. "When I was playing for Gonzaga we did that once on a frozen field, borrowed them from our basketball team, and we went out and beat a team a lot better than us." Owen wisely took him up on the idea (see sidebar) and dispatched the now quasi-immortal Abe Cohen to procure some.

The paid attendance was officially only 35,059, but according to *The New York Times* there were approximately forty-six thousand fans shivering in the stadium at kickoff time. The Giants posted the only score in the first period when Strong booted a 38-yard field goal. Both teams were sliding all over the field, as Abe Cohen was still uptown trying to round up sneakers.

The power of the larger Bears proved to be the factor in the second quarter. They were able to push the Giants down the slippery field, with Nagurski the prime mover on a long drive that did not end until he bucked in for a touchdown. Later in the period, the scenario was replayed, and the Bears marched all the way to the Giants' 10-yard line. The drive stalled there, but Manders came on to boot the field goal. The score at the half was the Bears 10, the Giants 3, and with another Manders field goal in the third period, Chicago was clearly in command.

But then, just before the fourth quarter began, Cohen showed up with the sneakers. The gym shoe–clad Giants took hold and suddenly ran around and away from the slipping and sliding Bears. Strong ran a punt back 25 yards. Danowski took to the air, and his receivers had little trouble getting free from the Bears defenders. Four straight completions to Flaherty, Burnett, Strong, and Ike Frankian, and the Giants had their first touchdown of the game.

On the next possession, Strong broke loose on a 42-yard touchdown jaunt, and New York had the lead. The Giants took the ball away from the Bears on an interception a minute or so later and marched down the field, with Strong adding another six-pointer. Then the Giants snared

The Giants tried desperately to earn the title of spoilers when they entertained the undefeated Bears late in the 1934 season at the Polo Grounds, but this field goal in the last minute by Jack Manders gave the Chicagoans a 10–9 triumph. The Bears went on to a 13–0 season, but the Giants got sweet revenge in the same stadium a few weeks later in the NFL title tilt. The two Giants defenders are tackle Bill Owen (No. 36) and end Red Badgro (No. 17).

still another interception from the stunned and stumbling Bears, and moments later Danowski carried the ball into the end zone. The 27-point fourth quarter gave the Giants a 30–13 victory over the Bears in what would be known forever after as the "sneakers championship."

In 1935 the Giants front office felt that Newman, who was still troubled with his back injury from the previous season, was making too much money because of the structure of his contract. Comfortable in the fact that Danowski had proven himself a most able passer, Mara decided the deal had to be changed, but it did not sit well with the talented tailback. As Newman later explained it, "In 1935, I had a contract dispute with the Maras. And I decided to hold out. In that last game that I'd played in, in 1934, the one against the Bears, we filled the Polo Grounds. Because I was on a percentage, they had to pay me a lot of dough. As a result they wouldn't give me the same kind of contract for the next

year. . . . I held out, but it didn't do me a lot of good. The season started, and I kept myself sort of busy scouting for coach Kipke back at the University of Michigan."

Newman did come back later in the season, but his playing time was limited. Guard Butch Gibson left in 1935. And the Giants' two All-Pro ends, Flaherty and Badgro, 31 and 32 years old, respectively, were thinking seriously about their own post-football careers. But there was a bright spot: a most promising newcomer, a raucous and outspoken end from West Virginia, Tod Goodwin. He not only won a starting job, but he became Danowski's favorite receiver.

The Giants started the season by demolishing the Pittsburgh Pirates, 42–7, before twenty-four thousand spectators—at the time the largest crowd ever to witness a game in Pittsburgh. The NFL East was acknowledged to be the weaker division—much weaker in fact—and the Giants were considered to be the only forceful team in it. The Western Division, with only four teams after Cincinnati dropped out of the league, was considered the class of the NFL. That would prove to be true.

The Giants lost only three games all season, and those were to Green Bay, the Chicago Bears, and the Chicago Cardinals—all from the NFL West. When the season was finished, the Giants (9–3–0) were the only team in the East with a record better than .500. The other Eastern teams posted a collective mark of 13–31–2. In the West all four teams had winning seasons.

The best in the West in 1935, as it turned out, was the Detroit Lions (7–3–2), which edged out the Green Bay Packers (8–4–0) for the divisional title. The Lions were anchored around triple-threat tailback Dutch Clark, who led the league in scoring that year with 55 points. They also had in the backfield another of the

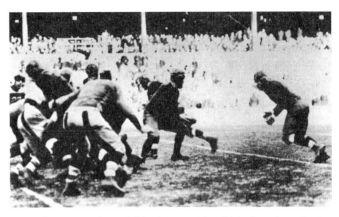

One of the most formidable things with which the Giants had to contend in the 1934 NFL title game—besides the ice-coated field—was the game's most powerful runner: 6'2", 235-pound Bronko Nagurski of the Bears, here about to take a pitchout from Carl Brumbaugh to test the mettle of the New York defense. The bruising fullback scored the game's first touchdown, which gave Chicago a lead they would not relinquish until Abe Cohen arrived at halftime with a dozen pairs of sneakers to transform a bunch of slip-sliders into sure-footed Giants. With 27 unanswered points in the fourth quarter, the Giants turned a 13–3 deficit into a 30–13 victory.

THE "SNEAKERS CHAMPIONSHIP," 1934

New York Giants		Chicago Bears
Ike Frankian	LE	Bill Hewitt
Bill Morgan	LT	Link Lyman
Butch Gibson	LG	Zuck Carlson
Mel Hein	C	Eddie Kawal
Potsy Jones	RG	Bert Pearson
Tex Irvin	RT	George Musso
Ray Flaherty	RE	Bill Karr
Ed Danowski	QB	Carl Brumbaugh
Dale Burnett	LH	Gene Ronzani
Ken Strong	RH	Keith Molesworth
Bo Molenda	FB	Bronko Nagurski

	1	2	3	4		T
Bears	0	10	3	0	—	13
Giants	3	0	0	27	—	30

Touchdowns—*Bears:* Nagurski; *Giants:* Strong (2), Frankian, Danowski.

Field goals—*Bears:* Manders (2); *Giants:* Strong.

PATs—*Bears:* Manders; *Giants:* Strong (2), Molenda.

game's most versatile backs, Glenn Presnell, and one of the most powerful fullbacks, Leroy "Ace" Gutowsky.

The Giants' strength was passing. Danowski led the league in three categories: completions (57), passing yardage (795), and touchdown passes (11). Goodwin caught the most passes in the NFL (26), and in receiving yardage he was only a single yard behind Boston Redskins end Charley Malone, who gained 433. Center Hein was named All-Pro for the third year in a row, and Danowski and tackle Morgan earned similar honors that year.

So for the third time in three years of NFL championship games, New York was the Eastern Division representative.

It rained off and on for four days before the game, and the field at the University of Detroit looked like the Florida Everglades. By game day the rain had turned into snow. Only about fifteen thousand stalwarts turned out for the title game, but the highly partisan Detroit fans were rewarded almost instantly. The Lions took the opening kickoff and marched 61 yards in six plays. They scored when Gutowsky bulled in for the touchdown. A little later in the quarter, Clark raced 40 yards for

SNEAKERS, ABE COHEN, AND A CHAMPIONSHIP

Hero of the New York Giants' first triumph in an NFL title game, the "sneakers championship" of 1934, was 5'2", 140-pound Abe Cohen. Wellington Mara tells of how Cohen achieved his immortality:

> At the Polo Grounds on Sunday morning, the field was completely frozen. We had a little fellow on the payroll named Abe Cohen, a sort of jack-of-all-trades. Abe was a tailor by profession, and he also worked for Chick Meehan, who was a famous coach at Manhattan College and was quite a showman in his own way. Meehan was the first coach to put what we call satin pants on a football team. He had done that first at NYU in the days of Ken Strong. Abe was his tailor and made the pants for the players so that they would fit properly. Steve Owen asked Abe to go up to Manhattan College, to which he had access—he had a key to their equipment room and the gym—and borrow the sneakers from the lockers of the basketball players and bring them over to the Polo Grounds for our players.

> Abe got in a taxi and went to Manhattan. I think he had to break into the lockers. At any rate he got back around halftime of the game with nine or ten pairs of sneakers.

Some of the players didn't want to put them on, but those who did had so much success that eventually most of our players put them on. Ken Strong, who kicked off for us, placekicked with the sneakers on, and he lost a toenail on his big toe. In the second half we began moving the ball. One of the Bears players went over to the sideline and told George Halas that we were wearing sneakers. "Step on their toes," Halas shouted to his players.

> The following week after the championship game—in those days you had barnstorming trips after the season was over—the Bears were playing an exhibition game in Philadelphia, and Steve Owen and I went down to see the game. We went into the Bears' dressing room, I guess to crow a little bit, and the first thing we saw was about 24 pairs of sneakers on top of the lockers. Halas said to us, "I'll never get caught like that again."

And as for Cohen, Lewis Burton summed it up best in the December 10, 1934, edition of the *New York American:* "To the heroes of antiquity, to the Greek who raced across the Marathon plain, and to Paul Revere, add now the name of Abe Cohen."

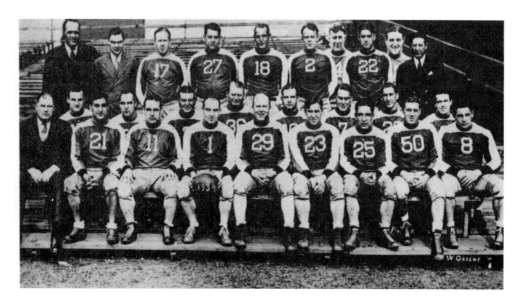

The NFL champion New York Giants of 1934. Top row, left to right: Charles Porter (trainer), Jack Mara (president), Red Badgro, Bill Morgan, Dale Burnett, Johnny Dell Isola, Stu Clancy, Ed Danowski, Harry Newman, Gus Mauch (trainer). Middle row, left to right: Elvin "Kink" Richards, Hank Reese, Len Grant, Bill Owen, Tom Jones, Mel Hein, Harrison Stafford, Willis Smith. Front row, left to right: Steve Owen (coach), Ike Frankian, Butch Gibson, Ray Flaherty, Cecil Irvin, Bo Molenda, Max Krause, Ken Strong, Bob Bellinger.

ABE COHEN WASN'T THE ONLY HERO

From *Pro Football Inquirer*, December 1976:

> When the water buckets froze during the "sneakers" game, trainer Gus Mauch thought of something else to give the Giants' players during time outs.

> "It was sometime during the fourth quarter," says Mauch. "I asked [team president] Jack Mara if he had a bottle of whiskey. I only wanted it for medicinal purposes . . . something to warm 'em up out there. During the next time out I poured some whiskey in each of the paper cups and took them out on a tray. On the next play, Ken Strong ran a reverse and took it all the way for a touchdown.

> "During the next time out, I did the same thing and we scored again," says Mauch. "By that time the bottle was empty. So Jack Mara went to some of his friends sitting in the field boxes right behind our bench. Judge Phelan, the boxing commissioner and Jack's father-in-law, was there. So was Mayor [Jimmy] Walker and Jim Farley, the postmaster general."

> Mauch says Mara returned with another bottle and the trainer made another visit to the players. "This time they told me, 'We've got this thing won now; we don't want to get drunk.' They chased me off the field."

EATING ON THE ROAD, THIRTIES STYLE

This is the menu from the dining car on a New York Giants road trip, December 1, 1935:

Pennsylvania Railroad Dinner

One Dollar and Fifty Cents

Puree of Tomato Soup, Croutons Consommé

Broiled Tenderloin Steak, Fresh Mushroom Sauce

Château Potatoes

New Stringless Beans

Assorted Bread

Lettuce and Beet Salad, French Dressing, Chopped Eggs

Mince Pie, *Hot or Cold*

Ice Cream

Chilled Grapefruit

Tea, Coffee, Milk

another Detroit tally. The Giants showed a little life in the third period when Strong scored on a 42-yard pass play from Danowski, but that and Strong's extra point proved to be New York's only points of that wintry afternoon. The Lions added a pair of touchdowns in the final quarter to give the them a 26–7 victory.

While this program was being hawked at the Polo Grounds, the Giants easily clinched the NFL East title. Their 13–0 victory over Pittsburgh gave them a 9–3 record for the season and the right to meet the Detroit Lions for the NFL title of 1935, the Giants' third consecutive battle for the NFL championship.

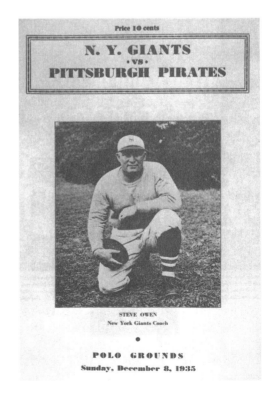

Price 10 cents

N. Y. GIANTS ·VS· PITTSBURGH PIRATES

STEVE OWEN
New York Giants Coach

•

POLO GROUNDS
Sunday, December 8, 1935

A DISAPPOINTING TITLE GAME, 1935

New York Giants		Detroit Lions
Ike Frankian	LE	Ed Klewicki
Bill Morgan	LT	Jack Johnson
Potsy Jones	LG	Regis Monahan
Mel Hein	C	Clare Randolph
Bill Owen	RG	Ox Emerson
Len Grant	RT	George Christensen
Tod Goodwin	RE	John Schneller
Ed Danowski	QB	Glenn Presnell
Ken Strong	LH	Frank Christensen
Kink Richards	RH	Ernie Caddel
Les Corzine	FB	Ace Gutowsky

	1	2	3	4		T
Giants	0	0	7	0	—	7
Lions	13	0	0	13	—	26

Touchdowns—*Giants:* Strong; *Lions:* Gutowsky, Clark, Caddel, Parker.

PATs—*Giants:* Strong; *Lions:* Presnell, Clark.

The Giants visited the Hollywood set of a motion picture starring James Cagney (front, center) in the midthirties on one of their exhibition tours to California. The cast, including actor and comedian Joe E. Brown (directly behind Cagney), posed with the Giants in front of a set of a prison.

A family and a friend—the brain trust of the Giants circa the late thirties. From right to left: Wellington Mara (secretary), Tim Mara (founder), Jack Mara (president), and Steve Owen (coach).

MORE NFL TITLE GAMES THAN ANY OTHER TEAM

The first NFL draft was held in 1936, and the Giants' first pick in it was Art Lewis, a tackle from Ohio University, who, as it turned out, would have only a one-year football career in New York. But the year before, a youthful Wellington Mara, then 19 and a student at Fordham University, went down to the nation's capital and recruited running back Alphonse "Tuffy" Leemans of George Washington University, an acquisition who would prove to be more valuable than any first-round draft pick over the next 15 years.

Although he was only a junior in college, Mara had already immersed himself in what was to become his career and avocation—that of an integral and guiding force in the New York Giants management. His special forte was finding talent. He kept files on hundreds of college players, scouring newspapers and magazines for information on them, writing letters to college coaches, friends, and Giants alumni for firsthand information about them. Leemans was one he thought had special potential even though he was playing for a small and unheralded college football team.

Wellington suggested to his father the efficacy of his going down and talking Leemans into a career in professional football. "Go ahead," Tim Mara told his son.

"I sent him a telegram setting up a meeting and signed my father's name to it," Wellington explained

later. "It was to be in front of the gymnasium at George Washington. When I got there, he thought I was a kid who wanted his autograph. He looked at me, strangely suspicious, and said he was meeting Tim Mara, the owner of the New York Giants. But I was able to eventually convince him that I was in fact a legitimate emissary, and he did listen to me. And, of course, we got him for the Giants."

The Giants lost three familiar names to the new American Football League: Ken Strong, Harry Newman, and Red Badgro. And Ray Flaherty resigned to take on the head coaching duties for George Preston Marshall of the Boston Redskins. Still, the Giants were favored to garner another divisional crown. Their vulnerability became apparent, however, early in the season with losses in their first two games to the hapless Philadelphia Eagles (which would turn out to be the Eagles' only victory in 12 games that year) and the Pittsburgh Pirates.

Chiefly behind the running of Leemans, who was fast proving to be one of the league's most effective rushers, Steve Owen's New Yorkers rebounded, winning four games and tying another. But then the Chicago Bears throttled them, 25–7, at the Polo Grounds. The next week it was the Lions in Detroit who battered them, 38–0. Then the Green Bay Packers came to Gotham and

RUNYON PREDICTS

The first night football game to be played at the Polo Grounds pitted the College All-Stars against the New York Giants in the 1936 preseason. It was a benefit for the *New York Herald Tribune* Fresh Air Fund, and Damon Runyon devoted one of his "Both Barrels" syndicated columns to it:

> It's our private opinion, and don't let it get around any more than you can help as it might affect the odds, that the College All-Stars will knock the spots off the New York Giants. . . .
>
> It is to be held at night on a light-flooded field, which in itself is a tremendous novelty in New York and may be the beginning of regular night football and baseball, too, here.
>
> They are presenting against the professionals a team of college stars that will include some of the most famous players in the United States, under the coaching of Bernie Bierman, who is accounted one of the smartest football generals alive.
>
> Neighbor Caswell Adams reports from Evanston, Illinois, where the College All-Stars are training, the presence of fellows like Wayne Millner and Bill Shakespeare of Notre Dame, Phil Hanagan of Holy Cross, Amerino Sarno of Fordham, and Dick Crayne, Sheldon Beise, Riley Smith and numerous others whose names and exploits threaded the football news last fall.
>
> Jay Berwanger, of Chicago, halfback selection on everybody's All-American is there. So is Joe Maniaci, Dick Pfefferle and Dale Rennebohm. . . . We think the collegians are a fair bet to beat the Giants.

The Giants won, 12–2.

His name was Elvin Richards, but he was better known around the Polo Grounds as "Kink" when he came out of obscurity (Simpson College in Iowa) in 1933 and worked his way into a backfield with such luminaries as Ken Strong, Harry Newman, and Dale Burnett. Richards became the second Giant to rush for more than 100 yards in a game, a feat he accomplished against the Brooklyn Dodgers in 1933 only a week after Harry Newman set the team's century standard. He led the club in rushing in 1935, with 449 yards, and stayed around through the 1939 season.

whipped the Giants, 26–14. A win over the Brooklyn Dodgers gave them a record of 5–5–1 going into the last game of the season, but as disappointing as the year had been, it could all be rectified at the Polo Grounds on December 6, 1936. That afternoon the Giants were scheduled to face the Boston Redskins, who had a record of 6–5–0. The Pittsburgh Pirates had already finished their season with a record of 6–6–0. So a win would put the Giants on top by dint of a 6–5–1 record.

But on a mud-soaked field with rain falling intermittently throughout the game, the Giants could not get going. Their offense was overwhelmed, most notably by Redskins All-Pro tackle Albert Glen "Turk" Edwards, who seemed to be in on every tackle, who recovered fumbles and blocked kicks. And halfback Cliff Battles stunned the well-dampened seventeen thousand fans at

Alphonse "Tuffy" Leemans, shown here carrying the ball against the Green Bay Packers, came to the Giants in 1936 after a teenage Wellington Mara went down to George Washington University to recruit him the year before. To prove Mara's sagacity, Leemans led the entire NFL in rushing with 830 yards as a rookie. Moving out to block for him here is Leland Shaffer (No. 20).

the Polo Grounds by weaving his way 74 yards to return a New York punt for a touchdown. That, and another touchdown by fullback Don Irwin, were enough to give Boston a 14–0 shutout and the divisional title.

New York's record of 5–6–1 marked only the third time in the franchise's 12-year history that it fell below .500. On an individual level, however, rookie Leemans led the entire NFL in rushing with 830 yards and was named All-Pro. The only other Giant All-Pro was center Mel Hein.

The Maras, unhappy at the sudden decline of their team, vowed some changes. And so when the Giants took the field in 1937, there were 17 rookies on the 25-man roster. That wasn't all that was new. New uniforms were fresh from the tailor, now with blue jerseys and silver pants. The offense was also revamped: Owen sent his team out with a backfield alignment he devised called the A formation.

The Giants' first-round draft pick in 1937 was consensus All-American tackle Ed Widseth of Minnesota. Two rookie backs, wingback Ward Cuff from Marquette and fullback/halfback Hank Soar of Providence, spent a lot of time in the backfield that year with Ed Danowski and Leemans. Jim Poole, out of Mississippi, replaced the retired Tod Goodwin at end,

FORESIGHT!

Arthur J. Daley wrote of this friendly encounter between NFL owners in 1938 in *The New York Times*:

> The Giants were playing the Redskins in Washington early this season before the largest crowd ever to see a professional football game in the capital. The youthful Jack Mara, president of the New Yorkers, strolled out on the field before the battle with George Preston Marshall, grand high mogul and panjandrum of the Redskins.
>
> With an innocence that was belied by the twinkle in his eyes, Jack turned to the Magnificent Marshall and asked, "Tell me, George, where are you going to put the extra seats for the playoff game?"
>
> George Preston took a running broad jump into the trap for a new Olympic record. "See those seats out in center field?" answered the Magnificent One with a grandiloquent wave of his hand. "We'll build extra stands in back of them and then we'll put more seats in right field and . . ."
>
> "Or maybe, George," interrupted Jack, "you'll come up to the Polo Grounds to see the Giants in the playoff."

As it turned out, the Giants did host the championship game that year, and Marshall did attend it, watching benignly as New York defeated the Green Bay Packers, 23–17.

the finale they were listed as a slight underdog by the oddsmakers. Marshall, the flamboyant owner of the Washington franchise, shrugged it off and said of his Redskins, "The Indians have come to reclaim Manhattan Island." And to support his contention he brought along a 55-piece marching band dressed in Indian costumes, as well as ten thousand fans who came by train and chartered buses. Marshall led them in a march up Broadway the day of the game.

The hype worked, at least in the second half. With the Giants only a touchdown behind midway through the third quarter, the Redskins suddenly went on the rampage and, behind the passing of Baugh and the running of Battles, raked off four unanswered touchdowns, turning a 21–14 contest into a 49–14 nightmare. And so the season ended for the Giants.

Danowski passed for 814 yards that year, second to sensational rookie Baugh, who became only the second passer in NFL history to throw for more than 1,000 yards (1,127). And Hein was named All-Pro center for the fifth consecutive season. The youthful team showed a lot of promise, Mara thought as he closed the books on the 1937 Giants; so did the game of professional football in New York, with the Giants attracting more than 260,000 spectators to their seven home games and their ledger solidly in the black.

Fullback Hank Soar was one of the 17 rookies to join the Giants in 1937, and he ended up as a starter. In fact, he gained the most yards rushing for the team that year: 442. Soar proved to be a dependable runner and blocker throughout his nine-year Giants career. After football, he went on to become a famous major league baseball umpire.

and Jim Lee Howell from Arkansas was slated for a good deal of work at the other end.

But for all the newness, the Giants again had to settle for the role of runner-up. And in almost a repeat from the year before, in the last game of the season they gave the title to the Redskins, who had relocated to Washington, D.C. The Giants were 6–2–2 when they hosted the Redskins on December 5, 1936, at the Polo Grounds. The Redskins were 7–3–0. The winner would claim the NFL East title.

The Redskins, deftly guided by rookie tailback Slingin' Sammy Baugh, had defeated the Giants in the first game of the regular season, 13–3, but going into

The 1937 Giants had a new look with 17 rookies on the 25-player roster, yet they just missed winning the NFL East title in the last game of the season. Top row, left to right: Charles Porter (trainer), Bo Molenda (assistant coach), Len Grant, Elvin "Kink" Richards, Ray Hanken, Stan "Bunny" Galazin, Ed Widseth, John Haden, Ed Danowski, Johnny Dell Isola, Mel Hein, Gus Mauch (trainer). Middle row, left to right: Jerry Dennerlein, Jim Lee Howell, Kenneth "Kayo" Lunday, Chuck Gelatka, Will Walls, Jim Poole, Ewell Phillips, Milt "Mickey" Kobrosky, Dale Burnett, Larry Johnson, Wellington Mara (secretary), Steve Owen (coach). Front row, left to right: Ward Cuff, Tony Sarausky, Alphonse "Tuffy" Leemans, Leland Shaffer, Ox Parry, Arthur "Tarzan" White, Hank Soar, Pete Cole, Jim Neill, Tillie Manton, Les Corzine, Orville Tuttle, Joe Carroll.

Perhaps "It seems I've heard this song before" should have been the refrain played by Marshall's marching band that again paraded up Broadway before the last game of the 1938 season. In the balance at the Polo Grounds for the third consecutive year was the Eastern Divisional crown. The young Giants sported a record of 7–2–1, and the Redskins were a shade behind at 6–2–2.

The New Yorkers' only two losses came in the second and third games of the regular season: 14–10 to Philadelphia and 13–10 to the Pittsburgh Pirates. After that the Giants soared, even topping the Redskins midway through the season.

The Redskins and their huge tribe of fans arrived and marched in Manhattan with the same exuberance they had the year previous. But their song ended on a distinctly different note in 1938. The tone was set in the first quarter when Soar burst through the Redskins' line and raced 42 yards for the Giants' first touchdown of the day. Thirty unanswered points after that, the Giants had

a 36–0 triumph, the NFL East title, and a sweet taste of revenge for the 49–14 drubbing they had received the year before.

Again Danowski had proved to be one of the game's most dangerous passers. His 70 completions were the most in the league

Ed Danowski did not have far to move when he went from Fordham, where he was a standout tailback, to the Polo Grounds and the Giants in 1934. The following year he took over as starting tailback, replacing Harry Newman, who was holding out for more money. Danowski kept the job until he retired after the 1939 season (he resumed the position for the 1941 season before going into the military).

Big Ed Widseth was a vintage addition to the Giants' front line in 1937. A consensus All-American tackle from Minnesota, he earned All-Pro honors his sophomore year in the NFL and played four years with the Giants.

CHAMPS A SECOND TIME, 1938

New York Giants		Green Bay Packers
Jim Poole	LE	Wayland Becker
Ed Widseth	LT	Champ Seibold
Johnny Dell Isola	LG	Russ Letlow
Mel Hein	C	Carl Mulleneaux
Orville Tuttle	RG	Buckets Goldenberg
Ox Parry	RT	Bill Lee
Jim Lee Howell	RE	Milt Gantenbein
Ed Danowski	QB	Herman Schneidman
Hank Soar	LH	Cecil Isbell
Ward Cuff	RH	Joe Laws
Leland Shaffer	FB	Clarke Hinkle

	1	2	3	4		T
Packers	0	14	3	0	—	17
Giants	9	7	7	0	—	23

Touchdowns—*Packers:* Mulleneaux, Hinkle; *Giants:* Leemans, Barnard, Soar.

Field goals—*Packers:* Engebretsen; *Giants:* Cuff.

PATs— *Packers:* Engebretsen (2); *Giants:* Cuff (2).

in 1938, and his 848 yards gained passing trailed only Clarence "Ace" Parker of the Brooklyn Dodgers and Baugh of the Redskins. Cuff kicked the most field goals (5) and extra points (18) in the NFL. And Widseth joined seemingly permanent resident Hein on the list of All-Pros.

The Green Bay Packers won the NFL West behind the passing combination of Cecil Isbell to Don Hutson and the powerful running of Clarke Hinkle. The Packers were a slight favorite to beat the Giants. The largest crowd to attend an NFL championship game up to that time—48,120—filled the Polo Grounds to watch the contest that was both suspenseful and savage. Arthur J. Daley described it this way in *The New York Times:*

The Giants and the Packers delved into the realm of fiction for a storybook football game at the Polo Grounds yesterday. . . .

Perhaps there have been better football games since Rutgers and Princeton started the autumnal madness 69 years ago, but no one in that huge crowd would admit it. This was a struggle of such magnificent stature that words seem such feeble tools for describing it. . . . What a frenzied battle this was! The tackling was fierce and the blocking positively vicious. . . . Tempers were so frayed and tattered that stray punches were tossed around all afternoon. This was the gridiron sport at its primitive best.

The Giants got on the scoreboard first. A Hinkle punt was blocked in the first quarter by Howell, and the Giants took over on the Green Bay 7-yard line. Three plays failed to score, and then Cuff booted a field goal. On the next series of downs, Isbell dropped back to punt for the Packers, and this time Poole knifed in to block it, giving the Giants the ball on the Green Bay 27-yard line. The turnover resulted in a touchdown a few plays later when Leemans lugged the ball into the end zone.

In the second quarter, it was the Giants' turn to make a mistake. Paul "Tiny" Engebretsen, a 6'1", 240-pound guard for the Pack, intercepted a Giants pass, and moments later Arnie Herber dropped back and rifled a 40-yard bomb to Carl Mulleneaux for a touchdown. The Giants redeemed themselves, however, with a concerted march down the field, highlighted with runs by rookie halfback Len Barnum and culminating in a 20-yard touchdown pass from Danowski to Hap Barnard. And still the first-half scoring was not over, although time was running out. Isbell hit end Wayland Becker with a short pass, and Becker scampered 66 yards before Soar could catch him and drag him to the turf at the New York 17-yard line. Then Hinkle hit the Giants' line five times in a row, finally smashing in for six Packers points. The score at the half was the Giants 16, the Packers 14.

During the first half, Hutson, Green Bay's great pass receiver, had to leave the game with an injured knee; Hein, kicked in the cheekbone, was diagnosed with a concussion; Johnny Dell Isola was taken from the field on a stretcher straight to St. Elizabeth's Hospital, where he was treated for a spinal concussion that was feared to be—but fortunately was not—a fractured vertebra.

Then came the second half. The Packers were on the move from the opening kickoff, a 63-yard drive all the way to the Giants' 5-yard line. That was as far as they went, so Engebretsen stood back and kicked a 15-yard field goal to give Green Bay its first lead of the day, 17–16. But the Giants were far from foundering, and they came right back with a march of 62 yards, the highlight of which was a picture-perfect pass from Danowski to Soar at the 6, where Soar shook off a tackler and stormed into the end zone.

Green Bay fought back magnificently in the fourth quarter, dominating the action. The Pack reached the New York 38 on one drive and the 17 on another. But the first was stalled, and the second resulted in a fumble. After that the Packers moved again, and Herber connected on a pass to end Milt Gantenbein at the Giants' 40-yard line, but the Packers' flanker back had edged up to the line of scrimmage, which made Gantenbein

MIXING METAPHORS

After the Giants whipped the favored Green Bay Packers, 23–17, for the NFL title of 1938, Arthur "Bugs" Baer, writing for the International News Service, had trouble containing himself:

> It was a game of vibrating behemoths against fermenting Goliaths. Every man on the field was six feet tall, three feet wide and a yard thick. There was every kind of official on the turf except the one they needed most. And that was a knock-down timekeeper.
>
> When the two lines rushed at each other it was like a freight train kissing the depot. You could hear the crash from the rockbound shores of Maine to far prettier places. The score, 23 to 17, sounds like the little-potato-hard-to-peel had met the lumberyard skullbusters who decided to mash them instead.
>
> It was a backwoods vendetta in the high-rent district. . . . With the winners getting about $135 extra per man, it was this extra bit of muscular bribery that made the lads go to town like a wolf in famine.
>
> The result: the boys were as earnest as a sneak thief in a lock-and-key store. And as tough as veal breaded in marble dust.
>
> They went at each other like dogs meeting in a sausage machine. And mixed like the stuff they put in a martini.
>
> It was a throwback to the apes. Twenty-two mugs got an assist on the play and the apes get credit for the put-out. . . .
>
> It was mostly a barroom fight outdoors. Close to fifty thousand innocent bystanders looked upon the resumption of gang warfare in America. It was terrific.

an ineligible receiver. The ball was turned over to the Giants at the point of the foul—the rule of the day—which was the Green Bay 43-yard line. The Packers still put together two more drives during the fourth quarter,

The way the Redskins came to town, circa 1938. This was the band and the followers of the Washington Redskins, whom George Preston Marshall, the flamboyant team owner, led "unobtrusively into New York" (in the words of New York sports columnist Bill Corum) to support their team against the Giants. It did not do them a lot of good, however, as the Giants lambasted the Redskins, 36–0, to secure the NFL East title that year.

both into Giants territory, but both were stopped. There were no points scored in the fourth quarter, but many observers said it was one of the most exciting, hard-fought periods in the history of NFL championship games. Both teams were brutally beaten as they left the field that December afternoon, and every player on the field knew that he had been in a truly savage football game. The final score stood at 23–17, giving the Giants victory and the right to be known as the first team to win two NFL championship games.

The season was not over for the Giants when they dragged their bruised and bloodied bodies from the Polo Grounds after the NFL championship melee. Ahead was the league's first Pro Bowl game, a contest to be staged across the country at Wrigley Field in Los Angeles. On January 15, 1939, the Giants took on a select cast of pro all-stars, which included such future Hall of Famers as Baugh, Hinkle, Joe Stydahar, and Frank "Bruiser" Kinard. But the Giants displayed for the California audience their championship form, coming back from a 10–3

OWEN'S FAVORITE

Arthur J. Daley wrote in *The New York Times* of Steve Owen's response when he was asked who of his old ball players he missed the most:

> "That's easy," he drawled. "Hank Soar. I rode him unmercifully every season, but I guess he was my favorite. He had such a blazing team spirit, such a will to win and such good humor at all times that I hate to see him gone."

> Hank was strictly a money player, at his best when the chips were down and the going at its very toughest. Never will any Giant forget that terrific battle with the Redskins a few seasons back when Slingin' Sammy Baugh was trying desperately to pitch to victory in the closing minutes.

> Soar, playing safety, kept glancing back at the clock. "Don't look at the clock," roared Stout Steve from the sidelines. "Watch the ball."

> Hank's classic answer was delivered with an annoyed wave of his hand. "Don't bother us, Steve," he shouted back. "We're busy out here."

deficit in the fourth quarter with a 22-yard touchdown pass from Danowski to Chuck Gelatka and a Cuff field goal to win, 13–10.

Their next encounter that year was another All-Star game, this one against the College All-Stars, a tradition begun by sports columnist Arch Ward and the *Chicago Tribune* in 1934. The idea was to pit the NFL champs from the year before against the best players coming out of college that year in a game at Soldier Field in Chicago before the start of the pros' regular exhibition season.

This was the Giants' first appearance in the spectacle, which annually drew seventy-five thousand to eighty thousand fans into cavernous Soldier Field. Since its inception, the pro champs had won only once, the All-Stars twice, and they had played to two ties. The collegians had won the two previous encounters, embarrassing the Packers and the Redskins respectively, and the pros were eager to regain their self-esteem.

Among the more notable college All-Stars that year were Heisman Trophy–winner Davey O'Brien of Texas Christian University, Marshall Goldberg from Pittsburgh, Bob MacLeod of Dartmouth, and Bowden Wyatt from Tennessee. It was a less-than-thrilling game, but the pros could once again look demeaningly upon their younger challengers as the result of a 9–0 victory by New York. The points came on two field goals by Strong, back in a Giants uniform for the first time since 1935 after his three-year adventure in other pro football leagues, and another from the toe of Cuff.

Strong was 33 years old, and his contributions were pretty much restricted to the kicking game. The Giants' backfield was spoken for, so to speak, with division title veterans like Danowski, Leemans, Soar, Barnum, and Cuff. And the defense, keyed by Widseth, Hein, and Dell Isola, was overwhelming. In fact, the Giants gave up an average of only six and a half points in their first six games of the 1939 season.

As it had been since 1936, the NFL East was a fierce battle between New York and the Redskins, one that would again go down to the very last game of the season. The Giants had lost only to the Lions, an upset out in Detroit, and had played Washington to a 0–0 tie while defeating eight other opponents. The Redskins had an identical record of 8–1–1, having lost only to the Green Bay Packers.

And so, as New York sports columnist Bill Corum observed, "At the head of a 150-piece brass band and twelve thousand fans, George Preston Marshall slipped unobtrusively into New York today," for what had become the traditional December NFL East title decider.

Ward Cuff was another rookie find in 1937, a multitalented halfback from Marquette, in the days when the Milwaukee school fielded a football team. Cuff quickly earned a steady job in the Giants backfield and led the team in scoring every year from 1937 through 1942. He could run with the ball, catch passes, and kick field goals and extra points; he was also a fine defensive back during his nine-year Giants career.

ONE TITLE TILT BETTER FORGOTTEN, 1939

New York Giants		Green Bay Packers
Jim Poole	LE	Don Hutson
Frank Cope	LT	Baby Ray
Johnny Dell Isola	LG	Russ Letlow
Mel Hein	C	Earl Svendsen
Orville Tuttle	RG	Buckets Goldenberg
John Mellus	RT	Bill Lee
Jim Lee Howell	RE	Milt Gantenbein
Ed Danowski	QB	Larry Craig
Kink Richards	LH	Cecil Isbell
Ward Cuff	RH	Joe Laws
Nello Falaschi	FB	Clarke Hinkle

	1	2	3	4		T
Giants	0	0	0	0	—	0
Packers	7	0	10	10	—	27

Touchdowns—*Packers:* Gantenbein, Laws, Jankowski.

Field goals—*Packers:* Engebretsen, Smith.

PATs—*Packers:* Engebretsen (2), Smith.

It was rainy that day, but to prove conclusively that professional football had come into its own in New York City more than 62,500 filled the Polo Grounds to see who would earn the right to represent the NFL East in that year's championship game. On a messy field, the game was a plodding one, with defense the overriding factor. The Giants proved the stronger through the first three quarters of play, holding the Redskins scoreless and maintaining a 9–0 lead on two field goals by Cuff and another from Strong. That lead was diminished in the final quarter, however, when tailback Frank Filchock threw to end Bob Masterson for a Redskins touchdown. The conversion brought them within two points of New York. Then, with less than a minute remaining, the Redskins, on the Giants' 10-yard line, lined up for a field goal. Bo Russell booted the ball, and the Washington players watching it began leaping in jubilation at what presumably was the game-winning, title-clinching three

points. But they were stopped in their proverbial tracks by referee Bill Halloran, who signaled that the attempt was not good. There was a lot of screaming and yelling from the Redskins players and their coach, Ray Flaherty, who raged after Halloran, and there was a small riot among players and spectators on the field after time expired. But the ruling held, and the Giants were the winner by the score of 9–7. The call was controversial and never proven correct or incorrect by later photos, the angles of some showing the kick to be good, and others showing it to be not good. Later Owen said, "I thought the call was right, but I didn't have the best angle to judge it." Flaherty said, "If that guy [Halloran] has got a conscience, he'll never have another good night's sleep as long as he lives."

The Green Bay Packers had narrowly edged out the Chicago Bears in the NFL West and were to serve as the host for the title tilt, not in their hometown, however, but instead at the State Fair Park in Milwaukee, which could accommo-

Green Bay fullback Clarke Hinkle meets a stubborn Giants defense in the second quarter of the 1938 title game and is brought down one yard from the goal line. On the next play, however, Hinkle bulled it in for a Packers touchdown. Still, the Pack ended up on the short end of a 23–17 score that December day. No. 17 on Green Bay is tailback Cecil Isbell.

Ed Danowski (left) and trainer Gus Mauch, two very familiar faces around the Giants locker room during the late thirties, share a little canned libation during Danowski's last year (1941) as a Giant. Danowski led the team in passing every year from 1935 through 1939 and was named an All-Pro twice (1935 and 1938).

date a larger crowd. The 9–2–0 Pack still sported the backfield of Isbell, Herber, and Hinkle, the dazzling pass catching of Hutson, a fine defense, and the able coaching of Earl "Curly" Lambeau.

It was a typically cold, windy December day in Wisconsin, but that hardly hampered the Packers. They were hot for revenge for the defeat the Giants had handed them in the championship match the year before. And the Giants were as cold as the frozen turf of State Fair Park. Green Bay scored midway through the first quarter on a pass from Herber to Gantenbein. The Giants had several opportunities to score, but two field-goal attempts by Cuff and another by Len Barnum were all unsuccessful. The Pack had a 7–0 lead at the halftime intermission. From that point on, the game was Green Bay's alone. Scoring 10 points each in the remaining two quarters and picking off pass after Giants pass (the Packers intercepted six passes that afternoon), Green Bay humbled the Giants by the most decisive score up to that time in NFL championship play, 27–0. The $455.37 each Giant took back to New York as shares of the gate was little consolation—each Packer received $708.97.

SIXTH TRIP TO THE CHAMPIONSHIP GAME, 1941

New York Giants		Chicago Bears
Jim Poole	LE	Dick Plasman
John Mellus	LT	Ed Kolman
Kayo Lunday	LG	Danny Fortmann
Mel Hein	C	Bulldog Turner
Len Younce	RG	Ray Bray
Bill Edwards	RT	Lee Artoe
Jim Lee Howell	RE	John Siegal
Nello Falaschi	QB	Sid Luckman
George Franck	LH	Ray Nolting
Ward Cuff	RH	Hugh Gallarneau
Tuffy Leemans	FB	Norm Standlee

	1	2	3	4		T
Giants	6	0	3	0	—	9
Bears	3	6	14	14	—	37

Touchdowns—*Bears:* Standlee (2), McAfee, Kavanaugh; *Giants:* Franck.

Field goals—*Bears:* Snyder (3); *Giants:* Cuff.

PATs—*Bears:* Snyder, Maniaci, Artoe, McLean.

Still, it had been a fine season, bringing the team its second straight divisional crown. The Giants allowed their opponents only 85 points in 11 games during the regular season and set an NFL record by kicking 14 field goals (Cuff's 7 were the most in the league that year). Four Giants made All-Pro: center Hein (for the seventh straight year), halfback Leemans, end Poole, and guard Dell Isola.

The New York Giants should have been overjoyed at not having to go to the NFL championship game of 1940; that was the one in which the Chicago Bears—Sid Luckman, George McAfee, Bill Osmanski, Ken Kavanaugh, Joe Stydahar, Clyde "Bulldog" Turner, Danny Fortmann, and "Automatic" Jack Manders—annihilated the Washington Redskins, 73–0, and undoubtedly shortened Marshall's life by a decade or two.

Danowski retired before the start of the 1940 season, and replacing him was Ed Miller from the University of New Mexico, who had been drafted by the Giants the year before. And there was a lot of hope for two rookie backs: Grenny Lansdell from the University of Southern California and Kay Eakin of Arkansas. But the spark that had fired the two previous divisional champs was not there, illustrated graphically in an opening-day tie with the Pittsburgh Pirates, who had had a record of 1–9–1 the year before and would be 2–7–2 at the end of the 1940 season. The Giants followed that performance by a 21–7 beating at the hands of the Redskins.

Midway through the season, and just before having to face the Chicago Bears, Leemans was lost for the rest of the year with a back injury. A pounding by the Bears, 37–21, and a loss to the Brooklyn Dodgers, 14–6, gave the Giants four losses at the end of the season against six wins and a tie—good enough only for third place. Hein was the only Giant to win All-Pro honors, accomplishing that for the 10th year in a row.

With a world war looming and a disappointing season to start the decade, the forties did not seem all that promising for the Mara family business.

The Giants, however, managed to put together a quite respectable team in 1941. Danowski was lured out of retirement, Leemans' back healed, and Hein was talked out of a potential retirement. The New Yorkers virtually sailed through their first five games, with only the Redskins coming within a touchdown of them as they outscored their opponents, 122–27. But the Brooklyn Dodgers, coached by Jock Sutherland and guided on the field by All-Pro tailback Clarence "Ace" Parker, dealt them their first loss of the season over at Ebbets Field. Then, after an upset by the cellar-dwelling Chicago Cardinals of the NFL West, the Giants got back on track.

By the last game of the season, the Giants had clinched the NFL East title with a record of 8–2. It mattered little that they lost that Sunday, December 7, 1941, at the Polo Grounds to the Dodgers, 21–7. It mattered much more, of course, that while they were playing that game Pearl Harbor was under attack by the Japanese. For the United States, World War II had begun.

The NFL title game two weeks later attracted little interest in a nation otherwise preoccupied. Only 13,341 spectators showed up at Wrigley Field in Chicago, the smallest crowd ever in the history of NFL championship games. The Bears, the pride of George Halas with a regular season record of 10–1–0, who had outscored their regular-season and playoff opponents (they had to defeat the 10–1–0 Packers for the divisional crown) 429–161, were a legitimate favorite. But by the end of the first quarter, they trailed the Giants, 6–3, the result of a 31-yard touchdown pass play from Leemans to George Franck.

The Bears' hibernation came to an end in the second half, however, with four touchdowns and almost complete domination. The final score was 37–9, and the Bears became the first team in NFL history to win back-to-back championships.

The Giants could find solace in the fact that they had rebounded respectably to win their sixth divisional title and held the honor of having played in more NFL championship games than any other team in the league.

Slated as the starting 11 for the 1942 Giants. Many would soon be gone, however, exchanging football uniforms for those of the military. Top row, left to right: the backfield—Ward Cuff, John Chickerneo, Merle Hapes, Alphonse "Tuffy" Leemans. Bottom row, left to right: the line—Will Walls, Al Blozis, Chuck Avedisian, Mel Hein, Ed Lechner, Frank Cope, O'Neal Adams.

TRYING TIMES IN THE FORTIES

The National Football League continued to operate during World War II, but many of the best players were in Europe and Asia fighting for their country. In all, 638 NFL players saw military duty during the war, and 21 of them were killed in action. Fifty-two New York Giants were in military service during the 1942–1945 period, and two did not return. A scant six weeks after playing in the 1944 championship game for the Giants, tackle and lieutenant in the U.S. Army Al Blozis was killed on his first combat mission in the Vosges Mountains of France on January 31, 1945. A little more than two months later, U.S. Marine lieutenant Jack Lummus, an end on the 1941 Giants team, was killed while leading an attack during the battle on Iwo Jima.

Joining the 1942 Giants was Merle Hapes, a running back from Mississippi, New York's first-round draft choice that year. He not only worked his way into the starting lineup, but he proved to be the club's leading rusher that year. At 6'6" and 250 pounds, Blozis, from Georgetown, became an immediate and imposing figure in the Giants front line. Alphonse "Tuffy" Leemans took on the duty of signal calling and the role of chief passer at quarterback in the decimated Giants backfield. The team was a mere splinter of the divisional championship team from the year before. "I took one look at the squad, and I felt like cry-

ing," Leemans said. "It hurt to see the Giants I loved having as miserable a group as we had there."

The season was a lackluster one, resulting in a 5–5–1 record and third place in the NFL East. Hapes was the leading ground gainer with 363 yards, but his average carry was only 3.8 yards. Leemans passed for 555 yards, the team standard in a year when Cecil Isbell gained 2,021 yards passing for the Green Bay Packers and four others threw for more than 1,000 yards ("Slingin'" Sammy Baugh of the Redskins, 1,524; Tommy Thompson of the Eagles, 1,410; Bud Schwenk of the Chicago Cardinals, 1,350; and Sid Luckman of the Bears, 1,023). Only guard Bill Edwards made All-Pro.

By the start of the 1943 season, the league was hanging on by several threads, with most well-known players gone, many empty seats on Sunday afternoons in the ballparks, and those taking the field often old or second-rate. The NFL dropped down to nine teams when the financially plagued Pittsburgh Steelers and Philadelphia Eagles combined forces to form a team called the Steagles (which would manage to beat the Giants in the opening game of 1943, 28–14, before folding after just one season).

In New York, rookie Bill Paschal from Georgia Tech was a nice addition to the backfield, Steve Owen

Sid Luckman, famed Chicago Bears T-formation quarterback, drops back to toss one against the Giants in November 1943. It was during this game at the Polo Grounds that Luckman, much to the chagrin of the Giants, set two NFL records—throwing seven touchdown passes and gaining 433 passing yards—in a 56–7 rout. No. 32 on the Giants is tackle Al Blozis; the Bears' No. 35 is tackle Bill Steinkemper.

admitted. And Blozis was playing All-Pro caliber at tackle, although there were no All-Pro selections officially made during the war years. But everything else was much the same. Leemans, 30 and in the last year of his playing career, was still at quarterback. Mel Hein, after 12 years with the Giants, retired to take a teaching and coaching job in upstate New York, but Owen

Tackle Al Blozis, from Georgetown, made an immediate impression on the wartime Giants, arriving in 1942 and quickly earning a starting berth. If All-Pro selections had been made during the war years, he would have been on two or three of them. Blozis played in the 1944 championship game, which the Giants lost to the Packers, 14–7, then was sent almost immediately overseas, where as a lieutenant in the army he was killed in action in France six weeks later.

talked him into coming back to the city on weekends to play (see sidebar). Because of the age of many of the starters and a general dearth of talent, the Giants of 1943 appeared to be not much better than mediocre.

By the time the Chicago Bears came to town in mid-November, the Giants were 2–2–1 and about to be shocked by the worst defeat in their 19-year history. Luckman, the Bears' outstanding T-formation quarterback, was a native of Brooklyn and had played his college football on Manhattan Island for Lou Little at Columbia. On November 14, he reappeared in New York before one of the largest crowds ever to watch a football game at the Polo Grounds, 56,591, and

SUNDAY CENTER

Mel Hein retired after the 1942 season to take the head coaching job and to teach physical education at Union College in Schenectady, New York. But because of the war, the school decided to disband its team for 1944. When Steve Owen heard of the decision, he phoned Hein and talked him into coming down to New York City to join the Giants on weekends. So the 35-year-old Hein taught classes all week, got on a train for Manhattan on Friday nights, worked out with the team on Saturdays, resumed his slots at center and linebacker on Sundays, and then commuted back to Schenectady on Sunday nights. One sportswriter dubbed him the "Sunday Center."

"It wasn't easy," Hein remembered. "That first game! I went into it without any physical contact before it that year. We were up in Boston, and our center, who had worked out with the team in the preseason, was supposed to start until I'd gotten myself into decent shape. But he got hurt in the last preseason game against the Bears. So I had to play the full 60 minutes, and I think it was the hottest day Boston ever had. What a toll it took. I could hardly get on the train to get to Schenectady that night. It took about three weeks to get rid of all that soreness. Still, the next week I had to go 60 minutes again."

put on an aerial exhibition unlike any the Giants fans had suffered before. Luckman passed for seven touchdowns to set an NFL record and gained 453 yards passing, breaking by a full 120 yards the previous mark set by Isbell of the Packers. The final score was 56–7.

The humiliation served an ironic purpose, however. After that, Owen turned his team around, and the Giants won the remaining four regular-season games, including back-to-back triumphs over the Washington Redskins, with whom, as a result, the Giants were tied for the divisional title. The playoff match was set for December 19 at the Polo Grounds, and after their two convincing victories on preceding Sundays, the Giants were the favorite.

For one reason or another, the Giants' pass defense reverted to its prior ineptness. Baugh came out slinging: three touchdown tosses and 199 yards gained on 16 passes. Besides that, Baugh intercepted two New York passes, running one of them back 44 yards to set up another touchdown, and got off a 67-yard quick kick at another point in the mismatch. The final score was 28–0, and the Giants' 1943 season was over.

Paschal led the league in rushing that year with 572 yards, an average gain of 3.9 yards per carry. His 10 touchdowns rushing were the most in that category, and the 72 points he scored were second only to Don Hutson's 117. Ward Cuff averaged 6.5 yards on each of his 80 carries that year, another NFL high.

With Leemans truly retired in 1944, the Giants talked former Green Bay Packers tailback Arnie Herber, at age 34, out of retirement and into a Giants jersey. They even coaxed 38-year-old Ken Strong back into a football uniform, something he had not donned since the 1939 season. Thirty-five-year-old Hein was commuting between Schenectady and New York City on weekends.

But if the Giants were antiquated, so were the other four teams in the NFL East. The only competition of note came from the Philadelphia Eagles, with their impressive rookie halfback Steve Van Buren, and the Washington Redskins, who were paced by Baugh and Frank Filchock. But as it turned out, the Giants defense prevailed.

The New Yorkers gave up only two touchdowns and a field goal in winning their first three games. The

Bill Paschal, like Alphonse "Tuffy" Leemans, was a halfback out of George Washington University. Paschal came to the Giants in 1942, then set a passel of club records in 1943, scoring 72 points on 12 touchdowns (10 rushing). During the war years, he was the team's most productive rusher and scorer. His Giants career ended during the 1947 season, when he was traded to the Boston Yanks.

Alphonse "Tuffy" Leemans, shown doing what he did so well in the late thirties and early forties, breaking through a hole to rack up some yardage for the Giants. When he retired after the 1943 season, Leemans had the distinction of being the Giants' all-time leading rusher (3,132 yards). He was inducted into the Pro Football Hall of Fame in 1978.

brunt of the offense was the running of Paschal, who had another noteworthy year, and Cuff. The only loss came in the fourth game of the season when the Eagles came up from Philadelphia and eked out a one-touchdown victory despite Paschal's rushing for 139 yards. The only stain on the rest of the season was a 21–21 tie with the Eagles.

When the season was over, the 8–1–1 Giants had five shutouts to their credit, including a 24–0 drubbing of the NFL West–champion Green Bay Packers. Collectively New York outscored its opponents, 206–75. Paschal carried the ball more often (196 times), gained more yards rushing (737), and scored more touchdowns rushing (nine) than any other back in the league.

Strong's elderly foot booted the most field goals (six) in the NFL and connected on 23 of 24 extra points. Howie Livingston, a rookie back from Fullerton Junior College, led the league with nine interceptions. The Giants were back on top.

In the division to the west, the champion Packers had lost only one other game besides the one to the Giants. The loss was another shutout, that time at the hands of the Bears, to earn the Packers an 8–2–0 record. Their source of success was the passing of Irv Comp, his 1,159 yards gained being the most in the NFL, and the pass catching of Hutson, who led the league in receptions (58), yards gained receiving (866), and touchdown catches (9).

The Giants had the homefield advantage, hosting the Pack on the same ground where they had humbled them by 24 points a few weeks prior. The Giants were a favorite among sportswriters and oddsmakers alike, although only a slight one, and they were confident going

<table>
<tr><td colspan="2">**WARTIME HUMOR**</td></tr>
</table>

WARTIME HUMOR

This story has been told by many and is probably close to being true. Steve Owen was riding down to New York from Camp Devens, Massachusetts, with one of his more prized possessions—former safety, now U.S. Army private, Hank Soar, who had been given a leave of absence to play in a Giants football game.

The ever-football-conscious Owen leaned over and asked Soar, "How's your pass defense these days?"

"Wonderful, Steve," was the answer from the ebullient Soar. He reached into his pocket and took from his wallet a piece of official-looking paper. "Here it is. No MP can stop me. A pass signed by Colonel Winfield Shrum himself. Good for three days, too!"

AN UNWELCOME SURPRISE, 1944

New York Giants		Green Bay Packers
O'Neal Adams	LE	Don Hutson
Frank Cope	LT	Baby Ray
Len Younce	LG	Bill Kuusisto
Mel Hein	C	Charley Brock
Jim Sivell	RG	Buckets Goldenberg
Vic Carroll	RT	Paul Berezney
Frank Liebel	RE	Harry Jacunski
Len Calligaro	QB	Larry Craig
Arnie Herber	LH	Irv Comp
Ward Cuff	RH	Joe Laws
Howie Livingston	FB	Ted Fritsch

	1	2	3	4		T
Packers	0	14	0	0	—	14
Giants	0	0	0	7	—	7

Touchdowns— *Packers:* Fritsch (2); *Giants:* Cuff.

PATs— *Packers:* Hutson (2); *Giants:* Strong.

into the rematch. But Curly Lambeau still felt the smarting of the earlier loss, and he did everything to ignite his Packers before the game.

Neither team could get going in the first quarter, but Green Bay got the spark in the following period. On one drive, highlighted by a 20-yard run by Joe Laws and another for 27 yards by Ted Fritsch, the Packers got to the 1-yard line. The Giants' respected defense repulsed them on three power plays, but on fourth down Fritsch bucked in for the score. Later in the quarter, the Pack moved

Howie Livingston goes up high in this sequence to intercept a Chicago Bears pass intended for end Ken Kavanaugh in the battle for the 1946 NFL crown. It helped for the moment, but in the end the Giants fell to the Bears, 24–14. No. 15, in the last panel, is Hank Soar of the Giants.

Don Hutson, the greatest pass catcher of his time, hauls one in for the Packers in the 1944 NFL championship game against the Giants. He did not catch a touchdown pass that afternoon, but he did kick two extra points in Green Bay's 14–7 victory. No. 24 of the Giants, here in frustrated pursuit, is Howie Livingston.

DeWitt "Tex" Coulter, an All-American tackle from Army, joined the Giants in 1946 and was a mainstay on the line until 1952. He was named All-Pro in 1951.

MARA STORIES

Bill Corum loved to tell stories of Tim Mara in his column for the *New York Journal-American*. Here is one of them:

This will give you an idea of how much loose money there is around. Along with most everybody else, Tim Mara, who owns the N.Y. Giants professional football team, is finding it hard to get help these days.

So last week before the Giants and Bear game, when his ticket seller was out of the office, Tim took over the window himself.

He hadn't been there long when a young man came along who wanted 25 box seats.

"The only box seats left are in the lower stands back of the goal posts," Mara told him.

"I'll take 'em," said the young man.

Tim counted out the tickets, and the buyer proffered a $100 bill. Tim made the change and was taken aback when the young fellow shoved a $10 bill back through the window, saying: "Stick this in your kick."

"Oh, no," said Mara, returning the bill.

"You mean, you don't want $10?" said the ticket buyer.

"Not as a tip," replied Tim. "You see, I happen to be the owner of the Giants."

"Are you Tim Mara?" asked the young fellow.

"That's right," replied Tim.

"Well, keep the $10 anyhow," said the surprised buyer. "It's worth that to meet you."

defensive back Paul Duhart picked off a Herber pass at the Green Bay 20-yard line. The game ended with the Giants on the low end of a 14–7 score. After seven trips to the NFL title game, the Giants had been disappointed now five times.

The good news in 1945 was that the war ended; the bad news, at least for the New York Giants, was that they posted their worst record since Tim Mara brought the team to life back in 1925. After an impressive win over the Pittsburgh Steelers in the regular-season opener, 34–6, it was all downhill. Paschal played only the last half of the season after coming home from military service, and Hein at 36, Strong at 39, Herber at 35, and Cuff at 32 had clearly seen better times on the football field. When the season mercifully ended, the Giants had a record of 3–6–1, the fewest wins in their 21-year history, ahead of only the 2–8–0 Pittsburgh Steelers in the standings. With the 1945 season over, Hein, after 15 years as a Giant (a team service record that has yet to be exceeded), retired for good. So did Herber, who had spent 11 years as a Green Bay Packer and two as a New York Giant. Both were headed for the Pro Football Hall of Fame, which was instituted almost two decades later.

For the Giants, the year 1946 was very different from the one that preceded it in a variety of ways. First, there was some competition at the box office. Across the Harlem River, Dan Topping's football Yankees were scheduled to play in Yankee Stadium in the new All-America Football Conference (AAFC), which materialized that year to challenge the NFL's monopoly on professional football. Second, the Giants would, for the first time, play a regular-season game against a team from California because the Cleveland Rams had relocated to Los Angeles. The 1946 season was also different because the Giants were once again a winning team destined to end up on top of their division, a rather striking turnaround from their worst season ever.

Finally, the Giants would be the focus of the first scandal to hit professional football.

The most important addition to the Giants of 1946 was quarterback Frank Filchock, acquired from the Washington Redskins. Filchock was not only a fine runner but would also reinstitute the Giants' passing attack, which had been sorely lacking since Danowski left.

Frank Filchock came to the Giants in 1946 to take over tailbacking duties after serving as Sammy Baugh's understudy with the Redskins. He did well enough that year in New York to win All-Pro honors.

again, this time on passes from Comp. First he hit Hutson, which got the ball well into New York territory. On the next play, he used the triple-teamed Hutson as a decoy, sending him down one side of the field and then tossing to Fritsch in the flat on the other side. Fritsch ran it 26 yards into the end zone. Along with two extra points from Hutson, the Packers had a 14–0 lead at the half.

The Giants moved in the second half and scored when Cuff carried it in from the 1-yard line on the first play of the fourth quarter. Late in the game, they marched again, only to see it come to nothing when

Frank Filchock (No. 40) is brought down here by Bears line-backer Clyde "Bulldog" Turner in the 1946 NFL title game. Filchock, a figure in a bribe offer before the game, was allowed to play because it was believed that a bribe had not been offered directly to him, only that he knew an offer had been made to teammate Merle Hapes. After the game Filchock was suspended indefinitely, like Hapes, when it came to light that he had, in fact, been offered a bribe.

Two other key figures were rookie tackles DeWitt "Tex" Coulter, a 6'4", 225-pound All-American from Army, and 6'2", 225-pound Jim White, who hailed from Notre Dame.

The Giants were 2–0 when they went to Washington to face Filchock's former teammates. Filchock especially wanted the win after so many years of existing in the shadow of Baugh, but it was not to be: Washington dealt the Giants their first loss of the year, 24–14.

At home afterward, New York pulled off two impressive wins against expert passing teams: the Chicago Cardinals with their hurler Paul Christman and the Chicago

Bears with Luckman. A loss in Philadelphia to the Eagles was avenged the following week at the Polo Grounds, when the Giants annihilated the Philadelphians, 45–17—their most explosive performance of the year. The Giants also lost to the Los Angeles Rams, who had come to the East Coast to introduce Bob Waterfield and Tommy Harmon, their two prize backs.

But when the regular season was over, the Giants were firmly entrenched at the top of the NFL East with a record of 7–3–1. Filchock had passed for 1,262 yards, the first Giants passer ever to toss for more than 1,000 yards, and his 87 completions and 12 touchdown passes set two other Giants standards. Filchock also led the club in rushing with 371 yards. It was enough to earn him All-Pro honors. White also made All-Pro in his rookie year.

So, for the eighth time since the NFL began holding championship games in 1933, the Giants had earned their way to the classic, and for the fourth time they faced the Chicago Bears, whom they had beaten once and lost to twice. The Bears, behind NFL passing leader Luckman (1,826 yards, 17 touchdowns), had easily taken the NFL West with a record of 8–2–1 (one of their only losses administered by the Giants at the Polo Grounds, 14–0—one of only two games that year in which the Bears did not score at least 21 points).

Merle Hapes, pictured here just after returning from military service in 1946, had been the club's leading ground gainer in 1942 before going off to war, rushing for 362 yards and leading the team in both punt and kickoff returns. Hapes was suspended indefinitely by Commissioner Bert Bell before the 1946 championship game between the Giants and Chicago Bears for not reporting a bribe that was offered to him and teammate Frank Filchock.

On Saturday, December 14, 1946, the day before the championship game, Giants owner Mara and coach Owen learned that two of their mainstays, Filchock and fullback Hapes, were under investigation for bribe offers in a scheme to get them to throw the championship game (see sidebar). Bert Bell, in his first year as NFL commissioner, was informed of the facts of the case, at least what was known of them at the time—that Hapes had been offered a bribe by gambler Alvin Paris, had not taken it, but had not informed his coach or team officials of the offer, and that Filchock had associated with Paris, but claimed that he had not been offered a bribe. Bell decided to suspend Hapes, but Filchock was allowed to play in the championship game.

The Bears did not look anything like the team that had been embarrassed at the Polo Grounds two months prior when, as one New York scribe called it, the "tainted title tilt" got under way. Luckman hit All-Pro end Ken Kavanaugh with a 21-yard touchdown pass in the first quarter; then Dante Magnani snatched a Giants pass and raced 19 yards for another touchdown in the same period.

But the Giants were far from out of it. Filchock, playing his heart out because of the scandal that hung over him that day, came back with a 38-yard bomb to end Frank Liebel. Then, in the third quarter, Filchock lobbed another to Steve Filipowicz in the end zone. With 40-year-old Strong's 2 extra points, the Giants had a tie at 14 points going into the final period.

In the fourth quarter, however, Luckman came up with a little razzle-dazzle that proved to be the Giants' undoing. He described it this way:

> We had a play called "Bingo keep it," where I ran with the ball. It worked like this. We had George McAfee at halfback, and he was such a tremendous threat as a runner, a breakaway back, that they always had to watch out for him. So, in the fourth quarter of that championship game, I took a timeout and asked coach Halas if I could call the "Bingo" play. He said OK. When I got the snap, I faked to McAfee, who went around the left end with the defense in hot

pursuit. Everyone was chasing McAfee, so I just danced around right end with the ball and then along the sidelines for a touchdown.

It was a 19-yard run, during which Luckman shook off a Giants tackler, and it proved to be the decisive play of the game.

The final score was the Bears 24, the Giants 14. From the wallets of the 58,346 fans who had passed through the turnstiles at the Polo Grounds that day, the gross gate of $282,955.25 was the most up to that time for an NFL title game. Each Giants player went home with $1,295.57, and each of the victorious Bears pocketed $1,975.82.

Frank Filchock played hard and well, despite having suffered a broken nose early in the game, to assure

EXCEPT FOR THE FOURTH QUARTER, 1946

New York Giants		Chicago Bears
Jim Poole	LE	Ken Kavanaugh
Tex Coulter	LT	Fred Davis
Bob Dobelstein	LG	Rudy Mucha
Chet Gladchuk	C	Bulldog Turner
Len Younce	RG	Ray Bray
Jim White	RT	Mike Jarmoluk
Jim Lee Howell	RE	George Wilson
Steve Filipowicz	QB	Sid Luckman
Dave Brown	LH	Dante Magnani
Howie Livingston	RH	Hugh Gallarneau
Ken Strong	FB	Bill Osmanski

	1	2	3	4		T
Bears	14	0	0	10	—	24
Giants	7	0	7	0	—	14

Touchdowns—*Bears:* Kavanaugh, Magnani, Luckman; *Giants:* Liebel, Filipowicz.

Field goals—*Bears:* Maznicki.

PATs—*Bears:* Maznicki (3); *Giants:* Strong (2).

everyone that the gamblers had had no influence on his performance. After the game, however, he too was suspended from professional football by Commissioner Bell when it became known that he had lied about having been offered a bribe by Paris.

The 1946 title tilt was the eighth in which the Giants had participated, but it was to be their last trip to the NFL championship for a decade.

It was a devastating drop for the divisional champion Giants of 1946 to the cellar of the NFL East in 1947—the first time in the franchise's history that the team hit that particular bottom. Filchock and Hapes were, of course, gone, and the Giants were virtually without a quarterback in the beginning of the season.

After tying the Boston Yanks, 7–7, in the season opener, New York lost seven straight games. Four games through the dreadful season the desperate Giants traded their most consistent running back, Paschal, to the Boston Yanks for their quarterback, Paul Governali. A graduate of Columbia, "Pitching Paul" was in his second year in the NFL and had already proven himself an accomplished passer. And he showed off those credentials from the start in New York. In the eight games he played for the Giants in 1947, Governali set two club records by passing for 1,461 yards and throwing a total of 14 touchdowns. He managed to get the Giants a pair of wins late in the season, one of which was over the Chicago Cardinals and their "dream backfield" of Christman, Charlie Trippi, Elmer Angsman, and Pat Harder—the team that would win the NFL championship that year. But that was certainly the only bright spot of 1947. The Giants' final record, the worst up to that time in the team's history, was 2–8–2.

As good a passer as Governali was, he lost his job in 1948 to a lanky, raw-boned All-American from Mississippi who was destined to become a fixture in the New York Giants' backfield: Charlie Conerly. From his rookie year through 11 additional seasons as a starting quarterback and two others as backup, Conerly would virtually rewrite the club's passing record book.

Conerly was not the Giants' first-round draft pick that year; he was, in fact, acquired from the Washington Redskins, who already had Baugh and Harry Gilmer to handle their passing game. The Giants' top pick in the 1948 draft was Tony "Skippy" Minisi, a halfback

THE CONERLY CONTROVERSY

Red Smith, writing for the *New York Herald Tribune* in 1948, reported the intracity squabble for the rights to Charlie Conerly, who had just finished an illustrious career at Mississippi and was ready to become a pro. It seems both the New York Giants and the Brooklyn Dodgers of the All-America Football Conference wanted his quarterbacking services:

> Branch Rickey [the Brooklyn owner], the most dangerous switch orator since Demosthenes, got carried away by his own eloquence yesterday. The effects threaten to be as far-reaching as his rich [baritone] voice. . . .

> [He informed] members of the Brooklyn Gridiron Club that he had offered $110,000 to a rookie football player named Charlie Conerly of the University of Mississippi. Then he hauled off and swung a haymaker at the football Giants, who expect to hire Conerly. . . .

> It was, the Reverend went on, the best offer Conerly received, but the kid had to turn it down because he was already committed to the National League Giants, interborough rivals of Rickey's All-America Conference Dodgers. So here, the orator thundered, was a case of a boy in a "free American sport" being unfree to accept the best offer for his services. Going oracular, the Reverend predicted the Giants would always have a "morale problem" with Conerly because he would remember that he had not been allowed to make a better deal. "It seems un-American to me," declaimed the Reverend, "and you can take that for what it's worth—in New York or Mississippi." . . .

> "Maybe," said [Tim] Mara, who had just finished reading about Rickey signing Ralph Branca to pitch for $14,000 [for the baseball Dodgers], "the kid figures he'll have greater security with the Giants than with an organization that puts such a price on a 21-game winner.

> "Maybe he's looked over the All-America Conference and realized that we've been in business here 24 years, whereas Brooklyn has had three-four owners. . . . I do not know where this guy gets off talking about morale problems and stuff, considering the business he's in. . . . A hundred and ten thousand dollars," he mused. "That would be out of our reach. I thought United Cigar Company coupons were out of print these days."

Conerly, of course, signed with the Giants and stayed around for 14 seasons—his first contract was reportedly for $62,500 over five seasons with a $10,000 signing bonus.

from Pennsylvania. They also signed All-American end Bill Swiacki from Columbia, who would prove to be the team's most productive pass receiver his rookie year.

There was also a notable milestone in 1948: the Giants signed the first African-American player in club history. The young man simply walked into the Giants office one day and asked for a tryout. He had played for the University of Toledo for one year, he told Wellington Mara, but he broke his neck. Then he had gone into the coast guard, and when he came out of that had played some ball at Iowa. He got his tryout, made the team, and Emlen Tunnell began a pro football career that eventually would land him in the Hall of Fame, recognized as one of the greatest defensive backs ever to play the game.

It was a year of rebuilding, according to stout Owen. But it soon became clear that one element was not taking to the reconstruction process: defense. In the second, third, and fourth games of the season, the Giants gave up 41 points to the Redskins, 45 to the Eagles, and 63 to the Chicago Cardinals. The 63–35 loss to the Cardinals set an NFL record for the most points scored in a game up to that time, 98, eclipsing the 87 scored the year prior when the Philadelphia Eagles beat the Washington Redskins 45–42. The 63 points were also the most scored against the Giants since the team was founded.

On offense, however, the rebuilding went nicely. Conerly proved to be a masterful passer and an inspiring team leader. Against the Pittsburgh Steelers, he set an NFL record of 36

68

Emlen Tunnell walked into the Giants offices one day before the start of the 1948 season and asked Wellington Mara for a tryout. No African American had ever worn a Giants uniform before, but Tunnell got his tryout, made the team, became a four-time All-Pro, set a variety of NFL records as a defensive back, and earned his way into the Pro Football Hall of Fame as one of the greatest safeties of all time. His records of 1,282 yards gained on interceptions and 258 punt returns were NFL standards, as were his 79 career interceptions. Tunnell ended his 11-year Giants career after the 1958 season.

Charlie Conerly was a lanky rookie when he lined up as a tail-back with the Giants A formation on a blustery December afternoon in 1948 at the Polo Grounds and gazed across the line of scrimmage at the menacing Pittsburgh Steelers. When the afternoon was over, he had thrown an NFL-record 36 completions out of 53 attempts. A consensus All-American back at Ole Miss in 1947, Conerly had been drafted by the Washington Redskins in 1945, but when he became eligible for the pros in 1948, they traded him to the Giants. Fourteen years later, at age 40 with the distinction of being the oldest player in the NFL, Conerly finally took off his Giants uniform for the last time. In all Giants history only Mel Hein and Phil Simms have played longer for the team. When he retired after the 1961 season, Conerly held virtually every club passing record.

completions, a standard that would remain until George Blanda completed 37 for the AFL Houston Oilers in 1964.

Because of their porous defense, the Giants could only manage to win four of their twelve games in 1948. But Conerly passed for 2,175 yards on 162 completions and threw 22 touchdown passes—all team records. The 10 touchdown catches made by Bill Swiacki tied the team record set by Liebel in 1945, and the 550 yards Swiacki gained on pass receptions were the second most in club history at the time.

The Giants needed some help in their running game, Owen was well aware, and, needless to say, a complete overhaul on defense. Things would be better the next year, he assured the Maras: rebuilding takes some time. He was right on that score.

The Giants were back to .500 ball in 1949 with a record of 6–6–0, the result of a rampaging offense and a slightly improved defense. They had added a fine defen-

Bill Swiacki, remembered for his diving, acrobatic catch for Columbia that enabled them to upset Army in 1947, came to the Giants in 1948 and played three seasons. Swiacki led the team in pass receptions all three years and set two team records in 1949, when he caught 47 passes for 652 yards.

sive tackle in rookie Al DeRogatis from Duke, a good offensive guard in Bill Austin from Oregon State, and an expert place-kicker who had defected from the AAFC, Ben Agajanian.

It was the year that Steve Owen decided to do away with his A formation and switch to the T. Conerly, he felt, would be a most effective T-formation quarterback. To aid in the transition, Owen hired Allie Sherman, an acknowledged T scholar, to work with Conerly.

At season's end, Conerly had completed 152 passes for 2,138 yards, including 17 touchdown tosses. Swiacki had set two team records by gaining 652 yards on 47 receptions. But the biggest surprise was Gene "Choo-Choo" Roberts, a halfback in his second year with the Giants, who led the entire NFL in scoring with 102 points on 17 touchdowns. The 634 yards he gained rushing were then the third most in Giants history, trailing only Leemans' 830 in 1936 and Paschal's 737 in 1944.

The renovation years were over. Both the NFL and the New York Giants had a new look for the fifties.

Fullback Eddie Price came to the Giants in 1950 from Tulane and averaged 5.6 yards per carry as a rookie, gaining 703 yards rushing (then the third-highest total in club history). The following year he led the entire NFL with 971 yards. Twice an All-Pro, Price stayed with the Giants through the 1955 season and ranks sixth in rushing in club annals with 3,292 yards. Photo courtesy of the Pro Football Hall of Fame.

BEGINNING OF A NEW ERA

The All-America Football Conference, founded by *Chicago Tribune* sports editor Arch Ward in 1946, had run its course in competing with the NFL after the 1949 football season. But the AAFC bequeathed three teams to the NFL—the Cleveland Browns, San Francisco 49ers, and Baltimore Colts—all of whom would make distinctive marks in the expanded league. The divisions were realigned and renamed, becoming the American and National Conferences instead of the Eastern and Western Divisions.

The New York Giants were assigned to the American Conference along with the NFL's reigning champion Philadelphia Eagles and the Pittsburgh Steelers, Washington Redskins, Chicago Cardinals, and Cleveland Browns. The Giants were no longer sharing the Polo Grounds with the New York Bulldogs, now known as the New York Yanks, who had moved their act over to Yankee Stadium.

Due to the demise of the AAFC, the cream of its talent was infused into the NFL. The Giants were especially rewarded, acquiring such AAFC veterans as tackle Arnie Weinmeister, guard John Mastrangelo and defensive backs Tom Landry, Otto Schnellbacher, and Harmon Rowe. In the college player draft they selected Auburn quarterback Travis Tidwell. Later they added fullback Eddie Price from Tulane and signed Philadelphia-drafted end Bob McChesney of Hardin-Simmons University.

The NFL was rife with offensive football talent in 1950. In the American Conference, the Eagles had Steve Van Buren, Tommy Thompson, and Pete Pihos; the Steelers had Joe Geri and Lynn Chandnois; the Cardinals had Charlie Trippi, Pat Harder, Elmer Angsman, and Bob Shaw; the Redskins had "Slingin'" Sammy Baugh, "Bullet" Bill Dudley, and Charley "Choo-Choo" Justice; and the Cleveland Browns had Otto Graham, Marion Motley, Dub Jones, Mac Speedie, and Dante Lavelli.

Over in the National Conference, the Los Angeles Rams featured Bob Waterfield, Norm Van Brocklin, Glenn Davis, Dick Hoerner, Tom Fears, and Elroy "Crazylegs" Hirsch; the Bears had Sid Luckman, Johnny Lujack, Ken Kavanaugh, and Jim Keane; the New York Yanks had George Ratterman, Buddy Young, George Taliaferro, and Zollie Toth; the Lions had Bobby Layne, Doak Walker, Bob "Hunchy" Hoernschemeyer, Cloyce Box, and Leon Hart; the Packers had Tobin Rote and Billy Grimes; the 49ers had Frankie Albert, Joe Perry, and Emil "Red" Sitko; and the Colts had Y. A. Tittle and Chet Mutryn.

The forte of the Giants in 1950, however, was defense, and therefore most of the preseason pundits

THE UMBRELLA DEFENSE

Steve Owen invented the defense that came to be known as the "umbrella," and he described its versatility:

> The nickname refers to the four backs, who roughly assume the shape of an open umbrella, with the two halfbacks shallow and wide and two safety men deep and tight. Then, when we have a 6–1–4 formation, there is the backer-up to suggest the handle of a bumbershoot.

> In general, it is the role of the umbrella to act as a sort of flexible basket and adjust itself to contain any attacking situation, by moving in one side or dropping back on the other, but always as a unit, and never without interdependence.

> To give another idea of variations on a basic formation, we use the umbrella most often in a 5–2–4 and work eight changes off it.

> 1. We can red-dog the backers-up through the line, with the ends holding to protect the outside.

> 2. We can send in an end from one side and a backer-up from the other, with the backer-up on the end side sliding off to cover, and the end on the backer-up side dropping a few yards to protect the vacated area.

> 3. We can send all seven linemen and backers-up charging in.

> 4. With a man in motion, we can wheel the umbrella to pull three men onto the strong side. We do that depending on the quality of the opposition.

> 5. We may play zone defense in the backfield, with backers-up dropping straight back watching out for hook passes.

> 6. We may play man for man in the backfield, with the backers-up covering the fullback and one flat. To give that a minor change-of-pace variation we sometimes slide an end out to cover the flat, in lieu of the backer-up.

> 7. We may go into a 5–1–5, with a combination of some men man-for-man and others in zone defense.

> 8. We may go into a 6–1–4, to shift rapidly into a 4–3–4, with a combination of man-for-man and zone, if a pass develops after the snap.

suggested that the team was doomed to a dull and mediocre season much like that of 1949. But Steve Owen devised a revolutionary defense called the "umbrella" (see sidebar), which immediately proved to be highly successful, especially against a passing offense.

The Giants opened on the road in 1950 with a win over Pittsburgh, 18–7. Then it was on to Cleveland, where the mighty Browns lay in wait. Paul Brown's magnificent 11 had won the AAFC title in each of the four seasons of the team's existence, compiling a record of 52–4–3 in the process. To open their maiden season in the National Football League, the Browns destroyed the Philadelphia Eagles, the team that had won the NFL championship the year before, 35–10.

Cleveland was heavily favored the day they faced the Giants, but Owen's umbrella was opened up for the first time, and the Browns were both mystified and frustrated. Pass after pass from Graham was batted away or intercepted. The invincible Browns were, to their uncharacteristic chagrin, totally vanquished, held scoreless for the first time in the team's history. Giants rookie Price, who had earned the starting berth at fullback, scored to give his team a 6–0 victory.

The Redskins were the next victim, 21–17, and the Giants sat at the top of the American Conference with a record of 3–0—a reign short-lived, however, when Pittsburgh surprised them the following week. When the Browns came to the Polo Grounds, they had a record of 4–1, and the Giants were 3–1 (the Browns had opened their season a week earlier). Again the Browns were the favorite among oddsmakers, most choosing to ignore the Giants' earlier triumph. And it looked as though they were correct, at least at the half, with Cleveland holding a 13–3 lead by dint of two Lou "the Toe" Groza field goals and a Giants turnover on their own 1-yard line that was converted to a Browns touchdown. But New York came back, the umbrella once again shutting down the Browns. And while the Giants defense held Cleveland scoreless in the second half, the Giants offense came alive. A touchdown in the third quarter brought them within three points of the Browns. Another touchdown in the fourth quarter gave the Giants a 17–13 win and undisputed claim to the top tier of the conference.

The Giants' rank was short-lived. The Chicago Cardinals dished them a loss at Comiskey Park in

Tom Landry poses in 1950, the year he went to the Giants from the New York Yankees of the AAFC. An outstanding defensive back for the Giants through 1955, he ranks sixth in all-time interceptions with 31, 3 of which he returned for touchdowns. Landry was an All-Pro in 1954, served as a player/assistant coach in 1954 through 1955, and was the Giants' full-time assistant coach for defense from 1956 through 1959 before moving to Dallas to take over the head coaching duties of the newly enfranchised Cowboys.

Chicago the following week, and again they were forced to share the lead with the Browns. And that's the way it remained for the rest of the season. Neither the Giants

nor the Browns suffered another loss. Among the impressive Giants wins were a 51–21 drubbing of the Cardinals at the Polo Grounds, a 55–20 devastation of the Colts down in Baltimore (at the time, the second highest number of points a Giants team had compiled in a single game, only 1 point less than the 56 run up against the Eagles in 1933), and a 51–7 shellacking of the New York Yanks. No one was remarking on the Giants' alleged lack of offense any longer.

At season's end the Giants and Browns each had records of 10–2. The title would be decided in a playoff game at Municipal Stadium in Cleveland.

December 17, 1950, was brutally cold: it was an icy, windy 17 degrees at game time. There were slightly more than 33,700 fans on hand to see if the New Yorkers could once again shut down the otherwise offensively volatile Browns.

Cleveland edged ahead in the first quarter when a drive was stopped at the 4-yard line and Groza drilled one through the uprights for a 3–0 advantage. That lead, in a totally defense-dominated game, lasted into the fourth quarter. And then the Giants had a wonderful chance to go ahead. Having driven to the Browns' 36, the Giants surprised the Clevelanders when Roberts took a reverse and scampered around the end all the way to the Browns' 4-yard line. Two running plays advanced the ball to only the 3, where on third down, Charlie Conerly rifled one to McChesney in the end zone. But a flag lay on the field, and the signal was that New York had been offside. Several plays and several penalties later, the Giants found themselves on fourth down at the Cleveland 13. Randy Clay came on and kicked the game-tying field goal.

As the fourth quarter wore on, the Browns ground away at the Giants. Finally, with only 58 seconds left in the game, the truest toe in professional football, Groza's, kicked a 28-yard field goal. Not too many seconds later, Conerly, looking for a receiver from his own end zone, was tackled by Cleveland All-Pro guard Bill Willis for an additional—but unnecessary—two points. The final score was 8–3, and the Browns won the right to represent the American Conference in the NFL championship of 1950.

It had been a fine year for the Giants, however: they were back above .500 for the first time since 1946. They had shown Cleveland—and the entire NFL, for that matter—how

KYLE ROTE

In 1950 Notre Dame's coach Frank Leahy called Kyle Rote the "most underrated back in football." A year later Steve Owen said, "He receives, runs, and kicks with power, polish, and determination."

Rote, coming from San Antonio and the heir at Southern Methodist to Doak Walker's tailback spot and All-American status, came to the New York Giants in 1951 as their first-round draft pick and stayed around for 11 seasons. Beleaguered by a knee injury his first year and shortly afterward overshadowed in the backfield by Frank Gifford, Rote was converted to a flanker in the midfifties by Jim Lee Howell.

As a prolific receiver of passes thrown by Charlie Conerly and later Y. A. Tittle, Rote played in four NFL championship games (1956, 1958, 1959, and 1961) and went to the Pro Bowl four times (1954–1957). He stands 10th in all-time scoring for the Giants, having toted up 312 points on 52 touchdowns (48 of them on pass receptions, still the team record). During his 11-year career, Rote caught 300 passes for a total of 4,797 yards—an average gain of 16 yards, the eighth most productive in Giants history.

The first-round draft pick of 1952 for the Giants was a providential one: halfback Frank Gifford from Southern Cal. He starred for the Giants for 12 years (missing 1961 because of a concussion suffered in the last game of the 1960 season), earning All-Pro honors four times and making eight trips to the Pro Bowl. The Giff is the third-leading all-time scorer for the Giants (484 points: 78 touchdowns, two field goals, 10 extra points), the fourth-leading pass receiver (with 367 catches for 5,434 yards), and the sixth-leading rusher (with 3,609 yards). He was inducted into the Pro Football Hall of Fame in 1977.

effective Owen's umbrella defense was in the hands of the game's finest secondary: defensive halfbacks Landry and Rowe and safeties Emlen Tunnell and Otto Schnellbacher.

Price rushed for 703 yards with an impressive 5.6-yard average per carry, and Roberts picked up another 483 yards on the ground. Weinmeister was the only Giants All-Pro in the last year before those selections would honor offense and defense separately.

Just as the New York Giants and the Washington Redskins dashed for the divisional title in the late thirties, the same scenario was taking shape in the fifties between the Giants and the Cleveland Browns—at least it would play that way through the first three years of the decade. In 1951, there would be virtually no other competition in the conference except for those two teams.

The Giants began 1951 on a note of good fortune. In those days, the very first pick in the college draft was a "bonus" pick; each team drew a slip of paper from a hat, one of which was designated the bonus, and the lucky winner got the pick of that year's crop regardless of where the team had ended up in the preceding year's standings. In 1951, as Wellington Mara remembers, "My brother Jack or I ordinarily drew from the hat, but that year I said something like, 'Let's see if we can change our luck if Steve does the picking.' So he reached in, and he sure in fact drew the bonus, and we promptly drafted Kyle Rote." An All-American tailback and Heisman Trophy runner-up,

Kyle Rote, an All-American tailback from Southern Methodist University, signs his first pro contract with the Giants in 1951 under the delighted watch of Wellington Mara. It signaled the beginning of an illustrious Giants career that would last through the 1961 season.

NEWSLETTER NOTES, 1952

From the Giants' official newsletter:

Em Tunnell has fully recovered from the dislocated shoulder he suffered in the Pro Bowl game in California last January. Em can't wait to rejoin Otto Schnellbacher on the back line. While he's waiting, Tunnell works as a beer salesman in his hometown of Garrett Hill, Pa. . . . Kyle Rote is a building contractor in Corpus Christi, Tex., in the off-season. . . . Bob Wilkinson, brand new dad of a daughter, has graduated from stunt stuff to a featured part in Hollywood. . . . Lots of news on Giants in service: Sonny Grandelius is a second looey at Fort Slocum in New Rochelle, N.Y. . . . Jack Stroud is at Fort Jackson, S.C. . . . Both Stroud and Grandelius are scheduled for Far Eastern service. . . . Ray Wietecha is with the Marines at Quantico. . . . Bud Sherrod starred with the Carswell Air Base national service champions. . . . Bill Milner is expected to be mustered out of the Marines by fall. . . . Milner coached and played with the Camp LeJeune team, which lost the Cigar Bowl game, 20–0, to Brooke Army Medical Center. . . .

Kyle Rote of Southern Methodist University had been a most capable successor to Walker's role as a triple threat at SMU, and Rote was touted as the best pro prospect that year, coveted by every team in the league. The acquisition of Rote was especially welcome in Giantdom because starting halfback Roberts had abandoned the team for the new Canadian Football League.

But the Giants' luck reversed itself in the preseason. First, Rote injured his knee and therefore saw only limited service during the regular season. Then Conerly aggravated a shoulder injury to his throwing arm, which hampered his passing considerably throughout the year.

The Giants were surprised in the first game of the regular season and held to a 13–13 tie by the Pittsburgh Steelers. It was not all doom and gloom, however, because the Browns had been soundly defeated the previous day out in California by the revitalized San Francisco 49ers. But any elation was soon ended because the Browns did not lose another game the entire season. Among their 11

Arnie Weinmeister takes on two white-shirted Giants blockers in a practice session during the early fifties. An All-Pro tackle in each of his four years with the Giants (1950–1953), Weinmeister was considered as fast as most of the backs in the NFL, despite his 250-plus-pound bulk. He was inducted into the Pro Football Hall of Fame in 1984.

One of the smallest players drafted by the Giants in 1955 was 6', 180-pound defensive back Jimmy Patton from Mississippi, who would turn out to be one of the most significant contributors to the Giants' awesome defense over the next decade. Patton made All-Pro five times, and his 52 interceptions are exceeded in franchise history only by Emlen Tunnell's 74.

consecutive victories were two over the Giants, the first a 14–13 squeaker in Cleveland and the next a more decisive 10–0 shutout at the Polo Grounds. As it turned out, those were the only two losses New York suffered that year, but they were enough to sentence them to second place once again. "If we could only have beat the goldarn Browns," Owen said later, "we would have been champs of everything that year [1951]. We could have beat the Rams [the National Conference champ], and anybody else except those Browns."

Still, it had been a most respectable season. Price led the league in rushing and set a Giants record with 971 yards gained on the ground, 141 more than Alphonse "Tuffy" Leemans toted up back in 1936. Price's 271 carries set an NFL single-season mark, eclipsing the 263 jaunts that Van Buren had for the Eagles in 1949 when he set the NFL rushing record of 1,146 yards.

Tunnell was the top punt returner in the NFL, with a total of 489 yards on 34 returns, then a club record. And Schnellbacher's 11 interceptions were the most in the NFL and also a Giants standard that still stands (tied by Jimmy Patton in 1958).

When the All-Pro selections were made, the Giants landed two players on the offensive unit: fullback Price and tackle DeWitt "Tex" Coulter. Five Giants made the defensive squad: tackles Weinmeister and Al DeRogatis, guard Jon Baker, and defensive backs Tunnell and Schnellbacher.

In 1952, with Rote's leg better and the addition of first-round draft choice Frank Gifford, an outstanding halfback from Southern Cal, the Giants proved that they could, in fact, beat the Browns. First they handed them a 17–9 shellacking in Cleveland and took over first place with a record of 3–0. But when they slipped by them, 37–34, in the last game of the season, it did not really matter because going into the game, the 6–5 Giants had already been mathematically eliminated by the 8–3 Browns.

It was a frustrating season after such a fine start. Losses to the Chicago Cardinals and the Philadelphia Eagles after knocking off the Browns had brought the Giants back to Earth with a thud. But the most bone-crushing defeat was yet to come. The sorry site was

Kyle Rote, with a look of grim determination, takes off around an end in this 1953 game. Rote was the team's leading pass receiver that year, but the Giants posted a dismal 3–9 record and ended up in fifth place in the NFL East. No. 31 is Giants fullback Eddie Price.

Pittsburgh, and the Steelers, a team that had won only three of nine games so far that year, were the perpetrators. The Giants were annihilated that afternoon, 63–7—the most points, at that time, ever given up by a New York Giants team. Conerly left the game with a re-wounded shoulder. Then his replacement, rookie Fred Benners from SMU, was knocked out of the game. Owen sent Landry in to quarterback the ballclub—a position he had not played since his days at Texas in the midforties. The Giants' record of 7–5 left them in a tie with the Philadelphia Eagles for second place in the American Conference—once again short of the Cleveland Browns.

There were only a few highlights from the 1952 season. Price rushed for 748 yards, second only to Dan Towler of the Rams, who picked up 894. Tunnell actually gained more yardage running on special teams and for the defense than any running back in the league. Between punt and kickoff returns and interception runbacks, Tunnell gained a total of 924 yards for the Giants. Three New Yorkers made All-Pro: fullback Price, defensive tackle Weinmeister, and defensive back Tunnell.

If 1952 was disappointing, 1953 could only be described as disastrous, despite the appearance of a number of new and promising faces in the starting lineup. Three rookies moved into the offensive line: tackle Roosevelt "Rosie" Brown from Morgan State, guard Jack Stroud of Tennessee, and center Ray Wietecha from Northwestern. In the backfield, another rookie, halfback Sonny Grandelius, would see quite a bit of action after Price and Rote were forced to sit out much of the season with injuries. Arnie Galiffa, an All-American at Army in 1949, was back in football as a Giant and was scheduled to be Conerly's backup. And Owen decided to use Gifford on offense as well as defense (as a rookie Gifford was used almost exclusively as a defensive back).

In a reversal of the season before, the Giants lost their first three games of 1953, solid defeats at the hands of the Rams, Steelers, and Redskins. With Cleveland winning its first three games easily, it became apparent that the Giants were not going to challenge the Browns for the title that year.

As it turned out, the Giants won only three games in 1953, two wins over the hapless Chicago Cardinals, the only team in what was now called the Eastern Conference to have a record (1–10–1) worse than the Giants that year, and an upset over the Philadelphia Eagles. Their record of 3–9 was the most dismal since

Steve Owen accepts a silver token of the franchise's esteem for his sterling career as coach of the Giants on the occasion of his retirement from the job after the 1953 season. Looking on are the Giants owners: (from left to right) Wellington, Tim, and Jack.

recording the 2–8–2 season of 1947. The most embarrassing afternoon came in the next-to-last game of the year when the Giants went out to Cleveland and were annihilated, 62–10, the second worst beating in their 29-year history.

Weinmeister was the only Giant to make All-Pro. He would be gone the following year, however, defecting to the Canadian Football League. And another one-time New York tackle would also depart, one who had spent the past 23 years patrolling the Giants sideline and guiding their on-field actions: Owen.

Don Smith, former publicity director of the Giants, wrote of perhaps the most difficult decision the Mara family had to make in the first 30 years of the team's existence:

> As much as the Maras—Jack, Wellington, and the late T. J.—hated to admit it, they had to agree that the gridiron parade had passed by their old warhorse. Never before had the Giants fired a coach. . . . During Owen's long and successful tenure, it was unthinkable that he would be the first to be replaced. Stout Steve was so close to T. J. Mara that neither had ever considered a signed contract

Defensive back Dick Nolan, from Maryland's national championship team of 1953, joined the Giants in 1954 and stayed through the 1957 season. Nolan played in the defensive backfield with Tom Landry and later served as an assistant to Landry in Dallas before moving on to head coaching jobs with the San Francisco 49ers and the New Orleans Saints.

into coaching, first as a line coach at Baylor down in Waco, Texas, and later as a defensive coach with the Philadelphia Eagles. The man selected to replace him was a surprise to just about everybody, especially Jim Lee Howell himself. But Howell, who had been serving as the Giants end coach, was the Maras' choice to guide the team.

Among the first things Howell accomplished was a most masterful selection of a staff. He hired one of Earl Blaik's assistant coaches at Army, Vince Lombardi, to handle the offense and appointed Landry to direct the defense as a player/coach.

Conerly, who had been battered and bruised for six long seasons as a pro, especially during the last

necessary. Steve and the elder Mara simply shook hands before each season.

The day after the humiliating defeat by Cleveland, Owen was summoned to the Giant office. All three Maras were there when big Steve heaved into a wicker chair and asked, "What's up?"

It was an awkward moment in the lives of all four men.

Jack Mara acted as spokesman. He told Steve of the decision to hire a new, younger coach. He also expressed a genuine hope that Steve would remain with the Giants as head of college personnel.

Owen did stay around the Giants front office in 1954, but attended to a few duties then left to go back

Ray Poole was one of three members of the famous football-playing Poole family of Mississippi who, at one time or another, donned a Giants uniform. An end, Ray played for New York from 1947 to 1952. His brother Barney, also an end, was an All-American at both Army and Mississippi and played for the Giants in 1954. The oldest brother, Jim, still another end, played for the Giants from 1937 through 1941 and again in 1945 and 1946.

Bill Svoboda became a Giant in 1954, acquired in a trade with the Chicago Cardinals. He held a linebacking slot until retiring from the game after the 1958 season.

AUTOMATIC BEN

They called Ben Agajanian "Automatic Ben," and they also called him "the Toeless Wonder," the reasons being that, first, he was one of the finest place-kickers in the game, and second, that he had only one toe on his kicking foot. How the latter came about is described by Gerald Eskenazi in his book *There Were Giants in Those Days:*

> He went to the University of New Mexico on a scholarship. But the scholarship did not pay his way. He was poor. He washed pots and pans, refusing to ask his parents for money. The dishwashing job sapped his strength, and he found himself too weak to work out with the club. So he quit for a softer job in a soda-bottling plant.
>
> One day he took the freight elevator, which was loaded with barrels of syrup. He did not realize that his right foot protruded a few inches over the edge of the elevator floor. Four toes were sheared off. Before the surgeon operated, he told him, "Don't worry, Aggie, I'll square off your stumps and you'll kick better than ever."

Agajanian played five years for the Giants (1949, 1954–1957).

few years when New York's offensive line was less than protective, announced he was retiring from the game. Howell, who had always had great faith in Conerly's abilities as a T-formation quarterback, promptly went after him. As he later explained:

> I tracked him down and found him somewhere in Missouri or Iowa. He was putting out fertilizer on his farm, wearing those high rubber farm boots. When I asked him about coming back, he told me he didn't want to be hurt anymore. I told him I'd get him a line that would protect him, that would be the first order of business, and Charlie said OK, he'd come back.

The next step was to rebuild the stale roster, Howell felt, and when the regular season opened there were quite a few newcomers in Giants uniforms. From

the college draft, Howell plucked a quarterback to back up Conerly and his troublesome shoulder: Bobby Clatterbuck from Houston. He also debuted quarterback Don Heinrich, whom the team had drafted out of Washington in 1952. Howell also selected a fine defensive back, Dick Nolan from Maryland, and a solid running back, Bobby Epps of Pittsburgh.

Howell also went to the trading table and acquired linebacker Bill Svoboda from the Chicago Cardinals. Then he signed a former All-American end at both Army and Mississippi, Barney Poole, from the Baltimore Colts, and another highly regarded end, Bob Schnelker, from the Philadelphia Eagles. In addition, Howell signed up two returning servicemen, end Ken MacAfee and linebacker Cliff Livingston.

It was a new look, and it was a better one. The Howell-led Giants won four of their first five games in

Two Giants, halfback Frank Gifford (left) and quarterback Don Heinrich (right), visit with then-Vice President Richard Nixon at West Point, where all three were attending President Eisenhower's Youth Fitness Conference.

1954. The snarling and the boos at the Polo Grounds disappeared, and more people began to take seats in the stadium on Giants-game Sundays. But the Giants once again had trouble with Paul Brown's dynasty from Cleveland. They fell to them twice in 1954, as the invincible Browns marched to their fifth consecutive conference title.

The Giants won seven of their twelve games in 1954, a much-improved record over 1953. And there was a lot to be optimistic about. Gifford was proving to be a valuable and versatile back on offense, posting an average gain of 5.6 yards on each rush that year before

being injured. Rote had become a capable receiver, complementing the passing game from his slot at halfback. Conerly was throwing well, and because his line was blocking effectively for him, he seemed happy to have resumed his career. Both ends, Schnelker and MacAfee, proved to be most able receivers. Only defensive back and defensive coordinator Landry made All-Pro from the Giants that year, but everyone agreed that things were looking up.

In 1954, NFL Commissioner Bert Bell stood before a special press conference and announced, "The war is on." The conflict of figurative arms to which he was referring was with Canada, the Canadian Football League to be precise, which had been raiding the National Football League for talent. It reached untenable proportions, Bell felt, when the Giants' Weinmeister, the finest

Dick Alban (No. 42) of the Redskins picks off a pass from Charlie Conerly intended for Frank Gifford (No. 16) in this 1954 game. The Giants destroyed Washington, however, in both their encounters that year—51–21 in the nation's capital and 24–7 at the Polo Grounds. No. 89 on the Redskins is defensive end Joe Tereshinski.

tackle in the league, and Redskins quarterback Eddie LeBaron were lured north of the border.

There were no prospects for peace or even a truce as the 1955 football season approached. Bell and some of the NFL owners made concerted efforts to bring the Canadian forays to an end but got nowhere. It had reached a point when owners asked that all college players selected in the NFL draft that year be immediately and personally contacted in an effort to persuade them to stay and play in America.

The Giants were especially hard hit when three key linemen—Bill Albright, Ray Collins, and Billy Shipp—

decided on Canada. The Maras had had it. "We've got to do something about it," Wellington Mara said. "We have to teach *them* a lesson, and I think I know how to do it. Let's go after the best they have. Let's turn the tide on them." And he did. The CFL's leading rusher and MVP in 1954 was powerful halfback Alex Webster of the Montreal Alouettes. Webster had been a star running back at North Carolina State, but had been cut from the Washington Redskins by Curly Lambeau before the 1953 season. In his last year of coaching in the NFL, Lambeau told Webster, "You're just not good enough to make it in the pros, son."

After an exceptional two years at Montreal, Webster was the most prized possession in the Canadian league. So Mara went after him and got him for the Giants, and although it was not—in the war between the leagues— the fall of Berlin, to the Canadian league, it was at least akin to the D-day landing.

ANDY ROBUSTELLI

Andy Robustelli, a native of Stamford, Connecticut, went to tiny Arnold College in Milford in his home state, hardly a breeding ground for future NFLers. But he made the pros—made it all the way, in fact, to the Pro Football Hall of Fame. Don Smith, of that illustrious organization, wrote:

> Andy Robustelli almost didn't make it to the Pro Football Hall of Fame for the really excellent reason that he almost didn't play pro football.

> Andy was drafted in the 19th round by the Los Angeles Rams in 1951 and the only "bonus" he received was his air transportation to the California training camp of the Rams. Even if he stuck with the club, his starting salary was set at $4,250!

> For long hours, Robustelli and his wife Jean weighed the possibility of a pro football career against a high school teaching job which "would offer more security." Even some of his closest friends advised him to take the job. . . .

> Once he made the decision to report to the Rams—camp opened on his second wedding anniversary—Robustelli immediately had reason to doubt the wisdom of his choice. He had been considered an outstanding offensive end in college, but with the Rams, he would have to compete with a host of talented veterans, including future Hall of Famers Tom Fears and Elroy "Crazylegs" Hirsch.

> How could a raw rookie from a small college beat out those guys?

> The answer, of course, was that he couldn't, and Rams coach Joe Stydahar immediately informed him of this.

> "If you make it *at all*," he instructed Robustelli, "it will be as a defensive end, and that is where we are going to give you your shot."

Robustelli was honored as an All-Pro defensive end seven times in his 14-year NFL career, five of them as a New York Giant. He was inducted into the Pro Football Hall of Fame in 1971.

The Giants' first-round draft pick in 1955 was a halfback from Notre Dame, Joe Heap, who would carry the ball for them eight times during the regular season, gain 29 yards, and then depart the pro game for good. But they fared much better with some of their later picks that year. There was Grier, a 6'5" defensive tackle from Penn State, who was somewhere between 260 and 280 pounds when he arrived at his first training camp, depending on who tells the story. Then there was fullback Mel Triplett from Toledo and defensive back Jim Patton, who had played for Mississippi. In a trade with the Los Angeles Rams, Mara picked up linebacker Harland Svare. They were handsome additions to a roster

Roosevelt "Rosey" Grier, after three years as the cornerstone of the Penn State line, joined the Giants in 1955. One of the most imposing defensive tackles of his time, Grier played seven years with the Giants, missing the 1957 season for military service, before going to Los Angeles to join the Rams' famous "Fearsome Foursome."

Alex Webster, recruited from the Canadian Football League by Wellington Mara, made his New York debut in 1955. For the next 10 years he would prove to be one of the Giants' all-time greatest running backs. When he retired, no one in team history had rushed for more yardage than the 4,638 he gained. He rushed for 39 touchdowns and caught passes for 17 more. Webster came back as head coach of the Giants from 1969 through 1973, compiling a 29–40–1 record.

that still boasted names like Gifford, Rote, Schnelker, MacAfee, Brown, Tunnell, and Landry.

There was a lot of hope for the Giants of 1955 in the front office. The team seemed to be truly taking shape. Jack Mara was quoted in *The New York Times*: "We are a strong team, capable of meeting and defeating any team in the league." The fans and the sportswriters were a little more skeptical, however, and that became evident both at the box office and in the space devoted to Giants football on the New York sports pages. In 1954, the Giants had drawn a little more than 190,400 fans into the Polo Grounds, far below the more than 326,000

that the Los Angeles Rams and the Detroit Lions had attracted to their stadiums, or the 269,000-plus credited to the San Francisco 49ers and the 243,000-plus to the Chicago Bears. In 1955, the Giants would drop to a figure of 183,847 in home attendance—one of the few teams in the NFL to lose at the box office that year.

Part of that problem was attributable to the Giants' awful start in 1955. Despite a seemingly stellar cast taking the field, they lost decisively in the opening three games to the Philadelphia Eagles, Chicago Cardinals, and Pittsburgh Steelers—all second-rate teams in their conference. Those three games were on the road, so when the Giants arrived at the Polo Grounds for their home opener against

Harland Svare was traded to New York by the Rams in 1955 and became a key Giants linebacker through the 1960 season, playing in three NFL title games. Svare served as an assistant coach with the Giants after retiring as a player and later went on to head coaching jobs with the Los Angeles Rams and the San Diego Chargers.

Mel Triplett, one of 17 children of a Mississippi sharecropper, honed his running skills at the University of Toledo before being drafted by the Giants in 1955. The powerful fullback played for the Giants through the 1960 season before moving to the Minnesota Vikings. Triplett rushed for 2,289 yards as a Giant.

the Cardinals, they were the only ones in the NFL Eastern Conference without a win to their credit.

The foremost power in the conference that year was the Cleveland Browns. Graham was still around, although he had threatened to retire before the season began, and he was backed up at quarterback by Ratterman. Also on the roster were Dante Lavelli, Groza, Frank Gatski, Abe Gibron, and Len Ford, as well as such promising newcomers as Fred "Curley" Morrison, Ed "Big Mo" Modzelewski, and Chuck Noll, among others. The Washington Redskins were another force with which to contend since LeBaron came back from Canada, and they also had former Heisman Trophy winner Vic Janowicz to carry the ball and kick field goals and extra points for them.

The Giants went into their first encounter with the Redskins with the undistinguished record of one win and four losses, but they proceeded to destroy the favored Redskins, 35–7. The next week, however, they fell to the Browns, a team that, at that point in the season, with a

Frank Gifford finds plenty of running room in this 1955 game against the Eagles, which was the next-to-last game that the Giants played at the Polo Grounds. They beat Philadelphia that day, 31–7. The other Giants are guard Jack Stroud (No. 66) and quarterback Charlie Conerly (No. 42); the Eagles are tackle Lum Snyder (No. 73) and linebacker Bob Hudson (being blocked by Stroud).

Giants defensive end Walt Yowarsky has the leg of Pittsburgh halfback Lynn Chandnois and is not about to let go of it in this 1955 game at the Polo Grounds. New York lost that day, 19–17, one of five losses against six wins and a tie during that third-place season. No. 61 of the Giants is defensive lineman Roy Beck.

record of 6–1, had virtually wrapped up the conference title, at least as far as the Giants were concerned.

There were five more games remaining in the 1955 season, and that was when the Giants offered the harbinger of what was to come. They stomped all over the Baltimore Colts and the Philadelphia Eagles, the defense allowing each team only a single touchdown. Then Cleveland came to the Polo Grounds for a game that would prove to be historic. It was to be the last Giants game played in the Polo Grounds, the team's home since its inception back in 1925. (The Maras had decided to move to the more spacious Yankee Stadium after the 1955 season.)

The game with the conference-leading Browns was a fitting cap to all the pro football excitement that had occurred on the grass beneath Coogan's Bluff during the 31 years the Giants held court there. Going into the fourth quarter, the score was tied at 21 apiece. The Browns marched in the final period and iced the drive with a touchdown when Modzelewski bucked in from the 1-yard line. But the Giants came right back with a drive of their own and climaxed it when Conerly rifled one to Rote in the end zone. The 28–28 tie did not last long in that volatile quarter. A few minutes later the Giants had the ball again, but Conerly's pass ended up in the hands of Cleveland linebacker Noll, who returned it for a touchdown.

An undaunted Conerly came right back, passing the Giants down the field until he culminated the drive with a touchdown pass to Gifford. The score stood at 35–35. Thirty-three-year-old Graham, playing out his last season as a pro, was not to be outdone, however. He moved the ball steadily against a desperately clawing New York defense as time wore down to the final seconds. Graham got the Browns just inside the New York 15-yard line, with fourth down and only a few seconds on the clock. In came Groza, at the time universally recognized as the finest place-kicker in the history of the game. The holder lined up just back of the 20-yard line, a straight line from him directly through the goal posts. But in a flash, after Groza's immortal toe sunk into the ball, Giants linebacker Pat Knight got high enough to slap it away, and the final score remained 35–35.

The Giants left the Polo Grounds for the last time that afternoon. They went out and won their last two games, beating a favored Redskins team and the Detroit Lions to round out a 6–5–1 season. The team had gotten its act together in midseason and had turned into a winning club and also a dominating force in the conference.

It was the beginning of a new Giants era. They would do justice to the house that Babe Ruth built over in the Bronx. Like the Yankees that ruled the baseball world so often, the football Giants would begin an eight-year epic of outstanding football in which they would lay claim to their conference title six times to become a fixture in NFL championship games.

Dick "Little Mo" Modzelewski was traded to the Giants by the Steelers in 1956 and took his place in a line that featured such stalwarts as Andy Robustelli, Rosey Grier, and Jim Katcavage. Modzelewski stayed with New York through the 1963 season, then went to the Cleveland Browns. "Little Mo" was anything but little—he weighed approximately 260 pounds during most of his Giants career.

THE FAMINE'S OVER

The last sporting event to which New Yorkers were treated at Yankee Stadium before the Giants made their debut in that illustrious edifice was the fifth game of the 1956 World Series, the one in which Yankees hurler Don Larsen pitched the only perfect game in Series history. When this fact was mentioned by one of the Giants coaching staff to the players during a session devoted to extolling their new home, one player allegedly remarked to head coach Jim Lee Howell, "And you want us to top that?" When Howell did not respond, the player added, "Do we get more than one game to do it?"

Jack and Wellington Mara, as well as coach Howell, were expecting good things from their ballclub that year. They had gone out and rounded up a number of new faces, in what would prove to be one of the most lucrative bounties of acquisition in the club's history. Their first draft choice, fullback Henry Moore, spent only a year on the Giants bench before being dealt to the Colts. New York also drafted Sam Huff, a 21-year-old linebacker from the coal-mining region of West Virginia who had made several All-America teams playing for the state university there. They also drafted a defensive end from Dayton, whose name was menacing but, as yet, largely unknown in the national football community—Jim Katcavage. They also drafted punter, place-kicker, and occasional half-back Don Chandler from Florida.

In trades, New York first acquired defensive end Andy Robustelli from the Rams. Next was Dick "Little Mo" Modzewleski from the Steelers, who told coach Howell on his arrival, "Last year, you know, Brown [Paul, coach of the Cleveland Browns] made a trade for my brother [Ed] and won the championship. This year it's your turn." And to augment the defensive backfield Ed Hughes was acquired, also from Los Angeles. Infusing this flush of savagery and talent into a defense that already boasted such stalwarts as Roosevelt "Rosey" Grier, Harland Svare, Bill Svoboda, Emlen Tunnell, Dick Nolan, and Jim Patton gave New York the foundation of what became one of the most legendary fortifications in pro football history.

The rookie and veteran defense was combined with an offense that featured Frank Gifford, Charlie Conerly, Alex Webster, and Mel Triplett in the backfield, along with receivers like Kyle Rote and Ken MacAfee, and a line to protect them peopled by the likes of Roosevelt "Rosie" Brown, Jack Stroud, Dick Yelvington, and Ray Wietecha. There was reason in New York City to be optimistic.

The Giants were scheduled to play their first three games on the road in order to accommodate the New York Yankees, the almost-perennial hosts of the World Series. The Browns and the Redskins had been the powerhouses

THANKS FOR A LATE PLANE

One of the most frequently told tales among Giants nostalgics concerns a pair of 21-year-old disheartened rookies in 1956, linebacker Sam Huff and kicker Don Chandler, whose professional careers almost ended before they ever began.

Huff, a third-round draft choice, and Chandler, a fifth-rounder, were not happy with the way things were going at the Giants training camp up at St. Michael's College in Winooski, Vermont. Huff had played tackle at West Virginia, but at 6'1" and 230 pounds, he was considered too small for that position in the pros. The rumor that a few of the coaches thought he was too slow for any other position got back to him, and he was, in his words, "disheartened, miserable, and homesick." Chandler was suffering from an injured shoulder and not doing well in camp, and therefore was often the butt of Jim Lee Howell's "bellering," as the players called the coach's remonstrations.

One day after workouts, the two decided it was hopeless and that they might as well go home. Line coach Ed Kolman heard about the situation and cornered Huff.

"You'll never forgive yourself if you leave now," he told him. "You'll feel like a quitter."

Huff shook his head "It's not working out. I'm just wasting my time here."

"I've seen some great ones," Kolman said. "And I think if you stick it out you could be one of them in a few years. You've got talent, and I mean it. Don't throw it away by leaving."

The vote of confidence was enough to persuade Huff to stay, but when the linebacker tried to talk Chandler out of departing, he couldn't. So he agreed to drive his friend to the airport in Burlington, Vermont. What happened there is described by Don Smith, former publicity chief of the Giants, in a book he wrote in 1960:

There they were informed that Chandler's flight would be late. It might be an hour or more before he could leave. The players drifted into the hot waiting room and plopped down on a bench. As the minutes ticked by, Huff began to wonder if he'd made the right decision; whether or not he should get his bags and join Chandler as they had originally planned. Despite Kolman's comforting words, Sam was losing his confidence again.

Just then a station wagon roared up to the terminal and out bolted [Vince] Lombardi. He dashed through the waiting room and pursued Chandler almost to the revved-up plane, which had just taxied up to the passenger gate.

"Hold on," Lombardi shouted in a voice that was disturbingly familiar to all Giant rookies. "You may not make this ballclub, Chandler, but you're sure as hell not quitting on me now. And neither are you, Huff, in case you've got any ideas about running out." With that, he packed the rookies into the station wagon and delivered them back to camp.

"If that plane had been on time," Huff recalls, "Chandler would have been on it. And maybe I would have gone with him."

of the NFL East the year prior. Cleveland, in fact, was the reigning NFL champ. But Paul Brown had lost Otto Graham to retirement, and many of his other old-line veterans had slowed noticeably. And Washington had lost Vic Janowicz, who had been severely injured in an automobile accident during training camp.

The Giants opened the season in San Francisco. The 49ers had had a miserable season the year prior and began 1956 under the tutelage of their former quarterback, Frankie Albert. They had Y. A. Tittle at quarterback and such running backs as Hugh McElhenny, Joe Perry, and John Henry Johnson, but their defense left much to be

ELECTRONIC QUARTERBACKS

There was an innovation in pro football at the start of the 1956 season, referred to in the press as "electronic quarterbacks." The electronics referred to were devices that allowed a coach on the sideline to communicate by radio directly to his quarterback on the field, who had a receiver in his helmet.

In the offices of the National Football League, especially the one belonging to Commissioner Bert Bell, the practice was "absurd, disruptive to the game, and takes away the human element." Still, many teams were using the devices as the season got under way, but not the Giants, at least not in the way the other teams were.

When the Giants traveled to Cleveland for the third game of the season, they brought some transistors of their own along. But not for Jim Lee Howell to talk from the sideline to Charlie Conerly on the field. Instead they were set to the wavelength that Cleveland coach Paul Brown was transmitting over to his quarterback, George Ratterman. End Bob Topp sat on the bench with earphones, picking up the plays Brown was sending to his quarterback. Topp quickly relayed them to defensive coach Tom Landry, who, in turn, shouted them to his defense on the field.

It only lasted for several plays, however, before Ratterman disconnected the receiver because he could no longer hear Brown over the roar of the crowd.

Commissioner Bell, a few days later, decided radio communications and electronic spying on the field was just too much and outlawed the whole thing. "It was a good thing," Giants end and chief spy Topp said later.

"If the trend continued, the number-one draft choice of the Giants next year would probably have been the valedictorian of MIT."

Don Chandler almost left the Giants before he was able to boot a single football, but the disillusioned kicker was brought back into the fold by assistant coach Vince Lombardi during training camp in 1956. Chandler place-kicked and punted for the Giants until 1964, when he was traded to the Green Bay Packers and reunited with Lombardi. He still holds the Giants record for the most extra points in a season (52). The "Babe," as he was called by some, holds the top career punting average in all Giants history (43.8 yards) and in a single season (46.6 in 1959).

desired. And the Giants took advantage of it, racking up 38 points while allowing the San Franciscans just 21.

The next game brought them to Chicago to face the Cardinals, who had surprised the NFL-champion Browns in their opener. Behind the running of Ollie Matson and the passing of Lamar McHan, the Cardinals proved they were a force to contend with that year by beating the Giants, 35–27. On to Cleveland and the faltering Browns, where the doom of the "electronic quarterbacks" was sealed (see sidebar). There, New York sent the longtime ruler of the NFL East reeling, a fall that would continue throughout the season and result in the team's first finish below .500. The score was 21–9, and as the Giants returned to New York to debut in their new Bronx home, there was a lot of ink in the local papers about the heartening prospects of this new New York Giants team.

The Steelers, who had finished last in the NFL East the year before, were in a state of reconstruction, or so their public relations staff stated. Quarterbacked by Ted Marchibroda, they upset the Redskins in their home opener but then lost the next two. The Redskins were to serve as the bow on which the Giants would break the bottle of champagne to christen Yankee Stadium.

By October 21, 1956, the Yankees had abandoned the stadium after trimming the Brooklyn Dodgers in the World Series, and such illustrious baseballers as Mickey Mantle, Yogi Berra, Billy Martin, Hank Bauer, Gil McDougald, Enos Slaughter, Whitey Ford, and Larsen had emptied their lockers so that the Giants could fill them with pads, cleats, and helmets. The Giants took the field that afternoon before 48,108 expectant fans who got what they came to see—a New York rout. With Conerly passing well, Gifford doing everything right, and the defense simply overwhelming the Steelers. the Giants walked off with a 38–10 victory to inaugurate what would become nearly a decade of exceptional football in New York.

The Eagles and the Steelers again fell to the Giants before the rejuvenated Chicago Cardinals came to Yankee Stadium. The Giants were 5–1, and so were the Cardinals—both well ahead of the rest of the division. Even that early in the season, it was clearly a two-team race for the divisional crown.

Coach Howell and his two assistants, Vince Lombardi and Tom Landry, knew that to win they had to stop the Cards' running game, most importantly that of the division's leading ground gainer, Matson, but also the power rushes of fullback Johnny Olszewski. The coaches felt that if the Giants could control the run, the Chicagoans' preferred method of attack, the game was theirs. Middle linebacker Huff was given the chore of keying on Matson, and after a series of brutal hits, he made it clear to the Cardinals running back that he was in for a painful day. And to Landry's everlasting joy it was his Giants defense that carried the day. Matson was held to a mere 43 yards rushing, and the Cardinals as a whole

The Giants' third-round draft choice in 1956 was linebacker Sam Huff from West Virginia. One of the key cogs in the Giants' fabled defense of the late fifties and early sixties, Huff was twice named All-Pro and four times went to the Pro Bowl as a Giant. After the 1963 season he was traded to the Redskins. Huff was enshrined in the Pro Football Hall of Fame in 1982.

to 10 points. Meanwhile the Giants offense put 23 points on the board and gained sole possession of first place in the NFL East. After the game, Huff, a rookie in only his third game as a starter, was asked by a New York sportswriter about the savagery with which he went after All-Pro Matson. "I learned right off," he said, "there's no room for nice guys in pro football. When I go out there on the field, I'm mad at everyone. The hell with them all. Tell them to look out for old Sam Huff. He's mean today."

The game had been an important one, and the Giants had prevailed. The letdown the following week against Washington was totally unexpected. The Redskins had gotten off to a miserable start, losing their

RAZZLE-DAZZLE, 1956 STYLE

From a Giants program of the time:

> The Giants must be the hardest team in the National League to scout. Every week, coach Jim Lee Howell and his staff come up with some fancy new offensive wrinkle. The "Belly 26 Reverse Pass" from Gifford to MacAfee that scored the first touchdown against Washington last Sunday was a real gem. It involved faked handoffs by Don Heinrich to Mel Triplett, plunging into the line, and then to Alex Webster, slicing toward his left tackle. Don then delivered the ball to Gifford, who had started to his left from left halfback, then wheeled back to the right. Led by Jack Stroud, who executed a reverse pull from right guard, Gifford headed out around right end. With an option to run or pass, he passed when he saw that MacAfee had a lead on Washington's left corner man, who had been drawn in by the faked runs to the other side, and threw a 35-yard strike to Ken in the end zone.

first three games, but they were on a roll when New York came down, counting three subsequent wins. And then they added a fourth consecutive victory with devastating force by crushing the Giants 33–7.

It was a game the Giants particularly wanted to win because the following week the Chicago Bears were coming to Yankee Stadium, bringing with them a record of 7–1. The Bears were tied for first place in the NFL West and naturally not anxious to jeopardize their race to the title with a loss to New York. The Bears offense was the best in the entire NFL that year, concentrated around the powerful running of fullback Rick Casares and the passes of Ed Brown to Harlon Hill and Bill McColl. The defense showcased future Hall of Famers end Doug Atkins and middle linebacker Bill George. But the "Monsters of the Midway," as they were called around Chicago, hardly seemed the stuff of their press clippings, at least through the first three quarters of the game that day at Yankee Stadium.

The Giants led 17–3 going into the final period and were confident their defense would maintain the lead. But the defense did not, and the two touchdowns the Bears scored before time ran out gave them a tie at the final whistle.

A rebound win over Washington was more than satisfying after the way the Giants had been treated down in the nation's capital two weeks prior. Next up was Cleveland, with a lowly record of 4–6. The Giants, playing at home, were a solid favorite. The team's chief scout, Jack Lavelle, a corpulent character about town, who, if he had not been real could well have been a creation from the pen of Damon Runyon or Paul Gallico, was wary, however, after having watched the Browns defeat the Eagles the week before. Lavelle wrote in an article for the game program:

> I have warned Jim Lee Howell to tell the boys to be ready to fight for their lives today. Those Browns will come to town with the sincere meanness that you develop when somebody takes something you own. They held the Eastern Conference title for so long that they figured it belonged to them permanently. I promise that they will not look upon the Giants with friendly eyes.

Lavelle was absolutely correct. The bloodthirsty Browns came and left with a 24–7 shellacking of the Giants. But, as it turned out, it didn't matter. Out in Chicago, the Cardinals fell to their crosstown rivals, the Bears, leaving them with a record of 6–5. The resurgent Washington Redskins would loose the following weekend to the Steelers, reducing their record to 6–5 as well. The Giants, standing at 7–3–1, clinched the division title with a victory the following Saturday over Philadelphia coupled with the Washington loss on Sunday. The win gave them their best record since 1951.

Not since 1950 had a Giants team earned its way to the NFL championship game. And not only were they there in 1956, but the oddsmakers gave them a slight edge over the Chicago Bears, whose record of 9–2–1 was just a smidgen better than the 9–3 Detroit Lions in the NFL West.

The afternoon of December 30, 1956, was bitterly cold in New York, as it had been all the previous week, and the field was a marble slab. The Giants were prepared for it, having obtained basketball shoes the day before (see sidebar). There were 56,836 bundled-up fans in Yankee

SNEAKERS CHAMPIONSHIP GAME II

If the Super Bowl warrants Roman numerals, so should the two classic "sneakers" games played between the Giants and the Chicago Bears. In 1934, little Abe Cohen was the hero of the hour; in 1956 it was somewhat of a joint effort.

Wellington Mara remembered the 1934 classic that was saved by his team wearing basketball shoes in the second half. And when he saw how frozen the field was the week before the 1956 title game, he talked with coach Jim Lee Howell about the situation and the shoes that might just make a difference.

Howell tested the turf. He sent back Gene Filipski out to run around wearing basketball shoes and defensive back Ed Hughes with cleated shoes. Hughes slid about on the frozen field, but Filipski ran smoothly. So Mara and Howell spoke with defensive end Andy Robustelli, who, on the side, had a sporting goods store, and asked him to put through a rush order for rubber-soled basketball shoes. As Robustelli recalls, "It was for four dozen pairs, sizes nine to thirteen."

The order came through in time, and the ever-responsible defensive end carted them to Yankee Stadium for the Giants. It helped once again. Perhaps even more in 1956: the Giants won, 47–7, while in 1934 they had only won by a score of 30–13.

THE FAMINE'S OVER, 1956

New York Giants		Chicago Bears
Kyle Rote	LE	Harlon Hill
Rosie Brown	LT	Bill Wightkin
Bill Austin	LG	Herman Clark
Ray Wietecha	C	Larry Strickland
Jack Stroud	RG	Stan Jones
Dick Yelvington	RT	Kline Gilbert
Ken MacAfee	RE	Bill McColl
Don Heinrich	QB	George Blanda
Frank Gifford	LH	Bob Watkins
Alex Webster	RH	John Hoffman
Mel Triplett	FB	Rick Casares

	1	2	3	4	T
Bears	0	7	0	0	—	7
Giants	13	21	6	7	—	47

Touchdowns—*Bears:* Casares; *Giants:* Triplett, Webster (2), Moore, Rote, Gifford.

Field goals—*Giants:* Agajanian (2).

PATs—*Bears:* Blanda; *Giants:* Agajanian (5).

Stadium for the opening kickoff. Gene Filipski returned it for the Giants 53 yards. Three plays later the Giants were at the Bears' 17-yard line. Triplett hit the middle of the line, shook off a tackle or two, and plowed straight through to the end zone. On the ensuing Bears' possession, Casares fumbled the ball, and New York recovered, capitalizing on it with an "Automatic" Ben Agajanian field goal—the first of two from him that period.

In the second quarter, the Giants increased their lead to 20–0 when Alex Webster plunged in from the 3-yard line. The Bears then got on the scoreboard when

Casares found a hole and bulled his way nine yards for a touchdown. But the Giants were in total control. One writer aptly put it, remembering the famous "sneakers championship" of 1934, "As some racehorses take to mud the Giants in title contention apparently took to ice." Two more New York touchdowns were scored before the half, and the Giants went to the locker room with a 34–7 lead.

The game was really over before the third quarter started. But the Giants kept going. Conerly, who had come off the bench in the second quarter, hit Rote for a touchdown and then found Gifford for the Giants' sixth touchdown of the day. The final score: Giants 47, Bears 7.

It was the Giants' first NFL championship since 1938, when they had drubbed the Green Bay Packers in the old Polo Grounds. In 1956, each victorious Giants player received $3,779.19 for his effort; back in 1938, the take had been only $504.45.

With the Yankees winning the World Series and the Giants winning the NFL championship, it had been a most worthy year in Yankee Stadium. No one on the Giants made individual history in the vein of the Yankees hurler Larsen, but the statistics were noteworthy. Gifford was the fifth most productive rusher in the league with 819 yards, and his 5.2-yards-per-carry average was outstanding; the Giff was the third top receiver in the NFL with 51 catches for 603 yards. He scored nine touchdowns and passed for two others, making him an easy choice for All-Pro.

Conerly threw for 1,143 yards, including 10 touchdowns, and was ranked third among all quarterbacks in the NFL that year. Huff was named Rookie of the Year. Besides Gifford, others achieving All-Pro honors included Tunnell, Robustelli, Brown, and Grier.

It would not have been surprising if Jack and Wellington Mara had closed the books on the year humming, "This could be the start of something grand."

It turned out to be less than grand in 1957, however, although it was still an exciting season until the last three games. There were essentially no new faces, the Giants having given up their first-round draft choice in an earlier trade, but there was a conspicuous absence: All-Pro tackle Grier had departed for the army and would spend the season at Fort Dix, New Jersey, instead of Yankee Stadium.

For the most part, preseason picks had the Giants repeating as the NFL champ. Most felt that the Eastern Conference runner-up Cardinals of the year before had played over their heads, and that would prove to be true. The Browns were certainly going to be helped by their first-round draft choice, a muscular 6'2", 228-pound, 21-year-old running back named Jim Brown, although no one then realized just how much a factor he would become in the NFL.

The Giants were wary of him, however. Landry went on record on various occasions to tout the danger Brown presented to any team he ran against, including the

1956 NEW YORK FOOTBALL GIANTS

First row: Ray Wietecha, Jim Patton, Herb Rich, Gene Filipski, Mel Triplett, Kyle Rote, Coach Jim Lee Howell, Bill Svoboda, Dick Mudzelewski, Walt Yowarsky, Sam Huff, Gerald Huth, Dick Yelvington, Wellington Mara, Pete Previte.

Second row: Alex Webster, John Bauguil, Dick Nolan, Jack Stroud, Frank Gifford, Charley Conerly, Don Heinrich, Ray Beck, Ed Hughes, Roosevelt Brown Jr., Henry Moore, Harland Svare, Ed Kolman, Jim Kavanaugh, Pete Sheehy.

Third row: Em Tunnell, Bill Cottrelback, Jim Katcavage, Andy Robustelli, Cliff Livingston, Alex Webster, Ken MacAfee, Roosevelt Grier, Bob Schnelker, Bill Austin, Don Chandler, Sid Moret, Tom Landry, Vince Lombardi.

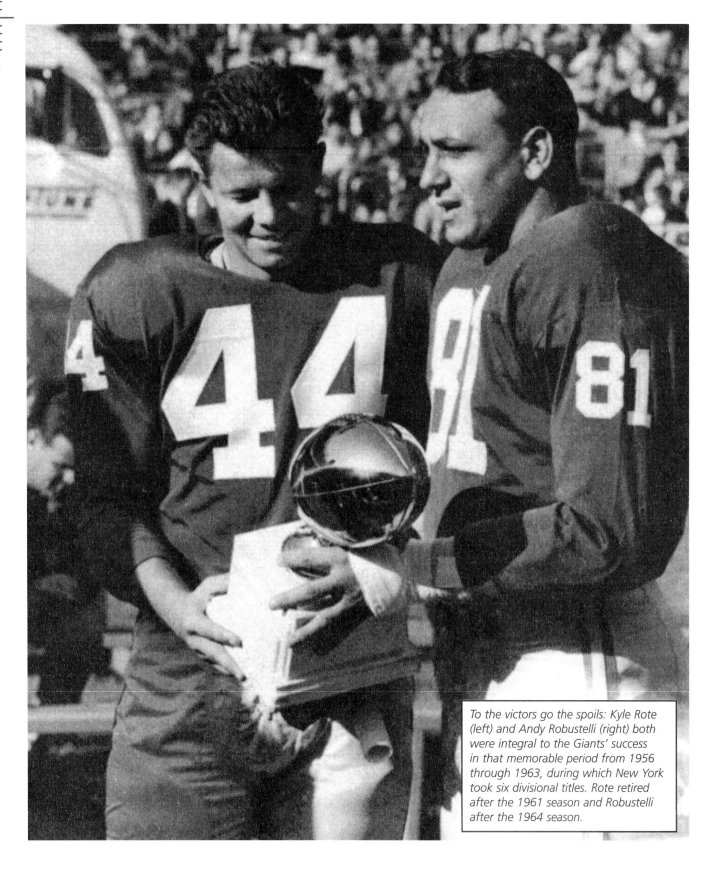

To the victors go the spoils: Kyle Rote
(left) and Andy Robustelli (right) both
were integral to the Giants' success
in that memorable period from 1956
through 1963, during which New York
took six divisional titles. Rote retired
after the 1961 season and Robustelli
after the 1964 season.

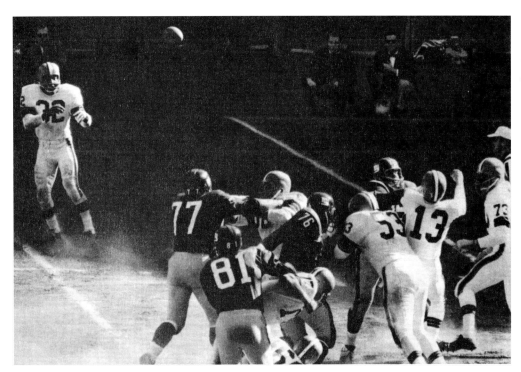

The Giants and the Cleveland Browns had some real roust-abouts over the years. One player who always contrib-uted a certain amount of discomfort was Jim Brown (No. 32), shown here awaiting a flat pass from Frank Ryan (No. 13). The Giants defend-ers are Dick Modzelewski (No. 77), Andy Robustelli (No. 81), Rosey Grier (No. 76), and Jim Katcavage, who is applying a bit of muscle to quarterback Ryan's upper torso.

vaunted defense of the Giants. Landry even designed a special defense to thwart him, basically having Huff key on Brown on practically every play.

With Jim Brown, Paul Brown's Browns quickly proved they were a restored champion. The Giants met them on opening day in 1957 in Cleveland, and the battle went right down to the last minute of the ballgame. Landry's special defense worked against the Browns—although Jim Brown gained 87 yards rushing and aver-aged more than 4 yards per carry—holding them to a mere three points until the last 20 seconds of the game. Unfortunately the Giants could post no more than three themselves, and with just a third of a minute left to play, the sure-footed Lou Groza came on to kick a 47-yard game-winning field goal.

The Giants rebounded with three straight wins over the Eagles, Redskins, and Steelers, but then were stunned by a fired-up Washington team in a 31–14 embarrassment. The loss was forgotten over the next four weeks, however, as the Giants rolled to four consecutive victories, giving them a record of 7–2, trailing Cleveland who sported a record of 7–1–1.

Then, for some still inexplicable reason, the foot-ball field fell out from under the Giants, and they lost their last three games to San Francisco, Pittsburgh, and finally Cleveland. In the Browns game, however, the Giants gave them a mighty fight despite already being out of any chance for the title. They lost, 34–24, but they left a distinct impression on Paul Brown that the Giants were the team to worry about in the upcom-ing season. "We beat them twice last year," he said before the start of the 1958 season, "but we were in two brutal battles. They're the team that will give us the most trouble."

New York ended up with a record of 7–5 in 1957. Gifford, Robustelli, and Rosie Brown were named All-Pro. Conerly had a good year, passing for 1,712 yards and 11 touchdowns, good enough to rank him number four among all NFL quarterbacks. Gifford led the Giants in rushing (528 yards, 3.9-yard average) and in receiving (41 catches for 588 yards). And Chandler led the entire NFL with a punting average of 44.6 yards, which also set a Giants record.

Although the season was a bit of a disappointment at the time, soon it would be nothing more than an intermis-sion between NFL championship games. The Giants were about to treat New Yorkers to six marvelous years of football in which they would prevail in their division five times.

Mel Triplett (No. 33) bulls his way through Philadelphia's line in the second game of the 1958 season. The Giants lost that day in the city of brotherly love, 27–24, one of three losses that year, but New York still ended up on top of the NFL East. No. 55 on the Giants is center Ray Wietecha. The two Eagles whom Triplett is dragging along are Eddie Bell (left) and Marion Campbell (right); No. 72 is Jess Richardson.

NEMESES EXTRAORDINAIRE

The year 1958 seemed filled with suspense and excitement on all fronts. The army launched the nation's first satellite, *Explorer I*, into orbit around the Earth to initiate the space age. President Eisenhower sent the U.S. Marines into Lebanon, the first real military action since the Korean War ended. The New York Yankees, trailing the Milwaukee Braves in the World Series three games to one, pulled off a miraculous comeback, thanks to the hitting of Bill "Moose" Skowron and Gil McDougald and the pitching of Bob Turley, and won the world championship of baseball, four games to three. And not to be outdone, the Giants treated New York football fans to one of the most heart-pounding, edge-of-the-seat seasons in the history of pro football.

For the Giants 1958 would not go down merely to the last game of the regular season—although it was an absolutely crucial game for them—but to a winner-take-all conference playoff game and the first sudden-death overtime championship game in NFL history.

It was the last year that Vince Lombardi and Tom Landry worked together as an assistant coach tandem for Jim Lee Howell. The next year Lombardi left to take the head coaching job in Green Bay, and the year after that Landry departed for the same position with the Dallas Cowboys. It was also the year that the Giants,

with noticeable jubilation, welcomed Roosevelt "Rosey" Grier back from the army. The Giants also aided their cause substantially with a few key acquisitions. From the Chicago Cardinals, they obtained defensive back Lindon Crow and place-kicker Pat Summerall, both of whom would make significant contributions in 1958. Al Barry, a fast, strong offensive guard, was picked up from Green Bay, and defensive back Carl Karilivacz was acquired to back up the four regular secondary defenders. From the draft, the most notable additions were Phil King, a hard-running, 6'4", 225-pound back from Vanderbilt, offensive tackle Frank Youso from Minnesota, and offensive guard Bob Mischak of Army.

The Giants lost five of six exhibition games, and Howell, Landry, and Lombardi scrambled to figure out what was going wrong with a team so filled with proven talent. The preseason was hardly a harbinger of what was to come, however.

The season opener with the Chicago Cardinals was set in Buffalo because the Yankees still occupied Yankee Stadium and the White Sox were playing at the Cardinals' home, Comiskey Park in Chicago. The Giants were a heavy favorite despite their awful exhibition season; the Cardinals had won only three games the year prior and had occupied the NFL East cellar.

GIFFORD'S VISITOR

While Frank Gifford was having his injured knee attended to in a New York hospital in 1958, he awoke at about 5:30 one morning to find a large, trembling young man at the foot of his bed. The immobilized Gifford watched as the man shook the bed and ranted, "What's the matter with your Giants? What's the matter with all of you, Gifford?"

The man walked over to the Venetian blinds and ran his hand up and down them to make noise. "What you need is someone like me, a killer. I was in Korea."

Gifford grabbed the water pitcher beside his bed. "If he was going to come at me, I was going to gong him," Gifford said later. The man didn't, but he also did not leave. He just stood there, running his hand along the blinds.

Gifford finally said to him, "If you really think you can help the team, get your ass down to Yankee Stadium. Tell them what you can do." The man sort of nodded and left, much to Gifford's relief.

However, the man did take the Giff's advice and went to Yankee Stadium. He managed to get into the locker room, where most of the players were suiting up for practice. The young man began screaming at 260-pound Dick "Little Mo" Modzelewski first, and then at some others. According to sportswriter Barry Gottherer, the man then began drop-kicking footballs around the room, castigating the team before several policemen arrived to take him away.

As he was leaving, Gottherer quoted him as shouting back, "All right, so you don't appreciate me. I'll go down to Baltimore and help Johnny Unitas out."

Their defense was considered among the more porous in pro football, and it lived up to that reputation when the Giants met them in the 1958 season opener: the final score New York 37, Chicago 7.

Despite the blowout, the Giants were far from the team they became later in the season. They were still struggling the following week when they fell to the Philadelphia Eagles, 27–24 (one of only two games the Eagles would win that year). The Giants next managed a one-touchdown win over a weak Washington Redskins team, but then were shocked in their home opener at Yankee Stadium by the Chicago Cardinals, 23–6 (also one of only two games the Cardinals would win in 1958). To add to the woe, Frank Gifford was hospitalized after it with a leg injury. A lot of soul-searching was going on as the Giants took their 2–2 record into a game with the Pittsburgh Steelers, especially when the standings showed that the Cleveland Browns stood at 4–0, having scored no fewer than 27 points in any of their four games.

The Giants dispatched the Steelers with relative ease and then went back to prepare for a major confrontation against the 5–0 Browns at Cleveland. Jim Brown was already on his way to a record-breaking season rushing—he would demolish Steve Van Buren's nine-year-old total-yardage mark of 1,146 yards by gaining 1,527 and set another NFL standard with 17 touchdowns rushing.

Charlie Conerly, who had been benched the week before, was back at quarterback to face the Browns. Sam Huff again had the assignment of stopping the powerful and elusive Brown. A record crowd in Cleveland filled Municipal Stadium, 78,404, to watch their allegedly title-bound team squelch the New Yorkers. Only it did not turn out that way. With Conerly having one of his finest days in some time, the Giants rallied all their forces and beat the favored Browns, 21–17. Mel Triplett even outrushed Brown, 116 yards to 113.

If the Giants had their hands full with the Browns, the following week promised an armload. Coming to Yankee Stadium were the Baltimore Colts, 6–0 in the NFL West and just coming off a 56–0 humiliation of the Green Bay Packers. The "Hosses," as they liked to be called in the late fifties, were coached by Weeb Ewbank and had improved steadily since he arrived in 1954. In five years, he had put together a team that was laden with famous football names: Johnny Unitas, Alan "the Horse" Ameche, Lenny Moore, Raymond Berry, Jim Parker, Gino Marchetti, Art Donovan, Gene "Big Daddy" Lipscomb, and Jim Mutscheller, among them.

The biggest crowd ever to watch a Giants game in New York City (with the exception of the Red Grange/

Chicago Bears encounter in 1925, attendance of which was estimated at more than 72,000) showed up at Yankee Stadium, a turnstile total of 71,163 (a record that would endure until the Giants moved to the Meadowlands in the late seventies). And again the Giants were ready, helped incidentally by the sidelining of Unitas, who had suffered some cracked ribs the week prior. The game was a seesaw battle, but the Giants were able to pull it out in the last quarter. With approximately two minutes left to play and the score tied at 21, Summerall came on for New York and booted a 28-yard field goal to give them the victory.

Cleveland lost that same day, a surprise at the hands of the otherwise unimpressive Detroit Lions, and so the Giants had earned their way to a tie for the conference with a record of 4–2. The Giants lost one more game before going into the last game of the 1958 season, a 31–10 sting by the Pittsburgh Steelers. The Browns (9–2) did not lose another game and led the Giants (8–3) by one game.

That last game of the year pitted the two against each other, and a Giants win would bring the NFL East

Alex Webster gains a few yards for the Giants in 1958 despite the efforts of the Cleveland defense. The Giants met the Browns three times that year—twice in the regular season and once in the divisional playoff—and defeated them all three times. The other Giants are tackle Frank Youso (No. 72) and center Ray Wietecha (No. 55). The Browns' defenders are Frank Costello (No. 50), Henry Jordan (No. 72), Bob Gain (No. 79), and Walt Michaels (No. 34).

title race to a dead heat and necessitate a playoff game to determine the champ. The Giants had the home-field advantage, if there was any such thing in the snow and ice that blanketed Yankee Stadium that bitter December afternoon. Wellington Mara took a look at the conditions and felt that the extremely inclement weather might turn the game one way or another on just a break or two. "Everyone is going to be stalled in this," Lombardi said before the game, and altered his offense accordingly.

No one, however, told Cleveland's Jim Brown that. On the first play of the Browns' first possession, Brown took a handoff from Milt Plum, slid out of Huff's grasp, and raced 65 yards for a touchdown.

It was the only score of the first period. The Giants got a field goal from Summerall in the second quarter, but Lou Groza matched it for the Browns to send them to the locker room at the half with a 10–3 lead. Neither team scored in the third period nor in the first four minutes of the final quarter. The game had turned into a plodding battle on a slippery, windswept field—not much more than an exercise in exchanging punts. But then the Giants got a break. Plum fumbled on his own 25-yard line, and Andy Robustelli fell on it.

The Giants took immediate advantage of it. On certainly the most exciting play since Brown broke loose in the first quarter, Gifford took a pitchout from Conerly and started around right end, but suddenly he pulled up

SUMMERALL'S MOMENT IN THE SNOW

Many unpredictable things have happened on professional football fields, but not many were less likely than Pat Summerall's miraculous 49-yard field goal in a dizzying snowstorm in 1958 to defeat the Cleveland Browns. The effort clinched a tie for the NFL East crown. Gerald Eskenazi described the astonishing deed in his book *There Were Giants in Those Days*:

> "I couldn't believe Jim Lee was asking me to do that," says Summerall. "That was the longest attempt I'd ever made for the Giants. It was on a bad field, and it was so unrealistic. Most of the fellows on the bench couldn't believe it either."

> Meanwhile, Wellington Mara was up in the press box in the upper stand . . . [and said] "That Summerall kick was the most vivid play I remember. I was sitting next to Ken Kavanaugh and Walt Yowarsky and we all said, 'He can't kick it that far. What are we doing?'"

> It is credited as a 50-yard [actually 49 yards] attempt but, according to Summerall, "No one knows how far it had to go. You couldn't see the yard markers. The snow had obliterated them. But it was more than 50 yards, I'll tell you that. . . .

> "I knew as soon as I touched it that it was going to be far enough. My only thought was that sometimes you hit a ball too close to the center and it behaves like a knuckleball, breaking from side to side. It was weaving out. But when it got to the 10, I could see it was breaking back to the inside."

In the locker room after the game, Tim Mara was as happy as his sons Jack and Wellington, coach Jim Lee Howell, and Summerall all rolled into one. "What a kick, " he said. "What a kicker. But what the hell, that's what I pay him for, and I'm glad to see he earned his money today."

and threw diagonally across the field to Kyle Rote, who was racing down the opposite sideline. Rote grabbed it and broke a tackle, finally being slung into the snow at the 6-yard line. Gifford took a handoff on the next play, but was knocked for a one-yard loss. On the next play, it was again a pitchout to Gifford, who pumped a fake to Rote then rifled the ball to Bob Schnelker, who had button-hooked just inside the end zone. Summerall's extra point tied the game at 10.

The Giants defense responded as well, not giving up a single first down the remainder of the game. The Giants staged a 45-yard march to the Browns' 25, but there Summerall missed the field goal with approximately five minutes remaining. A few minutes later, after a shanked punt, the Giants got the ball at what was estimated as the Cleveland 43- or 44-yard line—no one could tell for sure because the field was totally covered with snow. Three passes from Conerly fell incomplete, and it was fourth down with a little more than two minutes remaining and the snow falling in a profusion that would have stirred Bing Crosby to song if he had been there. A punt, and the game would surely end in a tie, and a tie would do the Giants no good. They could try for a first down, but that was 10 yards away, and the chance of it being made was quite remote. The only thing perhaps more remote was a field goal, somewhere around a 50-yarder through the swirling snow. Howell, to almost everyone's dismay, yelled to Summerall to go in and boot it. Perhaps it was the shock of being told to do it under the conditions that fueled the adrenaline release, but whatever it was, it spurred Summerall to kick the longest field goal in his Giants career, officially logged as a 49-yarder (see sidebar). The Giants won it in the snow, 13–10.

The two teams had a week to rest, recover, and prepare for a repeat meeting. The coin toss to determine who would host the playoff game was won by the Giants, and therefore the teams reconvened at Yankee Stadium. The snow had stopped in New York, but the biting cold remained, and the field was frozen.

That time Jim Brown did not start the game with a flourish. In fact, the Giants' stoked-up defense shut him down completely the entire day, not to mention the rest of the Cleveland attack. It was the Giants who burned the Browns in the first quarter of this game. The play was unorthodox, to say the least, but it worked. New York had gotten to the Cleveland 19-yard line, and Lombardi sent in a special play. Conerly took the snap and handed off to Alex Webster, who then, on a double reverse, gave the

What a kick! Pat Summerall boots a 49-yarder in a snowstorm to defeat the Browns, 13–10, and force a playoff game to determine the 1958 NFL Eastern Conference champion.

ball to Gifford. The Giff made his way past the line of scrimmage, then at the 8-yard line, as he was about to be tackled, lateraled to 37-year-old Conerly, who ran it in for the score. "The double reverse didn't surprise me," Paul Brown said after the game. "But the lateral to Conerly? That couldn't have been planned. What the hell was he doing there?" Conerly was elated with the touchdown. "I don't know when I scored last. But it was great for an old guy like me to run it in." He also explained that it was not a fluke, either: "The lateral was an option. Vinnie [Lombardi] came up with the play just for this game."

That was all the Giants needed that day, although Summerall added a field goal in the second quarter. The final was 10–0, and the stats from the game tell the story of the invincibility of the New York defense that December afternoon.

As Paul Brown put it after the game, "We were soundly defeated by a team that was in an inspired state of mind, that's all." And so the Giants, with five All-Pros (Rosie Brown, Ray Wietecha, Robustelli, Huff, and Jim Patton), were headed to the NFL championship game for the club's 10th appearance since the league began playing the classic back in 1933—more than any other team at that time in the NFL.

The squad the Giants faced, to no one's great surprise, was the awesome Baltimore Colts, which had won its division with a record of 9–3. The Giants had beaten them during the regular season, but they were well aware of how explosive the Colts offense was. The Colts' average of 31.8 points per game with a total of 381 points scored was the best in the entire NFL. In fact, Baltimore led in almost all categories of offense that year. In addition, the Colts defense was acknowledged to be one of the league's strongest and most consistent.

Before he became one of pro football's most popular broadcasters, Pat Summerall spent his time putting his toe to the football. He played for the Detroit Lions and the Chicago Cardinals before going to the Giants in 1958, where he stayed through the 1961 season. He is the ninth-leading scorer in Giants history, his 313 points coming on 59 field goals and 136 extra points.

NOTES AND QUOTES FROM THE NFL EAST PLAYOFF, 1958

Mel Triplett, explaining the events that led to his ejection after a fight in the second period: "No. 86 [Paul Wiggin] kicked me, and Don Colo grabbed the bar on my mask. That's when we started to go at it. It was just one of those things. But the officials ought to know it takes two to make a fight."

Paul Brown, after being informed that the Browns had been shut out for the first time in 114 consecutive NFL games: "If you're going to lose, you might as well be shut out. Now maybe we can start another streak." (Note: 114 games earlier, in 1950, it was the Giants who shut them out 6–0 in Cleveland.)

Jim Lee Howell on his defense: "I have never seen a game where two equal teams were playing, where one defense overpowered the other team so completely. Landry and the defense deserve the credit. Andy Robustelli is a real money player, and Dick Modzelewski played his heart out. [Jim] Katcavage and [Sam] Huff are newcomers: they don't know the meaning of defeat."

And, from the *New York World Telegram*: "Giant fans were so confident of victory that many of them left in the third quarter to go outside and stand in line for tickets to the championship game next week."

There was more than the usual hype for this title game, perhaps because television was boosting professional football up to a level of national interest that the game had never experienced before. Perhaps too because the Giants had amassed a large and devoted following. Giants fans were thoroughly enraptured with the team that had come from behind to snatch the conference crown on Summerall's seemingly impossible field goal.

Baltimore was equally thrilled with its team, its first ever to go for the NFL title. As a matter of fact, the last time a Baltimore team had won a major professional sports crown was back in 1897 when Ned Hanlon's old Orioles were baseball's tops, and that was six years before the World Series was ever played. Sixty-one years later, "Coltaphrenia" was what the sportswriters called the sports madness sweeping Baltimore, which had been so intense during the regular season that one writer referred to Baltimore's Memorial Stadium as an "outdoor insane asylum." Fifteen thousand of those fans traveled by train, bus, and automobile to New York to become a frenzied and vocal part of the more than sixty-four thousand fans assembled to watch the Colts take on the Giants at Yankee Stadium.

It was expected to be a close game, a classic confrontation of Baltimore's great offense and New York's magnificent defense, and it was as close as any game could possibly be.

Defense prevailed in the first quarter, the Giants systematically held off the Colts' balanced rushing/passing attack. Summerall drove a 36-yarder through the uprights for the only score of the period, but the Giants' lead was a brief one.

Offense took charge in the second quarter as the Colts started a drive that ended on the Giants' 2-yard line, where Ameche bulldozed in to give the Colts the lead. Later in the same period, Baltimore began another march, one from its own 14-yard line. At the Giants' 15-yard line, 25-year-old Unitas dropped back and found Berry for another touchdown, and the Colts had a 14–3 lead at the half.

Again in the third quarter the Giants' renowned defense bent to the pressure of the Unitas-led attack.

This momentary ballet features Frank Gifford with one of the foremost blockers in Giants history, tackle Rosie Brown (No. 79). Both were instrumental in bringing New York six divisional titles between 1956 and 1963.

The Colts surged all the way to the New York 3-yard line, but there the Giants' defense lived up to its reputation. Three plays failed to gain a yard, and when, on fourth down, Ameche tried to bruise his way through to the end zone, as he had earlier, linebacker Cliff Livingston met him in the backfield and dropped him at the 5-yard line. The Giants took over, suddenly revitalized by the goal-line stand. After a pair of running plays, Conerly threw long to Rote, who grabbed the ball at the Colts' 40 and ran it as far as their 25 where, as he was being dragged down, he fumbled the ball. It bounced crazily, but Alex Webster managed to scoop it up and race for the goal line. He made it to the 1-yard line, and moments later Triplett carried it in for the score. The Giants were right back in the ballgame, trailing by only four points.

The momentum changed, no doubt about it, and Conerly took advantage of it. At the start of the fourth quarter, he hit Schnelker for 17 yards and on the following play for 46 more. With the Giants at the Baltimore

SUDDEN DEATH, 1958

New York Giants		Baltimore Colts
Kyle Rote	LE	Raymond Berry
Rosie Brown	LT	Jim Parker
Al Barry	LG	Art Spinney
Ray Wietecha	C	Buzz Nutter
Bob Mischak	RG	Alex Sandusky
Frank Youso	RT	George Preas
Bob Schnelker	RE	Jim Mutscheller
Don Heinrich	QB	Johnny Unitas
Frank Gifford	LH	L. G. Dupree
Alex Webster	RH	Lenny Moore
Mel Triplett	FB	Alan Ameche

	1	2	3	4	OT		T
Colts	0	14	0	3	6	—	23
Giants	3	0	7	7	0	—	17

Touchdowns—*Colts:* Ameche (2), Berry; *Giants:* Triplett, Gifford.

Field goals—*Colts:* Myhra; *Giants:* Summerall.

PATs—*Colts:* Myhra (2); *Giants:* Summerall (2).

15, Conerly changed targets and fired a sideline pass to Gifford at the 5, who shook off two tacklers and scored. Summerall's extra point gave New York a 17–14 lead.

There were a little more than two minutes remaining in the game when the Giants were faced with a third-and-four situation. With Baltimore looking for a pass, Conerly pitched to Gifford on a sweep to the right. Marchetti was outside for the Colts, so Gifford slashed in off tackle. Marchetti grabbed him and brought him to the ground, but not until after it appeared he had made the first down. As they went down, however, Lipscomb—all 290 pounds of him—fell across Marchetti's leg and broke it. Amid the screams of pain and the scramble by everyone to get off Marchetti, the referee neglected to mark the ball. When the chaos subsided, the ball was finally placed down, but it was about a foot and a half behind where it should have been marked, according to most observers and *all* members of the Giants organization.

"I know I made that first down," Gifford said later. "The referee was so concerned about Marchetti that he forgot where he picked up the ball. I saw him pick it up at his front foot, but he put it down where his back foot was." The ensuing measurement showed the Giants six inches shy of a first down.

At their own 43-yard line, Howell had no desire to take a chance at that late moment in the game and sent Don Chandler in to punt. It was a fine kick, and Baltimore was back at its own 14-yard line with two minutes to go. After two incompletions, it appeared the game was securely in the hands of the Giants. But then the ice-cold engineer Unitas went to work. It took seven plays in just about a minute and a half for the crew-cut quarterback to move the Colts all the way to the Giants' 13-yard line. Highlights of the journey were three completed passes to Berry for a total of 62 yards—all while Berry was double-covered. With only seven seconds remaining, Steve Myhra came on to boot the game-tying field goal.

And so, for the first time in NFL history, the title had to be decided in a sudden-death overtime period. The Giants won the toss and chose to receive. They were stymied, however, and forced to punt. Unitas and his "Hosses" got the ball at their own 20-yard line. Unitas carefully interwove runs with his passes and moved the ball steadily down the field. The most significant play was a 23-yard run by Ameche that brought Baltimore to the Giants' 20 and within field-goal range. But, as it turned out, the surging Colts did not need a field goal. They continued the march all the way to the 2, then Unitas gave the ball to Ameche, who simply slid through a gaping hole between tackle and end on the right side of the line, opened by perfectly executed blocks by tackle George Preas and end Mutscheller.

The most exciting NFL championship up to that time in history came to a close with the Giants on the short end of a 23–17 score. As the lead line in *The New York Times* the next day pointed out, "Time and fortune finally ran out on professional football's Cinderella team, the New York Giants." It was a heartbreaker indeed for the Giants, but there was still an abundance of pride. Howell said in the locker room after the game, "I'm very proud of my men. This team went a long way this season. Our kids were always straining against teams which

The coaching staff in 1959. From left to right: Johnny Dell Isola, Tom Landry, Ken Kavanaugh, Jim Lee Howell (head coach), Walt Yowarsky, and Allie Sherman.

should have been better than they were. We were only 20 seconds and a few inches away from winning it all today." And mountainous Modzelewski added, "We did pretty good for a team that was so low after we lost five exhibition games. You can't come any closer to winning the championship than we did. We outfought Baltimore, but they outplayed us."

And so ended a suspenseful and exciting 1958.

The year 1959 began on a sad note in the Giants organization with the death of founder Tim Mara on February 16. The elder Mara had been a major force in the development of professional football and was honored as a charter member of the Pro Football Hall of Fame when it was created in 1963. Through the hardest of times he kept the NFL franchise in New York, his mission to provide the people of New York with a good professional football team and leave a bequest to his

two sons that he knew they wanted so much. For 34 years he was the titular head of the Giants while they won three NFL championships and took eight divisional titles.

In 1956 Lombardi also left to launch his dynasty at Green Bay, taking over a Packers team that had finished last in the NFL West the year before with a record of 1–10–1. Allie Sherman, who had organized the T formation for the Giants some years earlier, was hired to handle the offense in Lombardi's stead.

With Conerly somewhere around 38 or 39 years of age—no one really knew for sure just how old the drawling quarterback was in those days—the Giants drafted a promising quarterback from Utah in the first round: Lee Grosscup. The Giants were faced with a plethora of quarterbacks because they still had Don Heinrich and had traded for George Shaw, who had been Unitas' backup at Baltimore the year before. In addition, gilded halfback Gifford announced his intention of trying out for the position at training camp. He said that he had always wanted to play that position in the pros—he had played it in high school and at the University of Southern California for a time—and had mentioned the desire to his roommate and good friend Conerly. The elderly Conerly did not mind; instead he seemed almost bemused by the idea. Coach Howell said, "Why not?" By the end of the preseason, however, Grosscup was relegated to the taxi squad, and Gifford was back at halfback, where he had already set so many club scoring, rushing, and receiving records.

The most important harvest from the draft that year was halfback Joe Morrison, although his contributions would not come until a few years down the line. By way of trade, the Giants picked up cornerbacks Dick Lynch from the Redskins and Dick Nolan, who was reacquired from the Cardinals. And offensive guard Darrell Dess came over from the Steelers.

The Los Angeles Rams, New York's opponent in the 1959 opener, were not a good team that year, one that would only win two games all season, but they were ready for the Giants and almost pulled off a major upset. No one in New York was worried about the Giants defense. As Lombardi had said when he was leaving for Green Bay, "Any team that hopes to get by in this conference somehow has to figure how to get past New York's defense. It may be the best in the history of the game." The offense was the worry: could Conerly, who despite his advanced age had won the starting slot at quarterback over all the 1959 competition, play championship-caliber ball? Could the Giants score when they had to? Would Conerly be able to bring them back in a game, like Unitas, when he had to? Those questions were, or at least should have been, put to rest after the Rams game out in Los Angeles.

Conerly came out passing, and the Giants built a 17–0 lead, but surprisingly the defense went stale in the second half, and the Rams scored three touchdowns to take a 21–17 lead. Without a lot of time remaining, Conerly passed the Giants 74 yards downfield, where Summerall came on to boot a field goal and narrow the margin to a single point. The defense returned the ball to the Giants offense, and Conerly started again. That time he was faced with a fourth-and-11 situation. It was too late in the game to punt, Conerly felt, and Howell agreed. So old Charlie dropped back in the pocket, faked a pass

to Gifford, then tossed the ball to Schnelker for the first down. Schnelker moved the Giants to the Los Angeles 18, where Summerall came on again and kicked the winning field goal. At game's end, Conerly had completed 21 of 31 passes for 321 yards, and Summerall was three for three from the field-goal tee.

Giants fans did not know it at the time, but they had seen a forecast of the upcoming season in microcosm that afternoon in Los Angeles. It was going to be a memorable year of Conerly's passes and Summerall's kicks, and, of course, a defense that was, as Conerly once put it, "as reliable as an old hound dog."

But the old hound dog must have dozed off the next week, when the Giants traveled to Philadelphia, because there the Giants were annihilated by the Eagles, 49–21. Not since the Cleveland Browns ran up 62 points against them in 1953 had a team scored so many points against a Giants defense.

Cleveland, with Brown, Bobby Mitchell, Plum, and Billy Howton, was the real concern for the Giants in 1959. But Huff and his brawling gang had found the way to handle them. Three times they had beaten them in 1958; in 1959 they would do it twice. The first was a simple 10–6 victory, the second a 48–7 humiliation in the next-to-last game of the season.

The latter trouncing stood a chance of not getting into the record books, however. As Tex Maule reported in *Sports Illustrated*:

> New York fans poured out of the stands about two minutes before the game ended and made a determined effort to tear down the goal posts while the two teams were going through the motions of finishing the game. Police were powerless to stop them, then the public-address announcer informed the unruly that unless they cleared the field, the game could be declared forfeit to the Browns. In the face of so grievous a contingency, the mob reluctantly squeezed itself behind the side and end lines and the game was played out.

After the game, Cleveland coach Brown, perpetrator of many similar devastations himself over the previous

10 years, said, "I wouldn't have asked for a forfeit even if the last two minutes hadn't been played. We didn't even belong on the same field with them today."

In between those two games with rival Cleveland, the Giants won six others and lost but one (14–9, to Pittsburgh), then capped the season with a win over the Redskins for a 10–2 record and easy access to the NFL East title for the second year running.

The Giants defense had given up an average of 14 points per game in the 12 regular-season contests, but discounting the anomaly that occurred in Philadelphia, New York's defense allowed only 11 points in each of the other 11 games. They, in fact, led in just about every major defensive category, most notably: fewest points allowed all season, fewest points per game, fewest first downs allowed, fewest rushing yards allowed, fewest passing yards allowed, and fewest rushing and passing touchdowns.

The worrisome offense offered little to worry about as it turned out, scoring a total of 284 points for an average of almost 24 points a game. Conerly ended up as the top-ranked quarterback in the entire league, completing 113 of 194 passes for 1,706 yards, including 14 touchdowns. The four interceptions he threw were the least a Giants passer had thrown since Alphonse "Tuffy" Leemans back in 1942. Summerall kicked the most field goals in the NFL—20 of 29—and his success ratio of 69 percent was also tops that year. Summerall was also 30 for 30 on extra points. Chandler's punting average of 46.6 yards per boot is still the best ever by a Giant, although it was second in the league that year to Detroit's Yale Lary (47.1). Gifford, proving his placement at halfback truly was proper, led the team in rushing once again (540 yards with a 5.1-yard average per carry), and in receiving (42 for 768 yards). All-Pro honors went to Gifford, Brown, Huff, Robustelli, and Patton.

The championship battle of 1959 once again brought together the Giants and the Colts. Baltimore had ended its season with a record of 9–3. Baltimore would host the event.

The Colts sent their ordinarily raucous fans into hysteria early in the first quarter when Unitas unloaded a pass to Moore that covered 59 yards and put the first six points on the scoreboard. But the frenetics wound down

ON SECOND THOUGHT . . .

Jimmy Cannon, one of the finest sportswriters of his time, proved his fallibility the week before the 1959 title game between the Giants and the Colts when he laid a prediction on the line in his column in the *New York Daily News*.

> The Giants are what all college football squads struggle to be but seldom achieve. That's why I think they will win the championship of the National League by beating the Colts in Baltimore this Sunday. They are the perfection of the team ideal.

> In all the seasons I have been reporting games at which men work for a living, I've never covered an athletic group that was closer. They belong together, each and every one, as if they were the brothers of an immense family connected by something more dramatic than a pay roll. . . .

> The defensive unit has been honored by the game's scholars as the best ever to function for wages. . . . I think the Giants will win because the Giants' defensive guys will be able to get to Unitas.

steadily as the Baltimore offense stalled under immense pressure from the Giants defense. Through the rest of that quarter, and the second and third as well, the Colts' ordinarily volatile offense was shut down. Meanwhile, for the Giants, Webster, Triplett, and Gifford ground out yardage, and Conerly connected from time to time. Even though they were unable to get into the end zone, they were able to get near enough in each of the three quarters for Summerall to kick a field goal. Going into the fourth quarter the Giants had a 9–7 lead.

The momentum, which the Giants seemed to have had on their side, took a dramatic reverse, however, when late in the third quarter New York, on the Baltimore 27 with a fourth-and-one-foot situation, disdained the field goal and went for the first down. Webster hit the line but was stopped. The Colts took over and proceeded to disembowel the Giants from that point forward. Unitas moved his team down the field, the highlight being a

End Bob Schnelker (No. 85) is ready to gather in a Charlie Conerly pass here in the 1959 NFL championship game. The Baltimore defenders are Johnny Sample (No. 47) and Andy Nelson (No. 80). Schnelker caught a touchdown pass late in the fourth quarter, but it was too little too late, and Baltimore triumphed, 31–16. Sample intercepted two Conerly passes that day and Nelson another on a less than memorable afternoon in New York Giants lore.

36-yard pass to Moore. When Unitas got the Colts to the Giants' 4, he faked a pass to Mutscheller and then carried it in unmolested for the touchdown.

The Giants came back passing, but a Conerly toss was intercepted by Andy Nelson and returned to the New York 17. A few plays later, Unitas hit rookie flanker Jerry Richardson for a 12-yard touchdown. Conerly, his day growing worse by the minute, went to the air again, and defensive back Johnny Sample picked it off and ran 42 yards for another Baltimore touchdown. The score stood at 28–9, Colts.

Not too much later, Sample did it to Conerly again, returning one for 24 yards, which set up a Myhra field goal. The Giants managed an inconsequential touchdown in the last minute of the game, but went down in defeat, 31–16.

FATAL FOURTH QUARTER, 1959

New York Giants		Baltimore Colts
Kyle Rote	LE	Raymond Berry
Rosie Brown	LT	Jim Parker
Darrell Dess	LG	Art Spinney
Ray Wietecha	C	Buzz Nutter
Jack Stroud	RG	Alex Sandusky
Frank Youso	RT	George Preas
Bob Schnelker	RE	Jim Mutscheller
Charlie Conerly	QB	Johnny Unitas
Frank Gifford	LH	Mike Somner
Alex Webster	RH	Lenny Moore
Mel Triplett	FB	Alan Ameche

	1	2	3	4		T
Giants	3	3	3	7	—	16
Colts	7	0	0	24	—	31

Touchdowns—*Giants:* Schnelker; *Colts:* Moore, Unitas, Richardson, Sample.

Field goals—*Giants:* Summerall (3); *Colts:* Myhra.

PATs—*Giants:* Summerall; *Colts:* Myhra (4).

If only the championship games of the late fifties had ended earlier, Giants fans must have thought: just seconds in 1958 and a quarter in 1959. If only. . . . But they did not; the Giants' nemesis Unitas and his loyal compatriots saw to that.

NFL Commissioner Bert Bell died during the 1959 season, and the job was held on an interim basis by acting commissioner Austin Gunsel. The owners were divided on giving him the job permanently, however, and after four days of meetings were still at an impasse. It was at that point that Giants vice president Wellington Mara offered a compromise candidate, the 33-year-old general manager of the Los Angeles Rams, Pete Rozelle, and the owners confirmed him.

Rozelle, of course, inherited a league in 1960 that was expanding—the Dallas Cowboys were entering it that year, and the Minnesota Vikings were scheduled to join the following year. The NFL was about to face the largest and most serious challenge of its then 40-year history: the well-organized and well-financed American Football League.

On the New York Giants home front in 1960, it was a year of ailments and injuries. Among those up, but mostly down, were Gifford, Conerly, Webster, Katcavage, and various others. Adding to the misfortune was the departure of defensive genius Landry, who returned to his home state to guide the fortunes of the maiden Dallas Cowboys.

The Giants got off to a decent start, winning their first three games, but dropped from first place after a tie with the Redskins and a loss to the now St. Louis Cardinals. They struggled through to the eighth game of the season, posting a record of 5–2–1, still definitely in the race. But in that game, Gifford suffered a severe concussion after a savage hit by Philadelphia Eagles' All-Pro linebacker Chuck Bednarik. It knocked Gifford out for the season, and the Giants folded after that, winning only one of their four remaining games. Their record of 6–4–2 left them in third place in the NFL East, behind the Eagles and the Browns.

Shaw had done the majority of quarterbacking for the Giants in 1960, relieving 39-year-old and often injured Conerly, and his stats were mediocre at best. Perennial All-Pros Brown, Robustelli, and Patton once again reaped that honor.

The Giants were far from over the hill, however, as the next three seasons delightfully proved. There were two important new faces: Sherman on the sideline as head coach replacing Howell, who chose to retire to the Giants front office, and a 34-year-old, bald-headed quarterback by the name of Y. A. Tittle.

And there would be three thrilling trips to NFL championship games.

Catches like this were the order of the day for Del Shofner in 1963. The adhesive-handed end gained more than 1,000 yards on pass receptions for the season, breaking the millenary mark for the third consecutive year. Chasing Shofner is Eagles defensive back Irv Cross (No. 27). The Giants annihilated Philadelphia in this meeting at Yankee Stadium, 42–14.

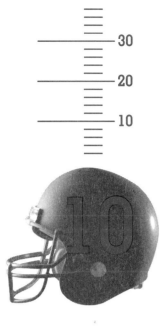

THE POTENTATES OF THE EAST

From 1961 through 1963 the Giants once again became the undisputed masters of the Eastern Conference. Although many of the veterans from the title teams of the late fifties were on hand for the new era of ascendancy, it was a markedly different offense that was to conduct come-from-behind victories game after game and season after season during a glorious three-year romp through the NFL.

Although 1960 was the only year during the previous three that the Giants did not end the season at the top of the Eastern Conference, the third-place finish resulted in substantial changes within the Giants organization. Jim Lee Howell, head coach since 1954, announced his retirement. The Mara brothers appointed him director of personnel and expressed hope that his move to the front office would make room for Green Bay's Vince Lombardi to rejoin the team in the capacity of head coach. But when Lombardi failed to accept the invitation to come back to New York, assistant coach Allie Sherman was promoted to the top slot.

Working with new NFL commissioner Pete Rozelle, the franchise owners lengthened the regular-season schedule from 12 games in 1960 to 14 in 1961. They also welcomed the league's 14th franchise, the Minnesota Vikings—an addition planned earlier as part of the same

expansion program that had brought the Dallas Cowboys into the league the previous season. To prove that were indeed a league addition, in the first game of the Vikings' first season, rookie quarterback Fran Tarkenton threw four touchdown passes and ran for a fifth in a 37–13 drubbing of the Chicago Bears. People in New York were impressed, but none surmised that "Sir Francis" would one day play for New York.

During the off-season, the Maras and coach Sherman worried that the floundering New York Titans of the struggling American Football League, now approaching its second season, might raid the Giants roster. However, the fears proved unfounded. With no major defections with which to contend, Sherman went to work reshaping the club's offense.

The elderly Charlie Conerly at last seemed to fade during the 1960 season. In a move that soon proved to be inspired, Sherman traded second-year tackle Lou Cordileone to the San Francisco 49ers in exchange for quarterback Yelberton Abraham Tittle.

"Who else did they get besides me?" Cordileone asked, shocked that a lineman was swapped for a seasoned All-Pro quarterback. But the San Francisco brain trust seemed happy with the trade. They were convinced that Tittle, 35 years old then (appearing even older because of his baldness), was no longer fast enough for the scrambling required by their newly installed shotgun offense. It was one of the grandest miscalculations in the history of pro football.

With the quarterback question settled, at least in Sherman's mind, the new coach turned his attention to another pressing problem. Frank Gifford, knocked out by a thunderous hit from the future Hall of Famer Chuck Bednarik of the Eagles during the 1960 season, had decided not to return for 1961. Sherman hoped to overcome the loss of Gifford by acquiring a pair of fine receivers. The most important of the acquisitions was a lean and lithe 6'3", 186-pound end named Del Shofner, a four-year veteran from the Los Angeles Rams. During the next three seasons, Shofner and Tittle combined to rewrite the Giants' and the NFL's record books in passing. Sherman also acquired an offensive end from Washington named Joe Walton.

As for the defense, all the great Giants stars were back: Andy Robustelli, Roosevelt "Rosey" Grier, Sam Huff, Jim Katcavage, and the rest—none had jumped to the AFL. And new to the defensive backfield was Erich Barnes, a three-year veteran acquired from the Bears. Barnes soon made his mark in the Giants' secondary, but at the start of the season his most distinguishing characteristic was the peculiar way he pronounced his first name: "It's *E-rich*," he insisted.

Mel Triplett was traded to the Minnesota Vikings, a move that ultimately reinstalled Alex Webster in the Giants' backfield. After a disastrous season in 1960, Webster worked hard to condition his legs and felt he was ready to resume an important role in the New York offense in 1961.

The unproven head coach had made his preseason moves, but by the end of the first game of the 1961 season, fans at Yankee Stadium sensed disaster. While Tittle watched glumly from the sideline, Conerly managed only nine completions for a total of 75 yards in a 21–10 loss to the St. Louis Cardinals in the season opener.

During the first half of the next game in Pittsburgh, the Giants offense was sluggish, to put it delicately. Some New York fans, watching their first televised game of the season, were already screaming for Sherman's head when he pulled Conerly and gave Tittle his chance to run the show.

Del Shofner literally ran out of his shoe after catching a pass from Y. A. Tittle in this 1961 game against the Eagles. He carried the ball in for a touchdown before retrieving the shoe. New York went on to win, 38–21. The Eagles are Glen Amerson (No. 46) and Jess Richardson (No. 72).

Shofner caught seven passes during that game, as it turned out, including one for a touchdown. Added to Joe Morrison's touchdown reception, the score was knotted at 14, paving the way for Pat Summerall's winning field goal. The come-from-behind victory was about to become a way of life for the New York Giants of the sixties.

When the Giants played their third game in Washington's new D.C. Stadium, Tittle again replaced Conerly, this time in the first quarter, with New York already down by two touchdowns. His first pass was intercepted, which allowed the Redskins to set up their third touchdown. But then the "Bald Eagle," as Tittle was sometimes called, settled down to engineer another come-from-behind miracle: a 24–21 win.

Out of uniform, the Giants offensive punch of the early sixties. From left to right: Joe Walton, Joe Morrison, Frank Gifford, and Del Shofner.

With Tittle wresting the starting assignment from Conerly, and with Rote, Webster, Shofner, and Summerall all in fine form, the Giants offense swung into high gear, posting impressive victories over the Cardinals, the Cowboys, and the Rams. Although he lost the starting job, Conerly proved to be a dependable backup. The Giants lost by 17–16 in the second game against Dallas, but they were back in form when they slaughtered Washington, 53–0, the following week. Helping to rack up the points were three touchdown passes from Tittle to Shofner.

The ninth game of 1961, played in Yankee Stadium on November 12 against the Eagles, was a bat-tle for first place in the East. Luck seemed to be with the Giants from the outset. Running for his life from a ferocious Philadelphia blitz, Tittle threw a wounded-duck pass toward Rote, but before it could reach him an Eagles safety tipped it high in the air toward the Philadelphia goal line. Diving for the ball, another Eagles player batted it back into the air, where Shofner grabbed it in mid-flight and carried it into the end zone. The final score was 38–21, and the victory put the Giants in first place.

Wins over Pittsburgh and Cleveland followed. In the Browns game, New York's tough defense managed to hold star running back Jim Brown to a total of 2 yards rushing in the second half, after having given up 72 yards to him in the first half. But just when it appeared

FROZEN OUT IN GREEN BAY, 1961

New York Giants		Green Bay Packers
Offense		
Del Shofner	LE	Max McGee
Rosie Brown	LT	Bob Skoronski
Darrell Dess	LG	Fuzzy Thurston
Ray Wietecha	C	Jim Ringo
Jack Stroud	RG	Forrest Gregg
Greg Larson	RT	Norm Masters
Joe Walton	RE	Ron Kramer
Kyle Rote	FL	Boyd Dowler
Y. A. Tittle	QB	Bart Starr
Joel Wells	HB	Paul Hornung
Alex Webster	FB	Jim Taylor
Defense		
Jim Katcavage	LE	Willie Davis
Dick Modzewleski	LT	Dave Hanner
Rosey Grier	RT	Henry Jordan
Andy Robustelli	RE	Bill Quinlan
Cliff Livingston	OLB	Dan Currie
Sam Huff	MLB	Ray Nitschke
Tom Scott	RLB	Bill Forester
Erich Barnes	CB	Hank Gremminger
Dick Lynch	CB	Jesse Whittenton
Joe Morrison	S	John Symank
Jim Patton	S	Willie Wood

	1	2	3	4		T
Giants	0	0	0	0	—	0
Packers	0	24	10	3	—	37

Touchdowns—*Packers:* Kramer (2), Hornung, Dowler.

Field goals—*Packers:* Hornung (3).

PATs—*Packers:* Hornung (4).

And it was elderly Conerly—not Tittle—who led the Giants to victory in the most important game of the season. Injured during the second quarter, Tittle watched from the sideline as Conerly dissected the injury-ridden Philadelphia secondary. Despite Sonny Jurgensen's NFL-leading aerial attack, the Eagles' weak running game and their injured and inexperienced defensive backs could not hold back the Giants. The final score was 28–24, New York; another three touchdown passes had been hauled in by Shofner that day.

Only a tie in the season finale was needed to clinch the Eastern Conference title for the Giants, and New York, as it turned out, indeed could do no more than that in that final game, played against Cleveland. Plagued by fumbles, interceptions, and missed field goals, the Giants managed only a 7–7 tie. But it was enough.

For the third time since 1958, the Giants were within one victory of the NFL championship. The last hurdle was the Green Bay Packers, champions of the Western Conference, who were in the infancy of the Lombardi dynasty that would put the Pack at or near the top of the NFL throughout most of the sixties. Green Bay, with six conference titles to its name, would host the championship game on December 31, 1961.

As 39,029 fans bundled up in freezing Lambeau Field, they saw their Packers give a chilly reception to the champions of the East. For a time, it seemed as if New York would take the lead. Kyle Rote, in his 11th and final season as a player, dropped a sure touchdown pass in the first quarter, which ended in a scoreless tie. It appeared he might score again in the second quarter when he broke free in the end zone for an option pass from halfback Bob Gaiters, but Gaiters overthrew him. The Giants were running out of opportunities, and the Packers took advantage of it. They scored three unanswered touchdowns in the second quarter, one on a Paul Hornung run, followed by two from Bart Starr passes. Then Hornung added a field goal. The score was 24–0 at the half.

In the second half, the Packers offense and crushing defense continued to dominate. The Giants running game was stifled, and Green Bay defender Jesse Whittenton did a fine job of covering the ordinarily elusive Shofner, allowing him only three receptions the entire game. When it was all over, Green Bay had racked

that the conference title was theirs, the Giants fell, 20–17, to the Green Bay Packers. The loss, coupled with a Philadelphia victory, put New York again in a tie with the Eagles. The Eastern Conference championship was on the line in the next-to-last game of the season when the Giants faced the Eagles in Philadelphia.

KYLE ROTE DAY!

The Kyle Rote Day Committee Wishes to Thank the Following Organizations for Their Participation—

N. Y. FORD DEALER'S ASSOCIATION—1962 Thunderbird Landau Coupe
DALLAS, TEXAS, FANS — 1962 Ford Ranch Wagon
PAN AMERICAN WORLD AIRWAYS—Transportation to and from Europe
AMERICAN EXPRESS WORLD TRAVEL SERVICE—Accommodations in Europe
WNEW RADIO—RCA Color TV, Stereo, AM-FM Radio Combination
HEREFORD ASSOCIATION—Champion Hereford Steer
PHILCO CORP.—2 1-ton Room Air Conditioners
FAIRCHILD CAMERA CORP.—16 mm. Sound Movie Camera and Projector
SAN ANTONIO, TEXAS, FANS — 20 cu. ft. Home Freezer
E. LEITZ, INC.—35 mm. Leica Camera
BULOVA WATCH CO.—Accutron Wrist Watch
SAMSONITE CO.—10 pieces Samsonite Luggage
JOHNSTOWN, N. Y., FANS—Leather Goods for entire family
WESTMINSTER PRINTING CO.—All Printing for Kyle Rote Day
MACK KENNETH CO.—Fur Trimmed Women's Coat
P. BALLANTINE & SONS — U. S. Treasury Bond
THE NEW YORK FOOTBALL GIANTS, INC.—Silver Tea Service
THE PARK PLAZA HOTEL—Meeting Rooms
ESKA CORP.—Power Driven Snow Thrower

THE GARDEN EQUIPMENT CO. — Snow Plower and Lawn Sweeper
THE PARKER CO.—Lawn Sweeper
MORSE ELECTRIC PRODUCTS CO.—Morse Sewing Machine
MILES & RILEY, INC.—Cashmere Top Coat
TRIPLER'S—$200 Gift Certificate
THE B.V.D. CO.—Complete B.V.D. Wardrobe
AMF PIN SPOTTERS—Bowling Balls, Bags and Shoes for Rote Family
VAN HEUSEN SHIRT CO. — Pleasurewear wardrobe
SAVIN BUSINESS MACHINE CO.—Portable Dictation Machine
THE EMERSON CO.—Portable TV Set
THE RAWLINGS SPORTING GOODS CO.—Golf Clubs and Bag
HARRY ROLNICK—$100 Resistall Texas Hat
SECTION 5 CLUB—Gold Money Clip
J. P. STEVENS CO.—4 pairs Slacks for Mr. Rote and 3 Sons
GOLET ORIGINALS—Coat for Mrs. Rote
PEPSI COLA CO.—1 year Supply of Pepsi Cola
L. ABLESON & SONS—Blazers for 3 Rote Boys
SIMPSON CLOTHES—Sport Jacket
LOUIS MARX & CO.—Toys for Rote Children
CANADA DRY CORP.—Soda Cooler
FINKLE & CO.—Washer Drier Combination
NEPTUNE STORAGE CO.—Storing, Insuring and Transporting All Gifts

1961 (New York Giants)

goals and another touchdown made it a certified rout. The Giants' hopes for a championship were frozen out in Green Bay by the final, embarrassing score of 37–0.

It was a disappointing end to an otherwise fine season for the New York Giants. Tittle, deemed "too old and too slow" to play in San Francisco, was named league MVP. Sherman was Coach of the Year in his rookie season. Barnes, Brown, Huff, Katcavage, Patton, Robustelli, Shofner, Tittle, and Webster were all invited to the Pro Bowl; and All-Pro honors were bestowed on six Giants: Tittle, Shofner, Brown, Patton, Katcavage, and Barnes.

The statistics from 1961 give solid evidence of the team's excellence. The Giants defense allowed three fewer points than Green Bay's, for a league-leading minimum of 220. The fleet-footed defensive backs gave up the stingiest percentage of pass completions in the NFL (45.6 percent), and the passing duo of Tittle and Conerly was third in total yards gained (3,035). The Giants netted the most first downs (275) and gave up the fewest (212). Shofner set a team record of 68 receptions during the season, and the defense led the league with 33 interceptions. One of the greatest pickoffs of the decade was made by newcomer

up a total of 183 yards rushing to 31 for New York. In the passing game, the Giants fared not much better. Tittle and Conerly threw for 119 yards, while Starr accounted for 164 for the Pack. Two second-half Hornung field

118

Aaron Thomas (No. 88) would have had this pass were it not for the interfering hand of St. Louis defensive back Bill Stacy (No. 24). Thomas gained 469 yards on his 22 receptions in 1963, but his best years with the Giants were when he led the club in receiving in 1964 (43 for 624 yards) and 1967 (51 for 877 yards).

Barnes in a game against Dallas that year. Intercepting a Cowboys pass in the end zone, Barnes scampered 102 yards for the touchdown—a new (and still-standing) Giants record.

Although Sherman and the Giants eventually proved them wrong, many sportswriters and oddsmakers saw the NFL East being dominated in 1962 by the Paul Brown–coached Cleveland Browns. Featuring the running attack of fullback Jim Brown, the perennial NFL rushing leader, they appeared to be even stronger with Heisman Trophy winner Ernie Davis, a halfback from Syracuse, selected in the first round of the college draft. What many thought could be the greatest one-two rushing attack in the history of pro football ended in tragedy before it ever began when Davis was struck down with leukemia before playing a single NFL game. And Jim Brown, as it turned out, finally was unseated as the NFL rushing champ. The Browns managed only a third-place finish in the East in 1962.

For the Giants, the pressure to repeat as conference champions fell squarely on Tittle's aging shoulders. Conerly, who had been so effective as Tittle's backup during the 1961 season, decided to call it quits at the age of 40. The new reserve quarterback was Ralph Guglielmi, a veteran from the Washington Redskins by way of the St. Louis Cardinals. Guglielmi's services were limited, however, because Tittle was starting a two-season, record-breaking passing streak that kept him on the field most of the time.

In addition to Conerly, two other Giants stars were gone by the start of the 1962 season. Rote, after 11 years of steady service, retired as a player to become backfield coach. Summerall also retired to pursue his already-burgeoning career in television and radio broadcasting. Don Chandler took over the place-kicks as well as punts. Gaiters was traded to San Francisco for end Aaron Thomas. Cliff Livingston went to Minnesota in exchange for defensive back Dick Pesonen, and Dick Nolan was sent to Dallas for a draft pick.

Rookies making the team were Bookie Bolin, an offensive guard from Mississippi; Jim Collier of Arkansas, an offensive end; a 5'10", 170-pound halfback from Illinois named Johnny Counts; and Bill Winter, a linebacker from St. Olaf. Of the four rookies, only Bolin managed to remain in the NFL longer than three years.

Gifford rejoined the team after sitting out the 1961 season. At the start of the season, Sherman decided to use Gifford as a flanker. Although he was no longer a rushing threat, Gifford hauled in enough passes in the 1962 season to rank second for total yards behind Shofner. Although they still had Webster's spirited rushing, the Giants knew that it would take another great passing season from Tittle—and consistent performance from the defense, still largely intact from the previous seasons—to capture the Eastern crown.

The Giants were put to the test in the first game of the 1962 season, held before a capacity crowd in Cleveland. The defense performed relatively well, but New York's aerial attack stumbled badly. Helped by three interceptions of Tittle passes, the Browns triumphed, 17–7.

The following Sunday, however, Cleveland began its long slide toward a disappointing 7–6–1 record in a close loss to Washington. Then in the Giants' second game of the season, with just one minute gone, it appeared as

Detroit Lions halfback Dan Lewis cannot free his leg from the grasp of Giants defensive back Allen Webb in this 1962 game at Yankee Stadium. New York won that afternoon, 17–14. Some of the other Giants are Erich Barnes (No. 49), Andy Robustelli (No. 81), Tom Scott (No. 82), and Jim Patton (No. 20).

if it might be a long season for New York as well: the Eagles' Jurgensen completed a 75-yard scoring pass to Timmy Brown. But it was a false alarm: it was the last Philadelphia touchdown of the afternoon. The defense stiffened, and Tittle, Shofner, Gifford, and the rest of the Giants' air force began their own blitzkrieg. New York trounced the Eagles that day, 29–13.

The third game of the season pitted two explosive offenses against each other: the Giants offense versus Bobby Layne's Pittsburgh Steelers. Tittle threw four touchdown passes to hit three different receivers: Shofner, Gifford, and Webster. It was too much even for the high-powered Steelers attack. Layne's final attempt at a game-winning drive ended when Barnes intercepted his pass in the New York end zone. The Giants won, 31–27.

The Giants' home opener did not come until the fifth game of the season, when the Steelers came to New York seeking revenge, and Layne and his cohorts found just that in a bruising 20–17 victory. For New York fans, the defeat was aggravated by an apparently serious injury to Shofner's shoulder late in the fourth quarter.

But by the next game, with visiting Detroit, Shofner was back and so were the Giants. Despite the fact that Tittle was forced to sit on the sideline for much of the first half following a fierce end-zone tackle at the end of a scoring bootleg early in the game, the Giants managed a 17–14 victory. It was the beginning of a nine-game winning streak that would extend through the last game of the regular season.

There was some question as to how seriously Tittle had been injured in the Detroit game, but the fears were put to rest the following Sunday when he tied a long-standing NFL record by throwing seven touchdown passes in an important New York victory over first-place Washington (see sidebar). It was the most astounding performance by a quarterback New Yorker fans had ever seen. The victory placed New York (at 5–2) one game behind the Redskins, whose record stood at 4–1–2.

By the time the season was over, Tittle had captured the imagination of every armchair quarterback in

TITTLE'S DAY

The game was at Yankee Stadium, October 28, 1962, against the Washington Redskins, and it was to be one of the most memorable afternoons ever to thrill the heart of a Giants fan. It was to be Y. A. Tittle's day.

Losing 7–0 in the first quarter, Tittle engineered a touchdown drive in the first half with passes to Del Shofner, Frank Gifford, and finally the 6-pointer to Joe Morrison. Then, after Erich Barnes intercepted a Norm Snead pass on the next Washington possession, Tittle again went to the air with two passes to Shofner and a short lob to Joe Walton for Tittle's second scoring toss of the day. As the two-minute warning approached in the first half, Tittle completed a 53-yard toss to Shofner, and after two futile running plays, fired a bullet to Morrison in the end zone to give the Giants a 21–13 lead.

On the first play following the Giants' kickoff to start the second half, Snead launched one to Bobby Mitchell for an 80-yard touchdown, his third of the game as well. On the next New York possession, however, Tittle moved a stride ahead of Snead by throwing his fourth touchdown pass of the afternoon.

The 36-year-old, balding New York quarterback was back at it again after the next Washington drive stalled, and the Giants took over at their own 49-yard line. He completed three consecutive passes, the last to Walton, who carried it into the end zone for passing touchdown number five.

In the press box, reporters were scrambling through their media guides to see just which records Tittle was approaching. Two loomed as possibilities: he had completed 11 passes in a row, and the NFL record was 13 (set by Minnesota's Fran Tarkenton the previous December); and there was the long-standing NFL mark of 7 touchdown passes in a single game (set by Sid Luckman of the Chicago Bears in 1943 against the Giants at the Polo Grounds and tied by Adrian Burk of the Philadelphia Eagles in 1954). Midway through the third quarter, Tittle was two completions shy of both records.

When the Giants got the ball again, Tittle completed his 12th consecutive pass with one to Alex Webster, but he lost his bid for the record when his next toss fell incomplete. He made up for it on the succeeding throw, however, with a bomb to Gifford that resulted in a 63-yard touchdown. Then in the fourth quarter came the record-tying pass. First, a 50-yard completion to Shofner brought the ball to the Redskins' 15-yard line. A few plays later, the "Bald Eagle" tossed a 5-yarder to Walton, who, after racing across the goal line, tossed the historic ball high into the air. The Giants were victorious that day, 49–34.

Late in the game, fans were screaming for Tittle to go for touchdown number eight, but he never did. "It would have been bad taste," Tittle was quoted in *The New York Times* the next day. "If you're leading by so much, it just doesn't sit right with me to fill the air with footballs. I'm the quarterback. It would be showing off."

When his record-setting day was over, Tittle shared the NFL standard of seven touchdowns in a single game and established a Giants' record of 505 yards gained passing (27 completions in 39 attempts), a mark that would stand until Phil Simms passed for 513 yards in 1985.

New York. He threw an NFL-record total (since broken) of 33 touchdown passes, eclipsing the mark of 32 held jointly by Johnny Unitas and Jurgensen. But Tittle's calm, steady demeanor in the pocket awed the Sunday audiences. Week after week he calmly picked out Shofner or Gifford for the bomb, Webster for the quick screen, and he even scrambled like a 25-year-old when he was forced out of the pocket. His completed passes went farther than anyone else's in the NFL that year, averaging exactly 16 yards each.

Dick Pesonen stops Redskins fullback Don Bosseler in a 1962 game at Yankee Stadium. The Giants pummeled Washington that day, 49–34. About to add his bulk to the situation is Rosey Grier (No. 76); in the background is Dick Lynch (No. 22).

The Giants' winning ways made them heroes in New York, helped by the fact that they were rapidly becoming the only football show in town. Playing before empty seats in the old Polo Grounds, the rival AFL's New York Titans franchise collapsed. As Tittle and the Giants passed and received their way into the record books, the Titans players' paychecks bounced at banks all over the metropolitan area. Fearing a total collapse of the American Football League should the New York team fail to finish the season, AFL commissioner Joe Foss was forced to run the Titans for the remainder of the year.

The Giants finished out their season with victories over St. Louis, Dallas, Washington, Philadelphia, Chicago, Cleveland, and Dallas to once again post a record of 12–2–0. The 41–31 Giants victory in the season finale featured six Tittle touchdown passes, the last one his 33rd of the year. Asked to comment on that record-breaking pass, he said, "I was going to run it in if I could."

Even before the regular season was history, the Giants could afford to joke. They had clinched their fifth Eastern Conference title in seven years with two full games remaining to be played when they edged out the tough Chicago Bears, 26–24, in early December. The remaining games were nothing more than warm-ups for the championship contest, which once again would be with Green Bay.

For New York fans, however, the final two games of the 1962 season were particularly frustrating. Both were played in New York. According to NFL rules in effect since 1954, all games played at home were blacked out from local television coverage. Adding to the fans' frustration was the fact that New York City was in the midst of a disastrous newspaper strike. While the Giants were wrapping up a sensational season, not a single daily newspaper was published in New York to document the achievement.

As they had for the past several seasons, thousands of New York fans flocked to area motels, where enterprising

ANOTHER DISAPPOINTMENT AT THE HANDS OF THE PACK, 1962

New York Giants		Green Bay Packers
Offense		
Del Shofner	LE	Max McGee
Rosie Brown	LT	Norm Masters
Darrell Dess	LG	Fuzzy Thurston
Ray Wietecha	C	Jim Ringo
Greg Larson	RG	Jerry Kramer
Jack Stroud	RT	Forrest Gregg
Joe Walton	RE	Ron Kramer
Frank Gifford	FL	Boyd Dowler
Phil King	HB	Paul Hornung
Alex Webster	FB	Jim Taylor
Defense		
Jim Katcavage	LE	Willie Davis
Dick Modzelewski	LT	Dave Hanner
Rosey Grier	RT	Henry Jordan
Andy Robustelli	RE	Bill Quinlan
Bill Winter	OLB	Dan Currie
Sam Huff	MLB	Ray Nitschke
Tom Scott	OLB	Bill Forester
Erich Barnes	CB	Herb Adderley
Dick Lynch	CB	Jesse Whittenton
Alan Webb	S	Hank Gremminger
Jim Patton	S	Willie Wood

	1	2	3	4		T
Packers	3	7	3	3	—	16
Giants	0	0	7	0	—	7

Touchdowns— *Packers:* Taylor; *Giants:* Collier.

Field goals—*Packers:* J. Kramer (3).

PATs— *Packers:* J. Kramer; *Giants:* Chandler.

school marching band to entertain at the half. Some pundits remarked that there were more fans glued to motel televisions in New York's Westchester County, Long Island, and Connecticut than there were spectators in Yankee Stadium.

While the Giants played out their season, the Green Bay Packers finished another spectacular year, posting a 13–1–0 record to earn a third-consecutive Western Conference title. With offensive standouts Starr, Hornung, and fullback Jim Taylor (who had just taken the NFL rushing crown from Jim Brown), Green Bay headed east fully expecting to face the respected aerial attack piloted by Tittle.

To the Giants' bitter disappointment, however, conditions at game time were far from favorable for the passing game. The 64,892 fans who jammed into Yankee Stadium on December 30, 1962, found the temperature at kickoff time was 19 degrees and falling; a 35-mile-per-hour wind, with gusts in excess of 40, precluded any passing threat that afternoon. Not a single passing point was scored by either team. Instead, a brutal ground game was fought in the trenches. Green Bay fullback Taylor and New York linebacker Huff had a particularly violent personal war going on. "Come on, can't you hit any harder than that?" Taylor chided Huff and the rest of the Giants defenders after nearly every run. And Huff and his associates made a concerted effort to oblige him.

The only sustained drive for either team in the first quarter ended in a 26-yard field goal by Green Bay's Jerry Kramer. In the second quarter, the Giants' Phil King fumbled on the New York 28, and the Pack recovered. On the next play Hornung threw to Dowler at the 7 on a halfback option. Only one more play was needed for Taylor to burst across the goal line. The score at halftime was Green Bay 10, New York 0.

The Giants' only score came in the third quarter, when Barnes blocked a Green Bay punt and end Collier fell on it in the end zone. Throughout the dismal afternoon, New York's normally productive offense, crippled by the wind and cold, failed to score a point. Two more Kramer field goals made the final score Green Bay 16, New York 7.

For the fourth time in five years, the Giants had made it to the championship game and had lost. The glorious season, the final game against Green Bay, the numbingly cold weather, an offense rendered ineffective:

owners had erected tall antennas capable of pulling in a television station in Hartford, which broadcast the game. So many fans crowded into some motel complexes that vendors and cheerleaders were attracted to the sites. One large motel presenting the Hartford coverage even brought in a high there was a bitter taste of déjà vu in that final game of 1962. From head coach Sherman down to the reserve linemen, the Giants took the loss personally. "I never saw a team that tried so hard and lost," said Rote, to sum it up the best.

For the season, Tittle had his records, and other Giants did too. Sherman was named Coach of the Year for the second consecutive year. For the 21st time in his career (including five years with the Rams), Robustelli recovered a fumble, tops in the NFL at the time. Chandler's 104 points for 1962 surpassed the Giants record set in 1949

On the sideline in 1963 head coach Allie Sherman confers with quarterback Y. A. Tittle and backfield coach Kyle Rote. Between the three, they molded a Giants offense worthy enough to occupy the same field with the team's magnificent defense and helped New York capture the NFL East crown that year.

by Gene "Choo-Choo" Roberts. Webster pushed his lifetime rushing total to 4,340 yards, at that time the highest ever for a New York Giants player. All-Pro players for the season included Barnes, Brown, Dess, Katcavage, Patton, Tittle, and Ray Wietecha.

There was a more ominous sign in the statistics of the 1962 season, however. For the first time in years, New York's aging defensive squad did not lead the league in a single important defensive category. Some said that the Giants were growing old.

Although coach Sherman may have been concerned about the advanced age of his players (10 starters were over the age of 30), he made only minor changes for the new year. The most prominent involved Grier, a fixture on the defensive line that had been intact for seven seasons. Grier was traded to the Los Angeles Rams in

A little like a Honda Civic waiting to be hit by a freight train, miniscule Cowboy Eddie LeBaron (5'9", 170 pounds) gets rid of the ball and grimacingly awaits the bone-rattling impact about to be dished out by Giants defensive tackle "Big" John LoVetere (6'4", 285 pounds). The Giants triumphed in this 1963 game, 37–21, at Yankee Stadium.

exchange for 6'4", 280-pound defensive tackle John LoVetere and a draft pick.

A familiar figure on the offensive line, four-time Pro-Bowl selection Wietecha, retired after a decade of service, and Greg Larson took over his job at center. Other new faces included third-string quarterback Glynn Griffing (who would spend just a single season in the NFL), linebacker Jerry Hillebrand, and tackles Lane Howell and Lou Kirouac. There was nothing new about the face of Hall of Fame–bound "Hurryin'" Hugh McElhenny, who put on a Giants uniform for the first time in 1963 after 11 years as a star halfback with San Francisco and Minnesota. McElhenny stayed with the

Giants for just a single season, and of the 12 new players on the Giants' roster in 1963, only Hillebrand and LoVetere spent more than two seasons with the team.

The city of New York's other professional football team, the AFL Titans, was undergoing massive changes in 1963. Sonny Werblin, a onetime president of Music Corporation of America, purchased what was left of the bankrupt team and immediately changed its name to the New York Jets. The name change did little to help the club's fortunes in the AFL East during that year, but when the season closed and the New York franchise had posted another last-place finish, its new owner revitalized the struggling league by negotiating a major television contract with NBC. The contract assured each AFL team of approximately $900,000 in television revenues yearly, just a scant $100,000 shy of the CBS guarantee to National Football League franchises. Werblin's deal made the AFL viable, and the Giants eventually felt the competition from his team. But not in 1963.

The biggest news in the NFL in 1963 was a gambling scandal involving Green Bay's Hornung and a half-dozen Detroit players, including All-Pro Alex Karras. Although Hornung and Karras never bet on their own teams, Commissioner Rozelle suspended them.

There was positive news as well. The NFL established its Hall of Fame in Canton, Ohio. Among the honored charter members was Tim Mara, in company with such legends as Jim Thorpe, Red Grange, Bronko Nagurski, George Halas, and Ernie Nevers (there were 17 charter members in all).

IRWIN SHAW ON Y. A. TITTLE

From *Esquire* magazine, 1965:

He almost always seems to be in desperate trouble, and almost always seems to get out of it at the last fateful moment. Whether the record bears it out or not, the Giants always seem to be behind, and in the good days, at least, Tittle put them ahead when all hope seemed lost. It's the Alamo every Sunday, with Davy Crockett sighting down his long rifle with the powder running out, and Jim Bowie asking to be carried across the line with his knife in his hand.

A newcomer to the Giants backfield in 1963, 34-year-old Hugh McElhenny picks up a few yards against the Cowboys. McElhenny came to New York in a trade with the Vikings after an illustrious nine-year career with the 49ers and two years with Minnesota, all of which earned him a berth in the Pro Football Hall of Fame. Trying to tackle him here is Dallas linebacker Harold Hays (No. 56).

For Tittle, 1963 was his finest season. The New York offense was flooded with capable receivers. Shofner, Gifford, Webster, Morrison, Walton, and Thomas were joined by the newly acquired McElhenny, who had already caught many a pass from Tittle when both played for the San Francisco 49ers. Complementing the offense was Chandler, whose accurate place-kicking enabled him to become the league's leading scorer in 1963.

But the brightest of the stellar attractions would be the come-from-behind quarterback himself, who had to rescue the 1963 season with yet another miracle finish. Although Tittle threw three touchdown passes for a 37–28 victory in the season premiere against Baltimore, his ribs were injured in the third quarter, and he was forced to spend the rest of the game, and the entire next game as well, on the sideline. Reserve quarterbacks Guglielmi and Griffing were of little help in game two, a 31–0 drubbing of the Giants at Pittsburgh. Fortunately for New York, Tittle recovered in time for the third game of the season.

In victories over the Eagles and Redskins, Tittle threw a total of five touchdown passes. The defense came alive as well, especially Lynch, who intercepted three Jurgensen passes in New York's defeat of the Eagles.

The Giants' home opener, perennially delayed by Yankee Stadium's baseball tenant, was the first critical game of the season. Jim Brown and the undefeated Cleveland team kept the Browns' perfect record intact and increased Cleveland's Eastern Conference lead over the Giants to two games with a 35–24 victory. With nine games remaining in the 1963 schedule, New York's 3–2 record did not seem particularly hopeful.

During the next five games, however, Tittle shifted the Giants' offense into overdrive, averaging an astounding 39.6 points per game. The sweetest of the victories was a 33–6 shellacking of the Browns in the face of eighty-four thousand stunned Cleveland spectators. Before a frustrated Jim Brown was ejected late in the fourth quarter for fighting with a New York defender, he had been held to a mere 40 yards rushing.

Of the final nine games in the 1963 season, the Giants lost only one: a 24–17 defeat by St. Louis in

Joe Morrison (No. 40) grinds out some yardage against the Cowboys in 1963. Morrison averaged 4.8 yards per carry that season for the Giants, gaining 568 yards rushing and another 284 on pass receptions. Bringing him to earth is Dallas linebacker Jerry Tubbs (No. 50). In a pile behind them are New York's Bookie Bolin (No. 63) and John Meyers (No. 78) of the Cowboys.

a game played at Yankee Stadium a few days after the assassination of President John F. Kennedy. (Commissioner Rozelle received broad criticism from many quarters for allowing the regular schedule to proceed on that bleak Sunday, for it had been set aside as a national day of mourning.) New York closed out the season with big wins over Dallas, Washington, and Pittsburgh, and the Giants captured their third consecutive Eastern Conference crown on the final Sunday of the season to finish 11–3–0, one game ahead of the Browns.

Throughout the autumn of 1963, the air above Giants football games virtually hummed with forward passes. The team had amassed 3,558 total passing yards, a mere 47 shy of the Baltimore Colts, who were led by Unitas. More importantly, Tittle led the NFL with 36 touchdown tosses, breaking his one-year-old single-season record of 33. But New York's passing game was to be severely tested by the league's acknowledged defensive leader: the Bears.

The Bears had not appeared in a championship game since 1956, when they lost to the Giants. In the interim, the Bears assistant coach George Allen developed a zone defense for the pass that shut down almost every passing attack it faced.

During the regular 1963 season, the Bears pass defenders led the NFL by allowing the fewest completed passes and the fewest total yards through the air. They also led the league with 36 interceptions—two more than the second-place Giants. The tough Bears defense gave up the fewest rushing first downs and the fewest total points in the league. Statistically, the game stacked up as a classic match-up: New York's record-breaking aerial attack set against the toughest pass defense anyone could remember. Oddsmakers polled by *Newsweek* magazine, apparently eschewing defense, rated the Giants a 10-point favorite for the December 29 game.

Joe Walton carefully cradles a pass from Y. A. Tittle in this 1963 contest with the Cowboys. Six of Walton's 26 receptions that year were for touchdowns. Looking on futilely is Dallas defensive back Jimmy Ridlon (No. 42).

Dick Lynch (No. 22) leaps to block a St. Louis Cardinals field-goal attempt that has just left the toe of Gerry Perry. The Giants squeaked by, 31–28—one of the conquests in New York's nine-game winning streak, which closed out the 1962 season and earned them the NFL East title. No. 20 for the Giants is Jim Patton, and No. 82 is Tom Scott.

As it had been in the two previous championship contests, the weather at kickoff time was brutal. More than forty-five thousand fans jammed into Wrigley Field on Chicago's North Side and shivered in the nine-degree cold. At first, it seemed as if the hot-air machines installed near both benches might thaw the Giants offense, which had been anything but warm in the 1961 and 1962 championship games, when Tittle drew first blood with a 14-yard scoring toss to Gifford. With the score 7–0 in the first quarter, Tittle later found Shofner in the end zone, but the usually sure-handed receiver saw the ball bounce off his cold fingers. On the next play Bears linebacker Larry Morris picked off a Tittle pass and ran it all the way to the Giants' 5-yard line. Chicago quarterback Bill Wade quarterback-sneaked across the goal line two plays later.

Dick Lynch corrals the ever-elusive Jim Brown in a 1963 game, but the Giants sustained one of their three losses for the year that day against Cleveland, 35–24. No. 13 of the Browns is quarterback Frank Ryan.

Seldom perceived as a scrambler, 36-year-old Y. A. Tittle (No. 14) is forced to hotfoot it around end against the Browns at Yankee Stadium in 1963. Tittle glowed with special incandescence that year at passing, becoming the first player in Giants history to toss the ball for more than 3,000 yards in a season (3,145). His 36 touchdown passes during the year were also a club record. In pursuit here is Cleveland linebacker Jim Houston (No. 82).

In the second period, the Giants drove deep into Bears territory, but had to settle for a Chandler field goal, making the score 10–7, New York. On the Giants' next possession, Tittle's knee was severely sprained when he was tackled by the Bears' Morris just as Tittle released a pass. Griffing was called on to finish the half for the injured Tittle.

During the halftime intermission, a doctor injected Tittle's knee with painkillers and wrapped it as tightly as possible, but the 37-year-old quarterback could barely walk as he took the field in the second half. Unable to set on his left leg, Tittle found his passing ability severely limited, and the fearsome Bears defense took control of the game. Chicago's defensive tackle Ed O'Bradovich intercepted a screen pass and ran it back 62 yards to the Giants' 14. Following a critical pass to Mike Ditka on third-and-nine that gave the Bears a first down, Wade scored on another quarterback sneak. Chicago had the lead 14–10 after the successful conversion.

In the frigid, defense-dominated battle, the score remained 14–10 deep into the final period of play, but with just 10 seconds remaining in the game, Tittle, who had been intercepted four times, still had one shot at pulling off a miracle finish. From the Bears' 39-yard line, he dropped back into the pocket and let fly with a desperation bomb to Shofner, who was streaking toward the end zone. The ball was overthrown, however, and landed in the hands of safety Richie Petitbon in the end zone for the Bears' fifth interception of the afternoon.

Overcome with exhaustion, pain, and grief, Tittle limped off the field and did not watch the final play of

A key turnover in the last game of the 1963 regular season: Giants defensive back Erich Barnes (No. 49) scoops up a Steelers fumble (upper left), writhes out of the grasp of Pittsburgh end Buddy Dial (upper right), races away from a diving Gary Ballman (lower left), and carries the ball for 30 yards (lower right). This fumble recovery was only one of the highlights in the 33–17 victory that assured the Giants of the NFL East championship on a cold December afternoon at Yankee Stadium.

DEFENSE TRIUMPHS, CHICAGO, 1963

New York Giants		Chicago Bears
Offense		
Del Shofner	LE	Bo Farrington
Rosie Brown	LT	Herman Lee
Darrell Dess	LG	Ted Karras
Greg Larson	C	Mike Pyle
Bookie Bolin	RG	Roger Davis
Jack Stroud	RT	Bob Wetoska
Joe Walton	RE	Mike Ditka
Y. A. Tittle	QB	Bill Wade
Frank Gifford	FL	Johnny Morris
Phil King	HB	Willie Galimore
Joe Morrison	FB	Joe Marconi

	Defense	
Jim Katcavage	LE	Ed O'Bradovich
Dick Modzelewski	LT	Stan Jones
John LoVetere	RT	Fred Williams
Andy Robustelli	RE	Doug Atkins
Jerry Hillebrand	LLB	Joe Fortunato
Sam Huff	MLB	Bill George
Tom Scott	RLB	Larry Morris
Erich Barnes	LHB	Bennie McRae
Dick Lynch	RHB	Dave Whitsell
Dick Pesonen	LS	Richie Petitbon
Jim Patton	RS	Roosevelt Taylor

	1	2	3	4		T
Giants	7	3	0	0	—	10
Bears	7	0	7	0	—	14

Touchdowns—*Giants:* Gifford; *Bears:* Wade (2).

Field goal—*Giants:* Chandler.

PATs—*Giants:* Chandler; *Bears:* Jencks (2).

the game. While Bears quarterback Wade grabbed the snap and fell to the ground to safeguard the Chicago victory, Tittle sat on the sideline wrapped in a parka, openly weeping over the game that, on paper at least, his team should have won. The Giants gained 128 yards rushing to Chicago's 93, 140 yards passing to the Bears' 129, and had accumulated three more first downs than their opponent had. But the five interceptions had been costly, and the NFL championship belonged to Chicago.

It had been a frustrating trio of championship games for the Giants from 1961 through 1963, disheartening to the players, coaches, and owners alike. But what they did not know as they left the unfriendly confines of Wrigley Field that day was that much harder times lay ahead.

Phil King bursts through the St. Louis line on the heels of a savage block by New York guard Darrell Dess (No. 62). King was the Giants' most productive ground gainer in 1963, rushing for 613 yards and adding another 377 yards on 32 pass receptions. New York lost this game, 24–17, the last of only three losses that year. The Cardinals in the picture are Marion Rushing (No. 52) and Joe Robb (No. 84).

A meeting of a pair of future Hall of Famers: linebacker Sam Huff grabs the leg of Cleveland's Jim Brown. Watching is New York's Jim Patton (No. 20).

FROM BOOM TO BUST

It was one of the more spectacular collapses in the history of the game. The proud Giants, champions of the NFL East in 1958, 1959, 1961, 1962, and 1963, suddenly found themselves finishing dead last in two of their next three seasons. By the end of the three-year period, almost all the great players from the championship Giants were gone: only Jim Katcavage, Del Shofner, and Joe Morrison survived the stretch. Head coach Allie Sherman, lionized in the early sixties, was now regularly excoriated in Yankee Stadium as the Giants lolled around the cellar of the Eastern Conference.

While the Giants' prospects were plummeting, the fortunes of the NFL—and the rival AFL as well—were soaring. Franchises in the older league were guaranteed $1 million annually in a two-year deal with CBS. Only the Dallas Cowboys and St. Louis Cardinals failed to show satisfying profits in 1964. To keep spectators tuned in to the multimillion-dollar broadcast schedule, CBS introduced the instant replay—a mixed blessing at best for the foundering Giants of the middle sixties.

The Maras and Sherman made some trades before the start of the 1964 season, but there were still a number of familiar faces around. The backfield of Y. A. Tittle, Alex Webster, and Morrison was still there, and so were end Shofner and flanker Frank Gifford. Phil King

had been traded to Pittsburgh. Two more unfortunate trades involved Sam Huff, who was sent to Washington, and Dick Modzelewski, dealt to Cleveland. For Huff, an important motivator for the entire defense and a favorite of the fans in his middle-linebacking position, New York acquired Dick James, a 5'9", 179-pound halfback and kick-return specialist who had performed well in Redskins games with New York. But James lasted only a year with the Giants. Coach Sherman hoped to replace both Modzelewski and Huff with younger players, but none were found that were as capable as the aging veterans. Huff recalled that he was "deeply hurt" by the trade. So were the Giants, who almost immediately felt the loss of both players.

Rookies joining the club were quarterback Gary Wood from Cornell and two running backs: 6'3", 235-pound Ernie Wheelwright from Southern Illinois, and 6', 180-pound Clarence Childs from Florida A&M.

The Cleveland Browns, ultimate champions of the East, finally fulfilled the experts' predictions. With rookie receiver Paul Warfield teaming with quarterback Frank Ryan to develop a deep pass threat to augment Jim Brown's rushing, Cleveland suddenly developed into the team everyone thought they would be in the early sixties. No small key to Cleveland's defensive success

A bone-jarring tackle by defensive back Clarence Childs separates St. Louis Cardinals flanker Billy Gambrell (No. 3) from the football in this 1966 game. Childs wore a Giants uniform from 1964 through 1967, before being traded to the Chicago Bears.

was the presence of former Giant Modzelewski on the line.

While the Browns opened their season by whipping Washington 27–13, the Giants got a shocking premonition of the year to come in their first game. They were destroyed, 38–7, by the Philadelphia Eagles—a team almost entirely rebuilt from the previous season, that would finish the year with a less-than-satisfying 6–8–0 record. The loss of Huff and Modzelewski seemed to demoralize the New York defenders, who, at the close of the season, had surrendered more points than any other squad in the NFL.

The Giants almost won their second game against Pittsburgh, but the porous defense allowed a 27–24 loss to the mediocre Steelers. The New Yorkers also lost more than the game. In the course of play, Tittle took a bruising hit in the ribs from the Steelers' John Baker, one from which the 38-year-old Bald Eagle would not bounce back. Two games later Tittle returned to face Detroit, but he was never again the same. Tittle who had led his team

Giants running back Danny Lewis (No. 41) follows the interference provided by guard Bookie Bolin (No. 63) against the Eagles at Yankee Stadium in 1966.

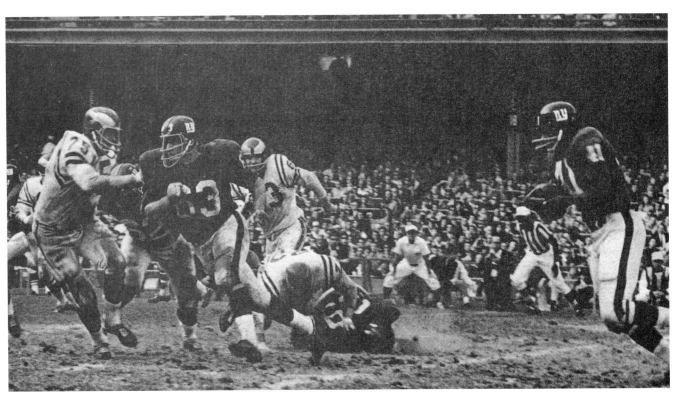

Life on the football field was a total and brutal commitment for 38-year-old Y. A. Tittle, a fierce and unyielding competitor. No words can portray his commitment more dramatically than this now-classic photo of a bloodied, frustrated, exhausted Tittle in the end zone after suffering an especially savage hit in a 1964 game at Pittsburgh. Photo courtesy of Morris Berman, Pittsburgh Post-Gazette.

to three consecutive Eastern Championships. He did not finish out the season as a starter; he was replaced by Gary Wood, whose unimpressive statistics ranked him next to last among NFL quarterbacks. A famous photograph taken by Morris Berman at the Pittsburgh game shows the fallen Tittle kneeling in front of the goal posts, bleeding from the head, and struggling for breath. That photo pretty much said it all about an illustrious career coming to an end.

The defense surrendered 399 points during the 1964 season, 20 more than the Chicago Bears (whose

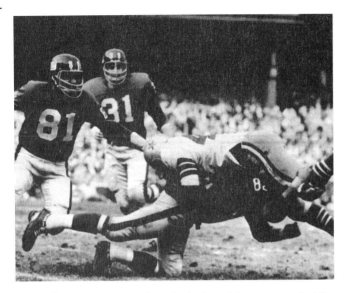

The defense in 1964 may have looked as vicious as ever, but it was not. Shown here is linebacker Tom Scott (No. 82) upending Dallas running back Don Perkins as Andy Robustelli (No. 81), in his last year as a Giants lineman, and linebacker Bill Winter (No. 31) converge on the play. The Cowboys prevailed, 31–21, in a game that was part of an altogether forgettable season.

A view from the opponent's backfield: Giants defensive back Jim Patton (No. 20) and linebacker Jerry Hillebrand (No. 87). The quarterback is Rudy Bukich of the Chicago Bears.

THOUGHTS ABOUT TITTLE

Offensive tackle Roosevelt "Rosie" Brown:

> Y. A. worried about you like your wife worries about you. He had the interests of the whole team on his mind all the time.

Offensive end Joe Walton:

> The greatest honor I've had in football is being a teammate and a friend of Y. A.'s.

Defensive back Dick Lynch:

> The measure of anyone's ability is results, and Y. A.'s results speak for themselves.

Frank Gifford, on Tittle's record-tying, seven-touchdown day in 1962:

> We were so far ahead that Tittle didn't want to pass anymore, but we knew he had a shot at the record. In the huddle we told him, "Throw the ball." We said if he didn't pass, we weren't going to play. That's how much his teammates thought of Y. A.

Fullback Alex Webster:

> He was the greatest.

defense had also fallen apart) for first place in that ignoble category. The Giants' final record was 2–10–2. For the first time in 17 years, the Giants had ended up last in their conference. The team's leading rusher, with 402 yards, was rookie Wheelwright. One of the few bright spots during the year was provided by Childs, who led the league in kickoff returns, averaging 29 yards per return. Other highlights were the consistent play of Erich Barnes, Rosie Brown, and Aaron Thomas, all of whom were invited to the Pro Bowl.

Two old New York favorites, Gifford and Webster, announced that they would not return for the 1965 season. Gifford, a versatile and productive fixture on the team since 1952, was on his way to the Pro Football Hall of Fame; Webster, the Giants' all-time leading rusher at the time, left his bold imprint on the team's history and would, of course, return to guide the team from the sideline in 1969.

On January 22, 1965, reporters and television crews crowded around a dais set up in Mama Leone's restaurant in New York for a lavish Giants press confer-

ALEX WEBSTER

In 1969 Alex Webster became the eighth head coach in New York Giants football history. "Big Red," as he was known to New York football fans, was well remembered for his performances on the field in a Giants uniform from 1955 through 1964. As a powerful running back, he was a key counterpoint to the passing of Charlie Conerly and subsequently Y. A. Tittle in the Giants offensive scheme.

During his 10-year career as a Giants player, Webster played in six NFL championship games. In regular-season play he carried the ball more often (1,196 carries), gained more yardage (4,638), and scored more touchdowns rushing (39) than any Giant up to that time. His average gain rushing was 3.9 yards, and he accounted for 336 points. Webster also caught 240 passes for 2,679 yards.

As a coach in New York, his career was shorter and less spectacular. Over five seasons (1969–1973), his teams won 29, lost 40, and tied 1. His best year at the helm was 1970, posting a 9–5 record—good enough for second place in the NFC Eastern Conference—and it earned him recognition as Coach of the Year by UPI (United Press International).

ence. At about noon, Tittle stepped up on the platform and, in his down-home but articulate manner, began to speak: "This is a moment I have dreaded," the great quarterback admitted. "I don't want to come back and be a mediocre football player again. I was one last fall."

He announced his retirement and told of future plans. "What I'll be doing exactly hasn't been decided. I suppose I'll be looking at college players the Giants are interested in." It was clear to everyone there that day that an all-too-brief but glorious era of Giants football had come to an end. Tittle returned to his suburban San Francisco home to pursue a successful career as co-owner of an insurance agency.

But the end of one era signaled the start of another: just a few hours after Tittle announced his departure from football, many of the same reporters who covered the event at Mama Leone's moved on to Toots Shor's restaurant. There the New York Jets had called a press conference to introduce the media to a senior from the University of Alabama named Joe Namath, whom they had signed to a $400,000 contract, setting off a very expensive bidding war between the two leagues.

It was a unique date for pro football. The other newsworthy event of the day was described in this Associated Press report:

> The Dallas Bonehead Club said today that Jim Marshall went the wrong way again and wound up in Chicago instead of Dallas, where he was supposed to receive the Bonehead of the Year Football Trophy.

> Marshall, a defensive end for the Minnesota Vikings, was selected for running 66 yards the wrong way in a Viking–San Francisco 49er National Football League game. The boner resulted in a safety for the 49ers, but the Vikings won.

138

"Wrong Way" Marshall, who jubilantly threw the ball into the air after he thought he had scored a Vikings touchdown, did indeed take a plane to Chicago instead of Dallas, but it was all part of a publicity stunt. The Vikings, with Fran Tarkenton, could afford to joke. In its few years of existence, the young Minnesota franchise was steadily working its way up the standings of the NFL West. For the Maras, however, it appeared that their franchise had, like Marshall, suddenly headed the wrong way.

In addition to Tittle, Andy Robustelli and Jack Stroud also retired. With the departures of Gifford and Webster at the end of the previous season, the Giants had lost many of their mainstays. Coach Sherman hoped that the Giants' first-round draft choice, 6'3", 233-pound Auburn running back Tucker Frederickson, would reju-

venate the Giants backfield. The Maras and Sherman had considerable faith in Frederickson. Because the Giants had placed last in 1964, they were awarded the first pick in the NFL draft, and they chose Frederickson, passing up Joe Namath, Gale Sayers, Dick Butkus, Craig Morton, and John Huarte. In defense of the Frederickson pick, many agree that he might have had a legendary career in the NFL had he not been plagued by injuries.

Despite increased pressure from the AFL, it was a good year for the draft. The Giants also selected Texas halfback Ernie Koy, Yale fullback Chuck Mercein, and cornerbacks Carl "Spider" Lockhart of North Texas State and Willie Williams from Grambling.

On June 15, well before the start of the 1965 season, Jack Mara died after having served as team president for 31 years. His brother Wellington succeeded him, and Jack's son Timothy was named vice president and continued to serve as treasurer. Wellington also functioned as chairman of the board of directors, which also included Mrs. John V. "Jack" Mara, Timothy, and Richard Concannon.

Carl "Spider" Lockhart joined the Giants in 1965 to begin an 11-year career with the team. An outstanding free safety, Lockhart was a 13th-round draft pick out of North Texas State. Here he races away from a Chicago Bear after picking off one of the many interceptions he made for New York (41 in all, the third most in club history).

THE ROOTS OF DESTRUCTION

All-Pro Players Lost by the Giants Between 1962 and 1964

Traded:

Defensive back Erich Barnes (to Cleveland after the 1964 season)

Offensive lineman Darrell Dess (to Washington after the 1964 season)

Linebacker Sam Huff (to Washington after the 1963 season)

Defensive tackle Dick Modzelewski (to Cleveland after the 1963 season)

Defensive tackle Rosey Grier (to L.A. after the 1962 season)

Retired After the 1964 Season:

Flanker Frank Gifford

Defensive end Andy Robustelli

Offensive lineman Jack Stroud

Quarterback Y. A. Tittle

Running back Alex Webster

A little more than a month later, Wellington and 42-year-old Sherman signed a new 10-year contract for the head coach's services. The agreement superseded a five-year deal that had been made in 1963 and gave the recently embattled coach a new vote of confidence, as well as a raise. "I think any coach in the business would envy me today," Sherman gleefully announced at the ceremony. And in 1965 it seemed as if Sherman once again had the team on the right track, although a major last-minute adjustment was needed.

Just a few weeks before the season began, Sherman lost confidence in quarterback Wood. He traded away Barnes and Darrell Dess in a three-way deal for Detroit quarterback Earl Morrall. The 31-year-old Morrall was a 10-year veteran of the NFL, with stints in San Francisco and Pittsburgh, as well as Detroit. He was no youngster, but the Giants' recent experiences with Tittle and even Charlie Conerly left them with little prejudice against aging quarterbacks. Kicker Don Chandler was also traded away, a move that put the Giants into a year-long

A key addition to the Giants in 1965 was 31-year-old quarterback Earl Morrall (No. 11), obtained from the Detroit Lions. Morrall completed 155 passes for 2,446 yards that year, including 22 touchdowns. He brought the Giants out of the cellar of the NFL East, where they'd finished the year before, into a tie for second place.

Ernie Koy (No. 23) takes a pitchout from Earl Morrall in this 1965 game against the Eagles. Koy, from the University of Texas, was another in the rich rookie draft of that year to secure a starting position with the Giants. His best year in New York was 1967, when he led the team in rushing with 704 yards.

search for a good place-kicker and eventually led to the signing of the AFL's Pete Gogolak a year later.

The new Giants offense performed relatively well throughout the 1965 season. Only twice in the 14-game schedule were the Giants held to fewer than 14 points, but once again the defense was weak. In the season opener, the Giants were slaughtered, 31–2, by Dallas. But Morrall settled the team down with victories over Philadelphia and Pittsburgh before bowing, 40–14, to Tarkenton's Vikings. During the erratic season, the Giants gave evidence of a credible if not explosive

offense, but they also had a defense that gave up 31 or more points per game no fewer than six times.

A sportswriter dubbed the young offensive backfield, which included such promising youngsters as Frederickson, Koy, and Mercein, the "Baby Bulls."

Near midseason a most promising offensive weapon joined the starting lineup, a lightning-fast, 6'2", 211-pound flanker from Texas Southern named Homer Jones. After his entry into the lineup, Jones gained 709 yards on just 26 receptions.

Although they were anything but the polished champions of the previous years, the Giants managed to finish the 1965 season with a 7–7 record, good enough for a second-place tie with Dallas in the Eastern Conference. In contrast to the Giants' many contributions to the Pro Bowl in previous seasons, only Brown

previously had been restricted to the enormously expensive draft battles.

"I have no qualms about signing him," said Giants owner Wellington Mara at the May 17, 1966, ceremony marking the acquisition of Gogolak. Mara defended an action many thought would greatly intensify the wars between the two leagues: "We honor the contracts of other organizations just like we honor the ones in our own league," he said. "We would not have talked to Gogolak, or any other player, prior to his becoming a free agent." The reaction was fierce, however. Newly elected AFL commissioner Al Davis set up a blue-ribbon task force to raid NFL teams for their established stars, and, before long, many were seriously considering moving to the AFL.

Joining the Giants roster in 1964 was wide receiver Homer Jones from Texas Southern. Nicknamed "Rhino," although he had the speed of a gazelle, Jones collected several team pass-catching records during his six-year career in New York, including the standards for most yards gained on receptions in a season (1,209 in 1967) and the highest average gain per reception over a career (22.6 yards) and for a single season (24.7). He is still credited with the Giants' longest touchdown reception (98 yards, from Earl Morrall in 1966 against the Steelers).

The Giants lured soccer-style kicker Pete Gogolak away from the AFL in 1966 to begin a career in New York that would last through the 1974 season. When it ended, Gogolak was—and still is—the Giants' all-time leading scorer, with 646 points (126 field goals, 268 extra points). No Giants kicker has booted more field goals or extra points than Gogolak has. Holding here is Tom Blanchard (No. 15).

and Frederickson were invited at the end of the year—Frederickson's first and only appearance. In retrospect, Sherman summed up the team's relatively strong comeback in 1965: "We were lucky," he said.

He must have been right. In 1966 the roof caved in.

The 1966 season was a historic one for the NFL and the New York Giants as well. That year Wellington Mara signed kicker Gogolak just as the soccer-style kicker's option ran out with the AFL's Buffalo Bills. The controversial acquisition threatened an all-out personnel war between the two leagues, whose skirmishing

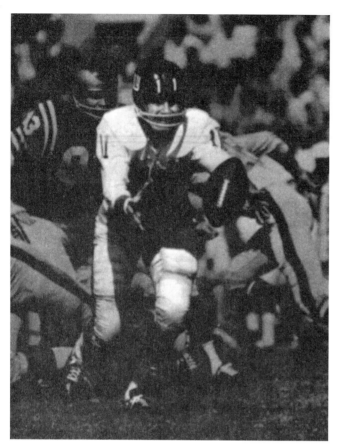

A view from a running back's eye: Earl Morrall (No. 11) shovels a lateral as Eagles defensive end Don Hultz (No. 83) lunges for him.

A peace treaty was signed before the war got out of hand, however. Dallas Cowboys general manager Tex Schramm and Kansas City Chiefs owner Lamar Hunt worked out the general terms of an AFL/NFL merger, and the agreement was announced on June 8, less than a month after Mara had signed Gogolak. Super Bowl I was to be played at the end of the season, a common draft would be held in January 1967, and the two circuits would begin playing a common schedule in 1970.

In the final year of the NFL/AFL draft wars, the Giants selected a tackle from Missouri named Francis Peay. In all, 20 new faces appeared on the Giants roster in 1966, many acquired in what proved to be a futile attempt to shore up the sagging defense. Only defensive tackle Jim Moran and defensive end and linebacker Freeman White remained on the team for more than a year or two. Frederickson sat out all of 1966 with a knee injury.

The first game of the 1966 season against Pittsburgh demonstrated what many had predicted: the Giants were a middling team with a decent offense led by Morrall with a weak defense. Still, few would have predicted the 34–34 tie in the opener would be the Giants' second-best effort of the entire season. There was one highlight in the first game, however: a 98-yard touchdown pass from Morrall to Jones, still the longest in team history.

The true nature of the disappointing year was demonstrated in front of sixty thousand Dallas fans on

JOE MORRISON

Dave Klein, in *Quarterback* magazine:

> Joe Morrison is not real. He exists in the minds of all the too slow, too small, too old former athletes who stand on street corners in every city in this country dreaming of what might have been, of how it should have been for them.
>
> Joe Morrison is not fast enough to be a running back in the National Football League. Furthermore, he is not big enough, either, and he runs straight up and he is 33 years old and he should not be able to make it as a flanker or a tight end. And you could probably stop him for a six-yard loss in the park Sunday morning, before everybody showers and changes and goes to the Stadium to see the Giants play.
>
> Forget it, Joe. Hey, somebody tell this guy to get packing. Go home to Ohio. . . . Leave the playing of this bone-snapping game to the younger men. Get serious, Joe. Before you get killed.

But Joe Morrison was serious. And he played 14 years for the Giants, from 1959 through 1972 (only Mel Hein and Phil Simms, who each played 15, have longer service with the club). His 65 touchdowns added up to 390 points, the fifth-highest total in Giants history, and only Gifford scored more touchdowns than Morrison's 65. No Giant had caught more passes (395, since exceeded) than Morrison had, and the 4,993 yards he gained catching passes are the third most in team annals.

the NFL's second Sunday. Knowing that he would need a massive offensive effort to help his weak defense, Sherman began the game by establishing an unbalanced offensive lineup with a single running back behind Morrall. Four receivers flooded the right side of the line in the hope of forcing the Dallas secondary into one-on-one coverage of receiver Jones.

For two plays, the unorthodox lineup worked, but then Dallas called a timeout and made adjustments to develop a two-man defense for Jones. It worked. The speedy receiver was limited to four receptions and one touchdown (the Giants' only score of the long afternoon). Dallas quarterback Don Meredith and receiver Bob Hayes, then holder of the world record for the 100-yard dash, had a field day dissecting the Giants defense. As the Cowboys' points piled up, happy Texas fans even began applauding Meredith when he threw an incomplete pass. The final score was 52–7.

The Giants defense set an NFL record in 1966 by allowing 501 points. In a freak accident during a training session in the second half of the season, Morrall fractured his wrist and was lost for the year. Backup quarterbacks Wood and Tom Kennedy couldn't get the offense moving fast enough to overcome the huge point totals Giants opponents amassed. On November 27 the Washington Redskins defeated the Giants, 72–41, to establish a new NFL record for the most points scored by a team in a single regular-season game (the Chicago Bears had run up 73 when they shut out the Redskins in the 1940 title game). The total of 113 points in a game was also a record. The Giants' only victory of the entire year had been over Washington earlier in the season. Other defensive embarrassments were losses of 55–14 to Los Angeles, 49–40 to Cleveland, and 47–28 to Pittsburgh. The Giants defense gave up 47 points or more five times.

By the end of the season, fans at Yankee Stadium had seen enough. On the final day of the regular NFL schedule, New York spectators carried thousands of blue-and-white banners with "Good-bye, Allie" printed on them into Yankee Stadium and then watched their team fall to Dallas, 17–7. The fans began singing "Good-bye, Allie" to the tune of "Good Night, Ladies."

New York's head coach, with eight full years remaining in his 10-year contract with the team, could do little but watch helplessly as New York finished the

Two New York defenders, Dick Pesonen (No. 25) and Dick Lynch (No. 22), bat away a pass intended for Washington's Joe Hernandez (No. 80) from Sonny Jurgensen in this 1964 battle at Yankee Stadium. The Giants won the game, 13–10, which turned out to be one of only two games they won during that dismal season.

season with a record of 1–12–1, the worst showing in Giants history. In response to the criticism, Wellington Mara told *Time* magazine, "Allie's going to be the coach next year, and, I hope, for many years to come." But rumors were sweeping Wall Street, the magazine pointed out, that the Mara family was interested in selling the team that had been part of the family since the earliest days of the NFL.

The rumors were unfounded, but Mara knew that a major change was needed. Only defensive back Lockhart was invited to the Pro Bowl at the end of the season. For the once-proud New York Giants, who just a few seasons earlier had perennially sent a small army of players to the Pro Bowl game, there was only one way to go.

Quarterback Fran Tarkenton (No. 10), a new face in the backfield in 1967, is flanked by veteran Joe Morrison (No. 40) and newcomer Bill Triplett (No. 38). Acquired from Minnesota, Tarkenton took command on the field and guided the Giants from a 1–12–1 season in 1966 to a 7–7 record and a second-place finish in the NFL East's Century Division in 1967.

THE TARKENTON YEARS

In February 1967, the sports pages of newspapers across the country carried stories about the resignation of Minnesota Vikings head coach Norm Van Brocklin, allegedly over a feud with star quarterback Fran Tarkenton, who also announced his intention to quit the team. Van Brocklin explained his side of the controversy to Dick Cullum, a Minneapolis sportswriter. "Tarkenton talked to players about his own situation," Van Brocklin said. "He made friends and supporters. This split the squad. If either one of us had quit and the other had returned, the squad would have continued to be split."

Wellington Mara took little time to capitalize on Van Brocklin's misfortune. Offering first-round draft choices in 1967 and 1968 and a second-round choice in 1967, as well as a fourth player to be named later, Mara acquired the 27-year-old quarterback from Van Brocklin's old team. The Giants' last-place finish the preceding season had given them first choice in the draft and the pick of graduating quarterbacks such as Bob Griese and Steve Spurrier, but Mara decided not to wait for a rookie quarterback to develop. "In New York, you've got to have a winner," he said. "We intend to have one."

With the trade complete, New Yorkers could boast of having two of the premier quarterbacks in profes-sional football: Joe Namath of the Jets and Tarkenton of the Giants. The comparisons came quickly. An article in *The New York Times* was headlined "The Swinger and the Square," referring, of course, to Namath's fondness for New York night life and the fact that Tarkenton, the son of a Pentecostal minister, declined to drink, smoke, or swear and was a quiet-living family man. On the football field, however, he was a proven crowd-pleaser. An accurate and highly mobile passer, Tarkenton had been nicknamed "the Scrambler," an appellation he vigorously disliked (see sidebar). But there was no denying the fact that, practically single-handedly, Tarkenton transformed the Giants from losers to contenders. From 1967 through 1970, the Giants managed second-place finishes every year.

The Giants' return to respectability following the dismal 1966 season coincided with the inauguration of the Capitol and Century divisions of the NFL Eastern Conference and the Coastal and Central divisions of the NFL West. The National Football League welcomed its newest franchise, the New Orleans Saints, to the Capitol Division of the Eastern Conference. To make room in the East and increase the Western Conference from an unwieldy total of seven teams to a more manageable eight, the Atlanta Falcons were moved to the Western Conference.

THE SCRAMBLER

The Giants' new quarterback, Fran Tarkenton, wrote a series of articles for *Sports Illustrated* when he first arrived in New York. In the first piece, published on July 17, 1967, he discussed his dislike for the moniker he had acquired playing in New York while still with the Vikings. He did not like to be called "the Scrambler."

Sure, I scramble. When everything else breaks down, I don't hesitate to roam out of the pocket. . . . These wild sideline-to-sideline scrambles have become my trademark, and people have forgotten the simple truth of the matter, which is that I'm basically a pocket passer.

After we beat the Giants in 1964 there was a lot of stuff in the papers about my scrambling. It seems to me that the name stuck after that. I don't think there was a reporter covering the game who didn't tell about the time I popped out of the pocket, roamed 40 yards behind the line of scrimmage, and finally completed a pass downfield for a 10-yard gain. And how many times do you think I scrambled in that ballgame?

Once.

After the tag "the Scrambler" had become mine, all mine, the public misconceptions about me seemed to multiply. I'd play a game away from home and I'd scramble maybe two or three times, which is my average, and after the game all the reporters would come in and say, "Why didn't you play your usual style?" and "How come you threw so much from the pocket?" And I would try to say, "I threw from the pocket because that's my style."

"No it isn't," they would say. "You're a scrambler."

"OK," I would say. "I'm a scrambler." Anything to get to the shower.

The "Four Cs" arrangement lasted only three years, until the league was reorganized once again in 1970 as part of the final integration of the NFL and the AFL into the National and American Football Conferences.

The history of the "Four Cs" organization was brief, but the Giants managed to keep it lively by changing divisions every year, beginning as a member of the Century Division in 1967, moving to the Capitol Division the following season, and returning to the Century circuit in 1969. In 1970 the team finally settled down to become part of the National Conference's Eastern Division, where it remains today.

An important acquisition for the defense in 1967 was Vince Costello, a 6', 228-pound veteran middle linebacker obtained from Cleveland in a trade. Costello brought talent to his position that had not been seen in New York since the heyday of Sam Huff. The Giants also picked up, for a draft choice, 6'6", 250-pound rookie defensive specialist Bob Lurtsema from the Baltimore Colts.

The Giants had something else going for them in the 1967 season. When visited by middleweight boxing champion Nino Benvenuti in Rome, Pope Paul VI recalled a visit the previous year by Allie Sherman. On June 2, using the prizefighter as an emissary, the pope sent his personal blessing to the Giants and their head coach.

On the down side, kicker Pete Gogolak, acquired from the AFL by Mara amid much controversy in 1966, was inducted into the army on January 25, 1967. The Giants scrambled for kickers during the first five games of the season, but eventually an agreement was worked out permitting Gogolak to play. A series of weekend passes allowed him to fly to New York on Friday evenings so as to arrive in time for Sunday games.

After the first 10 games of the season, the Giants had won 5, including a 38–34 heart-stopper over the Century Division–leading Cleveland Browns. As it had in the previous three seasons, the defense continued to give up large point totals, but the offense blossomed with Tarkenton quarterbacking. Aaron Thomas, Joe Morrison, Ernie Koy, and Tucker Frederickson were frequently on the receiving end of Tarkenton passes, but the most exciting receiver was still Homer Jones. The speedy end habitually discarded the intended pattern and roamed through the opposition's secondary trying to get free. Often enough, with the scrambling Tarkenton and the roving Jones, both ends of the passing connection were so unpredictable that it was nearly impossible to plan a defense against them.

He was known everywhere as "the Scrambler," and no one did it better than Fran Tarkenton (No. 10), rolling out here against the St. Louis Cardinals. Blocking for him are fullback Junior Coffey (No. 34) and guard Pete Case (No. 65).

148

Bart Starr of the Packers, a true nemesis who addled New York defenses until he retired after the 1971 season, unloads a long one here. No. 57 is Giants linebacker Vince Costello, acquired from the Browns in 1967.

Coach Allie Sherman talks a little strategy with a fiercely loyal fan, New York Senator Robert Kennedy, who had played some football himself during his undergraduate days at Harvard in the late forties.

The nimble Fran Tarkenton did not always get away with scrambling, as evidenced here, with Washington linebacker Chris Hanburger (No. 55) trying to disrobe the Giants quarterback as he brings him to Earth at Yankee Stadium.

The highlight of the Giants' season came on the NFL's 11th Sunday in a game against the Eagles. Philadelphia head coach Joe Kuharich plotted to stop New York's now-potent aerial attack by blitzing Tarkenton from the outside to "cut off his escape routes," and by double- and even triple-teaming Jones. It didn't work. New York scored the first seven times it had the ball, including two touchdown receptions by Jones.

New York's 44–7 victory over the Eagles set the stage for a dramatic confrontation in week 12, when the Giants traveled to Cleveland to play the first-place Browns. A victory would give the Giants a share of the Century Division lead, but it was not to happen. Cleveland no longer had star running back Jim Brown, but halfback Leroy Kelly was taking up much of the slack. Ex-Giant Erich Barnes added a new punch to the defensive secondary. Cleveland's rugged, but sometimes inconsistent, defense toughened up enough to hold the Giants to 14 points, and with the 24–14 loss, the Giants fell two games behind Cleveland.

New York finished the season with a 30–7 loss to Detroit and a 37–14 victory over St. Louis. Their final 7–7–0 mark was good enough for second place in the Century Division — a marked improvement over 1966. The defense, somewhat improved, especially in the second half of the season, was still the Giants' big weakness. Tarkenton had thrown for 3,088 yards and 29 touchdowns to become only the second Giants quarterback to pass for more than 3,000 yards (Tittle did it in 1962 and

1963). Three touchdown passes by backup quarterback Earl Morrall and one by Koy gave the Giants an NFL-leading 33 scoring tosses. (Washington's Sonny Jurgensen led the league in the individual passing statistics, however, with 3,747 total yards and 31 touchdowns.) Thomas caught 51 passes, 9 of which were for touchdowns, but Jones led the NFL with 13 touchdown receptions. He had a total of 49 catches and led the league with a 25-yard-per-reception average. Tarkenton, Jones, and Koy were invited to the Pro Bowl, and the freewheeling Jones also got All-Pro acknowledgment.

Considering that they had started from the cellar at the end of the previous season, it had been an excellent year for the Giants. The "Good-bye, Allie" chorus at Yankee Stadium was quieted.

Rookie running back Ronnie Blye (No. 22) from Notre Dame carries several Washington tacklers, including Jim Carroll (No. 60), for a few yards in this 1968 game. The Giants won that game at Yankee Stadium, 48–21, on their way to a second consecutive 7–7–0, second-place season.

150

A number of former Giants greats retired prior to the 1968 season, including Huff, Del Shofner, and Don Chandler, although only Shofner ended his career in New York. The team's draft picks had been depleted by the Tarkenton trade, and there were few new young faces on the Giants squad.

There was talk of an intracity confrontation between the Giants and the Jets (see sidebar). And the idea seemed exciting enough because in 1968 the Jets franchise came of age. After Sonny Werblin sold his interest in the team to four partners, Namath led the Jets to the AFL championship and a 16–7 victory over Baltimore in Super Bowl III. As "Broadway Joe" triumphantly proclaimed in the locker room following the Super Bowl victory, "The AFL and the Jets have arrived." The victory over heavily favored Baltimore was even sweeter because, at a Super Bowl banquet earlier in the week, the Jets quarterback had "guaranteed" a victory for New York.

Compared to the other New York team, the Giants' performance in 1968 was only average, but the season was not without its thrills. Behind Tarkenton's passing, the Giants won their first four games with an offensive onslaught that produced 34 points each against Pittsburgh and Philadelphia, 48 points against Washington, and 33 against New Orleans.

Talk of a title in the Capitol Division, which was dominated by the Dallas Cowboys, began to sweep New York. But the hopes faded when the Giants lost three of their next four games, including a 24–21 loss to Atlanta, which gave the Falcons one of their only two victories of the season. To have a chance of catching the division-leading Cowboys, the Giants needed to pull off a miracle in week nine by defeating the Cowboys, who, at that point, had suffered only one defeat.

If the Giants were to pull off an upset, they would have to do it the hard way—in Dallas. The New Yorkers got off to a solid start by scoring first when Tarkenton, searching for Jones in the end zone and finding him well covered, scrambled for a 22-yard touchdown run. Later in the game, with the score tied at 14, Tarkenton sensed a Cowboys blitz and called an audible at the line. He sent Jones slanting in toward the middle of the field and quickly threw a soft lob in his direction, arcing the ball over the onrushing Dallas defenders. Jones caught it and

GIANTS VERSUS JETS

Early in 1968 there were high hopes that New York's two professional football teams could at last play a game together. Wellington Mara and the Jets' Sonny Werblin agreed in principle to play a preseason game at Yankee Stadium in 1968 and another exhibition contest at Shea Stadium, which the Jets shared with major league baseball's New York Mets, the following season.

But the plans came to a halt when New York Mets president Donald Grant issued these stipulations for the use of Shea Stadium:

1. The game had to be scheduled at least five days before the next Mets' home game;

2. the mayor of New York had to make certain that the field would not be damaged;

3. all profits from the game had to be given to charity; and

4. no further requests could be made in the future for nonbaseball events that could, in any way, damage the field during baseball season.

In a joint statement, Mara and Werblin called the demands a "one-shot, don't ever bother us again" proposal and terminated the plans.

But the Giants and Jets did get together in the 1969 preseason at the Yale Bowl in New Haven to decide the in-town champ out of town. The Jets won, 37–14, and launched a preseason meeting at the Yale Bowl that would continue annually until 1975.

raced 60 yards for a touchdown. In all, Tarkenton completed 16 out of 24 passes for 187 yards and two touchdowns against one of the toughest defenses in the NFL, and the Giants beat mighty Dallas, 27–21.

Going into week 10 of the NFL schedule, the Giants had just one more loss than the Cowboys had. A sweep of the remaining five games, including the final

Putting the crunch on Dallas quarterback Roger Staubach is New York linebacker Ralph Heck (No. 55), who had a six-year NFL career with Philadelphia and Atlanta before joining the Giants in 1969.

game of the season which would bring Dallas to Yankee Stadium, would ensure the Giants of at least a tie for first place in the Capitol Division.

New York continued in high gear in week 11, winning a 7–6 defensive squeaker against Philadelphia—the same day, incidentally, that NBC television infamously decided to discontinue coverage of the close New York Jets–Oakland Raiders game in the final two minutes so that the network's presentation of the movie *Heidi* could be seen in its entirety.

While Namath passed the Jets to the Super Bowl, the Giants began to fall apart. Many fans had hoped that the final game of the regular NFL season would be a battle between the Giants and the Cowboys for the Capitol Division crown, but for the Giants, the 1968 season ended abruptly. They lost all four of their remaining games, including the final matchup with Dallas, when the standings had already been decided.

The Giants had to settle for another 7–7–0 record, good again for second place in the Capitol Division, but not good enough to give Dallas a scare of any sort. Statistically, Tarkenton had another good season, completing 182 passes in 337 attempts for 2,555 yards and 21 touchdowns.

Jones led the Giants receivers with 45 catches and seven touchdowns, and again led the NFL with an average gain of 23 yards per reception. But the Giants' rushing attack was just average, with leading ground gainer Frederickson gaining only 486 yards. Defensive back Carl "Spider" Lockhart and center Greg Larson were standouts, and they, along with Tarkenton and Jones, went to the Pro Bowl.

During the 1969 preseason, a much-anticipated exhibition game between the newly crowned world champion New York Jets and the New York Giants finally took place. Following through on the Mara-Werblin promise of the previous year to "remain committed to an early beginning of this series, if not in New York then in another city," the venue agreed upon was New Haven's Yale Bowl, where, on August 17, the Jets won easily, 37–14.

When the Giants lost their next and last preseason game to Pittsburgh in a cold and nearly empty stadium in Montreal, the event marked the end of a winless warm-up to the regular schedule. Mara had seen enough. With the approval of most New York fans, he removed Sherman as head coach.

"I expect Allie and I will be two of the highest-paid spectators in Yankee Stadium," Mara joked, referring to the five remaining years on Sherman's 10-year contract. Then Mara named former Giants fullback Alex Webster as the new head coach of the team.

The selection of Webster to replace Sherman was a popular choice among Giants fans, who remembered well the steady backfield performances "Big Red" Webster turned in on the championship teams of the early sixties. But Webster, with just a week remaining before the start of the regular season, faced a formidable task in rejuvenating the team.

To augment the cast of regulars in 1969 was running back Junior Coffey, a five-year veteran acquired in a trade from Atlanta. The first-round draft pick was a 6'6", 239-pound defensive end from San Diego State named Fred Dryer.

A new man in charge: the Giants' former star running back Alex Webster took over the head coaching duties from Allie Sherman in 1969. Over five years, Webster compiled a record of 29–40–1 and proved to be more beloved as a player than as a coach. However, he did earn Coach of the Year honors in 1970, his one winning season in New York (9–5).

At a news conference called before the regular season began, Webster was asked what kind of record he would like to have in his first year as a coach. "Fourteen and oh," he replied. The new head coach's wish was still a possibility after the first game of the season, when the Giants sneaked past Minnesota, 24–23, in an offensive thriller. But the offense died the following week, and Detroit beat the New Yorkers, 24–0. The Giants won their next two games, giving their new head coach a nice 3–1 start, but then a series of injuries and lackluster performances by stars such as Jones took their effect. With Jones off his usual touchdown pace and the backfield as slow as ever, the Giants lost seven in a row.

Even in the depths of the losing streak, New York fans and players stood behind Webster. Sherman had been controversial among Giants players as well as among their fans, and the entire team seemed to

have more fun playing for Webster. The Giants salvaged a respectable season by winning their last three games, including the finale against the Century Division–champion Cleveland Browns. New York's 6–8–0 record was good enough, once again, to place second in the division.

The greatest mystery of the year was Jones' performance. He registered only a single touchdown reception all season. Morrison, Don Herrmann, Thomas, and Koy all managed to pull in at least three scoring tosses. As usual, Tarkenton had an excellent year, completing 220 passes for 2,918 yards and 23 touchdowns.

But perhaps the biggest news was hardly noticed at first. Previously, on January 26, 1969, just two weeks after the Jets had won Super Bowl III, a short article from UPI was buried in the sports pages of a number of New York dailies. According to New Jersey State Senator Frank J. Guarini, the Giants management was actively considering moving the team away from Yankee Stadium. Guarini said he had met with Tim Mara and Giants general manager Ray Walsh to discuss the possibility of building a new stadium for the team in the Hackensack Meadowlands of New Jersey. "They indicated serious interest," Guarini told the UPI reporter, and agreed to "take a tour of the meadows probably within a week."

The 1970 season finally integrated the playing schedules of the old NFL and its rival AFL, now combined into the National and American conferences of the National Football League. The teams were all the same from the 1969 season, but the Baltimore Colts, Cleveland Browns, and Pittsburgh Steelers were moved over to the AFC so that each conference would have 13 teams. The Giants became a member of the Eastern Division of the National Conference.

Another historic first occurred the same season as ABC television began broadcasting a series of 13 games during prime viewing time on Monday nights. Commentators for the first year of *Monday Night Football* were Keith Jackson, Don Meredith, and Howard Cosell. It was not until the second season that Jackson was replaced by the Giants' former halfback and flanker Frank Gifford. With approximately $8 million from ABC, the three television networks were now spending nearly $150 million annually for the right to broadcast NFL football.

The Giants acquired veteran wide receiver Clifton McNeil from San Francisco and traded Jones, who had

Summer camp in 1969. Tight end Butch Wilson (No. 86) takes a turn on the blocking sled. Looking on is former Dallas receiver Pete Gent (No. 35), who had been released by the Cowboys after the previous season. Before the 1969 season began, Gent turned in his pads and helmet for a typewriter and sat down to write the best-selling football novel North Dallas Forty. *No. 81 is Freeman White.*

been a disappointment for the past season and a half, to Cleveland in exchange for halfback Ron Johnson and defensive tackle Jim Kanicki. Johnson, just a youngster of 22, would prove to be a valuable acquisition over the years. Another soon-to-be valuable addition was rookie tight end Bob Tucker from Bloomsburg State in Pennsylvania.

The 1970 season turned out to be the Giants' best since the championship years in the early sixties.

Although they finished second again, the year was filled with excitement. Some claimed the Giants had an easy schedule, but after the New Yorkers lost the first three games of the regular season to Chicago, Dallas, and even lowly New Orleans, it looked as if no schedule would be easy enough for Webster and the Giants. But then Tarkenton, along with Johnson, McNeil, and Frederickson— the latter, for once, relatively free of injuries—turned things around, and the Giants won six games in a row, their longest winning streak since the days of Y. A. Tittle. They even beat both the Jets and the Cowboys.

In the upset over Dallas at Yankee Stadium on November 8, 1970, kicker Gogolak had field goals of 40, 42, and 54 yards, the last a Giants record then. But it was Johnson's running, as much as anything else, that

Establishing himself as a defensive end of much repute in his rookie season, Fred Dryer from San Diego State fends off a block by Baltimore's Bob Vogel. Dryer, the Giants' first-round draft choice in 1969, played in New York through the 1972 season before being traded to the New England Patriots, who sent him to the Los Angeles Rams.

The legendary Johnny Unitas, in the twilight of his Baltimore Colts career in 1971, still has his inimitable form as he gets one off at the last second against the Giants. Applying the pressure is New York safety Joe Green (No. 33).

helped the Giants achieve the victory and beat the fierce Dallas pass rush. Time after time, Johnson and other backs ran draw plays, slipping past the Dallas defenders racing toward Tarkenton.

With the exception of the early minutes of the third quarter, when the Cowboys recovered a Frederickson fumble deep in Giants territory and took advantage of it with a field goal, the New York defense held Dallas scoreless throughout the second half. And in the final minutes of the game, the Giants rushing attack had finally opened up the passing game to Tarkenton. Three completions for a total of 49 yards set the pace for New York's final winning drive, which was capped by a 13-yard

scoring toss from Tarkenton to Johnson with just three minutes remaining to give the Giants a 23–20 triumph. It had been a fine day for Johnson, who rushed 23 times for 136 yards and gained 59 more with four pass receptions.

The victory placed the Giants (5–3) in a tie for second place with Dallas in the NFC East. They were one game behind St. Louis, which led the conference with a 6–2 record. New York chalked up its sixth consecutive victory the following week against Washington, but the string was broken in week 10 by a 23–20 loss to Philadelphia. However, the Giants bounced back with three victories in a row, capped by a 34–17 win over the Cardinals. Going into the final week of the regular

Ron Johnson (No. 30), shown carrying against the Redskins, was acquired from Cleveland in 1970 and promptly became the first New York Giant to rush for more than 1,000 yards in a season (1,027). Two years later he broke his own record by gaining 1,182 yards, a Giants mark that stood until Joe Morris rushed for 1,336 in 1985. In the background is quarterback Fran Tarkenton (No. 10).

season, the New York Giants had won nine out of their last 10 games, good enough for a first-place tie with Dallas. For the first time since 1963, they were just one game away from a conference championship.

An impressive come-from-behind season ended sadly, however, on the last Sunday of the football year when the Giants fell, 31–3, to Los Angeles, while the Cowboys whipped Houston, 52–10. A 9–5–0 record placed New York, for the fourth consecutive time, second

in their division, but it was their best effort since 1963. The Giants offense led the NFC in total first downs, first downs by passing, and pass completions. Johnson rushed for 1,027 yards—the first time any Giants player had run for 1,000 yards or more in a single season. Tarkenton and Johnson were invited to the Pro Bowl.

The 1971 season is one that almost all New York football fans would like to forget. For the Giants, it was as unsuccessful as it was tumultuous. Before the first preseason contest, a Monday night game with the Oilers in Houston, the Giants announced that Tarkenton had retired over a salary dispute. "I really think Fran's retiring," *The New York Times* reported Wellington Mara as saying. "We've been discussing salary for some time, but I don't think Fran's bluffing." Earlier, Mara had explained that the All-Pro quarterback had been seeking

The Giants had to scout tiny Bloomsburg State in Pennsylvania to come up with tight end Bob Tucker (No. 38), signing him as a free agent in 1970. Here he shows some fancy footwork, but pass catching was his truest talent. To illustrate the Giants' serendipity, Tucker became the first tight end in NFL history to lead the conference in pass receptions (59 in 1971), won All-Pro honors the following year, and is sixth in career receptions for the Giants (327 for 4,376 yards and 22 touchdowns).

a half-million-dollar loan from the Giants, much of it for his educational foundation devoted to vocational training for underprivileged people. Tarkenton told Mara that he would play in the game against Houston if he was needed but would then step aside. Head coach Webster declined the offer and named backup quarterback Dick Shiner as starter.

"There is no rancor," Mara said, referring to his relationship with Tarkenton. "But I haven't seen him since." After the Tarkenton-less Giants were routed by Houston, 35–6, the star quarterback headed toward his

home in Atlanta. His absence lasted only four days. "When I did what I did in Houston, it seemed to me I was doing the right thing," Tarkenton said upon his return to the Giants. "But now I admit it was a hasty move." Tarkenton signed a 1971 contract that was estimated to be worth $125,000. Both the quarterback and his head coach agreed that Tarkenton's leadership would not be affected by the incident.

For some New York fans, there was far worse news just two weeks later. On August 26, 1971, Mara and New Jersey Governor William T. Cahill announced that the Giants had signed a 30-year lease to play all home games, beginning in 1975, in a new stadium being built in the Meadowlands, actually a 750-acre parcel of land in the town of East Rutherford, New Jersey. Mara said that the Meadowlands stadium would give the Giants their first real home and would be more convenient to many of their fans. "New York is not losing a team, but gaining a sports complex," he added. While it was true that the Meadowlands would be easier to reach for many fans living in Westchester County, Connecticut, and the New Jersey environs, some residents of New York City regarded the move as little less than treason.

The most vociferous of all was New York Mayor John Lindsay, who took the news in much the same way a general in wartime might feel about a deserter. "The Giant management crossed the line that distinguishes a sport from a business," he said. "I am today directing the corporation counsel to initiate proceedings to restrict the right of the Giants to call themselves by the name of the city they have chosen to leave." Just to make sure no one missed the point, Lindsay characterized Mara's decision as "selfish, callous, and ungrateful." He further announced that he would meet with NFL Commissioner

Bob Hyland (No. 70) attended to the duties of center for much of the period from 1971 through 1975 after coming to the Giants in a trade with the Chicago Bears.

Pete Rozelle to investigate the possibility of bringing a new or existing professional football franchise to the city; that he would plan a suit in federal court to attack football's exemption from antitrust laws should a new franchise fail to develop; and that he would ask New York Representative Emanuel Celler, chairman of the House Judiciary Committee, to conduct a broad investigation into the matter. In the unkindest cut of all, he suggested that New York might prohibit the Giants from playing in Yankee Stadium while their new park was being built. "We made them a successful operation," he added, "and now they want to leave. If they want to play in a swamp, let them play in a swamp right now."

The Giants' first-round draft choice in 1971 was a halfback from West Texas State, Rocky Thompson, who could do little to improve the standing of an injury-laden team. Most missed were Johnson, the running sensation of 1970, who sat out much of the year with a thigh injury, and Frederickson, who reinjured his knee. Defensively, a number of injuries hampered the secondary, and veteran defensive back Bennie McRae, acquired from the Chicago Bears at the age of 31, seemed to have lost much of his effectiveness.

The Giants lost all their preseason games in 1971 and, after winning two out of their first three regular-season contests, lost all but two of their remaining games. The 4–10–0 record put them in last place in the NFC East. The defense surrendered 64 more points than any other team in the conference. With only 11 touchdown passes all year going into the final game, Tarkenton was benched in favor of backup quarterback Randy Johnson. New York lost the season finale to Philadelphia, 41–28. For the first time in history, no New York Giants player was invited to the Pro Bowl.

Tarkenton never again played in a Giants uniform. It was the end of an era in which, except for the chaotic final season, the Giants were respectable enough to be contenders, but just not good enough to win a division title. And, unfortunately, there were to be more hard times ahead during the remainder of the seventies.

Norm Snead, shown here throwing in the snow, came to the Giants in a trade in 1972 that sent Fran Tarkenton back to the Minnesota Vikings. Snead captained the offensive attack through that and the following season. His best effort came in 1972, when he completed 60 percent of his passes, tops in the NFC, while gaining 2,307 yards passing.

ORPHANS OF THE NFL

Sportswriter Red Smith looked back on the chaotic seasons between 1972 and 1976 and referred to the team as the "New York–New Haven–Long Island–New Jersey Giants."

The renovation of Yankee Stadium, begun in 1973, forced the team into a public search for a temporary park, which led to stays in Connecticut's Yale Bowl, as well as a season sharing Shea Stadium in Queens with the Jets, before the Giants finally settled into their permanent home in New Jersey in 1976. They were the most highly visible orphans in the NFL, and it apparently had a deleterious effect on the players. The Giants managed a winning season in 1972, but finished last the next two years and next to last in 1975.

The New York Giants began their four-year scramble for a place to play without their scrambling quarterback Fran Tarkenton. Before the final game of the 1971 season, Tarkenton asked to be traded, providing Wellington Mara and coach Alex Webster a list of five acceptable teams. The well-publicized problems faced by the Giants were in obvious contrast to the stability developing in the NFL as a whole. With the difficulties of interleague rivalries finally behind them, NFL owners and officials settled down to refine the rules, a process that, in just a few seasons, brought the game very close to its present state.

In an attempt to diminish the effectiveness of zone defenses and thus open up the passing game, new rules for 1972 decreased the distance between the hash marks by six yards. At least partially in response to a dilemma faced by the Giants in 1973, the U.S. Congress passed a bill that prohibited blackouts of home games sold out 72 hours in advance.

Other major changes were put into effect in 1974: to cut down on long field goals, the goal posts were moved back 10 yards to the back line of the end zones, and missed kicks from outside the 20 were awarded to the opposing team at the original line of scrimmage rather than at the 20. In the same year, the first of several rulings on the defense now called "bump and run" were put into effect, allowing defenders a single hit on receivers heading downfield. Reserve teams, dubbed "taxi squads," were abolished in 1975.

Word of the Giants' upcoming real estate problems surfaced during a New York Yankees off-season promotion tour in January 1972. As officials from the Yankees' business office toured cities in Connecticut, New Jersey, and upstate New York to drum up ticket sales, they brought news of a major facelift of Yankee Stadium to be performed during 1973 and 1974. The arrangement, first suggested by New York Mayor John Lindsay, involved

Wide receiver Bob Grim holds onto a Norm Snead pass despite the efforts of St. Louis defender Larry Wilson (No. 8) in this 1972 game. Grim came to New York along with Snead when Fran Tarkenton was dealt to the Vikings. The Giants beat the Cardinals in both their encounters in 1972 to post an 8–6 record, a third-place standing in the NFC East.

the purchase of the structure and grounds of the stadium by the City of New York from Rice University and the Knights of Columbus, its previous owners. While their stadium was being rebuilt, the Yankees would share Shea Stadium with the Mets, but few New York officials seemed concerned with helping the Giants.

The Maras' problems were also compounded by difficulties in raising funds for the Meadowlands, a problem so significant that there was litigation and the possibility of a major delay in the start of construction work. "Officially, we haven't been informed about any of this," Wellington Mara said to reporters in early 1972, regarding the renovation of Yankee Stadium. "We've talked a little among ourselves about what we would do, but we haven't made any sort of real plans. You might say we'll cross that bridge when we come to it, but under the circumstances that might be a poor choice of words."

At around the same time he was talking to the press about Yankee Stadium, Mara was burning up the phone lines to Minnesota, hammering out a trade with Vikings general manager Jim Finks. The agreement sent Tarkenton back to Minnesota in exchange for 11-year veteran quarterback Norm Snead (who had been in and out of the Vikings offensive lineup the previous season), offensive end Bob Grim, running back Vince Clements, and two draft choices.

Jack Gregory, a defensive end, was acquired from Cleveland. Notable rookies from the draft included a pair of monstrous defensive tackles: 6'1", 255-pound John Mendenhall from Grambling and 6'6", 260-pound Larry Jacobson from Oklahoma. Tucker Frederickson retired following the 1971 season, unable to overcome the knee injuries that had ruined a potentially great career.

COSELL AND ROZELLE ON THE MOVE TO THE MEADOWLANDS

On June 19, 1972, commentator Howard Cosell launched a verbal tirade against the Giants' announced move to the New Jersey Meadowlands.

"The Giants have sold every available seat for 15 straight years," Cosell said. By moving across the Hudson River, he continued, the Giants were harming the people of New York City, who had supported them so loyally over the years, and they were contributing to the city's image as an "unlivable" place.

One of the members of the viewing audience was Senator Marlow W. Cook, a Republican from Kentucky. The senator was so moved by Cosell's remarks that less than a week later he brought NFL Commissioner Pete Rozelle to Washington to answer pointed questions about the proposed move.

"The new Giants Stadium will be 6.9 miles from Times Square," Rozelle testified. "Yankee Stadium is 6.6 miles. The same fans will have tickets. Some will have a somewhat longer ride, but others will have a shorter ride. The same fans will watch all Giant road games on the same New York television stations."

A RECORD-SETTING ROUT

The Giants, their collective eye still on a playoff berth as a wild-card, rampaged into Yankee Stadium on November 26, 1972, to play the Philadelphia Eagles. With quarterback Norm Snead, running back Ron Johnson, and receiver Bob Tucker all in top form, it was hardly a contest. On New York's first possession, they scored on a 15-yard pass from Snead to Tucker. The next time the Giants had the ball, they scored again, that one on a 35-yard run by Johnson.

On the first play of the second quarter, Snead passed to fullback Joe Orduna for a five-yard touchdown. Not much later, Pete Gogolak nailed a 25-yard field goal. Tucker then made his second touchdown reception of the day on a 29-yard pass from Snead, and Johnson added yet another on a 1-yard run. At halftime, the score was 38–10, New York.

Later in the game, reserve quarterback Randy Johnson took over for Snead, and a host of other Giants replacements took to the field. For Philadelphia, it was just one of those days. In the final 18 minutes of the game, Johnson hit Don Herrmann twice in the end zone with touchdown tosses, and even ran in once for a score. The final score, 62–10, set team scoring records for the Giants and the Eagles as well—Philadelphia had never before given away so many points in a single game. Gogolak also set a team game record when he kicked his eighth extra point. Johnson rushed for 123 yards before he was pulled in the third quarter. Tucker caught eight passes for 100 yards.

A group of disgruntled Philadelphia fans planned to use the game as evidence in their lawsuit against the Eagles. The season-ticket holders went to court demanding their money back because they alleged that the Philadelphia team failed to provide football entertainment at a big-league level.

Economic and political problems were still swirling around the team's proposed new home in New Jersey, which was only in the planning stages, when Giants management took the first step in the move by setting up training camp at New Jersey's Monmouth College. At Monmouth, head coach Webster let everyone—veterans and rookies alike—know that his days as a nice guy were over. Hard training and discipline replaced the rather easygoing approach that Big Red had adopted before the lackluster 1971 season.

Perhaps in part because of Webster's new, hard-nosed approach, the Giants responded with a season better than anyone expected. After losing their first two games to Detroit and Dallas, the Giants won the next

four. Leading the way was quarterback Snead, who, by the end of the season, could boast of the highest pass completion average in the NFL. Halfback Ron Johnson returned to the lineup in good shape

Defensive end Jack Gregory (No. 81) makes the Cowboys' Roger Staubach painfully aware of his presence, although the Dallas quarterback managed to get rid of the ball. Gregory was obtained from the Cleveland Browns in 1972. Gregory played for the Giants through the 1978 season. No. 62 for Dallas is John Fitzgerald.

following a nearly season-long recovery from a leg injury in 1971. And tight end Bob Tucker was playing his position as well as anyone in the league. Following a 23–16 loss to the first-place Washington Redskins in week nine of the NFL schedule, New York bounced back to defeat St. Louis, 13–7, giving the Giants a record of 6–4, three games behind the 9–1 Redskins.

The Giants were two games behind Dallas in a bid for an NFC wild-card berth when they returned to

Yankee Stadium on November 26, 1972, to play the less-than-lustrous Philadelphia Eagles (2–7–1). The Giants indicated what kind of afternoon it would be when they scored touchdowns on their first two plays from scrimmage. The 62–10 triumph was the highest score ever posted by the Giants and the most points ever surrendered by the Eagles (see sidebar). More importantly, Dallas lost to San Francisco the same week, putting New York only a single game behind the NFC's leading contender for the wild-card playoff spot. Because the Giants were scheduled to travel to Dallas for the final game of the season, they had, as sportscasters are wont to say, control over their destiny in the playoff race.

Four days after the humiliation of the Eagles, New Jersey governor William T. Cahill officially broke ground for the Giants' new Meadowlands stadium in East

Rutherford. The ceremony took place in bitterly cold weather at a site surrounded by mountains of garbage and rusty automobile carcasses, and the speeches were continuously interrupted by a group of demonstrators opposed to the project. A spokesman for the "Save the Meadowlands" committee argued that the ceremony itself was illegal because litigation was still pending to stop the entire project. Mara and ex-Jets owner Sonny Werblin, now chairman of the Meadowlands project, put on brave faces and smiled for photographers.

In the final game of the season, the Giants beat Dallas, 23–3, and would have earned a wild-card spot in the playoffs had they not lost the two previous games to the Cincinnati Bengals and Miami Dolphins. Nevertheless, New York's 8–6–0 season was judged to be reassuringly good considering the team's poor showing in 1971. Snead had completed 196 of 325 passes for a 60 percent completion rate, tops in the NFL. Overall he was ranked second in the NFC, right behind Tarkenton of the 7–7–0 Vikings. Halfback Johnson rushed for 1,182 yards, a new Giants record, and led the NFL with nine touchdowns rushing. Tucker was Snead's top receiver with 55 catches, followed by 45 for Johnson. Tucker and defensive end Gregory made All-Pro, and Gregory, Snead, and Johnson went to the Pro Bowl.

For New York's professional football fans, much of the excitement in 1973 took place before the start of the season. For Mara and the rest of the Giants management it became a nightmare as they were forced into a highly public search for a ballpark in which to play their home games. Although Mayor John Lindsay had proposed that the city of New York buy Yankee Stadium before refurbishing it, a group of investors, many from Cleveland, eventually acquired the stadium. Nevertheless, the city decided to proceed with its plans for a major renovation.

There is evidence that the ensuing eviction of the Giants was part vendetta—a little something in return for their plans to move to New Jersey in a few years. The executive director of the NFL stated that it should have been possible to schedule all seven Giants home games in Yankee Stadium by November 4, 1973, but city officials insisted that the work would have to begin by October 1 for the park to be ready by the start of the 1976 baseball season, about two and a half years away.

City Hall informed the Giants that the team would have to be out of Yankee Stadium after the first two home games in 1973. Dave Anderson of *The New York Times* reported that a high-placed, but unnamed, New York City official was overheard to say, "We're not going to do the Giants any favors. We're going to throw them out as soon as the Yankees' season ends."

In March the Maras learned that the Yale Corporation had decided against allowing the Giants to play in New Haven's Yale Bowl for the 1973 and 1974 seasons. The main difficulty reportedly revolved around the NFL's blackout rule for home games, which would have prevented Hartford's television station WTIC from covering the games. Just a day or two later, Princeton University in New Jersey also turned down the Giants' request to play in that school's Palmer Stadium for two years.

By the end of April, the NFL was forced to release its official schedule without naming the site of Giants home games. Faced with a mounting crisis, Commissioner Pete Rozelle suggested that, "as part of a continuing experiment," the blackout restriction could be rescinded for the five games the Giants might play in the Yale Bowl. The plan was heartily approved by the Yale Corporation, but chairman John Pastore of the U.S. Senate's Communications Subcommittee, which was studying alleged unfair practices by the television networks, labeled the plan "unsatisfactory." On May 24, 1973, the Giants announced that they would play five home games in the Yale Bowl, but that the question of television coverage remained "unresolved."

The situation was finally put to rest in the fall session of the U.S. Congress. Legislation that lifted the home-city blackout on games sold out at least 72 hours in advance of kickoff time was passed and signed into law by President Richard Nixon.

On July 11, Jersey City Mayor P. T. Jordan signed a two-year contract to allow the Giants to practice in that city's Roosevelt Stadium. The team still called the New York Giants would practice in New Jersey and play all but two of its home games in Connecticut.

With the excitement of the spring and summer over, the Giants got ready for the 1973 season. Their first draft pick (in the second round) was linebacker Brad Van Pelt

Johnny Roland (No. 23) struggles for a few yards in this 1973 meeting with the Cowboys, but cannot get out of the clutches of Dallas linebacker Lee Roy Jordan. Roland was in the last year of his career, coming to the Giants that year after seven fine seasons with the Cardinals. He gained 142 yards for the Giants in a lackluster 2–11–1, last-place season. No. 74 on Dallas is defensive tackle Bob Lilly.

from Michigan State. In marked contrast to the regular season, the Giants went 6–0 in the preseason, including a 45–30 victory over the Jets on August 19 in the Yale Bowl.

In the closing weeks of the preseason and the early weeks of the regular schedule, yet another ballpark problem arose: New Jersey authorities had difficulty floating bonds to cover the costs of building the Meadowlands stadium. On November 1 Wellington Mara told reporters that he had given the New Jersey Sports and Exposition

Authority until December 1 to show that the money for the stadium could be raised. But following the general elections in November, New Jersey's new Governor-elect Brendan T. Byrne clouded the issue even more by announcing that he would not necessarily support Governor Cahill's backing of the project—at least not without a renegotiated contract with the Giants. Word of the governor-elect's stance was met with enthusiasm in Albany, where New York's Governor Nelson Rockefeller renewed his efforts to block the building of the stadium and force the Giants to remain in New York City.

Wellington Mara, barely over the crises of the summer, had to throw more energy into the Meadowlands project, supposedly settled more than two years prior. But on November 27, Byrne, a month and a half away from taking office, announced that he had come to terms with the Maras and the Giants. Governor Cahill was

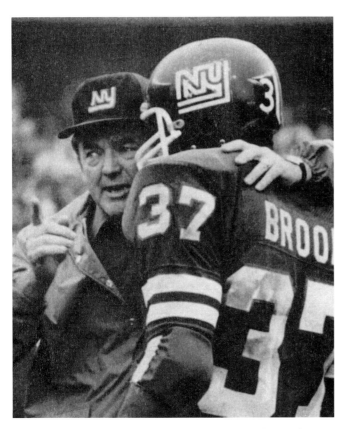

Bill Arnsparger, the new head coach in 1974, confers with defensive back Bobby Brooks, also a Giants newcomer that year. Arnsparger replaced Alex Webster and remained at the helm for three seasons, posting a disappointing record of 7–28–0.

lavish in his praise of the new agreement, and the Maras must have breathed a great sigh of relief.

There was no relief on the playing field for the Giants, however. After an impressive preseason, the Giants won the opening game of the year in Yankee Stadium by defeating Houston, 34–14. In the second week, the team played its final game in Yankee Stadium, battling Philadelphia to a 23–23 tie. But then the Giants went on the road, so to speak, and the nomadic lifestyle seemed to destroy them. They lost 11 of the remaining 12 games, managing but a single victory in the Yale Bowl over the St. Louis Cardinals. One of the biggest losers was Webster, who resigned as head coach before the final game of the season, a 31–7 loss to Tarkenton and the Vikings in the Yale Bowl.

Ron Johnson had another good year, rushing for 902 yards and scoring nine touchdowns, six rushing and three on pass receptions. Snead completed 56 percent of his passes, but far too many of them fell into the hands of opposing players. He was intercepted 22 times against only seven touchdown tosses. Backup quarterback Randy Johnson, who announced that he was quitting the team, played in many of the games. The defense, which had shown signs of coming alive in 1972, gave up a total of 362 points, just 31 shy of the NFC-leading Eagles in that inglorious category. No one from the team was invited to the Pro Bowl.

The 1973 Giants did not have much of a season, but there was no lack of help in shaping it. The president of the United States, the U.S. Congress, the governor of New York, the mayor of New York City, numerous courts, two Ivy League universities, the commissioner of the NFL, and two New Jersey governors all had their hands in Giants affairs that year.

On January 16, 1974, Andy Robustelli, who had been named Giants director of operations a month earlier, held a press conference at New York's 21 Club to introduce the team's new head coach, 47-year-old Bill Arnsparger. Although he had never played football professionally, Arnsparger brought solid credentials to his first head coaching position. Most recently, he had spent four years masterminding the Miami Dolphins' cham-pionship defenses as assistant coach to Don Shula. "[Arnsparger's] got the job of coaching football," Robustelli said at the conference. "He's going to tell me what he needs, and I'm going to try and get it for him."

After the new head coach had completed his remarks, he was asked if he would be "satisfied with a .500 season." His answer came quickly: "No." Arnsparger's first goal was to rebuild the aging offensive line, which had not done enough to protect Snead the previous season. Work began at the NFL draft held two weeks later. In the first round, Arnsparger selected All-American offensive guard John Hicks from Ohio State. To a chorus of boos from the crowd watching the proceedings during the second round, he chose another offensive lineman, Tom Mullen, from Southwest Missouri State. Despite the reaction of the audience, both new-comers were good enough to step into the starting lineup.

Unfortunately, the reinforced offensive line was not enough to help the Giants to a respectable season. In the first 7 games of the 14-game schedule, the New

Guard John Hicks (No. 74), adding a little something to a hit on Washington's Diron Talbert, was New York's first-round draft pick in 1974. The former Ohio State All-American made the NFL All-Rookie team and was one of the Giants' finest blockers through the 1977 season.

Doug Kotar, obtained from the Steelers during training camp of his rookie year in 1974, landed a starting job in the Giants backfield right away. Kotar remained with the Giants through the 1981 season, gaining a total of 3,378 yards on 900 carries, enough to rank him seventh on the all-time Giants' rushing ledger. His best year was 1976, when he gained 731 yards, averaging four yards per carry.

Yorkers were 1–6, scoring just 68 total points, to 141 for their opponents.

The Giants' road loss to the Washington Redskins in week six was indicative of the first half of the 1974 season. The previous Sunday, the Redskins and their 18-year-veteran quarterback, Sonny Jurgensen, had engineered a come-from-behind victory against the Miami Dolphins. Before 53,879 roaring spectators, Jurgensen (who, ironically, had been acquired from Philadelphia for Snead) picked apart the Giants secondary, completing the 249th, 250th, and 251st touchdown passes in his professional career. For the third consecutive game, Snead and the New York offense were unable to get anything going, and the final score was 24–3, Washington.

A 21–7 loss to Dallas in the Yale Bowl the following Sunday proved conclusively that the Giants offense was in deep trouble. The solution, Arnsparger thought, was to be provided by 32-year-old Craig Morton, who came to New York from the Dallas Cowboys. Morton had

signed a contract to join the Birmingham Americans of the new World Football League (WFL) the following season, but, after acquiring Kenny Stabler, the Birmingham team traded Morton's rights to a struggling WFL franchise in Houston. Gambling that Morton would be able to get out of his WFL contract, the Giants acquired him from Dallas in midseason, and Snead was traded to San Francisco.

Morton, who relieved interim quarterback Jim Del Gaizo in the eighth game of the season after only three days with the club, immediately brought new vitality to the Giants offense. The team that had scored just 68 points in the first half of the season managed to put 127 points on the board during the second half, but even the

About to make a spectacular catch is wide receiver Walker Gillette (No. 84), who was picked up on waivers from the Cardinals in 1974. His best year with New York was 1975, when he led the team with 43 receptions for 600 yards. He left the squad after the 1976 season.

Veteran quarterback Craig Morton (No. 15), acquired in October 1974 from Dallas, was the hope on which the restoration of the Giants passing game was based. Here he fires one off against Dallas as New York's John Hicks (No. 74) and Willie Young (No. 69), as well as Pat Donovan of the Cowboys, watch. Morton quarterbacked the club for three seasons. His best year was 1975, when he completed 186 passes for 2,359 yards and 11 touchdowns.

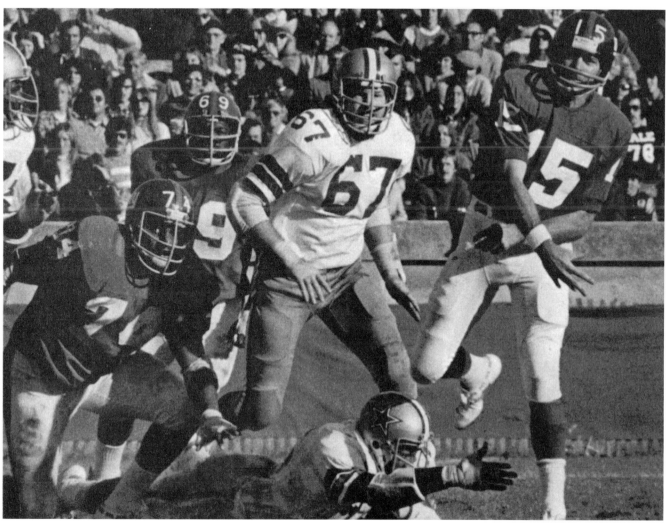

much-improved offense under Morton was not enough to rescue a poor season. The defense was unable to hold opponents to fewer than 16 points in any of the last 10 games. The final 2–12–0 record was made even poorer by the fact that the Giants lost every home game in 1974. The record for nearly two full seasons at the Yale Bowl was 1–11.

Although work on the new Giants Stadium in the New Jersey Meadowlands was progressing, it was clear that the park would not be ready by the 1975 season. Officials at the Yale Corporation were surprised when, on December 19, 1974, Abraham Beame, still in his first year as mayor of New York City, announced that the Giants would be playing their home games in Shea Stadium during the 1975 season. Beame apparently did not share former Mayor John Lindsay's feelings toward the team. He also announced that the Giants were given an option to play in refurbished Yankee Stadium during 1976 in the event that the Meadowlands stadium was still unfinished. "We understand it is a stopgap measure," said a spokesman for the NFL, which then faced the difficult task of scheduling Giants games in a stadium shared by the Mets and Yankees as well as the Jets.

The Giants, who had traded their number-one draft choice in 1975 to Dallas the previous season in exchange for Morton, selected offensive tackle Al Simpson from Colorado State in the second round. Simpson was used extensively on special teams during the 1975 season and remained with the Giants for only one year.

The Houston Texans, the WFL team that owned Morton's 1975 contract, moved to Shreveport, Louisiana, and later folded. Stating that he had no further commitments with the WFL, the former Dallas quarterback

Bobby Brooks (No. 37) puts the shoulder to Eagles wide receiver Charlie Smith in this 1975 game. Moving in to help are George Martin (No. 75) and Brian Kelly (No. 55); Stan Walters is the horizontal Eagle in the foreground.

Pressuring Dallas quarterback Roger Staubach is defensive end Dave Gallagher, who came to New York in 1975 in a trade that sent Bob Grim to the Chicago Bears. He remained through two seasons.

OPENING AT SHEA STADIUM

When the Giants met Dallas on October 12, 1975, at Shea Stadium in New York, it had been two years since the Giants played in New York City. It was an inauspicious homecoming. On the game's first play from scrimmage, New York quarterback Craig Morton fumbled, setting up a 24-yard field goal by Dallas' Toni Fritsch. Two first-half drives by the Giants ended in Dallas interceptions. In the third period the New Yorkers went ahead, 7–3, but another Morton fumble, this time at his own 32, set up a second Dallas field goal, making the score 7–6, New York.

The Giants defense performed well all day, limiting Dallas quarterback Roger Staubach to eight completions in 22 attempts and sacking him three times. But late in the game, another error by Morton led to a Dallas victory. The Cowboys' Mark Washington intercepted a Morton pass thrown into the end zone and ran the ball all the way back to the New York 17-yard line. A short scoring toss from Staubach sealed the Cowboys' come-from-behind victory, 13–7.

signed a three-year contract with New York in April. In May the Giants acquired linebacker Bob Schmidt, a free agent after playing the 1974 season with the WFL's Portland franchise.

On July 23, 1975, came the sad word that former Giants great and Hall of Famer Emlen Tunnell had died the day before of a heart attack. At the time of his death, he was working as a scout for the Giants organization.

For nearly a year, NFL Players Association president Ed Garvey had battled with owners and Commissioner Rozelle over the "Rozelle rule," which limited the movements of free agents playing out their options. The dispute led to a brief strike during the 1975 pre-

season, but seemed, still unresolved, about to threaten the regular season in 1975. On September 13, just one day before their final exhibition game, the New England Patriots went out on strike. Within the next four days, officials for both the Giants and the Jets, as well as the Washington Redskins and the Detroit Lions, found their players also walking away from them as a response to the controversy over the Rozelle rule. On September 18, just three days before the start of the regular season, a peace pact was signed to allow the regular season to commence without a final decision on the controversial rule, but courtroom battles over free agent status continued well into 1976.

In the meantime, the Giants started the 1975 season on a high note. More than sixty-five thousand fans watched the Eagles take an early lead in the September 21 season opener in Philadelphia, but the Giants bounced back with two short scoring rushes by Ron

Rondy Colbert (No. 35) enters the open prairie after fielding a New Orleans punt, on his way to a 65-yard touchdown return. A rookie in 1975 out of Lamar University, he proved to be an adept defensive back as well as a fine kick-returner. No. 28 of the Giants is Robert Giblin.

Johnson and a 41-yard George Hunt field goal to give New York a 16–7 lead in the third quarter. The Giants defense performed well, sacking Eagles quarterback Mike Boryla three times and intercepting him twice. In the fourth quarter, Boryla was replaced by Roman Gabriel, who managed a two-yard touchdown toss, but it wasn't enough. The final score was 23–14, New York.

The joy of a season-opening win was short-lived, however. The Giants were slaughtered, 49–13, the following Sunday in Washington and lost, 26–14, in week three at St. Louis. Things looked far from rosy as the New Yorkers prepared for their home opener at Shea Stadium against Dallas on October 12.

Following a 13–7 loss to the Cowboys, the Giants upset previously undefeated Buffalo in a 17–14 Monday night thriller the next week, despite 128 rushing yards gained by O. J. Simpson, but fell, 20–13, to St. Louis the following Sunday. In week seven, Morton and the rest of the offensive squad put on a fine show, defeating San Diego 35–24 in the Giants' first victory at Shea Stadium. But the team fell from contention in the NFC East by losing the next five games in a row. Only victories in the final two games over New Orleans and San Francisco enabled the Giants to post an improved record of five wins against nine losses.

Although the team improved, there were few bright spots in the year-end statistics. Fullback Joe Dawkins, with just 438 yards, was the team's leading rusher. Quarterback Morton, with only 11 touchdown passes and 16 interceptions, was ranked eighth in the NFC. The defense gave up a total of 306 points, the third worst in the conference.

There was, at least, some good news. Although the entire Meadowlands sports complex was running millions of dollars over the projected $302 million budget (it also included a horse racing track and an arena), the new Giants Stadium in New Jersey was finally taking shape. There were signs, at least, that the orphans of the NFL were about to have a real home, the first in their history.

Joe Dawkins, acquired from Denver in 1974, dives over the New Orleans Saints line for a first down. Dawkins led the Giants in rushing for two seasons before moving on to Houston. The Giants won this game, 28–14.

Dallas quarterback Roger Staubach seems to be either saying something nasty or crying out for mercy as New York's John Mendenhall (No. 64) and George Martin (No. 75) zero in on the fallen Cowboy. But the Super Bowl–bound Cowboys won that day, 24–10.

A STADIUM OF ONE'S OWN

The United States celebrated its 200th birthday in 1976, and the festivities were a nationwide patriotic pageant. The New York Giants, on the other hand, were only entering their 52nd year of existence, but they were able to celebrate that milestone with a brand-new home. No more baseball parks or college bowls—they now had a football stadium of their own replete with their name on it in enormous, boldface letters: Giants Stadium.

But that was about all the organization had to celebrate, having just come off three losing seasons in which they had posted a collective record of 9–32–1. Bill Arnsparger was beginning his third year as head coach and predicted that "1976 is the year we break .500, the first real step on our way back up."

In the preceding years the Eastern Division had been fairly well dominated by three other teams: Tom Landry's Dallas Cowboys, which showcased quarterback Roger Staubach and a defense approaching legendary status; Don Coryell's St. Louis Cardinals, which featured the two-fisted attack of Jim Hart's passing and the running of Jim Otis and Terry Metcalf; and George Allen's Washington Redskins, with their punishing defense and conglomerate of very old but still very good pros, not the least of whom was quarterback Billy Kilmer. The Giants had not been in the same class with their division competitors for some time.

The league itself was undergoing some changes. Welcomed into the fold were the Tampa Bay Buccaneers and Seattle Seahawks, bringing the number of franchises to 28. The 30-second clock became a feature in all NFL stadiums. And the World Football League was no longer any threat, gone to the same burial ground as so many other rival leagues that preceded it.

The biggest name to join the Giants in 1976 was Larry Csonka, the bone-crushing fullback who had battered his way through several Super Bowls for the Miami Dolphins in the early seventies and who spent the 1975 season playing for the WFL's Memphis franchise. The Giants signed Csonka after giving him, according to Dan Jenkins in *Sports Illustrated*, "most of Wall Street." Then just before the start of the regular season, the Giants reacquired quarterback Norm Snead, age 37, from the San Francisco 49ers. From the draft, the Giants picked up defensive tackle Troy Archer from Colorado, defensive lineman–turned-linebacker Harry Carson from South Carolina State, and running back Gordon Bell out of Michigan.

Anticipating a last-minute scramble to get the Meadowlands stadium ready for the 1976 season opener,

Fullback Larry Csonka (No. 39), signed by the Giants in 1976 after the demise of the WFL, carries the ball across an icy field and prepares to meet Chicago Bears linebacker Doug Buffone (No. 55) in the last game of the 1977 season. Csonka played only three seasons for New York. No. 87 for the Giants is tight end Gary Shirk.

the NFL schedule-makers put the Giants on the road for the first four games of the year. The New York coaching staff dearly wanted to win the first game of the season, hoping to upset the strongly favored Redskins in Washington. And the Giants almost pulled it off. With only about a minute and a half remaining in the game, they led, 17–12.

But the offense stalled, and the Redskins' fleet wide receiver Eddie Brown fielded a New York punt and broke loose on a 45-yard return. Two Kilmer passes later, the Redskins had the score they needed and had eradicated the Giants' bid for an upset with a heartbreaking 19–17 come-from-behind victory.

Rookie defensive end Troy Archer, the Giants' number-one draft choice from Colorado in 1976, snares Roger Staubach for a loss on opening day at Giants Stadium in 1976.

This opening day crowd of 76,042 christened brand-new Giants Stadium in the Meadowlands of East Rutherford, New Jersey, on October 10, 1976. Ground was broken for the edifice back in November 1972.

The road show moved on to Philadelphia, Los Angeles, and St. Louis, but the story in each city was unfortunately much the same, at least in terms of the final score.

When the Giants finally traveled to New Jersey to make a long-anticipated debut in their new stadium, they brought with them a record of 0–4. Despite that, 76,042 fans jammed Giants Stadium to watch the new

tenants take on the powerful Dallas Cowboys. There was, of course, color and controversy as the new home of the Giants was christened that October afternoon (see side-bar). Notable were the new Giants helmets, with the long-familiar *NY* removed from the side and replaced by the word *Giants*. When the game began, Staubach and the rest of the Cowboys demonstrated why they were the only undefeated and untied team in the NFL as they moved smartly downfield with nine consecutive first downs and two touchdowns on their first two possessions. The second Dallas score was a 40-yard touchdown strike from Staubach to Drew Pearson. "We

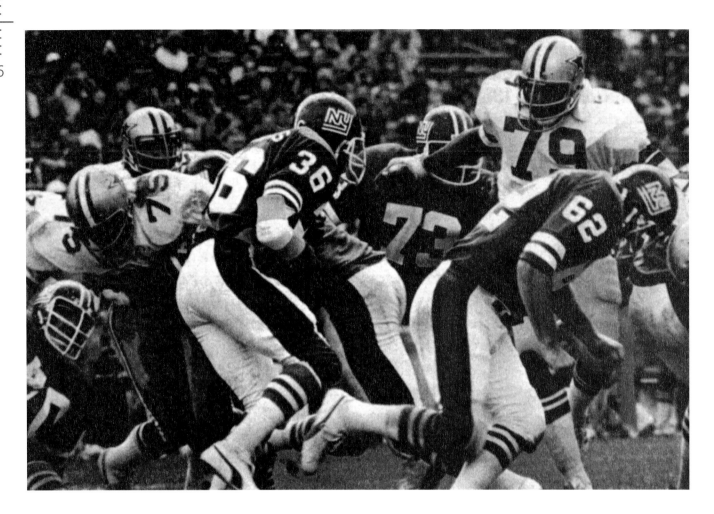

Larry Watkins (No. 36) hits the line against Dallas, but await-ing him is monstrous defensive end Harvey Martin (No. 79) during the Giants' home opener in 1976 at Giants Stadium in New Jersey. Other Giants are Tom Mullen (No. 73) and Ron Mikolajczyk (No. 62). No. 75 on the Cowboys is Jethro Pugh.

played very well in the first quarter," sportswriter Red Smith quoted Dallas head coach Landry as saying, "and then we began to work on our running game, which hasn't been going very well lately." While the Cowboys spent the remainder of the contest practicing their rushing attack, New York managed to make the final score look respectable. After a Dallas field goal upped the score 17–0 at halftime, New York finally scored in the third quarter on a 30-yard pass from Craig Morton to wide receiver Jimmy Robinson, who had been signed as a free agent prior to the start of the season.

Halfway through the final quarter, Dallas put its third touchdown on the board soon after intercepting a Morton pass. Just minutes later, Morton was sacked for the fifth time during the afternoon and left the game with a minor leg injury. Replacement Snead completed four consecutive passes to give the Giants their final score of the day, but it wasn't enough. Sadly, the handsome new stadium was christened with a 24–14 Dallas win. And for the first time in club history, the Giants opened their season with a pitiful five consecutive losses.

Two more losses—a 24–7 lacing by Fran Tarkenton's Super Bowl–bound Vikings and a 27–0 shut-out by the world champion Pittsburgh Steelers—doomed head coach Arnsparger. On October 25 director of opera-tions Andy Robustelli announced that Arnsparger had been fired and that 45-year-old assistant coach John McVay had been moved up to the top slot. "He is not an interim coach in the strict sense of the word," Robustelli

This sequence records the Giants' first touchdown in their new stadium. Wide receiver Jimmy Robinson gathers in a pass from Craig Morton, wheels around, and races off to the end zone, eluding a diving tackle by the Cowboys' Aaron Kyle (No. 25). Unfortunately for the Giants, the Cowboys scored more touchdowns that day, and a field goal to boot, and won 24–14.

OPENING DAY COLOR AND CONTROVERSY

"I haven't missed a Columbus Day parade in years," said New Jersey governor Brendan T. Byrne, trying to explain why he chose to attend a local parade rather than the pregame dedication ceremonies at brand new Giants Stadium in the Meadowlands. But there were other explanations.

"He didn't come because he didn't want to get booed," *The New York Times* quoted an unnamed official from the New Jersey Sports and Exposition Authority. "He got booed pretty badly when the race track opened last month."

Former governor William T. Cahill, one of the guiding forces behind early plans for the sports complex, answered, "No comment," when he was asked to speculate on why the current governor chose not to attend. Outside the stadium, several hundred demonstrators carried placards demanding that the sports authority pay a larger share of taxes.

Although a few fans were disappointed that their seat locations made it impossible to see either of two huge electronic scoreboards, most agreed that the three-tiered stadium, dedicated solely to football, was a comfortable place to watch a game. In the audience and participating in the pregame festivities were former Giants from the 1956 championship team, including Charlie Conerly, Kyle Rote, Rosey Grier, and Alex Webster. Bob Hope, Peggy Cass, and other celebrities were also in attendance.

Said Sonny Werblin, former Jets owner then chairman of the New Jersey sports authority, "I'm as excited as I can be because everybody said that it would never happen."

Robert Meyner, another former New Jersey governor, waxed even more enthusiastic: "Even from the time of William Penn and Ben Franklin, we were considered a state between New York and Philadelphia. I'm pleased to see it's worked out, and it augurs well for the identity of New Jersey."

But the Giants did not get off on the old right foot. While a group of fans displayed a banner reading "Brand New Stadium—Same Old Giants," the New Yorkers lost to Dallas, 24–14.

Some veterans of past football wars who wore the Giants colors with special brilliance are honored at the new Giants Stadium. From left to right: Ben Agajanian, Andy Robustelli, Rosey Grier, Herb Rich, Jim Katcavage, Kyle Rote, Charlie Conerly, and Jack Stroud.

Midway through the 1976 season, with the Giants shamefacedly sporting a record of 0–7, John McVay was brought in to replace Bill Arnsparger as head coach. McVay's record for the remainder of the season was 3–4. He remained in command through 1978, but could not come up with a winning season and logged a collective record of 14–23.

A New York intracity battle was waged in New Jersey as the Giants and Jets met at Giants Stadium during the 1977 preseason. In this scene, quarterback Jerry Golsteyn (No. 12) tries to pick up some yardage on a quarterback draw while guard Bill Ellenbogen appears to be blocking in a way that might catch a referee's attention. The Jets won that day, 10–0.

said, implying there was more than a little pressure on the new head coach.

Wellington Mara, after living through all the relocation controversy and the bitter disappointments of his team in recent years, sounded a bit world-weary when he said, "I feel we've reached the point where it's imperative to see if the people we have can respond to a personality other than Bill."

McVay's number one objective was to get the faltering Giants offense rolling again, and his ability to work with offensive teams was undoubtedly part of the reason he was given the head coaching position. When he had directed the WFL's Memphis Southmen two seasons earlier, his team led that league in most offensive categories and won 17 games.

Doug Kotar (No. 44) carries for the Giants as Bill Ellenbogen (No. 65) moves in to lay a block on Dallas defensive tackle Larry Cole in the first game to be played in the new Giants Stadium at the Meadowlands, October 10, 1976.

But in McVay's debut at Giants Stadium on October 31, the offenseless New Yorkers were shut out, 10–0, by the Philadelphia Eagles, a team destined to win only four games that year. Morton was sacked six times. Things were not much better at Dallas the following week, as the 0–7 Giants became the 0–8 Giants in a game they should have won.

The defense had not allowed Dallas a single touchdown all afternoon, and with the score 9–3 favoring Dallas and only one minute left to play, the Giants had the ball on the Cowboys' 6-yard line. There, with a Dallas defender all over potential receiver Bob Tucker in the end zone, Morton was hit hard before he could get rid of the football. He fumbled and Dallas got the ball—and the game.

Then, as the NFL moved into the second half of its schedule, the Giants dropped to 0–9 by losing to Denver, 14–13.

New York finally won its first game of the year in NFL week 10. With Snead at quarterback, the Giants upset Washington, 12–9, to mark not only the first win for the team in Giants Stadium, but also McVay's first victory as head coach and the first victory in 15 attempts for the Giants over a George Allen–coached team. McVay and the Giants won two of the remaining four games, giving them a final 1976 record of 3–11.

One of the few standouts on the squad was linebacker Brad Van Pelt, who had been the team's second-round draft choice in 1973. As he would be for the next five years in succession, Van Pelt was invited to the Pro Bowl, and it was the first time any Giants player had been selected since 1972.

Running back Doug Kotar, who had been acquired from the Pittsburgh Steelers in 1974, led the team with

Hall of Fame–bound Walter Payton (No. 34) carries the ball for the Chicago Bears but runs into an irresistible force in Giants linebacker Brian Kelley (No. 55). Ensnaring Payton's leg is George Martin (No. 75). The Bears eked out a 12–9 win in overtime on that wintry day. Some of the other Giants in the picture are Troy Archer (No. 77), Jack Gregory (No. 81), John Mendenhall (No. 64), and Harry Carson (No. 53).

Defensive tackle John Mendenhall (No. 64) wrestles Philadelphia running back Herb Lusk (No. 32) to the AstroTurf in this early 1977 match. Mendenhall, a third-round draft choice from Grambling in 1972, was a mainstay on the Giants front line for most of the seventies and earned All-Pro honors in 1974. Linebacker Brad Van Pelt (No. 10) is shown fighting off the block of Eagles fullback Mike Hogan (No. 35). The Eagles won, 28–10, on a rain-soaked field.

731 yards rushing. Csonka, although sidelined much of the time with injuries, gained 569 yards. Tucker again led the Giants receivers with 42 catches.

On December 14, 1976, McVay signed a two-year contract to continue as head coach, his record of 3–4 considerably—but not excitingly—better than what the Giants had been experiencing.

The Giants traded Morton to Denver in 1977 for quarterback Steve Ramsey, but the major acquisition, management felt, was free agent Joe Pisarcik, who had spent three years with the Canadian Football League's Calgary franchise. The 6'4", 220-pound athlete arrived at training camp as the number five quarterback, but he eventually won the starting job. The first-round draft choice was defensive lineman Gary Jeter of the University of Southern California.

The Giants opened the 1977 season on September 18 in a game against Washington before a then-record crowd of 76,086 at Giants Stadium. Midway through the first period, New York defensive end George Martin intercepted a pass from Kilmer and rumbled 30 yards for a touchdown.

The score stayed at 7–0 until the third quarter, when a 64-yard New York drive was capped by an apparent touchdown that was called back by a penalty. The New Yorkers had to settle for a 22-yard Joe Danelo field goal.

With the score at 10–0 at the start of the final quarter, the Washington offense exploded. A 3-yard touchdown run by Mike Thomas, a short, scoring toss from Kilmer to John Riggins, and a 51-yard Mark Moseley field goal gave the Redskins 17 unanswered points and a 17–10 lead late in the final period.

Defensive end Jack Gregory (No. 81) snags 49ers quarterback Jim Plunkett as Troy Archer (No. 77) lunges to provide the leveling factor in a 1977 encounter. The 49ers watching are Jean Barrett (No. 77) and Randy Cross (No. 51). The Giant on the ground is Gary Jeter. The Giants won the game, 20–17.

Cleveland's Greg Pruitt gets loose with the ball and scampers around end moments after almost having his jersey torn from him. In pursuit are New York linebacker Dan Lloyd (No. 54) and defensive back Bill Bryant (No. 21). The Browns won this 1977 game, 21–7.

But the Giants came back in one of their finest finishes of the time. Quarterback Jerry Golsteyn, a youngster out of Northern Illinois who had been New York's 12th-round draft choice in 1976, led a tremendous 74-yard touchdown drive on four plays, knotting the score at 17. With less than two minutes remaining, defensive tackle Archer stripped the ball from Washington running back Thomas, and Giants middle linebacker Carson recovered the fumble. With seven seconds remaining, Danelo kicked the winning field goal.

At Canton, Ohio, in July 1978, former Giants great Alphonse "Tuffy" Leemans smiles from the official escort car on his way to the ceremony to formally induct him into the Pro Football Hall of Fame. The great halfback died six months later.

DISTANT REPLAY

The ambulance that stood by in New York's Central Park was not needed, despite the 90-degree heat, as the stars from the Colts and Giants 1958 championship game played touch football on July 7, 1978, a game that was to be broadcast later in the season by CBS television.

Colts players included Johnny Unitas, Alan Ameche, Gino Marchetti, Lenny Moore, Raymond Berry, Jim Parker, Art Donovan, and Steve Myhra. The Giants players hoping for revenge were Charlie Conerly, Frank Gifford, Kyle Rote, Alex Webster, Rosie Brown, Ray Wietecha, Dick Modzelewski, and Pat Summerall.

Myhra brought a six-pack of beer to the Colts bench for pre-game refreshments, but soon referee Sonny Jurgensen had the players, six to a side, on the field. After just a few plays from scrimmage, Unitas threw a scoring spiral to Moore in the end zone. Jurgensen declared the score 7–0 without a point-after attempt.

Conerly's first pass was intercepted. "Same old Charlie," cracked Webster. To round out the scoring in the first half, Unitas hit Berry on two touchdown bombs, and Gifford took over quarterbacking responsibilities for Conerly, nearly 60 years old at the time.

In the third quarter, the Giants resorted to subterfuge to get on the scoreboard: Rote hid on the sideline and just before the ball was snapped, he ran into the end zone, where he pulled in a toss from Gifford. Later, Gifford threw another touchdown pass, that time to Webster, and for a time it looked as if the Giants might pull off an upset by tying the game. But with less than one minute left to play in the second 30-minute half, Unitas intercepted a Gifford pass and ran it back all the way for a touchdown. And the Colts had won again.

A view of the area between the uprights, that coveted space where Joe Danelo's kick is about to enter. This kick, booted in 1979, was Danelo's 18th consecutive field goal, a Giants record that still stands today. The previous record of 14 straight was set by Pat Summerall in 1961. Danelo joined the Giants in 1976 and handled the kicking chores through the 1982 season, ending up as the fourth all-time Giants scorer with 482 points (104 field goals, 170 extra points). He also holds the club record for the most field goals kicked in a single game, six, against Seattle in 1981.

The 20–17 upset marked the second time in a row that the Giants had surprised the Allen-coached Redskins. The season, which had begun on such a high note, however, ended with an all-too-familiar sad refrain, with the New Yorkers winning only 4 of their remaining 13 games.

The club's record of 5–9 was an improvement over the dismal 3–11 1976 season, but it had been a year marred by dropped passes—Pisarcik and Golsteyn managed only 134 completions in 311 attempts. Still, the defense ranked third in the conference against the rush and showed definite promise. Linebacker Van Pelt was

the only Giants player named All-Pro and invited to the Pro Bowl in 1977.

To many the highlight of the 1978 preseason came on July 7, when many of the stars of the unforgettable 1958 Giants-Colts championship game were reunited for a game of touch football for the benefit of CBS cameras. The Colts, who won their first championship in the NFL's first sudden-death overtime period 20 years earlier, won the geriatric contest as well.

The Giants' 1978 first-round draft choice was a 6'6", 275-pound offensive tackle from Stanford named Gordon King. A surprise from the fifth round was little 5'10", 197-pound cornerback Terry Jackson from San Diego State.

The Giants would need all the help they could get that year because the NFL season was expanded from 14 to 16 games in 1978, while the preseason was cut from 6 games to 4.

The first game of the regular season was against Tampa Bay and their rookie quarterback, Doug Williams. When Williams stepped onto the field, he became the first black quarterback in NFL history to start a game. But his debut was spoiled when he was intercepted in the first minute of play by Jackson, the Giants rookie, who ran 32 yards for the touchdown.

Throughout the remainder of the first half, however, Tampa Bay's offense outplayed the Giants' offense, which recorded its initial first down only midway through the second quarter. But by the end of the half, the Giants had arisen, and when Danelo kicked a 42-yard field goal, the Giants had a 10–10 tie at the intermission.

In the second half, Pisarcik, who replaced Golsteyn, connected with wide receiver Johnny Perkins on a long, scoring toss. Both teams made one more field goal, which left the Giants with a 19–13 victory. Pisarcik had been reasonably impressive, completing 9 of 15 passes.

For the first eight games of the season, Pisarcik led the Giants to a respectable 5–3 record, including big wins over the Kansas City Chiefs and the San Francisco 49ers and a 17–6 upset of the first-place Washington Redskins in front of a record 76,192 cheering fans at the Meadowlands. But after the big win over Washington, the team fell apart, losing all but one of the year's final eight games.

Perhaps the most embarrassing point in a truly disappointing football decade was reached in NFL week 12 of the 1978 season, when the Giants led the Philadelphia Eagles, 17–12, with just 20 seconds left to play and the ball in New York's possession. To run out the clock and win the game, the Giants only had to snap the ball and fall on it. Instead, mystifyingly, they tried a handoff. The ball was fumbled, and a Philadelphia defender recovered it, then proceeded to run it back for the winning touchdown.

The only victory in the second half of the season was in a game against St. Louis on December 10, 1978, at Giants Stadium. But after the streak of six losses ruined a 5–3 start to the season, New York fans were dissatisfied, to put it somewhat mildly. The biggest applause at the 17–0 shutout of the Cardinals that day was reserved for the pilot of a chartered airplane who flew above the stadium trailing a banner that read: "15 Years of Lousy Football—We've Had Enough." Fans huddling in the cold at Giants Stadium picked up the message and began chanting, "We've had enough, we've had enough, we've had enough."

In the game, running back Kotar became the first Giants player to rush for more than 100 yards in a single game all year, and the offense, for the fourth consecutive time, scored 17 points. "We're still stuck on 17, but that's all right as long as we get shutouts," said head coach McVay.

"I guess this means I can take my wife out to dinner now. I can be seen in public." McVay was fired just eight days later.

One day after the final game of the season, a 20–3 loss to the Philadelphia Eagles, director of operations Robustelli announced that he would resign on December 31, 1978. "What made this year so hard to accept," admitted Mara, "was the knowledge that we were losing Andy." Robustelli resigned only partly because of the Giants' dismal record: with a successful travel agency and extensive real estate holdings in the Caribbean, he had many responsibilities outside the Giants organization.

Carson and punter Dave Jennings were named All-Pro and invited to the Pro Bowl, and Van Pelt went to the All-Star classic in Hawaii for what would be his third year in a row.

Mara expressed the hope of luring Joe Paterno away from Penn State to become the Giants' new head coach, but said that he would follow "the rules of common decency" and not contact him until after Penn State's appearance in the Cotton Bowl. Mara was unsuccessful in his bid for the college coach, but major help was on the way.

In the early months of the year, it hardly looked as though 1979 would set the Giants on the comeback trail. Soon after the new year began, Giants vice president Tim Mara, a nephew of Wellington and half owner of the club, announced that the Giants would hire a new director of operations by February 1. But when that day came and went, there were rumors that the Maras, both 50 percent owners of the club, were not in agreement over the choice.

On February 8 the disagreement that had been quietly smoldering heated up. Wellington Mara called a press conference and announced that he would appoint a new head coach before the two owners would agree on a replacement for director of operations Robustelli. "As president I have the full decision-making responsibility," Wellington said.

George Young was hired in February 1979 to replace Andy Robustelli, who had resigned his post as the Giants' director of operations. Young, the new general manager and vice president, previously spent 11 years with the Baltimore Colts and Miami Dolphins and was rightfully known as Don Shula's right hand. Young's first job was to find a new coach for the club, and his overriding mission was to turn the Giants into a contender. He succeeded at this. New York, in Young's first eight years, earned its way into the playoffs in 1981, 1984, 1985, and 1986, including an NFL championship at Super Bowl XXI.

Ray Perkins, hired by George Young in 1979, became the 12th head coach in New York Giants history. Replacing John McVay, Perkins had been the offensive coordinator for the San Diego Chargers the season prior and was credited with the development of the Chargers' outstanding quarterback Dan Fouts. Perkins remained through the 1982 season, compiling an overall record of 23–30 before accepting the head coaching job at the University of Alabama.

There was a definite reason why Wellington Mara called the press conference, although the reason did not surface at the time: "I thought that as a result of the difficult time we were having in agreeing on a general manager and the delay it was going to cause us, we would lose our top choices for a new coach. They probably would not be available by the time a general manager was hired. I was afraid we would end up with a second-rate coach."

Later Wellington observed that of his three top prospects (which were Robustelli's choices as well), two have since managed to take their teams to Super Bowls.

Tim Mara disagreed and called in NFL Commissioner Pete Rozelle to act as an arbitrator (which had already been tried a few weeks earlier, before the squabble became public knowledge). "I just wish my father, God rest him, had given 51 percent to either Jack [Tim's father] or myself," Wellington remarked.

Tim Mara said, "I want to have a winner. Well wants to have a winner, his way, but Well's way has had us in the cellar the last 15 years."

Fortunately, the public family feud lasted only a few days longer before the Maras, still without the head coach Wellington had threatened to hire, agreed on the selection of George Young as the new general manager. Young had been hired by Don Shula on two separate occasions to act as his director of personnel with Baltimore and then later with Miami. Shula described him as his "right-hand man," and it didn't take long for Young, hired February 14, to solve the Giants' head coaching problem.

In a matter of days, both of the Maras were interviewing Young's choice for the new head coach. They approved, and at a February 22 press conference at Giants Stadium, 37-year-old Ray Perkins was formally introduced to the media.

"This situation was made for me," the former wide receiver for the Baltimore Colts remarked. During the 1978 season, Perkins had been offensive coordinator for the San Diego Chargers and helped develop the anemic squad there into the top passing team in the NFL.

Perkins may have thought the job was made for him, but it only lasted through the 1982 season. Bad luck and a rash of injuries hurt the team and spurred him to accept the head coaching job at the University of Alabama in 1983.

The truly significant acquisition of 1979 came at the NFL draft held in May. At the Waldorf-Astoria Hotel in New York, a number of spectators booed as the Giants selected a relatively unknown quarterback from Morehead State University, 6'2", 216-pound Phil Simms. The fans were hoping that their team, desperately in need of offense, would be able to select Washington State's quarterback, Jack Thompson. But Thompson went to the Cincinnati Bengals, and when the Giants' turn came four selections later, spectators in Manhattan were surprised as the choice of the Giants' brain trust was announced. Who was Phil Simms? And why was he chosen ahead of established college stars like Kellen Winslow and Charles Alexander? The pros knew what the amateurs didn't: Simms had labored at Kentucky's Morehead State

University, where a 2–6–1 record and a ball-control offense left Simms with relatively modest statistics. Most professional scouts expected the blond quarterback not to last into the second round.

Those who were unhappy with the Giants' first-round draft choice were only partly placated by their second selection—a 6'3", 195-pound wide receiver from Memphis State named Earnest Gray. The speedy receiver (4.5 seconds for the 40-yard dash) had averaged 29.5 yards per reception in his junior year, breaking an NCAA record, and a year later was named to several All-America teams. Additionally, he was invited to both the Senior Bowl and the East-West Game.

With Simms sitting on the bench, the Giants lost their first four games of 1979. A diversion in the early season came at a Monday Night affair in which the Giants' No. 78, Gus Coppens, misidentified by Howard Cosell's crew as Gordon Gravelle, missed some blocks. According to *The New York Times*, Cosell so excoriated No. 78 that Gravelle's wife was mortified enough to lodge a complaint.

"Cosell is a pompous, senile idiot," Gravelle concluded following the offending broadcast. Cosell explained later that he never actually mentioned Gravelle's name on the air. According to *The New York Times*, Cosell attributed the incident as being "all Frank Gifford's fault anyway."

The Giants' fifth game, against New Orleans, brought their fifth loss, but Simms appeared briefly in a relief role that was impressive enough to win him a start in game six. With Simms at quarterback, the Giants won four straight contests, and six out of the next eight before dropping the final three games of the season to Dallas, St. Louis, and Baltimore.

The Giants ended the year with a 6–10 record, identical to that of the previous season. But for the first time, there seemed to be new hope in the New Jersey Meadowlands. Simms was a unanimous choice for the All-NFL Rookie team honors and runner up to the Cardinals' Ottis Anderson for NFC Rookie of the Year. Wide receiver Gray was also named to the All-NFL Rookie team. As they had in 1978, Van Pelt, Carson, and Jennings went to the Pro Bowl.

It was deeply hoped by fans and team insiders alike that the eighties would be very different from the seventies. "I would not mind a return to the style of the early sixties," Wellington Mara said when asked about the Giants' prospects for the coming decade. A lot of Giants fans felt the same way.

Mark Haynes covers a Rams receiver like a proverbial blanket. The Giants' first-round draft choice in 1980, the cornerback hailed from Colorado and made his mark impressively in New York with three All-Pro berths and a second-team All-Pro mention in his first five years with the team. No. 55 and No. 57 on the Giants are, respectively, linebackers Brian Kelley and Byron Hunt. Photo courtesy of Fred Roe.

SOME NEW BLOOD

The eighties began with many firsts in sports. The United States, for the first time in the history of the modern Olympics, chose to boycott the summer games in Moscow; the Philadelphia Phillies won their very first World Series on the arm of Steve Carlton and the bat of Mike Schmidt; the New York Islanders captured their first Stanley Cup with one of the youngest teams ever to take the hockey title; "Doctor of Dunk" Darrell Griffith led Louisville to its first NCAA basketball national championship; and Georgia, behind the running of spectacular freshman Herschel Walker, took its first NCAA national title in football. Unfortunately there was nothing as satisfyingly new as that around Giants Stadium in 1980.

Coach Ray Perkins and general manager George Young hoped for a noticeable improvement over the club's fourth-place finish the year prior in the five-team NFC East. So did Wellington Mara, hounded by the fans' discontent, which seemed to become more vocal and vitriolic with each loss.

The first Giant to be drafted in the eighties was cornerback Mark Haynes from Colorado, who was highly regarded by all pro scouts and had earned invitations to both the Senior and Hula Bowls after the 1979 college football season. Curtis McGriff, an immense defensive

tackle from Alabama, made the team as a free agent and was eventually elected to the NFL All-Rookie squad.

Phil Simms, then in his second year, showed signs of brilliance. In the September 7 season opener at St. Louis, he threw five touchdown passes in the Giants' 41–35 victory. Earnest Gray, the Memphis State receiver drafted right after Simms in 1979, caught four of the touchdown tosses, establishing an all-time Giants single-game record.

But after the victory over the Cardinals, the Giants began to self-destruct, losing eight games in a row and falling far out of contention in the NFC East. The losing streak was finally broken by a 38–35 victory over Dallas on November 9 in the Meadowlands, a game in which Simms threw for 351 yards and three touchdowns. Remarkably, he would have had five touchdown passes and a total of 402 yards through the air if two of his strikes had not been called back because of penalties. But two games later in San Francisco, the young quarterback was sacked by the 49ers 10 times, tying a club record, in a 12–0 loss.

Simms had to sit out the final three games of the 1980 season because of a shoulder injury. His replacement was rookie quarterback Scott Brunner, a sixth-round draft choice who had had but one season

Throwing here against the Los Angeles Rams is Scott Brunner, a sixth-round draft choice from Delaware in 1980. He took over the quarterbacking for the Giants late in the 1981 season after an injury sidelined Phil Simms, and he did the majority of the passing for New York over the following two seasons as injuries continued to plague Simms. Brunner's best year was 1983, when he completed 190 passes for 2,516 yards and nine touchdowns. Some of the other Giants are guard Billy Ard (No. 67) and guard J. T. Turner (No. 68). Photo courtesy of Fred Roe.

as a starting quarterback at Delaware, then an NCAA Division II school. Under Brunner, the Giants managed one victory in their final three games, but many were impressed by the poise of the relatively inexperienced rookie.

What was not impressive was the 4–12 record of the Giants. It left them in last place in the NFC East, a notch lower than in coach Perkins' first season at the helm the year before.

There was a remarkable turnaround in 1981, and it started amid controversy. In January some players went on record objecting to the public criticism they received from Perkins. But the biggest flap came in April, just a few days before the NFL college draft.

"I haven't been part of any type of discussion," Brad Van Pelt said, "but I know about it." The Giants' All-Pro linebacker was referring to a threat among New York veterans to walk away from the team if Giants management agreed to pay planned first-round draft choice Lawrence Taylor the $750,000-per-year salary his agent was reportedly demanding (see sidebar).

But by the time the NFL draft began on April 28, all was apparently forgiven. The 6'3", 245-pound linebacker from North Carolina signed with the Giants and began a magnificent career of terrorizing all of New York's opponents.

Not easily recognizable here, as he is balanced precariously—and probably painfully—on his head, is linebacker Lawrence Taylor, in the process of sacking Jets quarterback Richard Todd. The Giants' first-round draft choice (number two in the entire draft) in 1981, Taylor had been a consensus All-American at North Carolina before beginning his illustrious pro career in New York. Photo courtesy of Fred Roe.

Jim Burt, famed for his tight-fitting jersey numbered 64, wrestles with a Kansas City blocker with an aim toward getting his hands on Chiefs quarterback Bill Kenney (No. 9). Signed as a free agent in 1981, the 6'1", 260-pound Burt soon developed into one of the finest nose tackles in the game. Photo courtesy of Fred Roe.

WELCOME, LAWRENCE TAYLOR

Lawrence Taylor's career in New York almost ended before it began when certain Giants players threatened a walkout over his agent's salary demands in the days leading up to the 1981 NFL draft. The consensus All-American linebacker from North Carolina talked about it to *The New York Times*:

> "I heard the talk that some of the Giants would walk out if I got a lot of money," the North Carolina linebacker said. "I didn't want people to get mad at me. So I sent the Giants a telegram Monday saying I would rather not be drafted by them. Monday night I got calls from some of the players, on the offense and defense, and some of the coaches. They said there was nothing to the story, and there would be no walkout. They said they wanted me here. That made me feel better."

Taylor arrived in New York on April 28, the same day the draft began. He seemed to enjoy his initial exposure to the Big Apple: "I'll enjoy New York," he said. "You've got a pretty good selection of TV up here. I watched *The Three Stooges*. I like them."

It would not be long before Taylor, clad in Giants uniform No. 56, began making opposing offensive linemen, quarterbacks, and running backs look a little like stooges themselves.

Taylor was certainly the standout among the new bodies donning Giants uniforms in 1981, but the rebuilding efforts hardly stopped there. Other significant draftees were defensive tackle Bill Neill from Pittsburgh, guard Billy Ard from Wake Forest, and linebacker Byron Hunt from Southern Methodist University. Free agents who came aboard and remained at least three seasons were linebacker Joe McLaughlin, running back Leon Bright, defensive tackle Jim Burt, safety Larry Flowers, defensive end Dee Hardison, and center Ernie Hughes. Veteran running back Rob Carpenter was obtained from Houston after the fifth game of the season, and safety Bill Currier was acquired from New England.

Doing what he did so naturally and repeatedly, Lawrence Taylor adds another sack to his statistics, in this instance leveling Pittsburgh quarterback Terry Bradshaw. One of the game's most fearsome pass rushers, Taylor had 9¹/₂ sacks in his rookie year, 1981. When he retired after the 1993 season, he had been credited with 142 sacks, by far the most in Giants history. The other Giants shown here are George Martin (No. 75) and Byron Hunt (No. 57). Photo courtesy of Fred Roe.

The rebuilt Giants lost the season opener to Philadelphia, 24–10, in a contest played at Giants Stadium. Although he completed 20 out of 37 passes for 241 yards, Simms was sacked six times.

The New York defense, feeling the impact of rookie linebacker Taylor, helped the Giants win their next two games against the Redskins and Saints, allowing only seven points in each of the two victories. But consecutive losses to Dallas and Green Bay dropped New York's record to 2–3. Running back Carpenter made his Giants debut in the second half of game six with the St. Louis Cardinals at the Meadowlands and, rushing for 103 yards on just 14 carries, helped his new teammates to a 34–14 win.

The hero of the next game in Seattle was place-kicker Joe Danelo, a graduate of Washington State and the Giants' regular kicker for six years. With his wife, his parents, and two dozen friends in the stands, Danelo kicked six out of six field goals, including a 54-yarder, helping the Giants to a 32–0 shutout of the Seahawks. No other Giant has ever kicked six field goals in a single game. Carpenter had his second straight 100-yard rushing game, and Harry Carson and Taylor led the revitalized defense. When the Giants won an overtime thriller in Atlanta, 27–24, the following week, their surprising 5–3 record clearly put them in the hunt for a playoff spot.

Three consecutive losses over the next three weeks, however, appeared to doom their chances. In the final contest of that three-game stretch, a heartbreaking overtime loss to the Redskins, quarterback Simms suffered a separated shoulder and was lost for the season.

Minus their starting quarterback and in the throes of a three-game losing streak, the Giants traveled to Philadelphia to play the winningest team in the NFL—

Louis Cardinals set the stage for the now-famous 1981 season finale.

Before New York's final game of the season, a Saturday affair at Giants Stadium against the Dallas Cowboys, who had already clinched the NFL East title (while fellow division-member Washington had secured the first wild-card berth in the NFC), the complicated wild-card picture took this shape: the Giants would become eligible for the playoffs only if they defeated Dallas and if the New York Jets beat the Green Bay Packers on the last weekend of the regular season. If those events took place, the Giants would enjoy post-season play for the first time since 1963—an 18-year famine. And it would mark the first time in history that both New York teams would enter the playoffs during the same year (the Jets were a wild-card in the AFC).

"When you hit the Cowboys early, and keep hitting them, they'll lose interest," said Giants All-Pro linebacker Carson, "particularly if it's a game they're not totally committed to." It was a good point. The Giants were riding high into the game, with obvious good reason; the Cowboys, on the other hand, had no real playoff advantage to gain in winning at the Meadowlands that Saturday afternoon. Still, they were the Dallas Cowboys, coached by Tom Landry; featuring the running of Tony Dorsett; the passing of Danny White; receivers like Drew Pearson, Tony Hill, and Billy Joe Dupree; and defensive stalwarts in the class of Randy White, Ed "Too Tall" Jones, Harvey Martin, Charlie Waters, and Dennis Thurman.

When the Cowboys and Giants took to the field on December 19 at the Meadowlands, the temperature was 25 degrees with a 20-mile-per-hour wind producing a wind chill just above zero. It was a defensive struggle in the first half, one as bitter as the weather. The New York defenders, led by linebackers Carson, Brian Kelley, and Taylor, held Dallas to 41 yards of total offense in the first half. But New York was frustrated as well, when two first-half drives fizzled in missed field goals by Danelo of just 21 and 27 yards. The first half ended in a scoreless tie.

New York finally scored in the third quarter on a 20-yard Brunner pass to tight end Tom Mullady. But the Cowboys came right back with a touchdown of their own, set up by a 44-yard pass from White to Hill. The score

Charging the Eagles defense is Rob Carpenter (No. 26), acquired from the Oilers in 1981. Carpenter led New York in rushing in 1981 with 748 yards and in 1984 when he gained 795. Photo courtesy of Fred Roe.

the 9–2 Eagles. In a stirring 20–10 upset, Carpenter rushed for 111 yards, and Danelo kicked two field goals.

Five turnovers to the Super Bowl–champion San Francisco 49ers in week 13 resulted in a 17–10 loss and diminished the odds for a successful bid for the wild-card in the NFC East. But there was still hope. Teams in the other two NFC divisions, except for the leader of each, were doing poorly (as it would turn out, none of the runners-up in either of those divisions would produce a record better than 8–8), and a 9–7 season might just do it. So the Giants were faced with three must-win situations in the final games of the regular season. The team, especially the defense—and, most particularly, Lawrence Taylor—rose to the assignment. A 10–7 victory over the Los Angeles Rams and a 20–10 triumph over the St.

Dragging Pittsburgh's Mike Kruczek (No. 15) to the ground is safety Beasley Reece (No. 29), who joined the Giants in 1977 as a free agent. About to add his 255 pounds to the situation is defensive end George Martin (No. 75). Photo courtesy of Fred Roe.

was knotted at 7 until Brunner's only interception of the day was converted to a Dallas field goal.

With less than three minutes remaining in the game, Staubach completed a 23-yard pass to Pearson, who held the ball high above his head after the whistle blew. Suddenly, New York cornerback Terry Jackson reached up and knocked the ball out of Pearson's hand. "Don't ever do that again," an official yelled at Jackson, but the defender had his reasons for the move. "Drew was showing us they had the game wrapped up," Jackson said later. "I was showing him we were still in it."

With just over two minutes to play and Dallas owning a 10–7 lead and the ball, Dorsett fumbled at his own 45, and New York defensive end Martin recovered. With 30 seconds remaining in the fourth quarter, kicker Danelo faced a stiff wind and booted a 40-yarder to tie the score at 10 and send the game into overtime.

In the sudden-death extra period, New York got a big break when Taylor stripped Dorsett of the ball and then recovered the fumble. But when the Giants went for a 33-yard field goal, Danelo's kick hit the upright and bounced away. Then during the next series of downs, New York rookie linebacker Hunt intercepted a White pass and ran the ball to the Dallas 24-yard line. With the playoffs again on the line, Danelo connected on a 35-yard, game-winning field goal.

The celebration, if there was to be one, had to wait another day, however, because the Jets and Packers were scheduled to meet the following afternoon. But on Sunday, December 20, the champagne bottles were opened in the press box lounge at Giants Stadium, where the team's staff and many of the players had gathered to watch the game. In an act of intracity brotherhood, the Jets trounced the Packers, and the Giants were on their way to the playoffs.

"They had a buffet set up for us. The bar stayed open the whole time," Giants free safety Beasley Reece told *Sports Illustrated*. "Kids were running around all over the place. Everyone was trying to play it loose, pretending to eat and not show too much concern, but I can assure you that all eyes were glued to that TV set. When [Jets quarterback] Richard Todd got intercepted early, you could feel a chill come over the room. Someone got a plate of food for me," Reece continued, "but until the Jets went ahead 28–3, I couldn't tell if it was roast beef or coleslaw that I was eating. That's how tight I was."

Giants punter Dave Jennings watched the game at home. "I'm glad it wasn't thrilling," he said. "I wasn't ready for two in a row like that."

But Jennings and the rest of the Giants had to be ready to face the defending NFC-champion Eagles at Philadelphia in just seven days. With the passing of Ron Jaworski to receivers like Harold Carmichael and the running of Wilbert Montgomery, the Dick Vermeil–coached Eagles posed a formidable roadblock.

But, for the 71,611 fans in Philadelphia, the first period of the game was an unrelenting nightmare. In the opening minutes of the game, New York was forced to punt. The Eagles' Wally Henry fielded the kick, but a bone-jarring tackle by Taylor separated him from the ball. New York's Reece recovered at the Philadelphia 25. Five Carpenter runs and a short Brunner pass to back Bright gave the Giants the first score of the game, but on the point-after attempt, the snap was fumbled.

On its next possession, New York marched 62 yards in 11 plays and scored on Brunner's second touchdown pass of the first quarter, a 10-yard bullet to wide receiver John Mistler. The extra point gave the Giants a 13–0 lead. On the ensuing kickoff, Henry bobbled the catch, then was hit by New York's Mike Dennis. The ball skittered into the end zone, where it was recovered by Haynes for the third Giants touchdown in the first period.

With the score 20–0 at the start of the second quarter, the Eagles were forced to play catch-up football for the rest of the game. With two and a half minutes remaining in the first half, they finally got on the board. A Brunner pass was intercepted at the Giants' 24-yard line, and shortly after, Jaworski threw a 15-yard touchdown pass to Carmichael. But Carpenter and the Giants retaliated immediately. Carpenter carried the ball for 40 yards on four plays, and Brunner capped the drive with a

22-yard scoring strike to tight end Mullady. The score at halftime was 27–7, New York.

The Giants did not score again in the game, but there was no need to add to their points. With an oppressive defense and a ball-controlling offense led by Carpenter runs, the Giants held the Eagles to a touchdown in each of the remaining two quarters. The surprising New York Giants, minus their starting quarterback, had won the first round of the 1981 playoffs by beating the favored Philadelphia Eagles, 27 21. Carpenter finished the game with 161 yards on 33 carries, 65 yards more than Brunner gained through the air. On the defensive squad, Carson had nine tackles, Taylor had eight and a sack, and defensive end Jeter had seven and a sack.

The Giants' next obstacle was the San Francisco 49ers, who had dominated the NFC West that year with a record of 13–3. Coached by offensive wizard Bill Walsh, the 49ers had one of the game's most devastating passing attacks. Quarterbacked by Joe Montana and with receivers the caliber of Freddie Solomon, Dwight Clark, and Charles Young, they had the inherent potential of breaking any game wide open. In addition, the San Francisco defense was the second stingiest in the league that year, having given up only 250 points (the Giants surrendered only 257, third best).

A chilly, steady rain fell on Candlestick Park's natural grass on the day of the game, a condition that could affect the Giants' blitzing defense as harshly as it could San Francisco's passing game.

Walsh's plan to control New York's intimidating defense centered on minimizing Taylor's effectiveness. "They blitz him or somebody on almost every play," Walsh said. So the 49ers head coach instructed his best blocker, guard John Ayers, to cover Taylor on all pass plays. But on runs, he told his tight end, Young, to anticipate Taylor's moves and lie in wait for him. It ultimately proved to be a successful strategy.

The 49ers got out to an early lead, driving to New York's 8-yard line in the first quarter. From there Montana found Young in the end zone. But the Giants bounced back sensationally when Brunner lofted a bomb to Gray, a picture-perfect, 72-yard touchdown pass play. The 7–7 tie taken into the second quarter did not last

AN ILL-TIMED PUNCH

When the first postseason play the Giants had enjoyed since 1963 ended on January 3, 1982, in San Francisco, no one on the team felt worse than defensive end Gary Jeter. After the New York defense had forced San Francisco into a third-and-18 situation in the fourth quarter, Jeter threw a punch at 49ers lineman Dan Audick. The ensuing unnecessary roughness penalty was just what San Francisco, leading 24–17, needed. Instead of a difficult third-down situation at New York's 41, the penalty gave them a first down at the Giants' 26. It took only three more plays for the 49ers to forge a two-touchdown lead.

"He was holding me," Jeter said afterward. "The play was over and he kept pushing me down field. . . . All linemen hold, but he was holding the whole game."

"The Jeter penalty was a big break," head coach Ray Perkins said, "but there were a lot of big plays in the game." He was asked if he had talked to Jeter about the penalty. "No," he said, "not yet."

long, however. A Montana-to-Clark pass netted 39 yards and set up a Ray Wersching field goal. Rookie safety Ronnie Lott then snatched a Brunner pass to return the ball to the 49ers, and Montana quickly took advantage of the turnover by unloading a 58-yard touchdown pass to Solomon.

New York's second-quarter misfortunes continued on its next possession when Bright fumbled the ball over to the 49ers in Giants territory. Again San Francisco capitalized: running back Ricky Patton broke loose for 25 yards and another touchdown. Danelo did manage a 48-yard field goal before the half ended to reduce the 49ers' lead to 24–10.

The Giants came even closer in the third period when Brunner hit Johnny Perkins with a 59-yard touchdown pass. The New York defense held throughout the period, not ceding a single point. And near the end of it, the Giants, trailing 24–17, worked their way downfield all the way to the San Francisco 4-yard line. But

there, instead of a score, came what coach Perkins later described as "the point where the game turned." Brunner dropped back and rifled one over the middle to Gray, who, for a moment, appeared to have the game-tying touchdown in his hands. But another pair of hands, belonging to a 49ers defender, got there at about the same time and knocked the ball away.

"I just tried to put it in there low," Brunner said later. "It would have been a great catch if he'd made it, but their cornerback, Eric Wright, came in from behind and stripped the ball." As a result of the incomplete third-down pass, the Giants were forced to settle for a field goal. But they did not even get that when Danelo's 21-yard attempt banged off the upright.

"That was a big factor, not getting any points on that drive down there," coach Perkins recalled. "Especially not getting a touchdown and then missing the field goal. If we'd got a touchdown there for 24–24, we would have had the momentum going for us."

The Giants were still not out of it, especially with the defense shutting down Montana and his colleagues. But just as they forced the 49ers into an apparent third-and-18 situation at the Giants' 41, with only a touchdown separating the two teams in the fourth quarter, a crucial mistake changed San Francisco's extremely difficult situation into one of especially good fortune. After the second-down play had been whistled dead, a flag was suddenly thrown. Defensive end Jeter had lost his temper and taken a swing at a 49ers player. The resulting penalty gave the 49ers a first down. They scored three plays later. Not too many moments after that, when Lott picked off a Brunner pass for the 49ers and ran it back for a touchdown, the demise of the Giants that day was final: the score was 38–24, San Francisco.

The Giants, in effect, had been just a few big plays shy of attending the NFC championship game, and they could look back on a reasonably impressive year. Their 9–7 regular-season record, although third in the NFC East behind Dallas and Philadelphia, was good enough to capture the newly created second wild-card spot in the NFC. It was the first season above .500 since 1972. Carpenter led New York rushers with 748 yards. Simms and Brunner combined for more than 3,000 yards passing. Although he did not yet

Joe Morris (No. 20), one of the Giants' greatest running backs, moves out behind a block by Billy Ard. Morris, out of Syracuse, was New York's second-round draft choice in 1982, but did not get full-time duty until after the departure of Butch Woolfolk in 1984. The following year, his first full season as a starter, Morris set two all-time Giants rushing records by gaining 1,336 yards and scoring 21 rushing touchdowns (the latter still, by far, the most in Giants annals). He also became only the second Giant to rush for more than 200 yards in a game (204 against Pittsburgh). Photo courtesy of Fred Roe.

lead New York's defenders in tackles or quarterback sacks, Taylor was the big defensive story for the Giants. The Associated Press named him Rookie of the Year and Defensive Player of the Year as well. The professional players themselves named him NFC Defensive Rookie of the Year and NFC Linebacker of the Year. By unanimous vote, he was selected, along with veteran linebacker Carson and cornerback Haynes, for the Pro Bowl. The same three, with punter Jennings (second team), were named All-Pro.

The Giants had to savor the 1981 season. Two difficult years loomed ahead.

The strike-shortened 1982 NFL season started disastrously for the Giants when Simms, the promising but injury-prone quarterback, tore the ligaments in his knee during the second quarter of a preseason game with the Jets. Doctors determined that surgery was necessary and that Simms would be lost for the entire season. It was the third consecutive year the young quarterback was benched by injuries.

The offense again was led by Brunner, who, despite relatively unimpressive statistics, had helped the Giants reach the second round of the playoffs the previous season. Hoping to add some punch to the backfield, the Giants chose two running backs in the first two rounds of the college draft: Butch Woolfolk of Michigan and Joe Morris from Syracuse. Soon after Simms went down with his preseason knee injury, the Giants acquired reserve quarterback Jeff Rutledge from the Los Angeles Rams to back up Brunner. In July, Doug Kotar, New York's starting halfback for most of the previous seven seasons, announced his retirement.

Jeff Rutledge was obtained from the Rams in 1982 as a backup quarterback, a role in which he has continued to play well over the ensuing years. His best games were in 1983, when he started for an injured Phil Simms and threw for 329 yards against Dallas, for 349 yards against Seattle, and for 324 yards against the defending NFL champion Redskins. Photo courtesy of Fred Roe.

THE FIRST MONDAY NIGHT, GIANTS STADIUM

When Giants alumnus Frank Gifford and the rest of the ABC television crew covered the first *Monday Night Football* game ever to be staged at Giants Stadium on September 20, 1982, it was hardly a happy occasion for football fans except, perhaps, those from Green Bay. According to the NFL Players Association, there would be no more games after it until a new contract was signed to replace the one that had expired on July 15. To add to the misery of New York football fans, the Giants blew a 19–7 lead in the third quarter and lost to the Packers by the score of 27–19.

To top off everything, not one but two of the East Coast's famous power failures occurred during the game, causing delays totaling 24 minutes and darker-than-normal conditions during another portion of the game. New York's disheartening loss was the final game played in the NFL for eight weeks.

Despite amassing 378 yards of offense, including two Brunner touchdown passes to wide receiver Gray, the Giants made some critical mistakes that led to a 16–14 defeat by the Atlanta Falcons in the season opener at Giants Stadium. When the Giants lost their second game, a Monday Night fiasco against Green Bay, the NFL Players Association had already announced its strike.

The Giants came back to the Meadowlands to face the eventual Super Bowl–champion Washington Redskins at the end of the eight-week players' strike, which had forced the NFL to dramatically alter the usual rules for postseason play.

Because of the shortened season, the concept of divisions within each conference was suspended. Rather than ending the season with six conference champions and four wild-card teams, it was decided that the eight top clubs in *each* 14-team conference would be invited to postseason play. With an extra week added to the original prestrike schedule, each club would play a total of nine regular-season games. The new playoff rules gave teams such as the Giants, who had gotten off to a bad start, a chance to come back and get into the playoffs.

The Giants, unfortunately, were not ready to take advantage of the reprieve granted them by the temporary postseason rules, and they fell to Washington, 27–17, to restart their NFL season. But the next game, nicknamed the "Lawrence Taylor Show," finally put the Giants into the win column.

In that nationally televised Thanksgiving Day contest at Pontiac, Michigan, against the Detroit Lions, Taylor put on an amazing defensive display. After sitting out much of the first half because of a minor knee ailment, the sophomore sensation entered the game with the Giants trailing, 6–0. First, he blitzed the Lions quarterback and forced a hurried throw that was intercepted by Carson and set up a Danelo field goal. On the next

Bill Parcells, talking with linebacker Brian Kelley, was named the 13th head coach in New York Giants history in 1983. A former head coach at the Air Force Academy, Parcells served as defensive coordinator with the Giants before taking the top job. After a disastrous, injury-riddled first year (3–12–1), he rewrote the scenario and took the Giants to the playoffs five times and won two NFL championships, in 1986 and 1990. Photo courtesy of Fred Roe.

Detroit possession, Taylor hit running back Billy Sims hard enough to jar the ball loose. Van Pelt recovered, setting up another Danelo field goal, which tied the score at 6–6. The next time the Lions had the ball, Taylor made an almost unbelievable one-handed sack of Detroit quarterback Gary Danielson, forcing a punt. In the fourth quarter, with the game tied and the Lions on the Giants' 4-yard line, Taylor intercepted a Danielson swing pass at the 3 and ran the ball back 97 yards for a touchdown. It was the third-longest interception return in club history. Taylor had almost single-handedly won the game for the Giants, 13–6.

The Giants won their next two games, against Houston and Philadelphia, and were back in the race

for a spot in the playoffs. But on December 15, just four days before a major showdown against Washington, news from Tuscaloosa, Alabama, surprised most football fans in New York. On that day, Paul "Bear" Bryant, at the time the winningest coach in the history of collegiate football, announced that he was retiring as head man at the University of Alabama. On the very same day, the Giants' head coach, Ray Perkins, who had been an All-American end in 1966 under Bryant at Alabama, announced that he would leave New York to take over Bryant's job. Perkins explained that he had been born and raised in Mississippi and had dreamed for years of returning to the South and coaching at his alma mater: "It's just something I've wanted to do very, very much."

On the night before those big announcements, Giants general manager Young was on the phone to Wellington Mara, who was attending an NFL owners' meeting in Dallas. Young had learned of Perkins' decision two days prior and had already decided on his replacement. Young also called Tim Mara to discuss his choice with the other half of the Giants ownership. "George told me that he wanted to name Bill Parcells [an assistant coach since 1979] the next coach," Tim Mara explained. "And he told me that he wanted to announce it the same day that Ray Perkins made his announcement so that there wouldn't be weeks of speculation as to who was going to be the next coach." By promoting the former defensive coordinator to the head position, Young was making certain that the Giants avoided the publicity and infighting that had led up to his own and head coach Perkins' appointments a few seasons earlier.

"For better or worse," wrote *The New York Times'* Dave Anderson, "George Young—not the coach, not the owners, not even Lawrence Taylor—has emerged as the foundation of the Giants' future."

When the whirlwind of announcements subsided, the Giants got back to preparing for the decisive game with the Redskins on December 19. With a three-game winning streak already behind them, the Giants seemingly were on their way to the playoffs.

At Washington, the Giants built a 14–3 lead by halftime. But on a broken play in the third quarter, the Redskins scored a touchdown. And with four seconds remaining in the game, Washington's Mark Moseley kicked his then-NFL-record 21st straight field goal from 42 yards out to give the Redskins a dramatic 15–14 victory.

On December 26, New York played its next-to-last game of the season in St. Louis. With just 40 seconds left to go in the game and the Giants ahead, 21–17, the Cardinals drove 70 yards in four plays to score the winning touchdown with just seconds on the clock. The second heart-wrencher in succession all but ruined any Giants' hope for a playoff spot.

Seasoned computer analysts explained a long series of events that could make a Giants playoff berth conceivable if New York won the final game of the season, but as the team traveled to Philadelphia for the year's finale, victory was considered nothing more than a mathematical possibility in a convoluted scenario.

The Giants won the season closer, 26–24, on a Danelo field goal with two seconds left to play. "It was kind of nice to win one in the last few seconds [rather] than the other way around," said Perkins of his final

game as the New York Giants' head coach. New York had won the game, but the complicated script required for a playoff spot failed to materialize. "Coming into this game," said quarterback Brunner, "we didn't hold any high hopes that we would get into the playoffs. We just wanted to send Ray Perkins away with a win."

New York's 4–5 record was not good enough for a playoff berth, but the fact didn't quite seem as important as in previous years. After all, it was not a real season anyway, rather a kind of patched-up scramble to earn some money for players, coaches, and owners. Taylor, Carson, Jennings, and Haynes were again recognized with invitations to the Pro Bowl and given All-Pro honors.

In the first and second rounds of the 1983 draft, the Giants selected safety Terry Kinard from Clemson and a defensive end from Louisiana State named Leonard Marshall. Way down in the ninth round they picked place-kicker Ali Haji-Sheikh, who had been a walk-on at Michigan and who shortly took the job from Danelo.

But major problems developed after the final preseason game when new head coach Parcells announced that Brunner was to be the starting quarterback instead of Simms or backup quarterback Rutledge. "To say I'm disappointed is the understatement of the world," said Simms, the team's number-one draft choice in 1979.

With Brunner as the starting quarterback, New York won two out of its first five games, and Simms made it clear he was extraordinarily unhappy in his role as a backup. On October 3 he asked to be traded. "I think it would be best for me and everyone concerned if it happened," he said. "If I stay, I'll work hard. But how long can I wait? We're pretty deep into our season. They've made a commitment to Scott Brunner. They have to play him. It's been six weeks since I've had a good look at anything."

Six days later, Simms replaced Brunner in the third quarter in a game against Philadelphia at Giants Stadium. A few minutes later, the more than seventy-three thousand fans must have experienced a collective and unpleasant sense of déjà vu. There was Simms, in obvious pain, leaving the field of play, lost for the season. It was the fourth year in a row that the promising but ill-fated young quarterback was beset with season-ending injuries.

Defensive end Leonard Marshall (No. 70) is two-timed by Chicago Bears blockers Jimbo Covert (No. 74) and Mark Bortz (No. 62). New York's second-round draft pick in 1983, hailing from LSU, Marshall set a then club record with 15 1/2 sacks in 1985 and was named All-Pro and the NFC Lineman of the Year that season. Photo courtesy of Fred Roe.

Ali Haji-Sheikh (No. 6) appeared to be the answer to any and all of the Giants' kicking problems when he arrived in 1983. In his rookie season, he set an NFL record by booting 35 field goals and was honored as an All-Pro. He also set the following team records that year: most points scored (127), most field goals attempted (42), highest conversion percentage (83.3), and the longest field goal (56 yards, twice). His career was stymied by a hamstring injury in 1985, and he left the Giants after that season. Photo courtesy of Fred Roe.

The Giants defense began to take on devastating proportions in 1983. Here All-Pros Lawrence Taylor (No. 56), Leonard Marshall (No. 70), and Brad Van Pelt (No. 10) converge on Jets running back Mike Augustyniak. Photo courtesy of Fred Roe.

Butch Woolfolk, shown here high-stepping it away from a fallen Cowboy, was the Giants' first-round draft pick in 1982. A highly regarded running back from Michigan, he immediately broke into the starting lineup in that abbreviated season and won NFC Offensive Rookie of the Year honors. He led the Giants in rushing during the 1982 and 1983 seasons before being traded away midway through the 1984 season. Photo courtesy of Fred Roe.

The Giants lost to the Eagles that day and went on to win only one of their remaining ten games. The dismal 3–12–1 record sank New York into the cellar of the NFC East and gave new coach Parcells a less-than-gleeful introduction to his new job.

There were some noteworthy performances that gave hope for the future, however. Haji-Sheikh kicked for 127 points, the most ever by any Giant, with his 35 field goals and 22 extra points. He also set a team mark when he booted a 56-yard field goal against Green Bay; then he did it again a few weeks later while facing the Lions. Another rookie, defensive back Kinard, lived up to his credentials and was a welcome addition. The linebacking trio of Taylor, Brian Kelley, and Carson contributed 88, 71, and 68 solo tackles, respectively. Gray caught 78 passes for 1,139 yards, the first Giants receiver to go over the 1,000-yard mark since Homer "Rhino" Jones in 1968. Taylor and Haji-Sheikh were named All-Pro, and both, along with Carson and Haynes, went to the Pro Bowl.

The quarterback situation was still shaky as the Giants looked to the 1984 season. Rushing left a little to be desired, although Woolfolk had gained 857 yards and Carpenter another 624. "Some changes are needed," Parcells said. "And we're going to make some. We are a much better team than last year's record indicates." In 1984, he was going to prove the truth of that statement. Better times—much better times—were just ahead.

The Giants' first pick in the 1984 draft brought linebacker Carl Banks from Michigan State. As a rookie, he joined All-Pros Lawrence Taylor and Harry Carson in the linebacking corps and quickly became a mainstay there. Photo courtesy of Fred Roe.

PLAYOFFS BOUND

The year 1984 signaled the 60th anniversary of New York Giants football. A full six decades had elapsed since that day before the 1925 season when Tim Mara put his signature on the franchise papers and his money on the proverbial line to give life to his belief that the city of New York was ready to host the quite controversial sport of professional football.

The Irish bookmaker had, of course, made a good bet: by 1984 the team had a history as illustrious as any in the National Football League. There had been 17 first-place finishes in divisional play, 14 trips to the NFL championship game, three league crowns, and 11 second-place seasons. At the end of 60 years, the Giants were able to boast a regular-season record of 407–343–32, having outscored their opponents 14,062 points to 13,140.

From the Polo Grounds to Yankee Stadium to Giants Stadium, the story had been played out on plains of grass, in muddy quagmires, on snow-packed, frozen fields, and finally on a carpet of AstroTurf. Players had become legends through their deeds on those fields: Henry "Hinkey" Haines, Steve Owen, Benny Friedman, Ray Flaherty, Morris "Red" Badgro, Ken Strong, Mel Hein, Ed Danowski, Alphonse "Tuffy" Leemans, Johnny Dell Isola, Bill Swiacki, Arnie Weinmeister, Eddie Price, Emlen Tunnell, Kyle Rote, Frank Gifford, Andy Robustelli, Rosie Brown, Rosey Grier, Charlie Conerly, Sam Huff, Alex Webster, Del Shofner, and Y. A. Tittle, among the many stars. Then there were the glistenings of some novas of the eighties like Lawrence Taylor, Harry Carson, Leonard Marshall, Phil Simms, and Joe Morris.

It was only appropriate, then, that the Giants start their seventh decade with a chance at a divisional crown, something they had once done regularly, but also something they had not accomplished since 1963. New York sportswriters were cautious in their optimism; after all, the Dallas Cowboys, Washington Redskins, and St. Louis Cardinals were highly regarded in the always-tough NFC East. But Wellington Mara expressed some feeling of comfort at the club's prospects. They were turning it around, he felt, and a resolution of the quarterbacking situation and a little more support from the running game might just make the difference.

First to be culled from the draft that year was linebacker Carl Banks from Michigan State. Another first-rounder, the selection obtained from the Redskins for the Giants' second- and fifth-round choices, was mountainous (6'5", 275 pound) offensive tackle William Roberts of Ohio State. Other draftees who made the squad were quarterback Jeff Hostetler from West Virginia, linebacker

Hauling in a touchdown pass against the Eagles is Lionel Manuel (No. 86), who was drafted in 1984 and took over as a starting wide receiver late that season. In 1985, despite missing four games because of an injury, he led the team in pass receptions (49) and yards gained receiving (859). Photo courtesy of Fred Roe.

Gary Reasons of Northwest Louisiana State, offensive tackle Conrad Goode from Missouri, wide receiver Lionel Manuel from Pacific, and offensive guard David Jordan of Auburn. Two free agents caught on: wide receiver Bobby Johnson from Kansas and wide receiver/punt returner Phil McConkey of Navy. Recovered and off injured reserve were cornerback Perry Williams and offensive tackle Karl Nelson. Five of the newcomers—Banks, Reasons, Johnson, Nelson, and Williams—would earn NFL All-Rookie team honors at the end of the 1984 season.

Annual All-Pro Brad Van Pelt, discontented, got his wish and was traded to the Minnesota Vikings, who, in turn, could not sign him and traded him to the Los Angeles Raiders. As part of the first deal, nine-year veteran running back Tony Galbreath came to the Giants and would prove to be a most valuable "third-down player," coming in on those downs to pose a threat as both a runner and pass receiver.

During the preseason, coach Bill Parcells shifted the quarterbacking duties between a healthy Simms and Jeff Rutledge, both of whom looked very good in three decisive wins over the New England Patriots, New York Jets, and Pittsburgh Steelers. In fact they even stood

Running back Tony Galbreath, making a diving catch of a Phil Simms pass, came to the Giants as part of the trade that sent Brad Van Pelt to the Minnesota Vikings before the 1984 season. A threat as a running back and as a receiver, Galbreath became a highly productive third-down specialist for the Giants after having played five seasons with the New Orleans Saints and three with Minnesota. Photo courtesy of Fred Roe.

Wide receiver Bobby Johnson (No. 88) widens the gap with a stiff arm against the Cowboys after grabbing a Phil Simms pass. Johnson came aboard as a free agent in 1984, won a starting berth, and earned NFL All-Rookie honors after leading the Giants with 795 yards gained on receptions. Photo courtesy of Fred Roe.

out in a loss to the Colts, who were playing their very first game at their new home in Indianapolis.

For the opener of the regular season, Parcells decided on Simms to lead New York against the Eagles at Giants Stadium, and at the end of the 60 minutes of play, the quarterbacking situation was resolved. The blond hurler from Morehead State, now in his sixth year in the NFL and coming off several injury-riddled seasons, put on an aerial display for the hometown fans such as had never before been witnessed at the Meadowlands. In fact, its like had not been seen in the Giants' domain since Tittle dazzled the fans at Yankee Stadium with his passes one day in 1962. Hitting Zeke Mowatt, Byron Williams, and Bobby Johnson with touchdown strikes in the first half, and adding another to Johnson in the final period to secure a 28–27 victory over the Philadelphians, Simms

had the most productive day passing for the Giants in 22 years. The 409 yards (23 completions in 30 attempts) he gained passing that afternoon stood, at that point, second in Giants annals only to the 505 Tittle chalked up against the Redskins in 1962. Simms had hit Williams five times for 167 yards and Johnson eight times for 137 yards, and he also completed passes to Mowatt, Rob Carpenter, Earnest Gray, Butch Woolfolk, Galbreath, and Morris. Although they did not need it that day, Simms also connected on a 66-yard touchdown that was called back because of a penalty.

Next to arrive in New York were the Dallas Cowboys, coming off a 12–4 season in 1983, the same year they decisively beat the battered Giants twice. The scenario was considerably different in 1984, however, and again it was Simms who set the tone of the day. A 62-yard bomb to wide receiver Williams, then a 16-yard bullet to rookie Manuel, gave New York a 14–0 lead in the first period.

Dallas then got going, moving all the way to the New York 6, but there Taylor broke through and separated

Cowboys quarterback Gary Hogeboom from the football as he desperately looked for an open receiver. Linebacker Andy Headen scooped up the fumble and carried it 81 yards for a Giants touchdown and a new club record, 9 yards farther than the fumble return by Wendell Harris against Pittsburgh in 1966.

The Cowboys never got into the game. Simms connected with Mowatt for another score in the third quarter, and the Giants ended the day with a 28–7 rout of their longtime nemesis from Texas. Taylor had three sacks, two of which resulted in fumbles that the Giants recovered, and a total of nine solo tackles.

It was down in Washington, however, that the Giants were brought back to the reality of the NFL East. The Redskins, who lost only 2 of 16 regular-season games the year prior and went all the way to the Super Bowl (where they lost to the Los Angeles Raiders, 38–9), still showcased the running of John Riggins, the passing of Joe Theismann, and one of the most overwhelming defenses in the league. But the Giants might have made it three in a row if not for a disastrous fourth quarter. Going into that period, New York held a 14–13 lead, the result of a one-yard Rob Carpenter plunge for a touchdown after a concerted Giants drive in the first quarter and a Simms-to-Johnson touchdown toss in the third quarter.

It appeared the Giants were moving toward another score in the last period, but Carpenter fumbled the ball away, and the Redskins turned around and marched until Mark Moseley booted a 21-yard field goal to give them the lead. Two mistakes later—a Simms pass picked off and returned for a touchdown and a Manuel fumble snatched up and lugged for another 6 points—and the Redskins had a 17-point quarter and a 30–14 win.

The following week, however, Simms and Taylor again combined to provide the winner's edge, as the Giants slipped by Tampa Bay, 17–14. They won principally on Simms' touchdown passes to Johnson and Mowatt and Ali Haji-Sheikh's first field goal of the season. Adding to his own flair, Taylor terrorized the Bucs' quarterback, Steve DeBerg, sacking him four times.

The Giants were 3–1 and looking good, but there was still a lot of concern about the running game. Parcells mentioned, "Carpenter had good games against Dallas and Tampa [87 and 70 yards rushing respec-

tively], but that's about all we've shown in four games. We're going to have to do better than that if we want to get in the playoffs this year."

Coach Parcells should have saved that statement for the following week. Out in Anaheim, against the Rams, the Giants gained only eight yards rushing all day, six of them picked up by Carpenter on nine attempts and two by Woolfolk on three carries. The entire game was played so poorly by the Giants that the club's own public relations staff wrote of it later: "Every NFL team has a highlight film. For the Giants this one game could have constituted an entire season's lowlight film." Not only was the rushing game nonexistent, New York had three safeties recorded against them (all, incidentally, in the third quarter), setting an ignominious NFL record. Haji-Sheikh missed two extra points and a field goal; the offense allowed Simms to be sacked five times; the defense let Eric Dickerson run for 120 yards, and 84 more were gained by other Los Angeles rushers; and the Giants special team watched Henry Ellard return a New York punt 83 yards for one of the Rams' touchdowns. The final score was the Rams 33, the Giants 12.

The next week it was the Super Bowl–bound San Francisco 49ers who came to Giants Stadium and displayed what would earn them diamond-encrusted rings a few months down the line. With three touchdowns in fewer than eight minutes of the first quarter, including a 59-yard bomb from Joe Montana to Renaldo Nehemiah and a 79-yard punt return by Dana McLemore, the game was securely in the hands of the 49ers with 52 minutes still remaining. It ended with another 21-point Giants deficit, 31–10. Mara noted that there appeared now more to worry about than merely the paltry running game (95 yards total that day, not counting Simms' 22 on scrambles). Scoring, punt-return coverage, protection for Simms, and a reenergized defense were obviously some of the things discussed at the Giants coaches' meetings.

A win over Atlanta and a surprise drubbing by the Eagles left the Giants with a 4–4 record at midseason, certainly better than the 2–5–1 standing of the year before, but disappointing after the hope engendered by the first two games of the season.

To start the second half of the season, the Giants found one of the things they had been lacking. Morris, with the build and tenacity of a pit bulldog, was given the starting assignment at running back in place of Woolfolk. The 5'7", 195-pound dynamo from Syracuse, in his third year with the Giants, exploded for three touchdowns rushing against the Redskins to tie a club record (no Giant had run for three touchdowns since Mel Triplett did it against the Chicago Cardinals back in 1956). His 68 yards on 15 carries produced the kind of average Parcells had been looking for from Woolfolk and had not been able to find. But it was not just Morris who enabled New York to decimate the Redskins that day, 37–13: Simms got some protection and completed 18 of 29 passes for 339 yards, including touchdowns to Gray and Bobby Johnson.

When combined with a victory over the Cowboys the following week, 19–7, the Giants boasted a 6–4 record and were right back in the race for the division title. It was, incidentally, the first time since 1963 that the Giants swept their two games with Dallas.

A surprise loss to Tampa Bay and a win over the Cardinals gave the Giants a 7–5 record and part of a three-way tie with the Cowboys and Redskins for the NFC East crown. These were followed by triumphs over the Kansas City Chiefs and New York Jets. Suddenly the Giants were the talk of New York and New Jersey. The talk turned a bit vexatious, however, when New York managed to lose the last two games of the year to the Cardinals and the New Orleans Saints, neither of whom was favored to win. But, as it turned out, it did not really matter for the playoffs. The Redskins had clinched the NFC East before the last game of the season, and the Giants were in contention for a wild-card berth with division mates Dallas and St. Louis, all three teams having records of 9–6. If New York beat the Saints, it would have the wild-card bid by dint of its divisional record; if the Giants lost (they did, 10–3), both Dallas and St. Louis would have to lose that weekend as well, which, considerately, they did. And the Giants were playoffs bound.

The Los Angeles Rams were the NFC's other wild-card and, because of their better record (10–6), were the designated host. So two days before Christmas the Giants trotted onto the field in Anaheim, where they had been demolished and demoralized almost three months earlier.

TRIVIUM

The New York Giants played their first "road game" at Giants Stadium on December 2, 1984, a contest hosted by the relatively new tenant New York Jets. The visitors shocked the perversely partisan Jets fans by running up a 17–0 lead by the third quarter and then triumphing, 20–10, with the show being stolen by Phil Simms' passing (18 of 28 for 252 yards), Joe Morris' running (17 carries, 83 yards), and the voracious defense of Gary Reasons (17 solo tackles) and Leonard Marshall (two quarterback sacks).

Once again, the Rams were counting on the running of All-Pro Dickerson, augmented by the passing of Jeff Kemp. "We can beat them if we control Dickerson," Parcells told his Giants the week before the game. Referring to the 33–12 loss to Los Angeles earlier in the season, Mara added, "We've got to put more than 12 points on the scoreboard if we want to win."

The Giants did both that sunny day in southern California—barely. They held Dickerson to one touchdown, caused him to fumble once, and deprived him of important first-down yardage several times. And they scored 16 points. The first tally was a 37-yard field goal by Haji-Sheikh after Simms passed the Giants into position on their first possession. Shortly after that Dickerson fumbled the ball to the Giants, and Simms connected on two passes to bring the ball to the Los Angeles 1-yard line, where Carpenter dove in for a touchdown.

At halftime the Giants held a 10–3 lead, then increased it by three points with a 39-yarder from the toe of Haji-Sheikh in the third quarter. Dickerson ran 14 yards for a Rams touchdown in the same period, but then Haji-Sheikh made it 16–10 with a 36-yard field goal. The Rams came within three with a field goal of their own in the final period, but as time was winding down, Taylor burst through and sacked Kemp, causing a fumble that was recovered by the Giants' Headen. And that was it for the day: 16–13 Giants, and a trip up the Pacific coast to face the San Francisco 49ers, winner of the NFC West with a 15–1 record.

A new linebacker in 1984, Gary Reasons (No. 55) was a fourth-round draft choice from Northwestern Louisiana State. Here he wrestles an Eagles ball carrier to the turf. Reasons broke into the starting lineup in 1985 and ended that season as the third-leading tackler on the team. Giant No. 56 is fellow linebacker Lawrence Taylor. Photo courtesy of Fred Roe.

During the regular season, the 49ers had followed the Rams with a decisive defeat of the Giants, and New York was looking to deal them the same kind of turn-around justice as they had Los Angeles. But Bill Walsh's San Francisco team was flying high. It had scored an average of 30 points per game during the regular season, and its defense—the best in the entire NFL—had given up 227, an average of only 14 per game.

Just as they had back in October, the 49ers grabbed the gold at the very start. Montana, that year's All-Pro quarterback, guided a 71-yard drive early in the first

quarter, capping it with a 21-yard touchdown pass to Dwight Clark. On New York's ensuing possession, a pass from Simms bounced off the hands of intended receiver Manuel into those of 49ers defender Ronnie Lott. Moments later, Montana found tight end Russ Francis in the end zone, and San Francisco had a 14–0 first-quarter lead.

But the Giants had no thoughts of surrender that day. In the second quarter, Reasons intercepted a Montana pass, which the Giants shortly converted into three points on a booming 46-yard field goal by Haji-Sheikh. In the same period, with San Francisco backed up to its own 5-yard line, the result of a splendid punt by Dave Jennings, Montana had another pass picked off, this one by linebacker Carson, who ran it in for a touchdown.

But the two point-producing interceptions did not deter Montana. He went to the air again and moved his team down the field later in the quarter. Montana culminated the drive with a 29-yard touchdown pass to Freddie Solomon, and the 49ers had a 21–10 lead at the end of the first half.

The Giants defense solidified in the second half and held the ordinarily prolific San Francisco offense scoreless. New York had a fair share of opportunities to score during the last two periods of the game, but something went wrong each time—an interception deep in 49ers territory here, a missed field goal there—and, like their opponents, the Giants were unable to post a point in the second half. A touchdown down, the Giants were eliminated from the playoffs.

Simms threw 25 completions that day for 218 yards. Montana completed the same number for 309 yards, and three of them were for touchdowns. Montana was also the game's leading rusher with 63 yards on three scrambles. And so the 49ers went on to the Super Bowl and won the NFL championship, and the Giants went home with the consolation of having appeared in two postseason games in 1984. They were prideful of the

fact that they had given San Francisco a true scare (as no other team was able to do in that year's playoffs).

When the season's statistics were tabulated, Simms had set two New York passing records, his 286 completions being 60 more than former title-holder Fran Tarkenton (226 in 1971), and the 4,044 yards gained passing far outdistanced the 3,224 toted up by Tittle in 1962. Both linebacker Taylor and cornerback Haynes were named All-Pro. Morris and Carpenter gave evidence that the running game was taking on some form and substance. It was enough to make even the more skeptical of fans optimistic for 1985.

The Giants convened at Pace University in Pleasantville, New York, on July 15 to begin the football fiscal year of 1985. There, 97 veterans and hopefuls sweated under the hot summer sun to earn one of 45 berths on the team. Heading the list of newcomers was first-round draft choice George Adams, a running back from Kentucky, and second-round pick Stacy Robinson, a wide receiver from North Dakota State. Neither landed starting jobs that year, but

Wide receiver Stacy Robinson beats San Diego Chargers cornerback Terry Lewis on the way to establishing himself as a full-fledged Giants starter. Robinson was a second-round draft pick from North Dakota State in 1985 and played six seasons for New York. Photo courtesy of Fred Roe.

tight end Mark Bavaro from Notre Dame did later in the season.

Other rookies who made the 1985 Giants included Herb Welch, a defensive back from UCLA; Lee Rouson, a running back out of Colorado; and center Bart Oates from Brigham Young and the USFL. Other players from the USFL were punter Sean Landeta and running back Maurice Carthon.

The Giants were scheduled for five preseason games because they were to kick off the season in the now-annual Pro Football Hall of Fame exhibition game in Canton, Ohio, to benefit that organization. And to reassure those who were thinking optimistically, the Giants won all five, defeating the Houston Oilers, Denver Broncos, Green Bay Packers, New York Jets, and Pittsburgh Steelers.

The opener of the regular season brought the Eagles to Giants Stadium, and New York extended its thus-far perfect season with an easy 21–0 victory. Two touchdowns in the first quarter, both set up by Phil McConkey's kick returns of 40 and 37 yards, set the tone of the game. The Giants scored again in the fourth quarter, although it was meaningless after the defense had totally dominated the Eagles. Morris had a fine day, earning 88 yards on the ground, including two touchdowns. Marshall sacked Eagles quarterback Ron Jaworski three times, and Taylor was credited with $2^{1}/_{2}$ sacks. And everybody agreed it was a good way to start the season.

The glamour faded the next week, however, with a 23–20 loss to the Green Bay Packers. And besides the loss of the game, there was another loss of major proportions. The Giants had a number of problems going into the second game of the season. All-Pro cornerback Haynes, although healthy, had been a contract holdout and had yet to don a Giants uniform for 1985. Tight end Mowatt was lost for the season after knee surgery. Fullback Carpenter, with a bad knee of his own, had not played a minute of football thus far. And Haji-Sheikh, beleaguered by a hamstring problem earlier in the season although he had been playing, had been worrisome to the Giants coaching staff. However, the worries turned to deep concern when, after kicking a 52-yard field goal in Green Bay, Haji-Sheikh aggravated the injury to an

extent that put him on injured reserve for the rest of the 1985 season. Going into their third game of the season, the Giants had to scurry to fill a key position.

The St. Louis Cardinals, having won their first two games of the season, were on top in the NFC East when they came to Giants Stadium, but when they left were in a three-way tie with the Giants and the Dallas Cowboys. Simms scorched them with three touchdown passes, and new place-kicker Jess Atkinson added a pair of field goals for a 27–17 victory. The Giants defense was brutal enough to prompt Cardinals running back Ottis Anderson, nursing multiple bruises and scratches after the game, to tell a sportswriter, "I'm going to leave my body to science next week."

The defense was overwhelming the following week in Philadelphia as well, allowing the Eagles only three points and 168 yards of total offense all afternoon. But the Philadelphians got a touchdown late in the fourth quarter when Herman Edwards snatched a deflected Simms pass and ran it in for a touchdown to send the game into overtime. There the defense won it for the Giants when, on the second play of the additional period, cornerback Elvis Patterson, playing for holdout Haynes, intercepted a pass from Jaworski and carried it 29 yards for a touchdown.

The Cowboys came to town the next week for a special, nationally televised Sunday night game, broadcast by the trio ordinarily seen on Monday nights: Frank Gifford, O. J. Simpson, and Joe Namath (Howard Cosell having put to rest his football microphone after the previous season). Since it joined the league in 1960, Dallas had been a most annoying factor in the Giants' world. This was to be their 46th encounter, and in their preceding meetings the Cowboys had triumphed 30 times, lost only 13 games, and tied the other two. And when they left for Texas that Monday morning, they had claim to 31 victories in the series, the result of a beneficent gift by the Giants.

In the third quarter, the Giants had a comfortable 26–14 lead. And, despite an uncharacteristic lapse on the part of the defense, which allowed Dallas 10 points, New York would still have won had it not been for two fourth-quarter fumbles by Simms that resulted in two Rafael Septien field goals, the game winner being a

AND THEY LOST?

Phil Simms had his finest day as a Giant on October 13, 1985, and then the second most productive passing game of any quarterback in the history of the National Football League, when he filled the air with footballs against the Cincinnati Bengals. The 513 yards Simms gained passing were second only to the 554 Norm Van Brocklin of the Rams threw against the New York Yankees in 1951.

The 62 passing attempts, 40 completions, and 513 yards gained remain to this day Giants record performances. Rookie tight end Mark Bavaro caught 12 of Simms' passes, also a Giants record, surpassing the mark of 11 shared by Frank Gifford, Del Shofner, Doug Kotar, Billy Taylor, and Gary Shirk (since exceeded by Tiki Barber's 13 in 2000).

The Giants offense set a team record of 34 first downs in the game and an NFL all-time standard of 29 passing first downs.

New York's defense held the Bengals to a mere 199 yards of total offense in the game, including minus-3 yards of total offense in the second half.

Still, astonishingly, the Giants lost that day to the Bengals, 35–30.

Drafted in 1985 from Notre Dame, tight end Mark Bavaro gains a few yards for the Giants against the Tampa Bay Buccaneers. Bavaro made the NFL All-Rookie team that year, and the following season he led the Giants with 66 pass receptions and 1,001 yards gained receiving. Playing through the 1990 season, Bavaro ranks ninth all-time in receptions for the Giants (266 for 3,722 yards and 28 touchdowns). The Bucs defender is linebacker Keith Browner. Photo courtesy of Fred Roe.

31-yarder with approximately two minutes remaining. The 30–29 setback dropped the 3–2 Giants into a tie for second place in the division with the Cardinals and gave the Cowboys (4–1) undisputed possession of first place. The fumbles tainted the most productive passing game Simms had had in his Giants career, 432 yards on 18 completions, including two touchdowns (to Manuel and a 70-yarder to rookie Adams).

If turnovers were a problem against Dallas, they were a disaster the following week at Cincinnati. Against the Bengals, two fumbles and two interceptions "accounted for a possible swing of 28 points," Parcells noted with grim astonishment after the game, which the Giants lost, 35–30. What made it more incredible was that it occurred in the same game that Simms virtually rewrote the Giants record book with his passing, while the team's defense gave up only 199 total yards all day.

After that, however, New York cleansed the butter from its collective fingers and won the next four games in succession, defeating the Washington Redskins, the New Orleans Saints, the Tampa Bay Buccaneers, and the Los Angeles Rams. And it was partly the result of a suddenly energized running game featuring Morris.

PROMINENT DEBUT

Place-kicker Eric Schubert made his debut with the Giants against Tampa Bay on November 3, 1985. He had been cut by the team back in August, but after Ali Haji-Sheikh's hamstring injury did not get better and Jess Atkinson, who had replaced him, was released, he got a telephone call from coach Bill Parcells three days before the game with the Buccaneers. The gist of it was to get over to Giants Stadium and put on a uniform.

Schubert, who was working as a high school substitute math teacher in Wanaque, New Jersey, did as suggested and reported for duty. That Sunday, in his premier appearance, Schubert kicked five field goals to become the first player in NFL history to boot that many in his pro football debut. The kicks of 24, 36, 24, 41, and 33 yards were only one shy of the club record of six set by Joe Danelo in 1981.

And the 15 points were a substantial contribution to New York's 22–20 victory that afternoon.

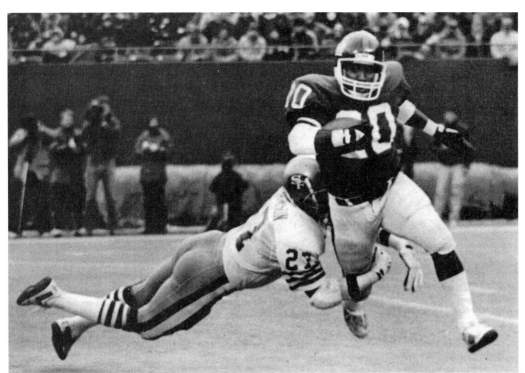

Joe Morris tries to break a tackle by diving San Francisco safety Carlton Williamson in the first game of the 1985 playoffs at Giants Stadium. Morris gained 141 yards rushing that day as the Giants defeated the defending Super Bowl champion 49ers, 17–3. Photo courtesy of Fred Roe.

On the ground is San Francisco quarterback Joe Montana, one of the four times he was sacked in the 1985 playoff game at Giants Stadium. Hovering over him are linebacker Lawrence Taylor (No. 56) and defensive end Casey Merrill (No. 71). No. 33 on the 49ers is running back Roger Craig. Photo courtesy of Fred Roe.

At the end of week 10 in the NFL, the Giants had a record of 7–3 and shared the division lead with the Cowboys. The top spot was still shared the following week when both the Giants and Cowboys lost. Despite three rushing touchdowns from Morris (56, 41, and 8 yards), tying the club record, New York was, in the words of one Giants coach, "fleeced out of it by Redskin flim-flam." He was referring to a fake punt and two unexpected onside kickoffs, the latter two converted into touchdowns that stood as significant contributions to the 23–21 win.

It was the first of a six-game, loss-win roller coaster ride for the Giants, which also saw the team slipping in and out of a tie with Dallas for the division lead. When the season finally closed, the Giants, with a record of 10–6, were actually in a three-way tie with the Cowboys and the Redskins. During that stretch, Morris became only the second Giant in history to rush for more than 1,000 yards in a season (Ron Johnson did it in 1970 and 1972). And the 21 rushing touchdowns Morris scored were not only the most in the entire NFL, but the player closest to him, Eric Dickerson of the Rams, had only 12.

The division title was awarded to Dallas because it had a better record within the division, and the wild-card berth was earned by New York because it had a better divisional record than the Redskins. And so for the second year running, the Giants were slated for postseason play as a wild-card team.

Their first opponent was the defending Super Bowl–champion San Francisco 49ers, who had ended their season with a 10–6 record, one game behind the Los Angeles Rams in the NFC West. The oddsmakers, perhaps remembering the 49ers' 18–1 record of the year before and the flashy Super Bowl rings the players sported as a result, gave San Francisco the edge. Sportswriters noted the volatile offense of the 49ers: Montana's passing to receivers Clark and sensational rookie Jerry Rice, and the presence of running back Roger Craig, who had just become the first player in NFL history to gain more than 1,000 yards each on rushing and on pass receptions.

What many pundits overlooked, however, was the New York defense, second best in the entire NFL, and

The proverbial frosting on the cake: tight end Don Hasselbeck (No. 85) holds the ball aloft in triumph after scoring the Giants' final touchdown of the day on a three-yard pass from Phil Simms in the 1985 playoffs against the 49ers. The win that afternoon enabled the Giants to go to Chicago to meet the Bears in the NFC title game. Photo courtesy of Fred Roe.

the undisputed leader in quarterback sacks (68). Another thing was the Giants' thirst for revenge after the two losses the year before, in which they had given up 31 points in the regular season and 21 in the postseason to the same San Francisco team.

Vengeance was theirs. New York allowed only three points that cold December afternoon at Giants Stadium. They sacked Montana four times and prompted Simms to say after the game, "That was the best I've ever seen our defense play." The offense was not bad either, putting 17 points on the board. Simms threw two touchdown passes to tight ends Bavaro and Don Hasselbeck, and Eric Schubert kicked a 47-yard field goal. Morris rushed for 141 yards on 28 carries. The Giants earned the right to travel to Chicago to play the Bears, the team with the best record in the NFL that year (15–1).

The Bears, of course, had the NFL's all-time leading rusher, Walter Payton. They also had the best total defense in the league; a quarterback named Jim McMahon, who got in trouble for wearing inscribed headbands and was considered something of an enfant terrible, but who had also come into his own as a passer and team leader; and a 308-pound behemoth called "the Refrigerator," William Perry, who played defensive tackle and occasionally filled in in the backfield as a rusher, pass receiver, and blocker for Payton. The latter prompted Taylor, when asked if he was worried about trying to tackle a 308-pound ball carrier, to remark, "I don't want to think about the Refrigerator. Or the stove. I'm going to throw all my appliances out of the house."

The site was Soldier Field on Chicago's lakefront, the former home of the College All-Star Game, a stadium known for its bitter cold and ice-needle winds in January. Before the game, Parcells admitted the team his Giants were to face was the most formidable one in the league. It was to be a battle of the two best defenses in the game.

With an appropriate if unappreciated pun, the Giants got off on the wrong foot when punter Landeta, trying to

A devastating force with which the Giants had to contend when playing against the Bears in the 1985 playoffs was the NFL's then all-time most productive rusher, Walter Payton (No. 34), shown here stiff-arming Lawrence Taylor (No. 56). Payton picked up 93 yards rushing that afternoon. Blocking New York defensive back Perry Williams (No. 23) is guard Mark Bortz (No. 62). Photo courtesy of Fred Roe.

Safety Terry Kinard corrals the Bears' Keith Ortego, who was returning one of New York's all-too-frequent punts in the NFC title in 1985. Kinard, the Giants' first-round draft choice of 1983 from Clemson, led the Giants secondary in tackles both in 1984 and 1985 and played for New York through the 1989 season. Photo courtesy of Fred Roe.

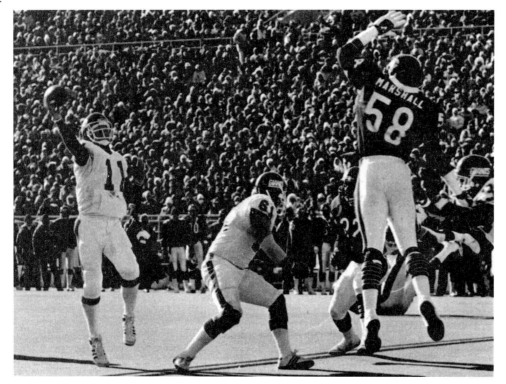

Phil Simms tries to loft one over leaping Chicago Bears linebacker Wilber Marshall (No. 58) in the 1985 NFL playoffs at Soldier Field in Chicago. Simms had a disillusioning day under the relentless attack of what was the NFL's top defense that year and completed only 14 of 35 passes (149 net yards passing, 129 of which were gained on New York's final two possessions of the game). Giants No. 61 is guard Chris Godfrey. Photo courtesy of Fred Roe.

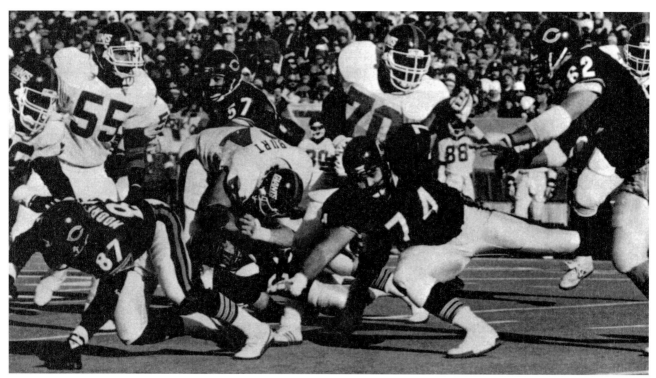

The trench, the battleground where so many games are won and lost. This one is in Chicago, where the Giants succumbed to the Bears in the 1985 playoffs. The New Yorkers waging war are linebacker Gary Reasons (No. 55), nose tackle Jim Burt (No. 64), and defensive end Leonard Marshall (No. 70); the Bears are tight end Emery Moorehead (No. 87), tackle Jimbo Covert (No. 74), and guard Mark Bortz (No. 62). Photo courtesy of Fred Roe.

kick from his own 5-yard line, only barely grazed the ball. Bears defender Shaun Gayle, who scooped it up and ran it in for the game's first touchdown, called it "a foul tip."

That was, in effect, enough to win the game for Chicago. The Bears defense totally shut down the Giants. Led by All-Pro defensive end Richard Dent (3½ sacks), Perry, and a host of other fierce and fired-up tacklers, Chicago held New York scoreless and to only 181 net yards gained all afternoon. Morris was able to gain only 32 yards, and Simms, sacked six times, completed only 14 of 35 passes. The final score was the Bears 21, the Giants 0.

Coach Parcells had been correct: the Bears were the most formidable team in the NFL in 1985. They proved that as they blithely went on to win the Super Bowl, barely contested. But the Giants had had a fine year, the best since 1963. Chicago's head coach, Mike Ditka, said later, "The Giants may have been the best all-around team we played all year."

Club records fell by the score in 1985. The Giants had found a running game and a passing game. They were a young team—25 active players with three years or less NFL experience, 15 of whom were starters—with untold promise. Among their accomplishments in 1985: they had consecutive winning seasons for the first time in 22 years; they had five players named to the Pro Bowl, the most in 22 years (Simms, Morris, Marshall, Carson, and Taylor); they had their second straight 6–2 record in games played at Giants Stadium (not counting the playoff victory); and they gave the fans good reason to look forward to the 1986 season.

RECORDS BROKEN, 1985

Individual
Most touchdowns scored: Joe Morris, 21
Most yards rushing, season: Joe Morris, 1,336
Most 100-yard rushing games, season: Joe Morris, 7
Most rushing touchdowns, season: Joe Morris, 21
Most touchdowns rushing, game (tie): Joe Morris, 3
Most passes attempted, game: Phil Simms, 62
Most passes completed, game: Phil Simms, 40
Most passing yards, game: Phil Simms, 513
Most games, 300 yards passing: Phil Simms, 11
Most pass receptions, game: Mark Bavaro, 12
Most punt returns, season: Phil McConkey, 53
Most fair catches, season: Phil McConkey, 18
Most fumbles, season: Phil Simms: 16
Most own recoveries, season (tie): Phil Simms, 5
Most own recoveries, game (tie): Phil Simms, 2

Team
Most yards gained, season: 5,884
Most yards rushing, season: 2,451
Most touchdowns rushing, season: 24
Most first downs, season: 356
Most first downs rushing, season: 138
Most first downs, game (vs. Cincinnati): 34
Most first downs passing, game (vs. Cincinnati): 29*
Most rushing attempts, season: 581
Most passes attempted, game (vs. Cincinnati): 62
Most passes completed, game (vs. Cincinnati): 40
Most yards passing, game (vs. Cincinnati): 513

* NFL record

Jim Burt (No. 64) hangs on the back of Bears fullback Calvin Thomas while safety Kenny Hill (No. 48) addresses his ankle. Adding a shoulder to the effort is linebacker Harry Carson (No. 53). But the Super Bowl–bound Bears gained 147 yards rushing to the Giants' 32, as they worked their way through the 1985 playoffs. Photo courtesy of Fred Roe.

One of the key factors in the Giants' demise in the 1985 postseason—besides, of course, the Bears' awesome defense—was a healthy Jim McMahon, here throwing one of his 11 completions of the day. The final score was Bears 21, Giants 0. Two of Chicago's touchdowns came on McMahon passes. The Giants are defensive end George Martin (No. 75) and linebacker Andy Headen (No. 54). Photo courtesy of Fred Roe.

The defense of 1986: ever-hungry, always punishing, continually relentless. Against the Eagles: George Martin (No. 75), Andy Headen (No. 54), Harry Carson (No. 53), Kenny Hill (No. 48); against the Cowboys: Lawrence Taylor (No. 56), Carl Banks (No. 58), Jim Burt (No. 64), Perry Williams (No. 23). Photos courtesy of Fred Roe.

YEAR OF TRIUMPH

The 1986 football season began for the Giants in midsummer under a bright, warm sun at their training camp at Pace University in Pleasantville, New York, and ended on January 25, 1987, under a similarly sunny sky some 2,800 miles away, in Pasadena, California. There, the midsummer night's dream of the team and the fans alike—of ultimate conquest in the world of professional football—became an eloquent and gratifying reality.

What turned out to be a joyous journey did not begin so well, however. The Giants reached the playoffs the year before, but there they were soundly shut out, 21–0, by the Chicago Bears. In 1986 the championship Bears were still intact and pundits were talking about a dynasty. And in the NFC East the Giants had brutal and talented competition awaiting them in the form of the Washington Redskins and the Dallas Cowboys, whose aspirations for a divisional title were as high as their own.

Coach Bill Parcells, in his fourth year at the helm, had a number of reservations. "In training camp I thought for a while we didn't have a chance. There were a lot of problems early on." There were some very major concerns. Pro Bowl running back Joe Morris was practicing only part time because of a contract dispute,

and there was talk of his sitting out the season. Lawrence Taylor had treatment for chemical abuse, although no one talked about it, and there was some concern that the problem might have an adverse effect on his future performance. Jim Burt was suffering from back problems that threatened his season. Running back George Adams had a chipped pelvis and would spend the year on the injured-reserve list. "And most of our high draft choices," Parcells pointed out, "reported late and didn't have a clue to what we were doing."

Others, however, were not quite so skeptical. An especially prescient Anson Mount, in *Playboy* magazine's pro football preview, predicted not only that the Giants would go to the Super Bowl, but that they would win it all at that spectacle by defeating the Denver Broncos. "This will be the year of the Giants," he wrote. "There are no obvious weaknesses anywhere. Quarterback Phil Simms has matured, the offensive line may be the best in the league, and the running game, with Joe Morris and George Adams, will be spectacular. Best of all is that the Giants are a stable franchise, with no internal bickering or jealousies."

Paul Zimmerman, writing for *Sports Illustrated*, offered an identical prognostication: the Giants to defeat the Broncos in Super Bowl XXI. "A good blocking line, a

As he did so often in 1986, Mark Bavaro gathers in a Phil Simms pass, this one against the San Diego Chargers. Bavaro caught five passes for 89 yards that September afternoon as the Giants dealt San Diego a 20–7 defeat. No. 54 on the Chargers is linebacker Billy Ray Smith. Photo courtesy of Fred Roe.

big booming fullback, Maurice Carthon, knocking people over for Morris . . . it's a good formula," he observed, "and it gets even better when the defense comes out and absolutely stuffs people."

It certainly did not look like a year of triumph for the Giants, however, when they left Texas Stadium in Irving after the first game of the regular season. On Monday night, September 8, 1986, before a national television audience, New York fell to the Cowboys and found themselves starting out in the cellar of the NFL East.

New York's highly regarded defense gave up 31 points that night, the most they would yield the entire season. But the offense made a game of it. Trailing 14–0 in the second quarter, the Giants bounced back with touchdown passes from Simms to Bobby Johnson and

Stacy Robinson. They even took the lead, 21–17, in the third quarter, when Morris bulled in from the 2-yard line, and again in the final period, 28–24, after Simms connected once more with Johnson on a 44-yard touchdown pass. New York's problem, however, was Herschel Walker, making his NFL debut after Tony Dorsett left the game with a sprained ankle. The most famous player from the dormant USFL averaged 6.4 yards on each of his 10 carries and scored touchdowns on 2 of them, the last a 10-yard burst up the middle with little more than a minute left in the game to give the Cowboys a 31–28 victory.

The fans who worried about New York's once vaunted, but lately seemingly leaky defense had their concerns wiped away at Giants Stadium the following Sunday. To kick off the season in New Jersey, the Giants defenders held the high-powered offense of the San Diego Chargers to a single touchdown and the Chargers' ordinarily prolific quarterback, Dan Fouts, to a mere 19 completions in 43 attempts. New York also intercepted five passes.

Simms gained exactly 300 yards on his 18 completions, one of them a touchdown toss to Lionel Manuel,

Stacy Robinson, very alone, awaits a Phil Simms pass in the 1986 game against New Orleans. Robinson gathered in four of Simms' passes that day for 66 yards as the Giants rallied to beat the Saints, 20–17. Photo courtesy of Fred Roe.

and Morris rushed for 83 yards, with one of his carries taking him into the end zone for his second touchdown of the season. Those scores, along with two field goals, were enough to give New York its first win of the year, 20–7. The most intimidating figure on the field that day was safety Terry Kinard, who was credited with six tackles, two interceptions, and a fumble recovery, which earned for him the honor of being named the NFC defensive player of the week.

Next on the agenda was a game in Anaheim, California, against another volatile offense, that of the Los Angeles Raiders, which featured the passing of

Jim Plunkett and the running of Marcus Allen. But the defense was again up to the challenge and allowed the Raiders only three field goals, holding Allen to a mere 40 yards rushing, and sacking Plunkett three times. Simms threw two touchdown strikes to Manuel in the second half, and that was enough for a 14–9 win. Morris registered his first 100-yard game of the season that afternoon when he picked up 110 yards on 18 carries.

Back at Giants Stadium the following week New York fans were astonished to find their team trailing the ordinarily lackluster New Orleans Saints 17–0 in the first half. Unfortunately for New Orleans, there was enough time remaining for the Giants offense to tote up 20 points and for the defense to definitively shut down the Saints. New place-kicker Raul Allegre booted two field goals, and Simms added two touchdowns to his

stats, hitting Bavaro with a 19-yarder and Zeke Mowatt on a 4-yarder.

At the quarter mark of the season, New York could boast a three-game winning streak and a record of 3–1, good enough, however, only for a second-place tie with the Cowboys behind the undefeated Redskins.

For their next assignment the Giants traveled to St. Louis to face the team that Jimmy "the Greek" Snyder predicted would win the Super Bowl. So far, however, the Cardinals had failed to win a regular-season game. A crowd of approximately forty thousand fans watched the ill-starred Cards extend their losing record to 0–5, as the Giants, with a 13–6 victory, moved to 4–1. The New York defense was especially effective that day, allowing St. Louis only 241 net yards and two field goals, and sacking Neil Lomax seven times. Carl Banks was credited with 10 tackles and two sacks, and Taylor and Leonard Marshall each had 6 tackles and two sacks.

If the Giants offense was a little on the quiet side in St. Louis, it came roaring back in the more obliging confines of Giants Stadium the next Sunday. There, the Philadelphia Eagles, under new coach Buddy Ryan

(best known for designing and guiding the defense of the Super Bowl–champion Chicago Bears the preceding year), were witness to New York's most productive offensive output of the season. In fact, the 35 points they tallied would be the most all year until the hapless Green Bay Packers showed up for the last game of the season. In addition, the defense was the stingiest it would be until the playoffs, giving up only a lone field goal.

Morris got things going by breaking loose on a 30-yard touchdown run, and Simms followed with a 4-yard scamper to give the Giants a 14–3 lead at halftime. In the third quarter, Simms hit wide receiver Solomon Miller for another touchdown. Then, a few minutes later, after a Giants drive stalled at the Eagles' 13, Allegre lined up to kick the field goal. But his foot never touched the ball. Holder Jeff Rutledge surprised everybody in the stadium by grabbing the ball and flipping it to linebacker Harry Carson, in the game supposedly to block but lined up as a legal receiver, for a 13-yard touchdown. Simms added the fifth and final touchdown of the day with a 37-yarder to running back Lee Rouson. The final: Giants 35, Eagles 3. Taylor, proving why he was a

The braintrust: Phil Simms on the field, Bill Parcells on the sideline. Photo courtesy of Fred Roe.

perennial All-Pro, was credited with nine tackles and four sacks.

There was some additional good news from down Dallas way. The Cowboys stunned the hitherto undefeated Redskins, 30–6, and so New York, now 5–1, moved into a tie for first place in the NFC East.

Residence at the top was short-lived, however. The Giants traveled out to the Kingdome in Seattle, where Simms experienced one of his most disappointing games in some time. Sacked seven times, he netted only 190 yards passing and was intercepted four times. The Giants managed a 9–7 lead at intermission, but the Seahawks regained the lead with a field goal, then converted an interception into a touchdown, the ball eventually lugged in by Kurt Warner. The final score found the Seahawks on top, 17–12, and the Giants back in a second-place tie in their division with the Cowboys, one game behind the Redskins.

Jeff Rutledge (No. 17) and Harry Carson (No. 53) admire the football they teamed up to use on a fake field goal against the Eagles that resulted in a touchdown. Holder Rutledge grabbed the snap, rolled up and out, and lobbed the ball to the ordinarily linebacking Carson, who was in the backfield to block, for a 13-yard touchdown. Carson earned his way to the Pro Bowl in 1987 for the eighth time in nine years. Photo courtesy of Fred Roe.

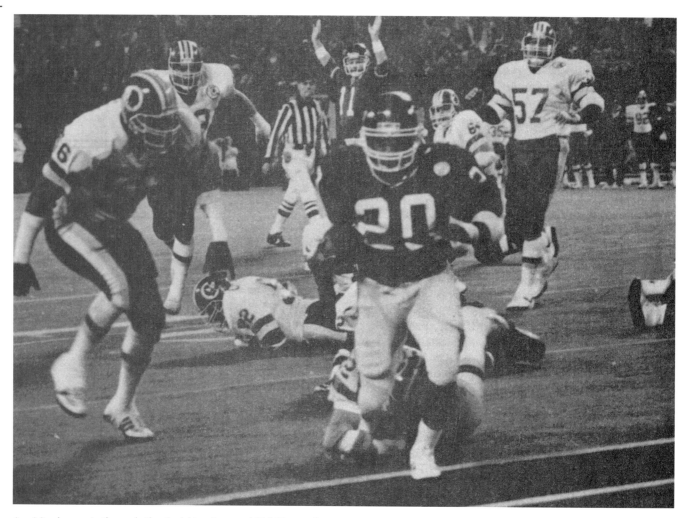

Joe Morris erupts through the Redskins line, and Phil Simms, in the background, signals touchdown, one of two Morris scored that day. Morris gained 181 yards rushing while the Giants racked up the first of three victories over the Redskins during the 1986 season. Photo courtesy of Fred Roe.

The stage was set for a most important confrontation, a nationally televised meeting on Monday night, October 27, 1986, between New York and the Redskins at the Meadowlands—a game that caused many football fans who were also following the seventh game of the World Series between the Red Sox and the Mets to spin their dials back and forth all night.

Allegre got the Giants off on the right leg, so to speak, by kicking a 37-yard field goal in the first quarter. Morris added six more points when he carried the ball 11 yards into the end zone. Another Allegre field goal and the Giants had a 13–3 halftime lead.

It appeared that the game might be taking on blow-out proportions in the third quarter when Simms connected with Johnson on a 30-yard touchdown pass to extend the lead to 20–3. But an unintimidated Jay Schroeder brought the Redskins back with a phenomenal passing performance (420 yards), racking up 17 unanswered points and tying the game late in the final period.

The Giants, however, launched a drive of their own, starting from their 19-yard line. With a little more than a minute and a half left in the game, they reached the Redskins' 13-yard line. There, Morris broke loose and carried the ball in for the winning score. The final: Giants 27, Redskins 20. And in the NFC East there was a three-way tie for the lead because Dallas had destroyed the Cardinals that weekend. Each of the leaders was sporting a record of 6–2.

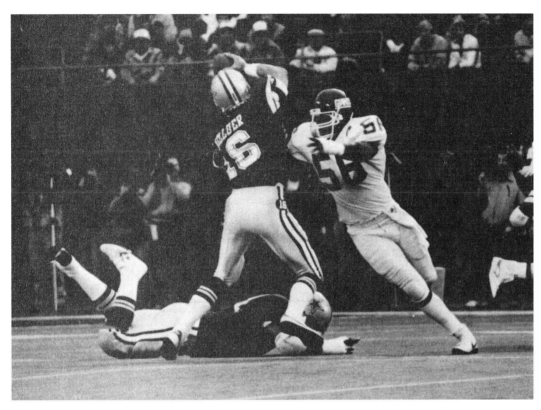

Accolades were merited in various corners that Monday night. Morris, who gained 181 yards on 31 rushes and added another 59 on pass receptions, was named the NFC offensive player of the week. Simms completed 20 of 30 passes without a single interception. And the defense was highlighted by Banks' 10 solo tackles, while Taylor was credited with six tackles and three sacks.

Six days later the Giants faced another formidable obstacle on the path to the playoffs. Dallas was coming to town in the hope of knocking New York back into second place in their division. The Giants, needless to say, wanted revenge for their opening-night embarrassment at the hands of the Cowboys, and all were aware of the heated three-team division race in which they were involved, one where a single loss might later prove to be disastrous for their playoff hopes.

Once again Allegre got the Giants off to a three-point lead in the first period with a 25-yarder. The Cowboys snatched it back the following quarter when Steve Pelluer, quarterbacking for Danny White, who had left the game with a broken thumb after a Carson sack, pitched a touchdown to Mike Renfro. But the Giants responded with a march that culminated in an eight-yard touchdown run by Morris, and it was 10–7 at the half.

Simms was having his worst day of the year (at day's end his stats would register just six completions in 18 attempts, for a negligible 67 yards), and so it was left to the Giants defense and Morris' running power to maintain control of the game.

Another touchdown by Morris in the fourth quarter, on a 6-yard run, gave New York a 10-point lead, but it was countered by a 23-yard touchdown run by Dorsett. Then the Giants gave the ball up to the Cowboys, who began a drive that they hoped would win the game in the closing minutes. Fortunately for New York, Dallas was slowed by several penalties, and when Rafael Septien attempted a desperate 63-yard field goal, it fell short. The final score was Giants 17, Cowboys 14.

Morris had certainly done his job, rushing for 181 yards and two touchdowns. And the defense had held Dorsett to 45 yards rushing and Walker to 34. Responsible for 13 tackles, Carson was the feature.

New York was not alone at the top, however, Washington having slipped past Minnesota, 44–38, in overtime. But what the Giants could boast of was a share of the best record in the NFC, 7–2, along with Washington, the Chicago Bears, and the Los Angeles Rams.

The Giants were a heavy favorite to beat the Eagles, their next opponent—after all, there had been a 32-point margin in their first encounter. But many of the Giants may have looked beyond the Eagles to what lurked in the ensuing four weeks: Minnesota (5–4 and in definite contention for a wild-card berth), Denver (8–1, the best record in the NFL), San Francisco (5–3–1 and battling for a playoff bid), and another confrontation with Washington.

Whatever the reason, the Giants looked lackluster in the first period that early November afternoon in Philadelphia. Neither team showed any sort of offense during the first 15 minutes, but Morris broke loose for an 18-yard touchdown run in the following quarter, and Allegre added a field goal to give the Giants a 10–0 lead at the half. Another Morris touchdown, a three-yard run in the third period, brought the score to 17–0, and every-

thing seemed wrapped up and ready to take home. But in the final period the Eagles came to life, as Randall Cunningham teamed with wide receiver Mike Quick on a 75-yard touchdown pass, then led an 87-yard march that culminated in another touchdown when he snuck the ball in from the 1. That was the scoring for the day, however, and the New Yorkers escaped with a three-point victory and a lesson in mortality and vulnerability.

Another lesson and another escape awaited them the following Sunday at the Metrodome in Minneapolis in what would prove to be one of the Giants' two most exciting games of the season. The Vikings, two games behind the Bears in the NFC Central and in a desperate duel with at least two teams from the East and West for a wild-card spot, truly needed to win the game. They were geared to stop the run: "Controlling Morris is the key to stopping the Giants, that and getting some points on the board against that defense," said Minnesota's new head coach, Jerry Burns.

And the Vikings did control Morris, holding him to a mere 49 yards on 18 carries. What they neglected to take into consideration was the talented toe of Allegre and the arm of Simms. In the first quarter, Allegre kicked his first field goal of the day, a 41-yarder. The Vikings responded in kind. Then Allegre booted a 37-yarder, but the Vikings came back with another of their own. The former Colts kicker then sent the Giants to the locker room with a 9–6 lead by kicking his third field goal of the day. Minnesota took the lead in the third period on a Tommy Kramer touchdown pass, but the Giants recaptured it with Allegre's fourth field goal and a 25-yard touchdown pass from Simms to Johnson.

Another Minnesota touchdown pass in the fourth quarter gave the lead back to the Vikings, 20–19. Then, with less than two minutes remaining in the game, it appeared that the Giants' last drive was stalled at their own 48-yard line on fourth down with a distant 16 yards to go for a first down. But Simms dropped back, found Johnson, and delivered the ball to him for a 22-yard gain. Five plays later, with 12 seconds on the clock, Allegre was perfect with a 33-yarder, and the Giants made their escape, 22–20.

Allegre's five field goals were one short of the club record set by Joe Danelo against Seattle in 1981, and Allegre was 15 of 21 for the season. "I feel like I'm involved in the team now," he said after the game. "I feel like I've made a contribution." Also contributing substantially that day, and much of the reason Allegre got close enough to kick his five field goals, was Simms, who completed 25 of 38 passes for 310 yards. Bavaro and Johnson caught four each for 81 and 79 yards, respectively.

Denver was still on top of the AFC West with a record of 9–2 when they came to the Meadowlands to meet the Giants. John Elway was getting rave reviews for his work at quarterbacking the Broncos, and running back Sammy Winder was on his way to leading the AFC in touchdowns scored. The game would prove to be the second of the Giants' two most heart-stopping encounters of the 1986 season, and the cast of heroes would be just about the same.

New York never trailed in the game, but with less than two minutes to go the score was tied, 16–16. Facing a third-and-21 situation at their own 18-yard line, once again Simms rifled it to Johnson for a first down. He followed that with a 46-yard pass play to Phil McConkey. Then, with six seconds remaining, Allegre again took center stage and drilled a 34-yarder to give the Giants a 19–16 triumph.

Allegre was successful with four field goals that afternoon, and Simms, although he registered only 11 of 20 passes for 187 yards, was perfect when he needed to be. Morris rushed for 106 yards. But perhaps the play of the day occurred when 255-pound, 33-year-old defensive end George Martin picked off an Elway swing pass and galloped 78 yards for a touchdown. It was Martin's sixth touchdown, an NFL record at the time for a defensive lineman. The smiling veteran of many football wars during his 14-year career with the Giants said of the feat, "When I caught the ball it was a bright sunny day. By the time I got to the end zone it was partly cloudy." Other defensive stalwarts of the day included Banks, who made 11 tackles, and Carson, who chalked up 10.

With the season three-quarters of the way over, New York had a record of 10–2—by far their best record since the championship years several decades earlier. But they still were not alone at the top of their division, for Washington was battling them win for win. The only other teams in the NFL to sport as good a record were

Brad Benson, the Giants Pro Bowl–bound tackle in 1986, was named NFC offensive player of the week after his performance in the second Washington game of the season, in which he blocked NFL sack leader Dexter Manley (17½ at the time) all day and held him to no sacks and just three tackles. The Giants won the game, 24–14. It was the first time in NFL history that a lineman was so honored. Photo courtesy of Fred Roe.

the defending NFL champion Bears and the surprising New York Jets.

Meeting San Francisco marked the Giants' third Monday night game of the season, and at the end of the first half it appeared to the national television audience that New York's five-game winning streak was about to come to an end. A remarkably recovered Montana, whose back surgery in September left questions as to whether he would ever play football again, led the 49ers on three sustained drives that resulted in a field goal and two touchdowns. And the San Francisco defense was devouring Morris (he gained only 14 yards on 13 carries that evening).

The second half was another story, a more-than-total reversal. Suddenly it was Simms engineering the drives. The first ended with a 17-yard touchdown pass to Morris, the next with a 34-yard scoring toss to Robinson. The third, set up by 49-yard completion to Robinson, was a simple 1-yard plunge by Ottis Anderson, the veteran running back acquired from St.

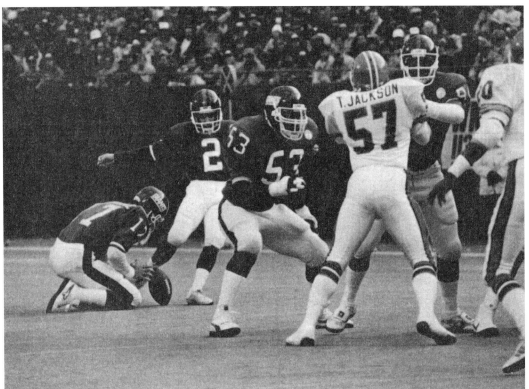

Raul Allegre puts toe to ball and drills one of the four field goals he kicked against the Denver Broncos in 1986. The 12 points he put on the board were instrumental in the Giants' 19–16 win that day, the winning margin of 3 points coming on his 34-yarder with less than one minute remaining in the game. Allegre's 105 points scored was seventh best in the NFL in 1986. No. 53 on the Giants is Harry Carson, and the holder is Jeff Rutledge. Photo courtesy of Fred Roe.

George Martin (No. 75) celebrates with nose tackle Jerome Sally after Martin picked off a Denver pass and carried the ball 78 yards for a Giants touchdown. It was Martin's sixth touchdown as a defender, an NFL record at the time. In his 12th year as a Giant, Martin was the oldest member of the Super Bowl champs. Photo courtesy of Fred Roe.

The NFL's Most Valuable Player of 1986, linebacker Lawrence Taylor (No. 56), has a Redskins running back in his crosshairs. Besides tackling Washington runners, he led the league in quarterback sacks with 20½. Photo courtesy of Fred Roe.

Louis a few weeks earlier. While all this was going on, the Giants defense completely shut down Montana and his fellow 49ers. The final score: 21–17, Giants.

This victory set up a showdown with the Redskins, who were tied with the Giants with an 11–2 record. Both teams were comfortably ahead of the 7–6 Cowboys. Washington had the home-field advantage, and in that city of extraordinarily loyal and fervid fans, it was indeed a distinct advantage.

Nothing happened in the first quarter, at least as far as the scoreboard was concerned. In the second period, Simms clicked with two scores, a nine-yard touchdown toss to Bavaro and one for seven yards to Johnson, to give the Giants a 14–7 edge at intermission. In the second half, Allegre added a field goal and Simms teamed with McConkey for Simms' third touchdown pass of the day. And the defense was simply overwhelming. A desperate Schroeder was forced to throw 51 passes, 6 of which were intercepted by the Giants, and on four other occasions he was sacked. The Redskins' rushing attack was held to 73 yards, and the usually volatile George Rogers picked up only 22 yards on 10 carries. It was a masterful game for both offense and defense, and, with the 24–14 victory, the Giants in 1986 had sole occupancy of the top floor of the NFC East for the first time.

The following two weeks were exercises in ennui. A 27–7 beating of the hapless St. Louis Cardinals (4–11–1 in 1986, to prognosticator Jimmy "the Greek" Snyder's ultimate chagrin) and a 55–24 annihilation of the even more hapless Green Bay Packers (4–12) ended the

Mark Bavaro (No. 89) snares a Phil Simms pass and carries it in for one of the two touchdowns he scored in the last game of the 1986 regular season against Green Bay. The Giants posted their season-high point total that December day as they routed the Packers, 55–24. The other Giants in the picture are center Bart Oates (No. 65) and tackle Karl Nelson (No. 63). Photo courtesy of Fred Roe.

Joe Morris made it happen in 1986: 1,516 yards, the most ever gained rushing by a New York Giant up to that time. Photo courtesy of Fred Roe.

Coach of the Year Bill Parcells makes a point from the sideline—and whatever points he made during the 1986 season certainly were effective, as the Giants rolled up a record of 17–2 and took the NFL title. Looking on are Harry Carson (No. 53), Phil Simms (No. 11), and Jeff Rutledge (No. 17). Photo courtesy of Fred Roe.

Giants' regular season with a nine-game winning streak and the most victories, 14, in the team's long history.

It was the New York Giants' first divisional title since 1963, and the long drought was finally over. It was also a record-breaking year of major proportion.

Morris had virtually rewritten the rushing-record log by gaining 1,516 yards on 341 carries and was the second most productive runner in the entire NFL, trailing only Dickerson of the Rams. Simms, who completed 259 of 468 passes for 3,487 yards and 21 touchdowns, ranked fourth among passers in the NFC with a rating of 74.6. Bavaro was the club's leading receiver with 66 receptions for 1,001 yards. Landeta was the top punter in the NFC with an average of 44.8 yards for his 79 punts. And Allegre was the fifth-highest point scorer in the

NFC, his total of 105 coming from 24 of 32 field goals and 33 of 33 extra points. Taylor led the league with 20½ sacks. The team's top tacklers in 1986 were Banks, with 120 (87 solos and 33 assists), and Carson, with 118 (87 solos and 31 assists).

Parcells was named NFL Coach of the Year, and Taylor was named NFL Defensive MVP. And a total of eight Giants earned their way to the Pro Bowl: Bavaro, Brad Benson, Burt, Carson, Landeta, Marshall, Morris, and Taylor.

With the best record in the NFC, and more wins within their division than the Chicago Bears, who also posted a 14–2 record, the Giants earned the home-field advantage for both playoff games—provided, of course, they triumphed in the first. They had to get by the San Francisco 49ers, whom they had come from behind to beat 21–17 during the regular season.

Montana said before the game that the 49ers were ready, hungry to redeem themselves. Coach Walsh was a little wary and expressed his concern

The hometown fans at Giants Stadium are informed of an honor well earned just before the team and Lawrence Taylor took on the San Francisco 49ers in their first playoff appearance of 1986. Photo courtesy of Fred Roe.

about the Giants' awesome defense, which he had seen firsthand. The Giants were a favorite, no doubt about it, but there was a lot of talk about the high-flying, ever-explosive 49ers, who had beaten three top teams (Jets, Patriots, and Rams) to round out their regular season.

The game, however, was a portrait of systematic destruction, with the final score 49–3. New York's offense was as imposing as its defense, a monstrous combination that led Parcells to say, "Not a perfect game, but it was pretty close to it." It did not look that way at the start, however, when Montana connected with Jerry Rice on a short pass and Rice broke loose. He streaked for the goal line with the Giants secondary in pursuit, only to fumble the ball in midstride. The Giants recovered it in their own end zone. After the game one of the 49ers was asked what would have been the outcome if Rice had not

fumbled. His reply was that "the final score would have been 49–10."

The Giants began with a touchdown pass from Simms to Bavaro in the first quarter and ended with New York's seventh touchdown in the third quarter. The defense limited the 49ers to a single field goal all day, holding Montana to a mere 98 yards passing before he left the game with a concussion. His replacement, Jeff Kemp, was held to 64. The entire San Francisco rushing attack gained only 29 yards all afternoon.

The Giants were on their way to the NFC title game. An all-time-record crowd turned out at Giants Stadium to watch New York take on the Washington Redskins for the third time of the season. The Redskins, a wild-card entry in the playoffs, got to the conference championship by defeating the Los Angeles Rams, 19–7, and then upsetting the defending title holders, the Chicago Bears, 27–13.

Despite defeating the Redskins twice during the regular season, Parcells was far from overconfident: "The Redskins are the best team we played this year," he told

New York sports reporters. "I thought they would beat the Rams in the wild-card game, and they did. I thought they would have a good shot against the Bears, and they beat them. A month ago Lawrence Taylor told me it was going to be us and the Redskins for the championship, and he was right."

As the two teams convened on the field in the Meadowlands, a poster showing a heart pierced by a Giants blue arrow said it all:

> The arrow that points to Pasadena
> Passes through the heart of Washington

The afternoon was a cold one, and winds gusted at about 30 miles per hour. Parcells knew the wind would wreak havoc on both the passing and kicking games. He felt the advantage lay clearly with the team that could

run, score first, and force the other team to throw the football. And he had extraordinary faith in his defense—the best in the NFL in 1986, most agreed. So when the Giants won the coin toss, the instructions were to kick off instead of receive to put the wind at their backs. It was a surprise to the more than 76,600 fans in the stands, and it was a tactic that, if it had backfired, would come back to forever haunt the head coach and his staff.

It did not, of course, backfire. And the defense lived up to their coach's expectations. The Giants stopped the Redskins summarily, and the Washington punt into that stiff Meadowlands wind carried only 23 yards. The Giants moved the ball to a position where Allegre, blessed by the same wind, kicked a 47-yard field goal. Again the Giants held, and again the Redskins had to punt. The wind held the second kick to 27 yards.

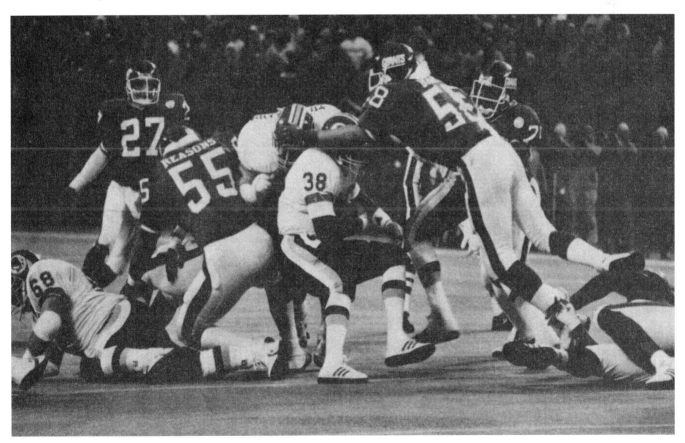

To say the least, the Giants defense was up for the Redskins in the NFC championship game. Here linebacker Carl Banks (No. 58) pummels Washington running back George Rogers (No. 38) to the turf. New York held the Redskins scoreless and limited them to 40 yards rushing and only 190 yards total offense all day. Other identifiable Giants are safety Herb Welch (No. 27) and linebacker Gary Reasons (No. 55). Photo courtesy of Fred Roe.

Lionel Manuel (No. 86) is all by himself in the end zone, happily taking possession of an 11-yard Phil Simms pass in the first quarter of the NFL title tilt with Washington. The Giants added another touchdown and a field goal to give themselves a 17–0 triumph and a ticket to Super Bowl XXI. Photo courtesy of Fred Roe.

Starting from an excellent field position, Simms moved the Giants down to the Washington 11-yard line, where he culminated the drive with a touchdown pass to Manuel.

In the second period, Washington had the wind, but they bobbled away the advantage. First Gary Clark got behind the Giants secondary and Schroeder threw a picture-perfect bomb that stunned Redskins fans when it went through the ordinarily sure hands of the team's top receiver of 1986. Then, after the Redskins moved the ball to the New York 34-yard line (but were held short of a first down), on the snap for the field-goal attempt the ball went through the hands of holder Schroeder and bounced to the Washington 49-yard line. From there Simms hit tight end Bavaro for a 30-yard gain and eventually moved the Giants to the Washington 1. From there Morris carried it in on a slant.

The halftime score of 17–0 remained unaltered through the following two periods. The Giants defense was as niggardly as Parcells had hoped (and believed) it would be. The Redskins were held to 40 yards rushing and 150 yards passing. Schroeder completed only 20 of 50 passes and was sacked four times. As he explained afterward, "We lost the game in the first quarter. We got behind, couldn't make the plays, and their defense was in control."

The next stop on the Giants' barreling express: the Rose Bowl in Pasadena, California. The event: Super Bowl XXI.

By the time the Giants deplaned in sunny Southern California, they were booked as 9½-point favorites over the AFC champion Denver Broncos. After conquering the AFC West with a record of 11–5 (one of those losses, of course, to the Giants), the Broncos disposed of the AFC East champs, the New England Patriots, 22–17, and then slipped past the AFC Central champion Cleveland Browns, 23–20, in overtime.

After a week of hype and hoopla, mammoth press conferences and media blitzes, and a pregame show that

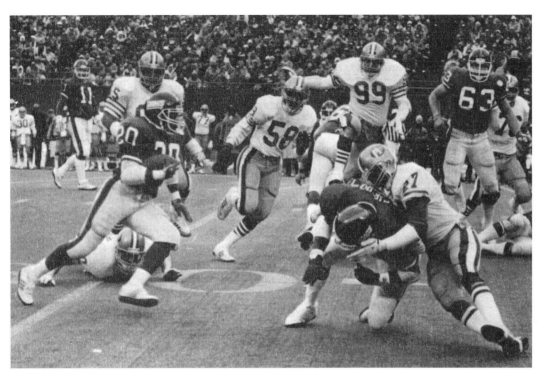

What helped Joe Morris (No. 20) gain 1,516 yards rushing in the regular season, 246 yards in two playoff games, and another 67 in the Super Bowl were shattering blocks like this one delivered by tandem running back Maurice Carthon. Morris gained 159 yards rushing as the Giants destroyed the 49ers, 49–3, in the NFC divisional playoff game. Other Giants in the picture are Phil Simms (No. 11), and Karl Nelson (No. 63). The luckless recipient of Carthon's block is safety Carlton Williamson. Photo courtesy of Fred Roe.

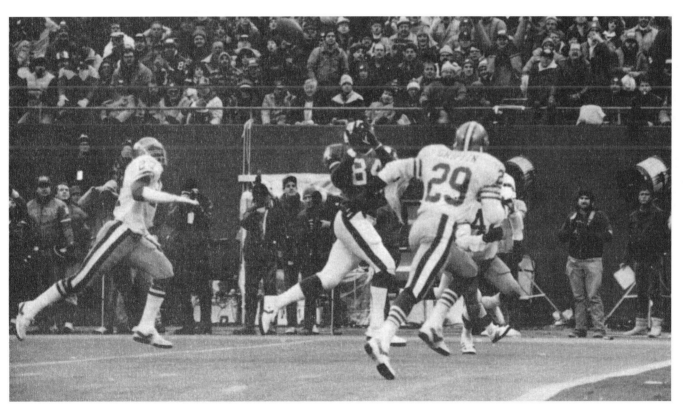

Zeke Mowatt (No. 84) gathers in a Simms pass and goes in for the Giants' sixth touchdown of the day against the 49ers. A seventh was added a little later, and, with a 49–3 victory, the Giants were in position to take on the Washington Redskins for the NFC title. San Francisco defenders are Carlton Williamson (No. 27) and Don Griffin (No. 29). Photo courtesy of Fred Roe.

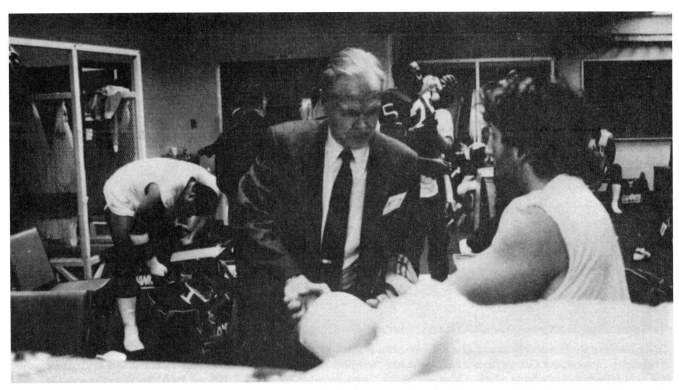

Club president Wellington Mara congratulates Mark Bavaro in the locker room after the Giants prevailed in the NFC East. They took the title and looked forward to their first Super Bowl appearance. Photo courtesy of Fred Roe.

An enthusiastic, ebullient Jim Burt joins his fans in the stands after the Giants' decisive conquest of the Washington Redskins, which gave them their first conference championship since 1963. Photo courtesy of Fred Roe.

NFC CHAMPIONSHIP GAME

Scoring

	1	2	3	4		T
Redskins	0	0	0	0	—	0
Giants	10	7	0	0	—	17

Giants   Allegre, 47-yard field goal

Giants   Manuel, 11-yard pass from Simms (Allegre extra point)

Giants   Morris, 1-yard run (Allegre extra point)

Individual Statistics

Rushing—*Redskins*: Bryant 6 for 25 yards, Rogers 9 for 15, Schroeder 1 for 0; *Giants*: Morris 29 for 87 yards, Carthon 7 for 28, Anderson 1 for 3, Rousson 1 for 2, Galbreath 1 for 1, Simms 7 for 2.

Passing—*Redskins*: Schroeder 20 of 50 for 195 yards; *Giants:* Simms 7 of 14 for 90 yards.

Receiving—*Redskins*: Monk 8 for 126 yards, Bryant 7 for 45, Warren 3 for 9, Griffin 1 for 8, Didier 1 for 7; *Giants:* Carthon 3 for 18 yards, Manuel 2 for 36, Bavaro 2 for 36.

would have impressed even P. T. Barnum, the captains of the Giants and the Broncos stood at midfield of the fabled Rose Bowl for the coin toss to launch the game that would determine the NFL champion of the 1986 season. Denver won the toss and, with no cyclonic winds in Southern California, chose to receive. Elway moved the team deftly. The Broncos' Rich Karlis, with a 48-yard field goal, put the first score of Super Bowl XXI on the board.

The Giants responded with an impressive march of their own. With Simms completing passes to Manuel, Bavaro, Morris, and Robinson, plus runs of 11 and 8 yards by Morris, the Giants moved from their own 22 to the Denver 6. From there Simms rifled one down the middle to Mowatt in the end zone, and the Giants took the lead.

In what was turning out to be a very offense-oriented game. Elway marched his Broncos back down the field. On third-and-goal from the 4, he surprised the Giants and just about everybody in the Rose Bowl by running a draw up the middle from the shotgun formation for a touchdown.

In the second quarter, however, scoring was not the name of the game. Denver was able to move the ball, but kicker Karlis, who had booted 20 of 28 field goals during the regular season for one of the best percentages in the league, missed a 23-yarder and a 34-yarder. The only score of the period came when old vet Martin broke through and chased Elway down in the end zone for a safety. At the half the Broncos clung to a fragile 10–9 lead.

Whatever Parcells had to say in the locker room while Walt Disney Productions entertained the halftime crowd with an extravaganza in which more than two thousand performers took part, or whatever super-adrenaline osmotically infiltrated the Giants players during the intermission, it produced a vibrant and violent Giants team that easily controlled the second half.

After Rouson returned the second-half kickoff to the 37, the Giants were stymied on fourth down and one at their own 46-yard line. But from punt formation, the Giants suddenly shifted on the Broncos' special team, and Rutledge moved up to take the snap from center and quarterback-sneaked the first down. After that, Simms completed four passes, the last of which a 13-yard strike to Bavaro for a touchdown, to give the Giants a lead they would not relinquish.

In the same period, Allegre added a 21-yard field goal. And Simms, who was playing one of the finest games of his career, stunned the Broncos with a flea-flicker, 44-yard pass to McConkey that brought the ball to the Denver 1. From there Morris carried it in for the score on the next play. The New York defense was equally aroused, not giving up a single first down, much less a score. By the end of the third quarter the Giants had a comfortable 26–10 lead.

To start the fourth quarter, New York cornerback Elvis Patterson picked off an Elway pass. And just to show that bad times sometimes run in streaks, a Simms pass to Bavaro in the end zone fell incomplete, but

Phil McConkey is about to make a key catch here for a 46-yard gain with less than a minute to go against the Broncos in the 1986 regular season. With the game tied, Simms' pass to McConkey set up the game-winning field goal by Raul Allegre. No. 45 on Denver is cornerback Steve Wilson. Photo courtesy of Fred Roe.

Denver was called for pass interference, which gave the Giants a first down on the Denver 1. Further proof of that maxim came three plays later when a Simms pass bounced off Bavaro's hands in the end zone and deflected into McConkey's.

Denver's Karlis managed a 28-yard field goal to bring the score to 33–13, Giants, but his onside kick-off failed. The Giants quickly took advantage of it and moved the ball down to the Denver 2-yard line, most of the yards coming on an 18-yard run by Rouson and a 22-yard bootleg by Simms. Anderson then bulled it in for the Giants' last score of the day.

With just over two minutes left, Elway connected with Vance Johnson on a 47-yard touchdown play, but the game was far out of reach by that time. When the gun finally sounded in the gray twilight of the Rose Bowl, the score stood New York Giants 39, Denver Broncos 20.

The Vince Lombardi Trophy, the symbol of professional football's ultimate

The symbol of ultimate triumph in the modern NFL. The Giants own two of them, for Super Bowls XXI and XXV.

A new tradition: Harry Carson, Gatorade, and a drenched coach Bill Parcells. Photos courtesy of Fred Roe.

triumph, belonged to the Giants. For the first time since 1956, the Mara family could claim an NFL championship. And Giants fans in New York, New Jersey, Connecticut—and everywhere else for that matter—were ecstatic.

Simms, who set two Super Bowl, records by completing an incredible 22 of 25 passes, 10 of which were consecutive, was the obvious choice for Super Bowl XXI's MVP award. Victory came, however, on the legs and shoulders of an entire team that combined an explosive offense with a magnificent defense and iced it with determination and spirit.

With more than 100 million people in the United States witnessing the team's splendid victory and with coverage by television or radio for fans in countries as diverse as China and England, it can surely be said that the Giants had added a handsome and rich landmark to the odyssey that began that Sunday back in 1925 when Tim Mara, on the sidewalk outside Our Lady of Esperanza Church, said, "I'm gonna try to put pro football over in New York today."

SUPER BOWL XXI, TRIUMPH AT THE ROSE BOWL

January 25, 1987, Rose Bowl, Pasadena, California
Attendance: 101, 063

New York Giants		Denver Broncos
Offense		
Lionel Manuel	WR	Vance Johnson
Brad Benson	LT	Dave Studdard
Billy Ard	LG	Keith Bishop
Bart Oates	C	Bill Bryan
Chris Godfrey	RG	Mark Cooper
Karl Nelson	RT	Ken Lanier
Mark Bavaro	TE	Clarence Kay
Stacy Robinson	WR	Steve Watson
Phil Simms	QB	John Elway
Joe Morris	RB	Sammy Winder
Maurice Carthon	RB	Gerald Wilhite
Defense		
George Martin	LE	Andre Townsend
Jim Burt	NT	Greg Kragen
Leonard Marshall	RE	Rulon Jones
Carl Banks	LOLB	Jim Ryan
Gary Reasons	LILB	Karl Mecklenberg
Harry Carson	RILB	Ricky Hunley
Lawrence Taylor	ROLB	Tom Jackson
Elvis Patterson	LCB	Louis Wright
Perry Williams	RCB	Mike Harden
Kenny Hill	SS	Dennis Smith
Herb Welch	FS	Steve Foley

	1	2	3	4		T
Broncos	10	0	0	10	—	20
Giants	7	2	17	13	—	39

Touchdowns—*Broncos*: Elway, V. Johnson; *Giants*: Mowatt, Bavaro, Morris, McConkey, Anderson.

Field goals—*Broncos*: Karlis (2); *Giants*: Allegre.

PATs—*Broncos*: Karlis (2); *Giants*: Allegre.

Safety—*Giants*: Martin, tackled Elway in end zone.

Joe Morris was the Giants' leading rusher in the strike-shortened 1987 season, compiling 658 yards after the regulars resumed play in weeks seven through fifteen. Photo courtesy of Getty Images.

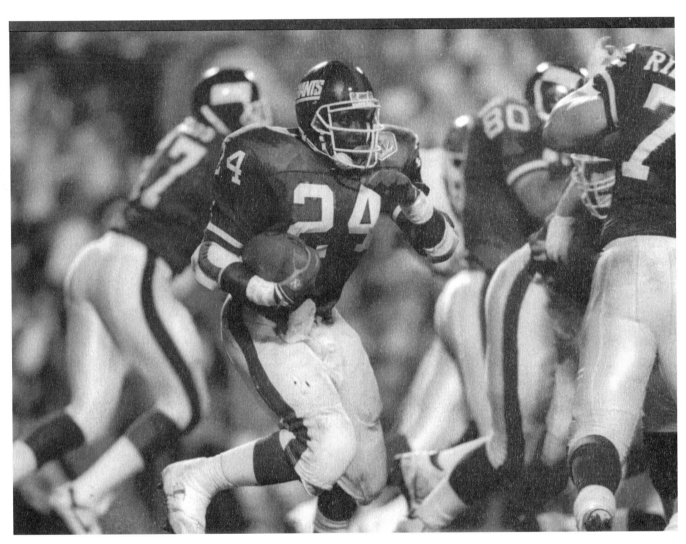

After seven and a half memorable seasons in St. Louis, running back Ottis Anderson came to New York and added six and a half more years to his career, including a 1,000-yard rushing season in 1989. Photo courtesy of Getty Images.

A STRUGGLE BACK TO THE TOP

If 1986 was a season to remember for the Giants and their fans, 1987 was one to forget, not just for Giants fans but for fans throughout the National Football League. At least most of that year, anyway. Despite a huge new set of television contracts with ABC, CBS, and NBC, and a brand new one with cable television's ESPN bringing multimillions of dollars to NFL franchises, the football season got off on the proverbial wrong foot.

After the second game of the season, the National Football League Players Association called a strike, and the games scheduled for the third week were cancelled. Play was resumed in the fourth week but, to the universal disenchantment of professional football fans, with replacement players for those on strike. The replacement-player teams took the field for the next two weeks as well, but finally, on October 25, 1987, the strike was settled and the players returned for week seven.

For the Giants, the reigning NFL champions, it was not only disheartening but downright disastrous. They had lost the first two games with their Super Bowl ring–bearing roster to the Bears by the embarrassing score of 34–19 and to the Cowboys, 16–14. Then, with replacement players, they lost the next three to the 49ers, 41–21, and the Redskins, 38–12, and finally an overtime loss to the Buffalo Bills, 6–3.

The Giants turned things around somewhat when the seasoned players returned for week seven, but it was really too late. They posted six wins against three losses to end the year with a 6–9 record, leaving them in the cellar of the five-team NFC East, their worst showing since 1983. Joe Morris led the team in rushing, gaining 658 yards, an average of 3.4 yards per carry. Once again Mark Bavaro was Phil Simms' favorite target, catching 55 passes for 867 yards and eight touchdowns. Simms was 163 of 282 for 2,230 yards, 17 touchdowns against nine interceptions, his 90.0 quarterback rating the highest thus far in his Giants career. Terry Kinard picked off five passes and returned them for 163 yards, the most yardage since Dick Lynch gained 251 on interceptions back in 1963. Lawrence Taylor had the most sacks—12. And despite the team's dismal showing, four players won All-Pro honors and invitations to the Pro Bowl: Taylor, Bavaro, Harry Carson, and Carl Banks.

The Giants were beginning to look like the team of 1986 as they breezed through the preseason of 1988 winning three of the four warm-ups and then opening the season at Giants Stadium with a 27–20 victory over the Redskins (the reigning NFL champions who had demolished Denver 42–10 back in January at Super Bowl XXII). All the franchise-player names were still there:

Taylor, Simms, Morris, Carson, and Leonard Marshall. Lionel Manuel and Stephen Baker had become fixtures at wide receiver. Eric Dorsey, out of Notre Dame and in his third year with the Giants, had taken over as defensive left end, and Pepper Johnson, from Ohio State and also in his third year with the club, had won the left inside linebacker slot.

What followed the successful preseason, however, was a roller coaster ride that lasted through the first six games of the season. After the heartening win over Washington, the Giants fell to San Francisco, 20–17, slipped by Dallas, 12–10, and then lost what would prove to be a crucial game in determining the playoff picture at the end of the regular season to the Los Angeles Rams, 45–31. To round out the roller coaster ride, New York again defeated the Redskins, 24–23, only to fall to Philadelphia, 24–13, one week later.

Starting with week seven, however, the Giants got on track, winning their next four games in a row, defeating Detroit twice, Atlanta, and Dallas. At 7–3, New York was very much in the race for the NFC East title. Their only clear competition was the Philadelphia Eagles. Then two losses followed, first to Phoenix then, in overtime, to the Eagles. Still, with Philadelphia having its own problems late in the season, three ensuing New York victories brought the race down to the last game of the season. With a record of 10–5 for the Giants, putting them one game ahead of the 9–6 Eagles, a win over the New York Jets would clinch the divisional title for the Giants. The Jets had won only seven games that year, had no chance to get into the playoffs, and were a decisive underdog that mid-December afternoon. But they didn't play like it, and to the chagrin of the Giants franchise and fans, the Jets pulled off a 27–21 upset.

With the Eagles winning that day, both Philadelphia and New York ended the regular season with records of 10–6, but the title went to the Eagles by dint of the fact that they had beaten the Giants twice during the year. And to make matters even worse, the Los Angeles Rams, runner-up in the NFC Western Division with a record of 10–6, got the wild-card berth as a result of having defeated the Giants in the fourth game of the regular season. So New York, with its best record since the Super Bowl year of 1986, had managed to play themselves out of the playoffs in 1988.

Morris regained his rushing eminence after the mediocre performance in 1987, becoming the first Giants running back ever to post three 1,000-yard rushing seasons when he gained 1,083 on 307 carries, a still mediocre average of 3.5 yards per carry. He also surpassed the club's all-time rushing record of 4,638 yards that had been set by Alex Webster back in 1964 (Morris' new record was 5,296). Manuel went over 1,000 yards receiving for the first (and only) time in his New York career, gaining 1,029 on 65 receptions, both team highs that year. Simms had a quarterback rating of 82.1, earned by completing 263 of 479 passes for 3,359 yards, with 21 touchdowns against 11 interceptions.

On defense, Taylor, to no one's surprise again led the team in quarterback sacks with 15½, winning his eighth-straight All-Pro recognition and eighth-straight invitation to the Pro Bowl. Marshall accounted for another eight sacks, and George Martin had 7½. Rookie cornerback Sheldon White, from Miami (Ohio), picked off the most passes—four—and returned them for 70 yards. Safety Kinard intercepted three while earning his first invite to the Pro Bowl.

Despite some outstanding individual performances, it was a truly disappointing season. The two defeats by Philadelphia, the wild-card-deciding loss to the Rams, and the upset by the Jets on the last Sunday of the regular season left the Giants and their fans unfulfilled and their postseason hopes dashed.

Still, it could be said that the Giants' 10–6 season in 1988 was a step in the right direction; 1989 would prove to be an even larger step in that annual quest for the Super Bowl.

There were some changes for the 1989 season. With Morris to miss the season with an injury, the rushing duties fell to 32-year-old Ottis Anderson in his third full year in New York after seven and a half memorable seasons with the St. Louis Cardinals. All-Pro tight end Bavaro would go down with a knee injury in the seventh game of the season and be replaced competently—but not by a player of All-Pro caliber—by Zeke Mowatt. In the fifth round of the draft, however, the Giants picked up running back David Meggett from Towson State, who would have an immediate impact on special teams.

Consummate pro Harry Carson earned his ninth and last trip to the Pro Bowl in 1987. Photo courtesy of Time Life Pictures/Getty Images.

The Giants again won three of their four preseason games, and again defeated Washington in the season opener, this time by a score of 27–24. But there was no roller coaster ride at the start of the 1989 regular season as there had been the year before. New York won the next three games in a row, and won them decisively, defeating Detroit 24–14, the Phoenix Cardinals 35–7, and Dallas 30–13. It was New York's best start since 1968, when they also won their first four straight. A squeaker of a loss to Philadelphia, 21–19, was the only spoiler in the first half of the 1989 season because the Giants bounced right back to win their next four in a row. They downed Washington again, this time by a score of 20–17, went out to San Diego to beat the Chargers 20–13, returned to the Meadowlands to clip the Vikings 24–14, and then whipped the Cardinals in Phoenix 20–13.

Tight end Mark Bavaro's 55 receptions in 1987 contributed to one of Phil Simms' better years statistically, but the team still struggled to a 6–9 record. Photo courtesy of Getty Images.

With a record of 8–1 in the first week of November, New York was comfortably on top of the NFC East, but Philadelphia and Washington were still very much in the running for the divisional crown. Then, things began to go terribly wrong. The Rams, who were desperately fighting the 49ers for the NFC West title, embarrassed the Giants in Los Angeles, allowing them only 10 points while scoring 31 themselves. New York rallied to defeat Seattle the following week, 15–3, but then returned to the West Coast for another drubbing, this time at the hands of the 49ers, 34–24. Another loss in week 13, to the Eagles 24–17 at the Meadowlands, left New York with a worrisome 9–4 record. But Bill Parcells got his Giants revved for the final run for the divisional crown. They beat the Broncos in Mile High Stadium, 14–7, then returned to Giants Stadium to knock off the Cowboys, 15–0, and the Los Angeles Raiders, 34–17. Their record of 12–4 was enough to give New York its second divisional title in four years. Philadelphia, with a record of 11–5, won a wild-card berth. But it was the Rams that the Giants were destined to face in the 1989 postseason,

Linebacker Carl Banks, in the snow at Denver's Mile High Stadium, became a force on the Giants' vaunted defense in the late eighties. Photo courtesy of Getty Images.

Dave Meggett amassed 1,807 all-purpose yards during the Giants' playoff season of 1989, including 582 yards on punt returns for a 12.7 average. Photo courtesy of Getty Images.

the same team that had decisively defeated them back in the first week of November.

The regular season had been a pleasant surprise. With Morris, Bavaro, and several other veterans out for either all or most of the year, it proved to be a year of overcoming adversity. And one of the key components in that effort was running back Anderson, filling in admirably for Morris by gaining 1,023 yards and scoring 14 touchdowns rushing. Another was rookie Meggett, who amassed a total of 1,807 all-purpose yards: 582 yards on punt returns (a 12.7-yard average), both club records; 577 yards on kickoff returns (a 21.4-yard average); 531 yards on pass receptions, including four touchdowns; and another 117 yards rushing. Simms had a good year as well, although he was beset by injuries through much of it and had to sit out two games; his quarterback rating was 77.6, but he was also an essential rallying force throughout the season. He completed 228 of 405 passes for 3,061 yards and 14 touchdowns. Odessa Turner caught the most passes: 38 for 467 yards and four touchdowns. Manuel hauled in another 33 passes for 539 yards and one touchdown.

On the defensive side, safety Kinard picked off five passes, returned them for 135 yards, and one for a touchdown. Cornerback Perry Williams and linebacker Johnson intercepted another three each. Once again Taylor led the team in sacks, 15 in 1989, with Marshall adding another 7½, nose tackle Erik Howard 5½, and linebacker Carl Banks 4.

The NFC playoff game was scheduled for January 7, 1990, at the Meadowlands. The Giants had not had home-field advantage when they fell so dramatically to the Rams during the regular season. Los Angeles, which ended the year three games behind the 49ers in the NFC West, had now to face the Giants before 77,025, most of whom were die-hard New York fans. And it appeared that having the home field was a factor. The Giants controlled the game through the first quarter, dominating possession of the ball and scoring twice on field goals by Raul Allegre, 35 and 41 yards respectively. But with the second period winding down and the Giants still seemingly in command of the game, a costly Giants turnover jarringly changed things in Giants Stadium. And with only seconds to play, Rams quarterback Jim Everett found

rookie wide receiver Willie Anderson and connected on a 20-yard touchdown toss. With the extra point, the Rams had a 7–6 halftime lead.

The Giants regained the lead in the third quarter after a drive resulted in Ottis Anderson carrying the ball in from the 2-yard line. But New York fans saw the 13–7 lead dissipate in the final period of play. Two field goals by Mike Lansford tied the game to send it into overtime. Then Everett again hooked up with Willie Anderson, this time on a 30-yard touchdown pass, to win the game and eliminate the Giants from the playoffs.

It was a disappointing conclusion to a season in which the Giants posted the second best record in the NFL. But it was going to get better the next year; in 1990 it was going to get infinitely better.

The preseason was a harbinger of what was to come as the Giants waltzed through the four games without a loss—the first time they had swept the warm-up games since 1985. Then began one of the most deliciously memorable seasons in Giants lore. New York defeated the Eagles in the regular-season opener at the Meadowlands, a team to which they had fallen in their last four encounters. They then went on to win their next nine games in a row. The 10–0 start in 1990 was the best in the team's then 66-year history (and still is).

Against Philadelphia in the opener, Simms exhibited all the finesse and productivity that was to mark one of his finest years as the Giants quarterback, although an injury would cut it short in the 14th week of the season. He rallied the Giants from a 10–6 deficit with a 12-yard touchdown pass to Rodney Hampton in the third quarter and a 41-yarder to Mark Ingram in the final period. That, along with a 68-yard punt return for a touchdown by Meggett and a pair of field goals from Allegre, was enough to give New York a 27–20 victory.

At Dallas the following week, with the temperature 96 degrees under a blazing Texas sun, the game was a breeze. After marching down the field on their first possession only to fumble the ball away at the 1-yard line, Simms led a 72-yard drive on the Giants' second possession and carried the ball in for the score himself from the 4-yard line. Another drive on the next possession was culminated with Ottis Anderson bucking it in from the 1. The Cowboys' Alex Wright returned the ensuing kickoff

90 yards for a touchdown, but that would prove to be Dallas' only score of the day. In the second half, Simms teamed with Bavaro on a 4-yard touchdown pass, and Taylor picked off a Troy Aikman pass and returned it 11 yards for the final score of the day: Giants 28, Cowboys 7.

Miami, whom the Giants had not encountered since 1972, the year the Dolphins, for the only time in NFL history, went undefeated through 17 regular-season and postseason games, was the next victim. Quarterbacked by Dan Marino, Miami was among the best of the AFC and destined to see postseason play in 1990. But the New York defense held the Dolphins to a mere 158 total yards, only 39 rushing, and just seven first downs. Anderson, who was the day's leading rusher with 72 yards, scored twice on short-yardage plays, and Allegre booted two field goals to give the Giants a 20–3 win.

The Cowboys then came to Giants Stadium and did not fare any better than they had down in Texas Stadium. After Aikman fumbled a snap and the Giants recovered the ball, Simms took six plays to put the first touchdown of the day on the scoreboard, a 12-yard pass to Ingram. Dallas got a field goal, but the Giants countered with one of their own from the toe of Matt Bahr, who was replacing the injured Allegre. Shortly thereafter Simms led the Giants on a 60-yard drive, capping it with a 7-yard pass to tight end Bob Mrosko. The lead at halftime was 17–3. Dallas began the second half with a touchdown, and the Giants remained quiet all of the third quarter. But the fourth quarter was all New York. Simms led a 72-yard drive, the last play of which was a 27-yard touchdown pass to Hampton. After the Giants intercepted Aikman, Jeff Hostetler came on for the resting Simms and added a final score by running it in from 12 yards out. The final: Giants 31, Cowboys 17.

The Giants' biggest test of the 1990 season came the following week in Washington. The Redskins had a collective eye on the NFC East crown and hoped to change the way things had been going between the two teams: the Giants had won the previous five encounters. Washington got on the scoreboard first with a field goal, but New York responded moments later with a spectacular 80-yard touchdown pass from Simms to wide receiver Baker. That was all the scoring in the first half.

The 'Skins started the second half with another field goal, but Simms responded almost immediately with a pass to Bavaro that covered 61 yards. A few plays later Anderson carried it in for a touchdown. Washington responded with a little razzle-dazzle, a 31-yard touchdown pass on a halfback option play from Earnest Byner to Ricky Sanders. Simms again came right back: a pass to running back Maurice Carthon netted 63 yards followed by a 2-yard pass for the touchdown. At the end of the third quarter the score was 21–13, but that was quickly reduced when the Redskins mounted a drive early in the fourth quarter that resulted in a touchdown to bring them within a single point. But Bahr clinched it late in the quarter with a 19-yard field goal. New York extended its winning streak over the Redskins to six games and its 1990 regular-season record to 5–0.

The Phoenix Cardinals came to Giants Stadium next. One of the weakest teams in the conference—they would win only five games that year—they gave the New Yorkers a very big scare. With Simms leaving the game early with an injury, Phoenix took a 16–10 lead into the fourth quarter and increased that to 19–10 with a field goal. With time ticking away and the Giants deep in their own territory, it looked like New York's perfect record was about to be marred. Hostetler, filling in for Simms, moved the team methodically up the field and into Cardinals territory. Then he connected with Baker on a 38-yard pass play, a touchdown that brought New York to within two points. The Giants defense held and, with less than two minutes remaining, forced Phoenix to punt. From his own 29, Hostetler, working the two-minute drill to perfection, moved the ball to the Phoenix 22. With four seconds remaining Bahr booted a 40-yarder to sustain New York's undefeated season. The final score: 20–19.

New York then continued its dominance over the Redskins by dispatching them easily, 21–10. Then, over the next three weeks, the New York defense, anchored by everyone's All-Pro linebacker Taylor, allowed only 14 points in three games. In the first of them, the Giants turned a 17–0 halftime lead into a 24–7 victory over the Indianapolis Colts, the defense holding All-Pro running back Eric Dickerson to just 26 yards rushing (the Colts gained only 55 yards on the ground and 160 in the air that afternoon). Out in Anaheim the following week, New York wreaked revenge on the Rams for the back-breaking loss that cost the Giants a playoff berth in 1989 by whipping them soundly, 31–7, with a touchdown pass from Simms to Bavaro and touchdown runs by Hampton, Anderson, and Lewis Tillman. Then, to round out the 10-game winning-streak, New York hosted the Detroit Lions and inhospitably shut them out, 20–0, with safety Greg Jackson turning in the best day of his career: eight tackles, one sack, and one forced fumble. The Giants defense as a whole limited All-Pro running back Barry Sanders to only 69 yards rushing.

The next week, however, the vaunted New York defense collapsed in Philadelphia, and with it ended the Giants' unprecedented, season-starting run of 10 straight victories. The Giants saw a 7–0 lead turn into a 31–13 disaster by day's end. Philadelphia ran all over them that day, gaining 176 yards rushing and another 229 on Randall Cunningham's passes, two of which were for touchdowns.

On the first Monday in December, the best teams in the National Football League collided in San Francisco. The Giants and the 49ers, both dominating their divisions in the NFC, captured the attention of football fans throughout the country. Simms was quarterbacking New York, and Joe Montana led the 49ers. Roger Craig carried the ball for San Francisco, and Anderson and Hampton toted it for the Giants.

It had all the makings of a most explosive game, but it was anything but that. Everything was decided by the two defenses. Neither team scored in the first quarter. In the second period New York got the ball on their own 44-yard line and moved it down to the San Francisco 3-yard line, where they had a first-and-10 situation. Three times they were thwarted, however, and had to settle for a Bahr field goal. Montana came right back, leading a drive that was highlighted by a 31-yard pass to Craig and culminated with a 23-yard touchdown pass to John Taylor. Both teams again were scoreless in the third period. In the fourth quarter, the Giants, down 7–3, had their chance. Simms engineered a drive that started at the Giants' 35-yard line; at the 49ers' 9-yard line, they had a first-and-goal. Needing more than a field goal, Simms passed on each of the four downs but could not put a score on the board. The game ended with the same score as the first half had ended, 7–3, San Francisco. Simms was just 14 of 32 for 153 yards, and Montana only 12 of 29 for 152 yards.

New York was brought back to the harsh realities of NFL football. The Giants' record, after two road losses, was 10–2 at the three-quarter mark of the 1990 season.

The Meadowlands proved to be much more gratifying as more than 76,100 fans turned out to watch their team take on the Minnesota Vikings. A sloppy first half left the Giants on the wrong end of a 12–10 score at the intermission. The Vikings extended their lead with a field goal in the third period, but the fourth quarter was all New York. Safety Jackson picked off a Rich Gannon pass that resulted in a 48-yard field goal by Bahr and brought the Giants to within two points of the Vikings, 15–13. The New York defense held and got the ball back in good field position. Simms then led a drive that ended with Anderson blasting in from the 2 to give the Giants their first lead of the day, 20–15. Linebacker Gary Reasons then stole another Gannon pass, and Bahr kicked a field goal to sew up the game. The final: New York 23, Minnesota 15.

Buffalo, sporting the best record in the AFC, came to Giants Stadium the next week. Some suggested that the game was the coming attraction for Super Bowl XXV about six weeks down the road. And the teams looked like Super Bowl–bound teams—in the first half anyway. After the opening kickoff, Simms guided the Giants on a 71-yard drive, 41 of which were picked up on a run by Hampton. The Bills responded in kind. Jim Kelly marched the Bills 74 yards, capping it with a touchdown pass to Andre Reed. Buffalo marched again in the second quarter, and Thurman Thomas bucked in from the 2-yard line to give the Bills a 14–7 lead. Before the half, however, Bahr booted a field goal. Also before the half, Buffalo quarterback Kelly went down with a knee injury and left the game for good. In the third quarter, Giants quarterback Simms suffered a game-ending and, as it turned out, season-ending injury to his right foot. Behind their reserve quarterbacks, both teams floundered, although the Bills were able to pick up a field goal in the final period while New York came up empty-handed. And so the Giants incurred their third loss of the season, 17–13.

Phoenix, which almost upset the Giants in week six of the season, hosted the Giants two days before Christmas and gave them another scare in a game that was not decided until the last two minutes. Hostetler was in charge, having replaced Simms, and he performed admirably, leading two drives in the first half. The first ended with a Bahr field goal, and the second with a two yard touchdown run by Hampton. The Giants had a 10–7 halftime lead. In the third quarter Hostetler hit Ingram with a 44-yard touchdown bomb, but the Cardinals came right back with a touchdown of their own. In the fourth quarter Hostetler led another drive, 63 yards, the last 4 of which he carried the ball in for New York's last touchdown of the day. But again Phoenix came back with a score of its own with just over two minutes left in the game. Phoenix then recovered its onside kick and suddenly the Giants appeared to be in trouble. But the Giants defense held, as did the 24–21 score.

Back on the right track, the Giants traveled to Foxborough, Massachusetts, to take on the hapless New England Patriots (who would end up 1–15 that year), and found more than they had thought they would. The Patriots played a tenacious game, and the Giants did not. All the scoring came in the first half: the Giants scored on a Hostetler-to-Meggett pass and two field goals by Bahr. New York's 13 points were 3 points more than New England could put on the board.

So the 1990 regular season came to a close. The Giants, with a record of 13–3, were three games ahead of the Eagles and the Redskins and could lay claim to their second-consecutive divisional title. The 13 triumphs were the most for New York since the Super Bowl season of 1986, when they won 14 games.

Simms, who had recorded his best performance ever as a New York quarterback, a rating of 92.7 (184 completions for 2,284 yards or 59.2 percent, and 15 touchdowns against only four interceptions), would remain on the sideline with his injured foot throughout the playoffs. Quarterbacking responsibilities were now firmly in Hostetler's hands. He produced a quarterback rating of 83.2 in the 2½ games he had held sway at the end of the regular season. A competent ball carrier when he had to be, Hostetler had engineered several important drives in those games.

Giants backs had rushed for 2,049 yards in 1990: Anderson for 784, Hampton for 455, Tillman for 231, Meggett for 164, Carthon for 143 (and Hostetler had 190). Meggett was also the team's top receiver with 39 receptions for 410 yards. Bavaro was second with 33 catches for 393 yards. To no one's surprise Taylor once again led the team in sacks with 10½, and Marshall was credited with another 4½. Former Dallas Cowboys cornerback Walls intercepted six passes, and safety Jackson picked off another five.

New York had earned home-field advantage for their first game in the playoffs. Their opponent was to be the Chicago Bears, who had won the NFC Central division that year with a record of 11–5 and then easily knocked off the New Orleans Saints in the first round of the playoffs by a score of 16–6. The Bears had made the playoffs every year except one since they won the NFL championship in 1985 with a team that was generally considered one of the most well-rounded—and perhaps even one of the greatest—in the history of the league. Mike Ditka was still the Bears' coach, but their great running back and then-holder of the NFL all-time rushing record, Walter Payton, had retired. Also gone from that team were quarterback Jim McMahon and such All Pros as defensive end Dan Hampton, linebacker Wilber Marshall, and safety Dave Duerson, now a Giant. But the Bears still had future Hall of Famer Mike Singletary at middle linebacker and one of the game's great pass rushers in defensive end Richard Dent. Neal Anderson had filled in well for Payton at running back (1,078 yards in 1990), but starting quarterback Jim Harbaugh had suffered a separated shoulder in the 14th game of the season and was now replaced by backup Mike Tomczak.

The largest crowd up to that time to attend a game at Giants Stadium, 77,025, were royally entertained that January afternoon. The Giants defense was overwhelming, holding the Bears to a mere three points and only 26 yards rushing and intercepting Tomczak twice. The offense put 17 points on the board in the first half with a field goal from Bahr and then two touchdown passes from Hostetler to Baker and tight end Howard Cross. New York added two more touchdowns in the second half on short runs by Hostetler and Carthon. The final score was 31–3.

The next matchup was not going to be quite so easy. And it was going to be far from home, across the country at Candlestick Park in San Francisco, where

When the 1990–1991 playoff season began the Giants were Jeff Hostetler's football team, the capable backup quarterback having replaced the injured Phil Simms late in the regular season. Photo courtesy of AP/Wide World Photos.

the 49ers awaited. The 49ers were the reigning NFL champs, who waltzed through the previous year's playoffs and then demolished the Denver Broncos in Super Bowl XXIV by the embarrassing score of 55–10. Having won 14 of their 16 games in 1990, they were now in pursuit of their third-straight NFL crown. Coached by Bill Walsh and quarterbacked by Montana, they had defeated the Giants in the same venue earlier in the season and were the oddsmakers' favorite going into the playoff game. It proved to be one of the great postseason matches in NFL history.

San Francisco scored first, a 47-yard field goal in the first quarter, but Bahr tied it with a 28-yarder. Both teams added another field goal in the second period, and the score was 6–6 at the half. When play resumed, Montana thrilled the hometown crowd with a 61-yard touchdown pass to wide receiver John Taylor. Bahr got his third field goal later in the third quarter, a 46-yarder to bring the Giants to within four points of the 49ers going into the final period of play. Midway through that period, however, Montana went down under a sack by New York defensive end Marshall and, injured, left the game and would not return. Shortly thereafter, with the Giants in a punting situation, coach Parcells pulled a surprise that would change the course of

Matt Bahr kicked the game-winning field goal against San Francisco, earning a trip to Super Bowl XXV and high praise from Hostetler. Photo courtesy of Getty Images.

NFC CHAMPIONSHIP GAME

Scoring

	1	2	3	4		T
Giants	3	3	3	6	—	15
49ers	3	3	7	0	—	13

49ers Cofer, 47-yard field goal

Giants Bahr, 28-yard field goal

Giants Bahr, 42-yard field goal

49ers Cofer, 35-yard field goal

49ers 61-yard TD pass, Montana to Taylor (Cofer extra point)

Giants Bahr, 46-yard field goal

Giants, Bahr, 38-yard field goal

Giants Bahr, 42-yard field goal

Individual Statistics

Rushing—*Giants*: Anderson 20 for 67 yards, Meggett 10 for 36, Reasons 1 for 30, Hostetler 3 for 11, Carthon 2 for 8; *49ers*: Craig 8 for 26 yards, Montana 2 for 9, Rathman 1 for 4.

Passing—*Giants*: Hostetler 15 of 27 for 176 yards; *49ers*: Montana 18 of 26 for 190 yards, Young 1 of 1 for 25 yards.

Receiving—*Giants*: Ingram 5 for 82 yards, Bavaro 5 for 54, Baker 2 for 22, Meggett 2 for 15, Anderson 1 for 3; *49ers*: Rice 5 for 54 yards, Rathman 4 for 16, Jones 3 for 46, Craig 3 for 16, Taylor 2 for 75, Sherrard 2 for 8.

the game. On a faked punt, the snap went to linebacker/ special team blocker Reasons, who carried the ball 30 yards and set up a 38-yard field goal by Bahr.

With the score 13–12, San Francisco leading, time running out, and the 49ers in Giants territory and moving the ball toward field goal range, things looked dismal. There were just over 2½ minutes left when Roger Craig ran into nose tackle Erik Howard, the impact knocking the ball loose. Taylor fell on it. Hostetler took over, and he began to move the Giants. Two key plays were passes

to Bavaro for 19 yards and Baker for 13. With virtually no time left on the clock, Bahr came back onto the field to attempt to make his fifth field goal of the day, a 42-yarder. He made it. The five field goals are still a Giants postseason record, although it was tied by Brad Daluiso in 1997.

The last-second score was the Giants' ticket to Super Bowl XXV.

*Lawrence Taylor recovers a fumble that helped seal the 15–13
victory over the two-time defending Super Bowl champion
49ers in the NFC Championship game on January 20, 1991.*
Photo courtesy of AP/Wide World Photos.

Hostetler celebrates a second-quarter touchdown against the Buffalo Bills in Super Bowl XXV. Photo courtesy of AP/Wide World Photos.

A WIN TO SAVOR

The NFL did not schedule an off week between the conference championship game and the Super Bowl, so there was barely time for celebration or for the Giants to catch their breath before they boarded their charter flight from San Francisco to Tampa for Super Bowl XXV. They didn't even bother going back home. It would have been a waste of precious time, and the Giants needed all of it to prepare for Buffalo's explosive offense.

It would be the most emotional and patriotic Super Bowl played up until that point. The Persian Gulf War was in its 12th day, security at Tampa Stadium was tight, and there was a stirring rendition of the national anthem by Whitney Houston. The game gave Americans four hours off from troubles abroad.

The Giants had just defeated the 49ers, which prevented San Francisco from becoming the first team to three-peat in the Super Bowl, which would have made a strong case for the Niners as the greatest team of all time. But apparently that NFC title victory on the road did not convince everybody the Giants were to be taken seriously. They were installed as 6-point underdogs against the Bills, whose unstoppable no-huddle offense had just humiliated the Oakland Raiders, 51–3, in the AFC Championship game.

Because this was one of the few times the NFL did not build in a week to rest before the Super Bowl, many of the Giants front office support staff arrived in Tampa the Thursday before the NFC title game to finalize plans in the event the Giants would be heading to Florida. A truck from New Jersey carrying the players' bags for Super Bowl week arrived in Tampa during the 49ers game. If the Giants had lost the game, the truck would have turned around and headed back north as the Giants flew home.

An advance scouting report yielded unfavorable reviews on the locker room setup at the local college where the Giants were assigned to practice, so they elected to turn one of the ballrooms at the hotel where the NFC team would be staying into a locker room. Those plans were not put into effect until Matt Bahr's field goal.

The 49ers felt no need to wait. The Giants support staff watched the NFC Championship game in the hotel, and when it was over, they headed to the offices where they would spend the week. San Francisco was a confident organization: it had already brought in furniture and had phone lines installed in the offices set aside for the NFC team before the playoff game was over.

The Giants were familiar with the Bills. They had played them on December 15 and lost 17–13. It was

262

the most costly loss of the season because Phil Simms suffered a season-ending foot injury. But the Giants gained confidence in Jeff Hostetler after he defeated the Cardinals and Patriots in the final two games of the regular season and then made enough plays to help them defeat the Bears and 49ers in the playoffs.

Hostetler had been frustrated in his role as Simms' backup, rarely getting an opportunity to play. He and Bill Parcells did not have the best relationship. In the days before unrestricted free agency, there was no way out for Hostetler, who was wasting valuable time sitting on the bench.

But the long wait was worth it. Simms' foot was in a boot, and Hostetler's team was in the most important game of his life. There would be a tremendous burden on him to get the Giants points and to put together time-consuming drives to keep Jim Kelly and Thurman Thomas and Buffalo's receivers off the field. Hostetler could not make any crucial errors that would create a short field for Buffalo. The Bills scored easily enough. The Giants did not need to help them.

Seeing the Bills just one month earlier gave Parcells and Bill Belichick, his brilliant defensive coordinator, a head start on preparing for Kelly and Co.

The Giants knew they had to control the clock on offense and find a way to clog the passing lanes on defense. The Giants had a defense in 1990 that was able to adjust. Having Taylor gave Belichick flexibility. Against the Bears, who relied on Neal Anderson running the ball, Belichick switched from the Giants' standard 3-4 to a more conventional 4-3. Anderson, who finished sixth in the league with 1,078 yards, managed only 19 yards against the Giants.

The next week against the 49ers, Belichick switched the Giants back to their 3-4 defense and they held the 49ers to only 13 points and knocked Joe Montana out of the game late in the fourth quarter. Next came the biggest challenge for the defense: how would they slow down Buffalo, which had scored 95 points in playoff victories over the Dolphins and Raiders?

The frenetic pace of the Bills' no-huddle offense was exhausting for any defense. So Parcells decided he would pound the Bills defense with running back Ottis Anderson to eat up time, and Belichick implemented a unique defense with only two down linemen, often put-

SUPER BOWL XXV, ANOTHER TITLE

January 27, 1991, Tampa Stadium, Tampa, Florida, Attendance: 78,813

New York Giants		**Buffalo Bills**
Offense		
Mark Ingram	WR	Al Edwards
Jumbo Elliot	LT	Howard Ballard
Eric Moore	LG	John Davis
Bart Oates	C	Kent Hull
William Roberts	RG	Jim Ritcher
Doug Riesenberg	RT	Will Wolford
Mark Bavaro	TE	Keith McKeller
Howard Cross	TE-WR	James Lofton
Stephen Baker	WR	Andre Reed
Jeff Hostetler	QB	Jim Kelly
Ottis Anderson	RB	Thurman Thomas
Defense		
Leonard Marshall	DE	Leon Seals
Erik Howard	NT	Jeff Wright
Carl Banks	OLB-DE	Bruce Smith
Pepper Johnson	ILB-DE	Darryl Talley
Lawrence Taylor	OLB	Cornelius Bennett
Mark Collins	CB-ILB	Ray Bentley
Reyna Thompson	CB-ILB	Shane Conlan
Everson Walls	CB	Kirby Jackson
Perry Williams	CB	Nate Odomes
Myron Guyton	FS	Mark Kelso
Greg Jackson	SS	Leonard Smith

	1	2	3	4		T
Bills	3	9	0	7	—	19
Giants	3	7	7	3	—	20

Touchdowns—*Bills:* D. Smith, Thomas; *Giants:* Baker, Anderson.

Field goals—*Bills:* Norwood; *Giants:* Bahr (2).

Extra Points—*Bills:* Norwood (2); *Giants:* Bahr (2).

Safety—*Bills:* B. Smith, tackled Hostetler in end zone.

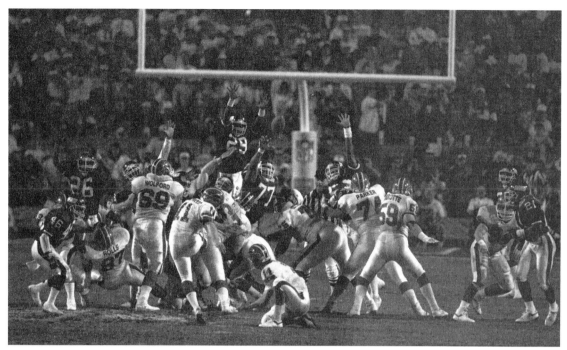

The fate of Super Bowl XXV rested on the leg of Buffalo kicker Scott Norwood, whose missed 47-yard field-goal attempt in the closing seconds secured the Giants' 20–19 win. Photos courtesy of AP/Wide World Photos.

ting the other nine players in coverage to slow down Kelly. He started with a 2-3-6 and then switched to a 2-4-5. That would open things up for Thomas, who rushed for 135 yards until the Giants decided that stopping Kelly was the first priority.

The plan worked to perfection. Anderson, named the game's MVP, rushed for 102 yards on 21 carries. As a team, the Giants rushed for 172 yards. They also held onto the ball for a Super Bowl–record 40:33. The Bills did manage 372 yards, but their offense was on and off the field so quickly many times that the Buffalo defense was subjected to a healthy helping of the Giants smash-mouth attack, which took its toll.

"They call us predictable and conservative," Parcells said after the game. "But I know one thing—and I've coached this game a long time—power wins football games. It's not always the fanciest way, but it wins games."

The Bills held a 12–10 lead going into halftime, but the Giants opened the third quarter with a 75-yard touchdown drive that consumed 9:29 as they converted four plays on third down. When the fourth quarter produced a Bahr field goal and a Buffalo touchdown, the Giants held a 20–19 lead.

That set up one of the most dramatic finishes in Super Bowl history. The Bills took over on their

10-yard line with 2:16 remaining. The Bills were trying to move into position for Scott Norwood, a reliable
kicker. Thomas nearly made Norwood unnecessary. He
came close to breaking a long run for a touchdown, but
Everson Walls made a game-saving tackle. Kelly was
able to drive Buffalo to the Giants' 29-yard line. There
were eight seconds remaining when Norwood lined up
for the kick that would make him a hero or, even if it was
unfair, make him a goat. It was no chip-shot field goal,
especially on a grass field. The Bills lined up on the
sideline holding hands.

Norwood had plenty of distance, but the kick barely
sailed wide right with four seconds left. The Giants exulted
on the sideline. After not even making it to the Super Bowl the
first 20 times it was played, they had just won two of the last five.

Hostetler took a knee to run down the last seconds. And
Parcells ran off the field arm-in-arm with Lawrence Taylor.

It would be the last time.

The 49-year-old Bill Parcells celebrated the Super Bowl win, but abruptly left the team during the off-season, setting into motion a coaching carousel that would continue through the next decade and a half. Photo courtesy of AP/Wide World Photos.

Partly due to the departure of coveted Parcells and assistants Bill Belichick and Tom Coughlin, Ray Handley emerged as Young's top choice to fill the head coaching vacancy in 1991. Photo courtesy of Getty Images.

A TEAM IN TATTERS

The day after winning the Super Bowl, the Giants were inundated with issues that would forever shape the franchise. Would Bill Parcells return as coach? And who would be the starting quarterback—Phil Simms or Jeff Hostetler?

When the Giants won their first Super Bowl five years prior, Parcells tried to work his way out of his Giants contract to become the coach and general manager of the Atlanta Falcons. The Giants were able to step in and stop Parcells, but after the win in Tampa, talk again centered on Parcells leaving the Giants. It was rumored that right after the Super Bowl, he would leave to take over as coach of the Bucs. The situation was repeated nearly one year later, and then again in 2002.

"Everything that has been written about me is a fabrication," Parcells said the morning after beating the Bills. "There is no truth to any of those rumors. I haven't talked to anyone about anything. Last time after we won this thing, I didn't give my owners or [general manager] George Young any time to savor the victory. That's not going to happen this time." But Parcells put his usual qualifier in at the end. "Just like every year, I'll sit down and evaluate where I am and what I want to do."

The year 1991 would turn out to be one of change and turmoil for the Giants. Wide receivers coach Tom Coughlin, a favorite of Parcells, had already accepted a job to become the head coach at Boston College. And then Bill Belichick, who was masterful in the playoffs, was hired to be the head coach of the Cleveland Browns. He and Parcells later hooked up and worked together again with the Patriots and Jets, but had an ugly parting after the 1999 season when Belichick, who was supposed to succeed Parcells as the Jets coach, instead quit after one day and went to New England.

The rumors persisted about Parcells stepping down as coach. Belichick appeared to be the natural successor, but even if he was an option, the word around the Giants camp was that general manager George Young wanted to promote little-known running-back coach Ray Handley.

The Giants entered the off-season not knowing for sure if the mercurial Parcells would be coming back or whether Simms or Hostetler would be the leader of the team. It was the first time quarterbacks who had won Super Bowls for the same team would be fighting for the same job.

The departure of Tim Mara in 1991 may have influenced Parcells' decision to leave. Mara and Parcells had developed a close friendship. Mara was Parcells' confidant in the organization. Not having him to rely on weighed on Parcells' mind.

CHANGING HANDS

Not long after the Giants returned from Tampa, co-owner Tim Mara, the nephew of co-owner Wellington Mara, sold his 50 percent share in the team to New York businessman Robert Tisch, the former postmaster general. The sale price for the transaction made in March 1991 was $75 million, which turned out be quite a bargain. Wellington and his nephew had a public falling out after the 1978 season because they couldn't agree on whom to hire as a general manager or coach. They each owned exactly half the team, and their stalemate was an embarrassment to the organization and prevented the team from getting on with its football business.

Mara and Tisch turned out to be perfect partners. Mara took a step back and involved his son John in the day-to-day operations of the club. And Tisch, more a football fan than football expert, became involved in the business side of the operation. Each owned 50 percent, a situation the NFL no longer allows, but in their case, the absence of a majority owner never once got in the way.

The longer the off-season went without Parcells leaving, the more it seemed he would stay. After the NFL held the draft at the end of April and Parcells was still in the draft room, it seemed certain he would return for his ninth season as the Giants coach. But word leaked the night of May 14 that Parcells would be stepping down the next day and would be replaced by Handley.

At the time, Parcells, who was just 49, gave no reason for his departure, although he denied he was burned out or it was health-related. "It's time to move on," Parcells said. "That's the best way I can say it. It's been a great eight years here. Who's been luckier than I have? In show business, you want to play the Palace. I was fortunate to play the Palace for a while." But the day after his Patriots qualified for Super Bowl XXXI, Parcells said there was only one reason he quit the Giants: his health. After leaving the Giants, he had two heart procedures and bypass surgery.

"Look, I didn't want to leave football, but I knew I had to do something," he said on January 13, 1997. "I knew I couldn't keep going like I was or I wasn't

Parcells' hasty exit (left) following Super Bowl XXV left a serious void in the organization, and a grim expression on general manager George Young's face (right). Photos courtesy of AP/Wide World Photos.

The quarterback controversy that emerged between Simms (above) and Hostetler after the Super Bowl victory would have been difficult even for Parcells to stomach, much less a rookie coach like Handley. Photo courtesy of AP/Wide World Photos.

going to make it. For a long time, I didn't know what was wrong. Quite frankly, it took six months to find out. I knew something was wrong because I could feel it even though it wasn't showing up on the tests."

Handley was an unlikely choice for the Giants. Parcells promoted him to offensive coordinator after the Super Bowl—after first talking him out of leaving the coaching business. Handley had planned to enroll in law school for the fall semester in 1991. On a staff that had high-profile assistants like Belichick and Coughlin, there was little talk of Handley, the studious-looking one who stood next to Parcells on the sideline and was considered a whiz at clock management. He had been invaluable to Parcells and was given the daunting task of replacing him. He followed one of the toughest acts in sports.

Handley only had the job a short while before he was bombarded with Simms-Hostetler questions, a subject that would overwhelm him during his two seasons on the job. "A week ago, I would have had an easy answer

to that question," Handley said the day he was hired. "I would have said I wanted an open and even contest in training camp and Bill would tell me who his quarterback will be. Today, I hope we'll have an open and even competition and that I'll decide who the quarterback will be."

Parcells' resignation shook up the players. Many figured that after the first few weeks of the off-season went by and Parcells was still the coach, he would remain the coach. But the players were missing a quarterback as well as their old coach, and now it was up to Handley, who had never been a head coach on any level, to deal with the most delicate personnel decision the Giants ever had.

Simms was 11–3 starting for the Giants in 1990 until he suffered his foot injury. But he was 36 years old and entering his 12th season. Hostetler was 30 years old and a career backup who took advantage of an incredible opportunity and made the most of it. Simms had the better arm. Hostetler was more mobile. They were both popular with teammates. It was a tough decision that dominated the off-season and training camp.

Handley struggled with the decision, and, at one low point, he considered a plan where both men could play. "I don't want anybody perceiving a loser," Handley said. "I have two number one quarterbacks, two guys I consider to be interchangeable. Either could have won the job based on performance so far. There are a number of ways to utilize both."

Handley tried to sell the idea to Simms and Hostetler individually and together. Neither liked it. They both wanted to start. They didn't want to share the job. Ultimately, Handley went with his gut and chose Hostetler to start the season opener against the 49ers in a rematch of the NFC title game.

The Giants opened the season on the big Monday night stage and went out and beat the 49ers again. This time, Matt Bahr hit a 35-yard field goal with five seconds left to give the Giants a 16–14 victory. It turned out to be one of the few highlights of the Handley regime.

After beating the 49ers, the Giants lost to the Rams and Bears. With four weeks remaining in the season, the Giants were 7–5 and in position to make a playoff run. Hostetler started all 12 of those games, but in the last one he suffered a fractured transverse process in his back and didn't play the rest of the season. Although he completed nearly 63 percent of his passes, Hostetler threw only five touchdowns.

Simms took over down the stretch, and the Giants lost to the Bengals, Eagles, and Redskins. They needed the victory they achieved over the Oilers in the final game of the season to avoid having a losing record again in a post–Super Bowl season.

Things only got worse in what turned out to be Handley's second and final season as the Giants head coach. Handley opened the season with Simms as his starter because of Hostetler's back injury. Handley had insisted all along Hostetler would be his starter in 1992. But after the Giants lost to the 49ers in the opener, Handley elected to remain with Simms, which infuriated Hostetler.

Simms suffered a season-ending elbow injury in the fourth game, thrusting Hostetler back into the starting role. But then Hostetler suffered a concussion in the 13th game, forcing him to miss the rest of the season. Rookie Kent Graham took over and was the starter when the Giants won their only game in the final six.

The veteran defensive players were not happy with the scheme employed by Handley's defensive coordinator, Rod Rust. Handley quickly lost control of the locker room, and the Giants finished 6–10—their second straight season in fourth place in the five-team NFC East. The Super Bowl in Tampa seemed like a long time ago.

It was their worst record since 3–12–1 in 1983, which was Parcells' first year. Fans chanted "Ray Must Go" at home games, reminiscent of "Good-bye Allie" of nearly 30 years prior.

Lawrence Taylor's season-ending injury nine games into the 1992 campaign effectively delayed his retirement by a year; it also probably expedited Handley's departure. Photo courtesy of AP/Wide World Photos.

It was a chaotic and dismal year. Lawrence Taylor tore his Achilles in the ninth game, which cost him the rest of the season. He had previously announced that he would retire after the 1992 season. But being helped off the field was not the way he wanted his career to end. Taylor subsequently announced during the off-season that he indeed would come back for the 1993 season.

Handley would not. Neither would Hostetler.

By the time the 1992 season mercifully came to an end, it was a foregone conclusion that Young would fire Handley. The players never responded to him as a coach. But it was not all his fault: the Simms-Hostetler controversy would have been tough even for Parcells to manage—not to mention a rookie coach. But too often he seemed miscast for such a huge job. When Handley walked off the field following a 20–10 loss to the Eagles in Philadelphia in the final game of the season, there was little doubt his career as Giants coach was over.

Two years after Young introduced Handley as Parcells' successor, he seemed genuinely hurt to announce he had fired him as well. Handley had held the job just 19 months. Handley elected not to comment on what went wrong in his two years as the Giants head coach, but the expectations were overwhelming.

"I think it had to do with progress and team chemistry," Young said. "I think the last two years were very difficult. Coming down from the mountain made it very difficult on the new coach and his staff."

It was the first time Young was forced to fire a coach. Ray Perkins left after four seasons to accept the job at Alabama, his alma mater. Then Parcells quit on him. Now he had no choice but to fire Handley.

Dan Reeves arrived in New York after having had greater control in Denver, and he never quite got used to the fact that he wasn't the number one decision maker in the Giants front office. Photo courtesy of AP/Wide World Photos.

ON THE ROAD TO WHOLENESS

The Giants had reached a critical stage. They were without a coach, and their team was growing old.

There were rumors that the Giants were going to bring back Parcells. One year earlier, Parcells came close to getting back into coaching in Tampa, but he changed his mind at the last minute. He did not return to New York. Parcells, newly confident about his health, indeed did take a coaching job in 1993, but he was hired by the Patriots, the worst team in the league.

General manager George Young knew exactly who he wanted to guide his team. But the coaching search soon turned into an embarrassment for the organization. Young offered the job to Tom Coughlin, the Boston College coach who had spent 1988–1990 as Parcells' wide receiver coach with the Giants. His philosophies were closely aligned with Parcells', and that appealed to Young, who never endorsed the idea of bringing Parcells back.

The Giants were certain Coughlin would say yes. But he had been at Boston College for only two years and felt an obligation to continue to build the program. Plus, with the Giants, he would not be in control of his own destiny. Under Young, no Giants coach had control over personnel. That philosophy was not going to change for Coughlin or anybody else. The Giants were stunned when Coughlin turned them down.

Young went to his backup plan. Cowboys defensive coordinator Dave Wannstedt, a protégé of Jimmy Johnson, was the hottest assistant in the NFL. Dallas was about to win the first of back-to-back Super Bowls, and Wannstedt was considered a rising star. But the Giants had competition: the Bears wanted Wannstedt. Chicago offered more control—Wannstedt would have much more power in personnel, something that could not happen with the Giants, who believed in a clear separation of coach and general manager powers. Also, by coaching for Chicago, Wannstedt would not have to compete in the same division as Johnson, his close friend.

When Wannstedt picked the Bears over the Giants, Young had to start over with his search. There was no Plan C.

Back in 1979, after he was hired as the Giants general manager, Young hired Chargers assistant Ray Perkins over Cowboys assistant Dan Reeves to be his head coach. Two years later, Reeves was hired by the Broncos and lasted 12 seasons, guiding the Broncos to three Super Bowl appearances with John Elway. Denver lost all three, including Super Bowl XXI, to the Giants. But now Reeves was available. He had been fired by the Broncos the same week Young fired Ray Handley. He was not high on Young's list—if he made the list at all. Reeves had the general manager powers in Denver, and

Young didn't believe Reeves could adjust to being only a coach. Reeves, however, publicly campaigned for the job, claiming he could embrace the Giants' way. Eventually, Young relented, with a strong nudge from ownership, and hired Reeves.

After two years of Handley and a mutiny by the players, bringing in an experienced and proven winner was just what the Giants needed. Reeves was decisive, and even though he surrendered the power he had in Denver, the fact that he wanted the job so badly convinced the Giants that Reeves would buy into their program.

Running back Rodney Hampton, the Giants' first-round pick in 1990, put together his third straight 1,000 yard season in 1993. Photo courtesy of AP/Wide World Photos.

They were right about Reeves for a while.

Nearly one month after taking the job and evaluating the personnel, Reeves declared that either Phil Simms or Jeff Hostetler would have to go. He didn't want to start off his tenure with a quarterback controversy. But who would stay? Simms was arguably the greatest quarterback in team history. Hostetler was six years younger. They each had won a Super Bowl. Simms had completed 22 of 25 passes against Reeves' Broncos team in the Super Bowl.

Reeves decided on Simms, and Hostetler signed as a free agent with the Raiders. They each had a team to call their own. Lawrence Taylor, recovered from his torn Achilles, was back for one more year. Reeves had a leader on offense and a leader on defense to help him through his transition period. But he upset veterans by bringing in many of his former players from Denver, which prompted some to call them the Denver Giants or the New York Broncos.

Reeves commanded respect, and his first season in New York added to his reputation as one of the best coaches in the league. The Giants started off 3–0, beating the Bears, Bucs, and Rams, before losing to the Bills, and then they beat the Redskins and Eagles.

The Giants were getting a big year from Rodney Hampton, the first-round pick in 1990, who was putting together his third-straight 1,000-yard season. Simms, after playing just a handful of games the previous two seasons, had a Pro Bowl year, throwing for 3,038 yards and 15 touchdowns. On defense, tackle Keith Hamilton developed into a force with $11\frac{1}{2}$ sacks. Taylor finished up with six, and then called it quits for good.

The Giants were in great shape at 5–1 before the offense shut down for two weeks in losses to the Jets and Cowboys. But then they made a terrific run in the second half of the season, winning six straight games. At 11–3, they were a lock for the playoffs, but wanted more. They lost to the Cardinals in the 15th game, but that didn't affect the winner-take-all showdown against the Cowboys in the final game of the season at Giants Stadium.

The winner would not only capture the NFC East, but also earn the number one seed in the conference, which meant getting a home-field advantage straight through the playoffs. The atmosphere was electric at

Giants Stadium, and the game lived up to all the hype. It was a tense struggle, with Dallas prevailing 16–13 in overtime. Dallas running back Emmitt Smith separated his shoulder in the first half but remained in the game and finished with 168 yards.

The Giants ended the regular season 11–5, and Reeves was named Coach of the Year. He may have been the third choice for the job, but he emerged looking like the best choice.

The loss to Dallas meant the Giants were stuck playing in the wild-card round against the Vikings instead of getting the bye week. They beat the Vikings 17–10, but from that moment forward, until Reeves was fired after three more seasons, the positive moments for the Giants were hard to find.

After beating Minnesota, the Giants closed out the Taylor era with a humiliating 44–3 loss to Steve Young and the 49ers. It was the most points the Giants ever allowed in the playoffs. The Giants had played some memorable playoff games against the 49ers in the past, winning three out of five matchups since the 1981 season—including the NFC title game just three years earlier. But they had no chance in 1993: the 49ers scored the first three times they had the ball to take a 16–0 lead.

During the regular season, the Giants allowed just seven rushing touchdowns. In the playoff loss, 49ers running back Ricky Watters set an NFL postseason record with five rushing touchdowns. The Giants' Hampton managed just 12 yards rushing.

Everybody knew the Gaints-49ers game was the final game of Taylor's brilliant 13-year career. But it also turned out to be the final game of Simms' 14-year career. The NFL had entered the new era of free agency, combined with a salary cap, and Simms became the first high-profile salary-cap casualty. When Reeves called him into his office in June, Simms thought the coach was going to ask him to autograph a football.

He was stunned. Reeves told him he had a choice: retire or be fired. Neither was appealing to Simms. The Giants were concerned about Simms' ability to come back from a shoulder injury, but were severely criticized for not showing loyalty to one of the best players to ever put on their uniform. Even Wellington Mara disagreed

The Giants' last victory of the Taylor era was a 17–9 playoff win over Minnesota on January 9, 1994. Steve Young and the 49ers effectively ended New York's Super Bowl dreams the following week with a 44–3 rout. Photo courtesy of AP/Wide World Photos.

that up with road victories in Washington and Cleveland. Beating the Bengals got them back to .500 at 7–7, and amazingly, a 16–13 victory over the Eagles sent the Giants into the final game of the season against the Super Bowl champion Cowboys with a shot at the playoffs.

To sneak in, the Giants needed to beat the Cowboys on the final Saturday, and then have the Bucs beat the Packers. The Giants held up their end with a 15–10 victory over Dallas, which already had its playoff seeding locked up. The winning points came after the Giants' Jessie Armstead sacked Dallas backup quarterback Rodney Peete at the goal line and the ball went through the end zone for a safety. But then the Giants sat and watched Green Bay's 34–19 victory over Tampa eliminate them from the postseason.

It was a season of streaks: three-game winning streak, seven-game losing streak, six-game winning streak. If nothing else, the way the season ended proved that the Giants did not quit on Reeves, and it gave them hope going into 1995. It proved to be false hope.

Before another disappointing season, the Giants received the sad news that Tim Mara, the former

with the decision made by Young and Reeves. Simms came close to signing with the Cardinals and then the Browns after the Giants released him, but in each case, elected not to play. He then retired.

The Giants could have used him the next season. Dave Brown, taken in the first round of the 1992 supplemental draft, had a tough act to follow when Reeves named him the starting quarterback in 1994. He was the first quarterback the Giants had taken in the first round since Simms in 1979. Incredibly, the Giants won their first three games, beating the Eagles, Cardinals, and Redskins, all NFC East opponents. But a 27–22 loss to the Saints in the fourth game started the Giants on a seven-game losing streak. Their record was pretty gloomy at 3–7. At halftime of the second loss, the Giants retired Taylor's No. 56 jersey. The way the season was progressing, it seemed that ceremony was going to be the only thing memorable about 1994 for the Giants.

But, somehow, they managed to finish the season with six straight victories and nearly snuck into the playoffs.

The winning streak started innocently in Houston in a 13–10 game on a Monday night. The Giants followed

Following the unceremonious release of Simms, Reeves pronounced Dave Brown his starting quarterback in 1994, and several seasons of mediocrity ensued for both coach and QB. Photo courtesy of AP/Wide World Photos.

co-owner of the franchise, had died from cancer on May 31, 1995, at the age of 59. He had sold his 50 percent share in the team to Robert Tisch in 1991. Mara's public disagreement with his uncle, Wellington Mara, over the direction of the franchise in 1979 led to George Young being hired as the compromise choice as general manager. And, of course, that led to two Super Bowl championships. Tim Mara was particularly close to Bill Parcells. The Maras, who feuded for years, finally reconciled, through the efforts of Frank Gifford, in the last year of Tim Mara's life.

"The thing that stands out from 1979 was the sadness of it all," former Giants public relations director Ed Croke told the *Daily News* after Mara's death. "It was tearing up the family. They were the best people." Croke described Wellington Mara as "a prince with a heart of gold, and loyal. Timmy was the same way."

The 1995 season opened on a Monday night at home against the Cowboys. Considering the way the previous season ended, the Giants were hopeful of picking up where they left off. To get things started, they retired Simms' jersey at halftime.

Otherwise, it was a forgettable night. The Cowboys beat up the Giants, 35–0, and things never really got much better. Losses to Kansas City and Green Bay got the Giants off to their first 0–3 start in a nonstrike year since 1979. They finally picked up their first victory against the Saints, but unlike the previous season, it didn't start a winning streak. They did win three of five before a four-game losing streak sent them on their way to a 5–11 season.

Kent Graham, who had competed with Brown for the starting quarterback job in 1994, was cut right before the season so that Reeves could sign Tommy Maddox, his former first-round pick in Denver. Maddox played only half of one game because Brown was entrenched as the starter. But it was becoming increasingly clear that Brown was not going to be the answer to all the Giants' problems.

The biggest question at the end of the season was whether Reeves would be back for the fourth year of his five-year contract. He was growing uneasy with the Giants structure. He wanted more input, but the Giants were not going to change for him. In mid-November, with the Giants stuck in their losing streak, Reeves said he

would not return to the team after his contract expired if the organizational structure didn't change. "The way things are right now, no, I wouldn't be interested," he told the *New York Daily News*. "If I had to go through two more years like the past two years, then no, I wouldn't be interested."

As the Giants finished up their second consecutive nonplayoff season, they debated whether they would pay Reeves for the final two years of his deal and start over once again. Just one week after the season concluded, Reeves had four days of meetings with the team's hierarchy. The result: status quo. Reeves would remain, and no organizational changes would be made. To emphasize that point, Young was given a contract extension.

Keeping Reeves turned out to be a mistake for the Giants. After finishing 5–11 in 1995, they were 6–10 in 1996, and for the second year in a row, they lost their first three games. It was the first time since 1982–1983 that they had consecutive losing seasons. They could not win more than two in a row, and by the time December arrived, the Giants were 5–7. Even though they had just defeated the Super Bowl–champion Cowboys, there was little hope for the playoffs as the Reeves era was coming to a close. They lost the next week to the Eagles, 24–0.

The Giants didn't show much life down the stretch, and as soon as the season was over, Reeves was fired. At the press conferences after Reeves was fired, some dirty laundry came spilling out. It was clear Young had been right about Reeves in 1993: Reeves was not the right man for the organization, although no one questioned his ability to coach.

The Giants offense needed work. In 1996 it was 30th overall and 30th in passing. In 1995 they had been 29th overall and 30th in passing. In the six seasons since Parcells stunned them by stepping down, the Giants were just 45–51, with one playoff appearance and just two winning seasons.

Once again, Young was off looking for a new coach. He also needed a new quarterback.

During the search for a new coach, Michigan State coach Nick Saban, who had worked with Young's assistant, Ernie Accorsi, in Cleveland, and Jim Fassel, who had been Parcells' quarterback coach, emerged as the frontrunners. But the deal to acquire Saban ran into

FASSEL'S TRAVELS

Jim Fassel, the Cardinals offensive coordinator, had been an assistant on Handley's staff with the Giants in 1991 and 1992. He was actually hired by Parcells as the Giants quarterback coach immediately following Super Bowl XXI, after Parcells promoted Handley to offensive coordinator. Parcells hired Fassel on Handley's recommendation. Fassel and Handley had worked together at Stanford. Fassel then became Handley's offensive coordinator. Fassel received excellent reviews from Simms even though it was a difficult time for the Giants.

When Reeves was hired, he elected not to retain Fassel, who then went to Denver to work as offensive coordinator for Wade Phillips, who had been promoted by the Broncos to replace Reeves. Fassel was on Stanford's staff when John Elway played there, and they had become close friends. Now Fassel was back working with Elway again, and Elway flourished in Fassel's offense. After Phillips was fired after two seasons, Fassel went to Oakland, where he was reunited with Jeff Hostetler. And from there, he went to Arizona.

He was the clear favorite to replace Reeves.

Then Kanell wrapped up the Giants' first division title since 1990 by beating the Eagles, Redskins, and Cowboys in the final three games. Kanell threw three touchdowns to beat the Eagles. He finished with only 11 touchdowns and nine interceptions, and completed just 53.1 percent of his passes, but his plays translated into victories. In the final three games, the Giants scored 81 points. Although the offense in general was hardly explosive, the defense more than held up its end. The Giants recorded a team-record 44 takeaways, which led the NFL, and they were number one with 27 interceptions and third with 54 sacks.

The Giants went from last place to first place, just the 15th team to accomplish that feat. They were 7–0–1 in division games, the first team to ever go undefeated in NFC East games. The one blemish was an unsightly 7–7 tie with the Redskins.

Fassel, just like Reeves four years prior, was named coach of the year in his first season as the Giants

roadblocks, and the Giants hired Fassel. They had faith that he could turn Dave Brown into a consistent, productive player.

Fassel named Brown the starter—there were limited alternatives—and the Giants got off to another dreadful start. Fassel won his first game for the Giants on his 48th birthday against the Eagles, but then lost three straight. It seemed inevitable that the Giants were headed for their third straight losing season.

In the sixth game, however, Brown was injured, and Fassel turned to Danny Kanell, the fourth-round pick from 1996 who had thrown just 60 passes as a rookie. Kanell turned out to be magic for the Giants. He won his first three starts, against the Cardinals, Lions, and Bengals, to give the Giants a five-game winning streak—their longest since the end of the 1994 season.

Like Reeves before him, Jim Fassel was named Coach of the Year in his first season with the Giants, leading the team to a 10–5–1 record in 1997. Photo courtesy of AP/Wide World Photos.

head coach. Young, as had been rumored, resigned as the Giants general manager after the season and took a job working for Paul Tagliabue in the NFL office in Manhattan. Young was replaced by Accorsi, who had been Young's assistant since 1994.

The Giants' 10–5–1 record was not good enough to get them a first-round bye, but it seemed like a moot point when they led the Vikings 19–3 in the second half of their wild-card playoff game. In keeping with the Giants' ability to force turnovers, Randall Cunningham turned it over three times in the first half. He fumbled on consecutive plays, setting the Giants up for two of Brad Daluiso's five field goals. A key fumble by New York rookie running back Tiki Barber at the Giants' 4 in the third quarter put the Vikings in easy touchdown range.

Defensive tackle Keith Hamilton, who had to be separated from teammate Michael Strahan during the game, reflects after New York's devastating 23–22 loss to Minnesota in the 1997 playoffs. Photo courtesy of AP/Wide World Photos.

Then tragedy struck for the Giants. Minnesota scored on a 30-yard touchdown pass from Randall Cunningham to Jake Reed with 1:30 left to make the score 22–20. Then Minnesota recovered the onside kick when Chris Calloway couldn't handle it. The Vikings then drove for the winning 24-yard field goal by Eddie Murray with 10 seconds remaining, taking the game, 23–22.

The Giants displayed a surprising lack of poise, fighting among themselves. Cornerbacks Phillipi Sparks and Conrad Hamilton argued on the field, and defensive linemen Michael Strahan and Keith Hamilton had to be separated on the sideline. "The biggest thing that helped us this year and held us together was the fact that we played together," Strahan said after the game. "When you had the arguments, that kind of tore us apart. The thing that helped us all year killed us."

It was a crushing loss, wiping out many of the good things that happened in Fassel's first year. Instead of building on what they accomplished in 1997, the Giants took a step back in Fassel's second season. In the third preseason game, Fassel decided to give Jason Sehorn—who had emerged the year prior as one of the best young corners in the NFL—an opportunity to return kickoffs. Sehorn might have been the fastest player on the team, and Fassel was looking to get some explosion into the return game. But on the opening kickoff of the third preseason game against the Jets, Sehorn tore his anterior cruciate ligament and was lost for the season. Fassel was criticized not only for risking one of his most important players on the kickoff team, but for doing it in a preseason game.

The Giants got off to a 3–7 start, which prompted Fassel to bench Kanell and replace him with Graham,

Wide receiver Amani Toomer (No. 81 in left photo), who had his first of five straight 1,000-yard seasons in 1999, and free-agent quarterback Kerry Collins (right), who appeared to have left his personal troubles behind in Carolina, were among New York's brightest spots heading into the 2000 season. Photos courtesy of AP/Wide World Photos.

who returned to the Giants after stops in Detroit and Arizona. The Giants finished strong to end the season at 8–8. By far, the highlight was beating the Broncos, who came into Giants Stadium at 13–0, three weeks away from becoming the first team in NFL history to finish 16–0. The game ended dramatically, with Graham hitting Amani Toomer in the back of the end zone with a 37-yard touchdown pass with 48 seconds remaining, to cap a six-play, 86-yard drive for a 20–16 victory. Denver had taken a 16–13 lead on Terrell Davis' 27-yard run with just over four minutes remaining.

After the Giants beat the Chiefs the following week, they were still alive, even at 7–8, in the wild-card race. They needed to beat the Eagles the final week, and they did, but they also needed the Bucs and Cardinals to lose. Both won.

But the season-ending, four-game winning streak once again brought optimism going into the off-season. Gary Brown rushed for 1,063 yards with six 100-yard games, and Jessie Armstead and Strahan were each picked for the Pro Bowl for the second straight season.

Two months into the off-season, Accorsi made a bold move when he signed free agent quarterback Kerry Collins, who in 1998 had been cut by the Panthers and then not re-signed by the Saints. Collins, the Panthers' first-round pick in their expansion year in 1995, had been embroiled in controversy when he was accused in Carolina of quitting on the team and directing a regrettable racial comment at a teammate. He also had a drinking problem. But Accorsi, who once worked at

Penn State and was very close to Nittany Lions coach Joe Paterno, decided Collins, who played at Penn State, was worth the risk of a four-year $16.9 million contract that included a $5 million signing bonus. At the same time, the Giants released Kanell.

Graham opened the season as the Giants starting quarterback, the third starter in Fassel's three seasons. But it was only a matter of time before Collins took Graham's job. By game 11, with the Giants at 5–5 and on their way to another nonplayoff year, Fassel made the switch, but Collins could not jumpstart the team. He lost to the Cardinals—he had started and lost a game earlier in the season at Arizona when Graham was injured—then beat the Jets 41–28 and the Bills 19–17, leading a last-minute drive for the winning field goal.

At 7–6, the Giants still had a shot at the playoffs. But they lost to the Rams, Vikings, and Cowboys, to finish the season a disappointing 7–9. Toomer was one of the few bright spots with his team-record 79 catches and the first of what would be five straight 1,000-yard seasons. The Giants thought they had something in Collins, but the three-game losing streak raised questions about just about everyone else, including Fassel. He was due to go into the fourth and final year of his contract in 2000, prompting management to extend his deal by one season so that he wouldn't be perceived as a lame duck. But clearly Fassel had to win in 2000 or it would be his last year. It was Young, not Accorsi, who hired him, and every general manager desires to have his own coach.

After a couple of losses dropped the 2000 Giants to 7–4, Fassel took matters into his own hands and made a public guarantee through the media that his team would make the playoffs. Photo courtesy of AP/Wide World Photos.

ALMOST VICTORIOUS

The Giants were active in free agency between the 1999 and 2000 seasons, knowing they had too many holes for the draft to fill. Accorsi signed big-name middle linebacker Mike Barrow, but primarily concentrated on improving the offensive line with veterans Lomas Brown and Glenn Parker. Finding moderately priced role players was a tactic the New England Patriots later used to win three Super Bowls in four years. Accorsi used it to turn around the Giants.

The pressure was on Jim Fassel going into the 2000 season. The mandate from management was to win—now. That was the unspoken message when he received just a one-year extension. The Giants responded by getting off to a 7–2 start, which included two victories over the Eagles, their main competition in the NFC East.

But then the Giants hit two major bumps: they lost back-to-back home games to the Rams and Lions. What made the St. Louis loss so distasteful was the Rams played without Kurt Warner or Marshall Faulk. The explosive Rams offense was still unstoppable, with Trent Green throwing four touchdown passes in a 38–24 victory. And when the Lions, an awful road team, stopped by for a 31–21 victory, the Giants were 7–4.

After the losses, rumors about Fassel's job security began once again. Then, three days after the Lions loss,

Fassel entered the media room for his usual Wednesday news conference. His announcement, however, was unusual. He said that he had told people in the front office he was going to publicly guarantee the Giants would make the playoffs. It helped that the next game was at Arizona, which was on its way to a 3–13 season.

Still, Fassel became a folk hero in New York because he was right about his playoff guarantee and because the Giants didn't lose another game until the Super Bowl.

The Giants beat the Cardinals, then beat the Redskins 9–7, holding on at the end in a crucial NFC East game. Then, on a roll, they beat the Steelers by 20 points. They finished up the regular season with victories over the Cowboys and Jaguars. The Giants were 12–4, their best record in 10 years, and, incredibly, had earned the NFC's number one seed.

Fassel suddenly was Joe Namath, following through on his guarantee. It helped that it was a down year in the NFC, but Giants fans didn't care. Their team now had a clear path to the Super Bowl: beat the Eagles, whom they had already defeated twice earlier in the season, and then most likely the Vikings, who had the second-best record in the NFC at 11–5.

They opened the playoffs with their ninth straight victory, a win over the Eagles to the tune of 20–10, even

A BOLD STATEMENT

On November 22, 2000, the Giants head coach, Jim Fassel, issued a gutsy proclamation in a press conference: "This team is going to the playoffs."

In an emotional speech, Fassel said, "I'm raising the stakes right now. If this is a poker game, I'm shoving my chips to the middle of the table. I'm raising the ante. Anybody that wants in, get in. Anybody that wants out, get out."

He clearly was putting the focus on himself to take the pressure off his team. "If you've got the crosshairs, if you've got the laser, you can put it right on my chest," he said. "I'll take full responsibility."

Fassel really had nothing to lose. He knew if the Giants failed to make the playoffs, he was likely to lose his job. He was popular with his players, so he elected to motivate them by putting the focus on himself.

It worked.

NFC CHAMPIONSHIP GAME

January 14, 2000, Giants Stadium, East Rutherford, New Jersey
Attendance: 79,310

Scoring

	1	2	3	4		T
Vikings	0	0	0	0	—	0
Giants	14	20	7	0	—	41

Giants   Hilliard, 46-yard pass from Collins (Daluiso PAT)

Giants   Comella, 18-yard pass from Collins (Daluiso PAT)

Giants   Manuel, 11-yard pass from Simms (Allegre PAT)

Giants   Daluiso, 21-yard field goal

Giants   Jurevicius, 8-yard pass from Collins (Daluiso PAT)

Giants   Daluiso, 22-yard field goal

Giants   Hilliard, 7-yard pass from Collins (Daluiso PAT)

Giants   Toomer, 7-yard pass from Collins (Daluiso PAT)

Individual Statistics

Rushing—Vikings: Smith 7 for 24 yards, Culpepper 2 for 10; *Giants*: Barber 12 for 69 yards, Montgomery 16 for 43, Dayne 10 for 29, Garrett, 3 for -3.

Passing—Vikings: Culpepper 13 of 28 for 78 yards; *Giants*: Collins 28 of 39 for 381 yards, Garrett 1 for 1 for 4.

Receiving—Vikings: Carter 3 for 24 yards, Walsh 3 for 23, Moss 2 for 18, Smith 2 for -2, McWilliams 1 for 9; Jordan 1 for 4, Hatchette 1 for -2; *Giants*: Hilliard 10 for 155 yards, Toomer 6 for 88, Comella 4 for 36, Barber 4 for 21, Dixon 2 for 62, Jurevicius 2 for 15, Dayne 1 for 8.

though they didn't score a touchdown on offense. But the win was never in doubt after Ron Dixon returned the opening kickoff 97 yards for a touchdown. It became 10–0 on a 37-yard field goal by Daluiso, and 17–0 when Jason Sehorn made a tumbling, acrobatic interception along the sideline of a pass by Donovan McNabb, got to his feet, and returned the ball 32 yards for a touchdown. The Eagles managed only 186 yards of offense and 11 first downs. The Giants were now one victory from their third Super Bowl.

The main concern for the Giants going into the NFC Championship game against the Vikings was how to stop Randy Moss. But Moss was never a factor in the ridiculously easy 41–0 victory. Kerry Collins hit Ike Hilliard with a 46-yard touchdown pass on the fourth play of the game; then, after the Vikings fumbled the kickoff, Collins connected on an 18-yard touchdown pass to fullback Greg Comella.

The rout was on. It was 34–0 at the half, in one of the most lopsided championships in NFL history. The Giants accumulated 518 yards on offense, Collins threw for 381 yards and five touchdowns, and Hilliard caught

10 passes for 155 yards and two touchdowns. Moss? He was limited to two catches for 18 yards. The Giants defense sacked Daunte Culpepper four times and intercepted him three times. Minnesota had just 114 yards on offense as it was outgained by 404 yards.

A 17–13 win over Dallas on December 17, 2000, celebrated here by Cedric Jones (No. 94) and Thabiti Davis (No. 82), gave the Giants the NFC Eastern Division title. Photo courtesy of AP/Wide World Photos.

Cornerback Dave Thomas (No. 41), flanked by teammates Michael Strahan and Cedric Jones, celebrates the missed field goal that enabled the Giants to hang on for a 9–7 win over Washington during their unlikely run to the 2000 NFC Championship. Photo courtesy of AP/Wide World Photos.

"I can't tell you how proud I am of this football team," Fassel said.

The trophy presentation took place on a stage at midfield as the players were showered with confetti. Even Wellington Mara, the 84-year-old patriarch of the franchise, got caught up in the moment. "This is the Giants team that was referred to as the worst team ever to win home-field advantage in the NFL," Mara said to the fans. "And today, on our field of painted mud, we proved we're the worst team ever to win the National Football Conference championship. And I'm happy to say in two weeks we're going to try to become the worst team ever to win the Super Bowl."

The Giants were clearly the best team in the NFC in 1986. In 1990, they were shoulder to shoulder with the 49ers, who had won back-to-back Super Bowl titles. But in 2000, coming off two nonplayoff seasons, not much was expected of the Giants.

That's why their trip back to Tampa, where they had defeated the Bills 10 years earlier in the Super Bowl,

Quarterback Kerry Collins threw five touchdown passes—this one to fullback Greg Comella—to lead a 41–0 rout of the Vikings on January 14, 2001, the most lopsided NFC Championship game in history. Photo courtesy of AP/Wide World Photos.

ONE WAY TO PLAY THE GAME

The Baltimore Ravens developed an interesting—and brutal—approach to winning games. "We go into every game trying to put the quarterback out," backup defensive tackle Lional Dalton told the *New York Daily News* in the days leading up to Super Bowl XXXV. "I think we put out three this year. The Super Bowl is the perfect setting for a fourth, just to show everybody—the whole world—how good we really are."

In the Ravens wild-card victory over Denver en route to the Super Bowl, they sacked Gus Frerotte four times, and at one point he left the game with a knee injury. The next week, the Ravens' Ray Lewis, the best defensive player in the league, was fined $7,500 for an illegal tackle on the Titans' Steve McNair, which knocked him out of the game for four plays. And in the AFC title game, Ravens defensive tackle Tony Siragusa was fined $10,000 for the way he handled Rich Gannon, injuring his left shoulder to put him briefly on the bench.

was such a joy to the organization. The game was to be played in Raymond James Stadium, the Bucs' new palace that was built next door to old Tampa Stadium. But unlike the Giants' two previous Super Bowls against the Broncos and Bills, who were both offensive teams, they would be facing the Baltimore Ravens, the most intimidating defense since the 1985 Bears.

The Ravens took pride in knocking quarterbacks out of games and considered it insulting when teams got into the end zone. They had their sights set early on Collins, who was coming off his five-touchdown performance against the Vikings.

"I don't have any special fears going into the game," Collins said. "I know they're going to be tough. I know they're going to come after me, but that's part of the game."

The nastiness of the Ravens defense contrasted with the good feelings between the organizations. Wellington Mara and Ravens owner Art Modell were best friends. Mara offered unwavering support to Modell when he was severely criticized for relocating the Browns

It had been 10 years since Giants fans had had anything to cheer about come Super Bowl time, and they gave their full support in the days leading up to the team's meeting with the Baltimore Ravens. Photo courtesy of AP/Wide World Photos.

from Cleveland to Baltimore in 1996. Also, Fassel's best friend in coaching was Ravens coach Brian Billick.

There was major-league trash-talking coming out of the Baltimore camp that week, which was the Ravens' style. The Giants just shrugged it off, but they knew the offense was in for the fight of its life. The good news was that the Baltimore offense was hardly high-scoring, meaning if the Giants could avoid turning the ball over and put together a drive or two, then they might win the game.

But the Giants didn't come close. They fell behind 7–0 when the Ravens' Trent Dilfer completed a 38-yard touchdown pass to Brandon Stokley, who beat Sehorn.

In the end, though, Baltimore's defense, led by Super Bowl MVP Ray Lewis (right), with more than a little help from wide receiver Brandon Stokley (below) and the rest of the offense, dominated the Giants in a 34–7 romp. Photos courtesy of AP/Wide World Photos.

In fact, if Dilfer had been more accurate, Sehorn might have given up a couple of more scores in the first quarter. He had what might have been the worst game of his career.

But it was a premeditated tactic that made things even tougher for the Giants. In his pregame meeting with the officials, Fassel advised them that when the Giants played the Ravens in the preseason, the Baltimore linemen had tackled the New York backs on screen passes. Fassel had sent those plays to the league office. But the warning backfired.

Early in the second period, Dilfer attempted to hit running back Jamal Lewis on a screen. Keith Hamilton, after fighting off a block from a Baltimore guard when it appeared he may have been held, was instead called for holding Lewis. Hamilton did slightly grab Lewis' arm, which happens all the time. When Dilfer attempted to hit Lewis, his pass sailed right into the arms of Jessie Armstead, who went 43 yards for what the Giants thought was the tying touchdown.

The Giants were horrified when the play was nullified on what they thought was a cheap holding call on Hamilton. Even if Hamilton had not touched Lewis, there didn't appear to be any way he would have come close to catching the ball. It was an awful throw by Dilfer. That one play may have changed the game.

The Giants were still down 7–0 and never got closer. They trailed 10–0 at the half, and when Duane Starks returned a Collins interception 49 yards for a score in the third quarter, the Giants were trailing 17–0. The Giants offense managed only 152 yards for the game, with only 11 first downs.

Yet, after Starks scored, Ron Dixon returned the kickoff 97 yards for a touchdown and suddenly the Giants fans got loud and had reason for hope. That didn't last very long as Jermaine Lewis then returned the Giants kickoff 84 yards for a touchdown. Back-to-back kickoff returns for touchdowns.

"The emotional flop had to be devastating to them," Billick said.

The Giants went on to lose 34–7, the sixth-most lopsided Super Bowl in history.

Collins completed only 15 of 39 passes for 112 yards with four interceptions. "This is the most disappointing loss I've ever been involved with," Collins

SUPER BOWL XXXV, BALTIMORE BLOWOUT

January 28, 2001, Raymond James Stadium, Tampa, Florida, Attendance: 71,921

New York Giants		**Baltimore Ravens**
	Offense	
Amani Toomer	WR	Qadry Ismail
Lomas Brown	LT	Jonathan Ogden
Glenn Parker	LG	Edwin Mulitalo
Dusty Ziegler	C	Jeff Mitchell
Ron Stone	RG	Mike Flynn
Luke Petitgout	RT	Harry Swayne
Ike Hilliard	WR/TE	Shannon Sharpe
Ron Dixon	WR	Brandon Stokley
Kerry Collins	WR	Trent Dilfer
Greg Comella	FB	Sam Gash
Tiki Barber	RB	Priest Holmes
	Defense	
Michael Strahan	LE	Rob Burnett
Cornelius Griffin	LT	Sam Adams
Keith Hamilton	RT	Tony Siragusa
Cedric Jones	RE	Michael McCrary
Michael Barrow	LLB	Peter Boulware
Jessie Armstead	MLB	Ray Lewis
Emmanuel McDaniel	CB/RLB	Jamie Sharper
Dave Thomas	LCB	Duane Starks
Jason Sehorn	RCB	Chris McAlister
Sam Garnes	SS	Kim Herring
Shaun Williams	FS	Rod Woodson

	1	2	3	4		T
Ravens	7	3	14	10	—	34
Giants	0	0	7	0	—	7

Touchdowns—*Ravens*: Stokley, Starks, Je. Lewis; *Giants*: Dixon.

Field goals—*Ravens*: Stover (2).

Extra Points—*Ravens*: Stover (4); *Giants*: Daluiso.

said. "I'm disappointed in the way I played. I didn't see the field well. They did a good job of disguising coverages."

A season that began with Fassel's job on the line produced "the Guarantee" and eventually the Giants' third Super Bowl appearance. But unlike the first two Super Bowls with Parcells, the Giants were outclassed. In time, they would appreciate the accomplishment of getting to the Super Bowl. But when they packed up their bags that night, the season felt like a failure. The longer the season extends, the more it hurts when it's finally over. Unless, of course, it ends with the Super Bowl trophy.

Behind Fassel's stoic leadership, the 2001 Giants—who were deeply affected by the September 11 attacks on the World Trade Center— poured a lot of their energies into rebuilding their community. Photo courtesy of AP/Wide World Photos.

BLEAK SEASONS

Free agency had turned the NFL into an up-and-down league. The Rams and Ravens, the past two Super Bowl champions, had not even made the playoffs the previous season. In fact, the Rams went from making the playoffs in 1989 to winning the Super Bowl in 1999 without a winning season in between. The Giants would have to try to avoid the fate of the previous two Super Bowl teams that failed to make the playoffs the season after making it to the big game.

Unlike their first two Super Bowls, the Giants were not concerned about their coach leaving. For getting his team to Super Bowl XXXV, Jim Fassel was rewarded with a new four-year, $10.8-million contract, and management gave out long-term deals to Jason Sehorn, despite his poor Super Bowl, and Tiki Barber, who was emerging as one of the best multipurpose backs in the league.

All during training camp in 2001, the Giants talked about their determination to prove they were not one-year wonders. They were picked to open the season on a Monday night, an honor bestowed on them after their first two Super Bowls. They were 1–1 in those games. And the opener would be their first Monday night opener since the 35–0 debacle against Dallas in 1995.

The NFL put them in Denver for the Broncos' inaugural regular-season game at their new stadium, where they lost, 31–20. But the loss was quickly forgotten. The Giants flew back on their charter flight to Newark Airport, landing in the early morning hours of September 11. Not long after they arrived, one of the four planes hijacked in the terrorist attack took off from Newark. It crashed in a field in Pennsylvania.

Out of respect for a nation in mourning, the NFL suspended all games for the weekend following September 11. The Giants players and organization rallied to help out their city in its time of need.

After the week off, the Giants went to Kansas City and received a warm welcome from the friendly fans in the Midwest on what turned out to be a very patriotic day around the NFL. Members of the Kansas City Fire Department passed their boots through the stands to take up a collection for the families who lost rescue workers. The Chiefs pledged to match the contributions.

The Giants were cheered by the Chiefs fans and were touched by the reception. Mike Barrow said he hadn't been cheered at an away game since he played Pop Warner. "What it showed is everything that happened just didn't affect New York," he said. "This is an American thing. Having people come out with their flags, it was like sports at its highest. We felt like one."

HELPING A CITY HEAL

Less than 12 hours after the Giants' loss in Denver in the season opener, nobody cared about the game. The NFL cancelled the games of the following weekend—the Giants were scheduled to host the Packers—as the nation mourned the loss of thousands of lives in the attacks on the World Trade Center in lower Manhattan and the Pentagon in Washington, D.C. The Twin Towers had been visible from the Giants practice field outside the stadium, and now they were gone. The hole in the skyline was a daily reminder of the tragedy.

In the aftermath of September 11, the Giants actively assisted in the recovery effort, visiting firehouses and Ground Zero, and helping to load supplies for rescue workers. Many of them set up foundations to help the families of the victims. About 20 players held a pizza party with about 30 children from three firehouses that had lost 12 members. "It was all very, very emotional," GM Ernie Accorsi said. "Those kids had been crying for a week. Somebody asked me, 'What do you say to them?' What can you say? You just go up and give them a hug."

After visiting rescue workers at Ground Zero, Fassel said, "So many guys said, 'Coach, the league did the right thing in canceling last week's games.' But they also said that they are really looking forward to the games this week. I think after what they've been through, they need a little diversion, and I think football can play its part in the healing process."

Defensive end Michael Strahan was the brightest light in an otherwise ordinary 2001 season, breaking the single-season sack record with 22½. Photo courtesy of AP/Wide World Photos.

The Giants won 13–3 and then went on to beat the Saints and Redskins. They played as if motivated to lift the spirits of New York. But after the hopeful start, they quickly lost three straight games to drop to 3–4, won two in a row, and then lost three in a row again. They finished 7–9, and the most notable accomplishment, by far, was Michael Strahan setting the single-season sack record with 22½—even though many thought Brett Favre handed him the last one to set the record. Kerry Collins became the first quarterback in NFL history to throw every one of his team's passes two years in a row. He set team records with 568 passes and 327 completions.

Coach Fassel was very happy when Ernie Accorsi moved the Giants up one spot in the first round of the 2002 draft to ensure the Giants would be able to draft Miami's flamboyant and talented tight end, Jeremy Shockey. He was an instant hit and headline-maker for what he did on the field and for what he did and said off the field.

Shockey helped Collins set team records with 335 completions, and they broke the team record with

ANOTHER LOSS FOR NEW YORK

The Giants were saddened in December 2001 by the death of their former general manager, George Young, of a rare neurological disease. After leaving the Giants following the 1997 season, he had been a valued advisor to Paul Tagliabue in the league's New York office. Young's arrival in 1979 signaled the start of a new era for the Giants. He had the wisdom to draft Phil Simms—the seventh overall draft choice—from tiny Morehead State in Kentucky in 1979. "Most people go for something safe, the big name, a nice satisfying thing for everybody," Simms said. "True to his character, he did what he believed."

Young was fortunate, picking second in 1981, when the Saints, picking first, drafted George Rogers over Lawrence Taylor. And he had the good sense to promote Bill Parcells from defensive coordinator to head coach in 1983 after Ray Perkins left for Alabama. Parcells said he would always be grateful to Young for taking a chance on him. "I just think George was really the consummate football guy," Parcells said. "He had tremendous respect for the history of the game, his predecessors, and the league. I feel very much that way myself. He was an upholder of the tradition, and I think people sometimes confuse that with being a little bit old-fashioned. I know I never did."

4,073 passing yards, 29 more than Simms had in 1984. Shockey, as a rookie, caught 74 passes, the fifth-highest total in team history, and he made the Pro Bowl.

But after the Giants lost to the expansion Houston Texans 16–14, and followed that with a disheartening 32–29 loss to Tennessee in overtime, their record dropped to 6–6. Were they going to play another meaningless December? Was Fassel on the way out?

Then the Giants offense began to click. The main reason Fassel had been hired was because he was considered an offensive guru. And in a three-week span, the Giants put up 27 points on the Redskins, 37 on Dallas, and 44 on the Colts.

Suddenly, the Giants' final game of the season against the Eagles became crucial in order to make the playoffs. The Giants beat Philadelphia 10–7 in overtime in one of the most compelling games in team history.

Tiki Barber had 276 yards of offense, and his 203 yards rushing was the second-highest total in team history. But he lost three fumbles and was fortunate to recover a fourth deep in Eagles territory in overtime. When Matt Bryant hit a 39-yard field goal to win it 5:10 into overtime, Barber sat on the bench and cried. He had one of the best games of his career—and one of the worst. "The gamut of emotions I went through were unbelievable," he said. "It's amazing I didn't have a mental breakdown on the sidelines afterwards."

The victory allowed the Giants to finish the season with a four-game winning streak and a 10–6 record. It also matched them up against the 49ers in the playoffs for the seventh time since 1981.

The Giants went into their game against San Francisco extremely confident. The 49ers also had finished 10–6, and were the NFC West champions. The Giants had lost to San Francisco, 16–13, in the league's inaugural Thursday night season opener, but the Giants offense was really clicking. The Giants went out and humiliated the 49ers for almost three quarters, thereby setting up the second-worst collapse in NFL playoff history.

The 49ers actually took a 7–0 lead at the outset, when Terrell Owens beat the Giants secondary on a 76-yard touchdown pass from Jeff Garcia. But then Collins caught fire, throwing four touchdowns in the first half, one to Shockey and three to Amani Toomer. It was 28–14 at the half, and the Giants kept pouring it on in the third quarter, with Barber scoring on a 6-yard run and Bryant kicking a 21-yard field goal with 4:27 left in the third quarter. Bryant's kick came after Shockey dropped a touchdown pass in the end zone. At the time, it seemed meaningless. What's the big deal—38–14 or 42–14? It became a very big deal.

Suddenly, the Giants offense shut down, and the defense couldn't stop the 49ers. Owens caught a 26-yard pass, then Garcia scored on a 14-yard run, then Jeff Chandler kicked a 25-yard field goal. The Giants clung to a 38–33 lead. And when Garcia threw a 13-yard touchdown pass to Tai Streets with one minute

The multitalented Tiki Barber has emerged as one of the best all-around backs in the league. Photo courtesy of AP/Wide World Photos.

remaining, the Giants, incredibly, were behind 39–38.

Delvin Joyce returned the kickoff 32 yards, and the Giants moved from their 48 to the 49ers' 23. Then, in the biggest botched play since The Fumble in 1978, the Giants attempted a 41-yard field goal for the win with six seconds left.

Trey Junkin, a 41-year-old, had been signed earlier in the week just to long snap. He sent the ball low and wide of holder Matt Allen. He could have quickly thrown it away—it was only third down—to give the Giants one more chance. Instead, he threw downfield to guard Rich Seubert, who was an eligible receiver. Seubert was deep in 49ers territory and wide open. He was interfered with on the play from behind by Chike Okeafor, but no flag was thrown. Instead, three officials flagged Tam Hopkins, another Giants lineman, for being an ineligible receiver.

It should have been off-setting penalties, giving the Giants another chance from the 41.

But the game was over. So was the Giants' season.

"This is about the worst loss I have ever felt in my entire life," Fassel said. "I'm not going to get over this one for awhile."

In fact, Fassel never did get over it.

The Giants opened the 2003 season by beating up Kurt Warner and the Rams. Warner fumbled six times and was sacked six times. But the next week, in Bill Parcells' return to Giants Stadium, this time as the coach of the Dallas Cowboys, the Giants came back from a 15-point deficit to take a 32–29 lead on Bryant's field goal with 11 seconds remaining.

But the kickoff rolled out of bounds, giving Dallas the ball at the Giants' 40. Quincy Carter then completed a 26-yard sideline pass to Antonio Bryant to set up Billy Cundiff's 52-yard field-goal on the final play of regulation. Cundiff hit the winning field goal, his seventh of the game, in overtime.

The problem was Fassel had not run enough time off the clock before he sent Bryant into the game. He admitted he was feeling "skittish" because of what happened on the field-goal attempt in San Francisco.

The following week the Giants came back and beat the Redskins in overtime, but then lost to the Dolphins and then the Patriots, for a record of 2–3 going into a huge home game against the Eagles, who were also 2–3.

It was the Giants' opportunity to make a statement to the Eagles, who had won the last two NFC East titles. They held Philadelphia to 134 yards of offense and only nine first downs, but ultimately lost another horrific game. The Giants led 10–7 until the Eagles' Brian Westbrook returned a punt 84 yards for a touchdown with 1:16 remaining.

The Giants came back the next week to beat the Vikings, and then they beat the Jets in overtime for a record of 4–4. But then the season fell completely apart. The Giants were decimated by injuries and lost their last eight games.

Two days after a humiliating 45–7 loss in New Orleans in a nationally televised game, Fassel asked management to confirm what he—and everyone else— already knew: he would be fired at the end of the season.

Fassel insisted on coaching the last two games, losses to the Cowboys and Panthers. He had made the playoffs three times in his seven seasons and took the Giants to the Super Bowl. In the up-and-down world of the NFL, it was not a bad run. He seemed relieved when the season was over and didn't complain about the organization not treating him fairly.

"It's time," Fassel said. "I need a change. They need a change. It's the right thing to do."

The Giants moved up in the 2002 draft to make certain they would get flamboyant tight end Jeremy Shockey out of the University of Miami. Photo courtesy of AP/Wide World Photos.

A NEW HOPE

The Giants—once more—needed a new head coach. On the day they announced that Jim Fassel would be fired after the 2003 season, team vice president John Mara, who had taken the lead role in the day-to-day operations of the club, said, "We're a franchise in trouble right now, and we need to make the right decision."

The 2004 off-season brought about some of the most eye-popping changes in club history. Tom Coughlin, who had shocked the Giants in 1993 when he turned down their head coaching job and elected to remain at Boston College, was hired to replace Fassel. Coughlin beat out Patriots assistants Charlie Weis and Romeo Crennel, both former Giants assistants.

Management craved the discipline and experience Coughlin brought to the table. If Fassel was a players' coach, then Coughlin was his opposite. He arrived with a well-deserved reputation of making things uncomfortable for his players. He had learned under Bill Parcells, who might have been the Giants' number one candidate if he hadn't gotten back into coaching the year before with the Cowboys.

"What we must be all about right now, immediately, is the restoration of pride—of self-pride, of team pride—and of the restoration of our professionalism and dignity with which we conduct our business," Coughlin said

at his introductory press conference on January 7. "We must restore our belief in the process by which we will win. And we must replace despair with hope and return the energy and the passion to New York Giants football."

Coughlin made his share of headlines even before training camp opened, when a handful of players complained to the union that the new coach was working them too hard. The players came off as whiners, and the public clearly sided with Coughlin. There wasn't much sympathy for players coming off a 4–12 season. He also created a stir during the regular season when he fined players if they didn't show up five minutes early for his team meetings.

The Coughlin headlines, however, paled in comparison to one of the most dramatic trades in team history. Ernie Accorsi drafted John Elway in 1983 when he was the general manager of the Baltimore Colts. Elway had insisted he would never play for the Colts, and Accorsi was willing to call his bluff. Colts owner Robert Irsay sent Elway to Denver. But Accorsi knew the value of a franchise quarterback, and when a second Elway-caliber player came along, he was consumed with trying to get in position to draft him. Accorsi sought Mississippi's Eli Manning, the younger brother of the Colts' Peyton and son of NFL veteran Archie.

Their 4–12 record slotted the Giants fourth in the annual draft. For weeks before the draft it was known the Chargers liked North Carolina State quarterback Philip Rivers better than Manning and would strongly consider trading out of their spot. The consensus was Manning was the better player and the Chargers would not risk losing Rivers by trading with the Giants.

But Accorsi and his San Diego counterpart, A. J. Smith, could not come to an agreement. A few days before the draft, Archie Manning informed Smith that his son Eli did not want to play for the Chargers. There was the possibility he would sit out the season and reenter the draft in 2005. Still, when Accorsi and Smith spoke the night before the draft, they were unable to bridge the gap on what the Chargers wanted and what the Giants were willing to give up.

The next day the draft began with San Diego on the clock. Smith never called Accorsi the morning of the draft, and Accorsi didn't pick up the phone, either. The Chargers selected Manning. Accorsi had heard a rumor in the hours leading up to the draft that San Diego's strategy would be to take Manning, then wait for the Giants to be on the clock before they reopened the lines of communication. The feeling was that in the 15 minutes each team is allotted to make its selection, the pressure would be on the Giants. And that's what happened. Smith called Accorsi just as he was talking to the Browns about moving down to the seventh spot, where New York would have taken Miami of Ohio quarterback Ben Roethlisberger.

The Giants quickly worked out a deal with San Diego: the Giants would get Manning and select Rivers for the Chargers. In addition, the Chargers received the Giants' third-round pick in 2004, and first- and fifth-round picks in 2005. It was a head-spinning day for Manning, who started off reluctantly wearing a Chargers cap and getting booed by fans at the draft in New York

Head coach Tom Coughlin (left) and rookie quarterback Eli Manning (right) were the headlining newcomers in 2004, and both endured growing pains during their first season in New York. Photos courtesy of AP/Wide World Photos.

and ended the day getting cheered by fans when he arrived at a draft party at Giants Stadium. He looked much more comfortable with the Giants cap.

It was a risky move by Accorsi. Kerry Collins had proven to be more than a serviceable quarterback and was popular in the locker room. But Accorsi believed Manning was one of the top quarterback prospects of the last 20 years, and was thus obligated to exhaust every possibility to make him a Giant. "I think he's got a chance to be a great quarterback," Accorsi said. "What I saw in Manning was a classic prospect—size, arm, tremendous athletic ability, poise, class. And probably more important than the obvious physical attributes is the fact that he lifted his team."

The Giants wanted Collins to remain for one last season to mentor Manning, but with no future in the organization, he was unwilling to restructure his contract and provide salary cap relief, thus forcing the Giants to cut him. Collins signed with the Raiders, and the Giants signed Kurt Warner, a two-time NFL MVP, to give them the luxury of easing Manning into the lineup.

Coughlin held an open competition between Warner and Manning in training camp, and the outcome was predictable: Warner won the job. That's what the Giants wanted. The classy Warner helped them get off to a surprising 5–2 start, but after losses to the Bears and Cardinals, two struggling clubs, Coughlin made the much-anticipated switch to Manning.

Manning did not hit the ground running.

He lost his first six starts, giving the Giants an eight-game losing streak to match the one that ended the 2003 season. He defeated the Cowboys in the final game of the season, which at least allowed him to go into the off-season not having to worry about when he was going to win his first game.

Once again the Giants had been decimated by injuries over the second half of the season. They finished 6–10—and the poor record was not Tiki Barber's fault. In his eighth season, Barber had a career year. He rushed for a team-record 1,518 yards, two more than Joe Morris' previous team record set in the Super Bowl year of 1986. Barber's total was fifth in the NFL, but he was first with 2,096 total yards from scrimmage, which was also a Giants record. He finished the season with 6,927 yards rushing for his career, putting him at the top of the Giants all-time list, ahead of Rodney Hampton, who finished with 6,897 yards on 291 more carries.

To date, Barber has caught 474 passes in his career, which is also number one on the Giants' all-time list. He is the only active player to be his team's all-time leader in rushing and receiving, and he joins Walter Payton of the Bears and James Wilder of the Bucs as the only players to hold that distinction.

Manning finished his rookie year with six touchdowns and nine interceptions. His play picked up in the final three games of his first season, giving the Giants hope that their investment in the future will pay quick dividends.

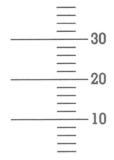

APPENDIX

Hall of Fame Giants

Enshrinee	Position	Year of Induction
Tim Mara	Founder/owner	Charter enshrinee, 1963
Wellington Mara	Co-owner	1997
Red Badgro	End (1930–1935)	1981
Rosie Brown	Tackle (1953–1965)	1975
Ray Flaherty	End (1928–1929, 1931–1935)	1976
Frank Gifford	Halfback (1952–1960, 1962–1964)	1977
Mel Hein	Center (1931–1945)	Charter enshrinee, 1963
Sam Huff	Linebacker (1956–1963)	1982
Tuffy Leemans	Halfback (1936–1943)	1978
Steve Owen	Coach (1931–1953)	1966
Andy Robustelli	Defensive end (1956–1964)	1971
Ken Strong	Halfback (1933–1935, 1939–1947)	1967
Lawrence Taylor	Linebacker (1981–1993)	1999
Y. A. Tittle	Quarterback (1961–1964)	1971
Emlen Tunnell	Defensive back (1948–1959)	1967
Arnie Weinmeister	Defensive tackle (1950–1953)	1984

Retired Jersey Numbers

1	Ray Flaherty
4	Tuffy Leemans
7	Mel Hein
11	Phil Simms
14	Y. A. Tittle
16	Frank Gifford
32	Al Blozis
40	Joe Morrison
42	Charlie Conerly
50	Ken Strong
56	Lawrence Taylor

Individual Records

Service

Most Seasons

15	Phil Simms	1979–1993
15	Mel Hein	1931–1945
14	George Martin	1975–1988
14	Joe Morrison	1959–1972
14	Charlie Conerly	1948–1961

Most Games

207	Howard Cross	1989–2001
201	George Martin	1975–1988
184	Lawrence Taylor	1981–1993
184	Joe Morrison	1959–1972
179	Greg Larson	1961–1973

Scoring

Most Points

646	Pete Gogolak	126 FG, 268 PAT
526	Brad Daluiso	123 FG, 157 PAT
484	Frank Gifford	78 TD, 2 FG, 10 PAT

Most Points, Season

127	Ali Haji-Sheikh	1983: 35 FG, 22 PAT
126	Joe Morris	1985: 21 TD
108	Matt Bryant	2002: 26 FG, 30 PAT

Most Points, Game

24	Rodney Hampton	9/24/95, vs. New Orleans
24	Earnest Gray	9/7/80, vs. St. Louis
24	Ron Johnson	10/2/72, vs. Philadelphia

Most Consecutive Games Scoring

61	Pete Gogolak	1969–1973
57	Ben Agajanian	1954–1957
47	Raul Allegre	1986–1991

Touchdowns

Most Touchdowns

78	Frank Gifford
65	Joe Morrison
56	Alex Webster

Most Touchdowns, Season

21	Joe Morris	1985
17	Gene Roberts	1949
15	Joe Morris	1986
15	Tiki Barber	2004

Most Touchdowns, Game

4	Rodney Hampton	9/24/95, vs. New Orleans
4	Earnest Gray	9/7/80, vs. St. Louis
4	Ron Johnson	10/2/72, vs. Philadelphia

Most Consecutive Games, Scoring Touchdowns

10	Frank Gifford	1957–1958
7	Kyle Rote	1959–1960
7	Bill Paschal	1944

Field Goals

Most Field Goals Attempted

219	Pete Gogolak	1966–1974
176	Joe Danelo	1976–1982
160	Brad Daluiso	1993–2000

Most Field Goals Attempted, Season

42	Ali Haji-Sheikh	1983
41	Pete Gogolak	1970
38	Joe Danelo	1981

Most Field Goals Attempted, Game

6   Many times, most recent:
    Raul Allegre, 11/16/86, vs. Minnesota

Most Field Goals

126	Pete Gogolak	1964–1974
123	Brad Daluiso	1993–2000
104	Joe Danelo	1976–1982

Most Field Goals, Season

35	Ali Haji-Sheikh	1983
26	Matt Bryant	2002
25	David Treadwell	1993
25	Pete Gogolak	1970

Most Field Goals, Game

6	Joe Danelo	10/18/81, vs. Seattle
5	Raul Allegre	11/16/86, vs. Minnesota
5	Eric Schubert	11/3/85, vs. Tampa Bay
5	Ali Haji-Sheikh	12/17/83, vs. Washington

Most Consecutive Games, Field Goals

18	Joe Danelo	1977–1979
15	Raul Allegre	1987–1989
15	Ali Haji-Sheikh	1983

Longest Field Goal

56	Ali Haji-Sheikh	11/7/83, vs. Detroit
56	Ali Haji-Sheikh	9/26/83, vs. Green Bay
55	Joe Danelo	9/20/81, vs. New Orleans

Extra Points

Most Extra Points Attempted

277	Pete Gogolak	1966–1974
176	Joe Danelo	1976–1982
159	Brad Daluiso	1993–2000
159	Ben Agajanian	1949, 1954–1957

Most Extra Points Attempted, Season

56	Don Chandler	1963
48	Don Chandler	1962
46	Pat Summerall	1961

Most Extra Points Attempted, Game

8	Pete Gogolak	11/26/72
7	many players	

Most Extra Points

268	Pete Gogolak	1966–1974
170	Joe Danelo	1976–1982
156	Brad Daluiso	1993–2000
156	Ben Agajanian	1949, 1954–1957

Most Extra Points, Season

52	Don Chandler	1963
47	Don Chandler	1962
46	Pat Summerall	1961

Most Extra Points, Game

8	Pete Gogolak	11/26/72
7	many players	

Most Consecutive Extra Points

133	Pete Gogolak	1967–1972
126	Pat Summerall	1958–1961
85	Brad Daluiso	1993–2000

Rushing

Most Attempts

1,824	Rodney Hampton	1990–1997
1,533	Tiki Barber	1997–2004
1,318	Joe Morris	1982–1989

Most Attempts, Season

341	Joe Morris	1986
327	Rodney Hampton	1994
325	Ottis Anderson	1989

Most Attempts, Game

43	Butch Woolfolk	11/20/83, vs. Philadelphia
41	Rodney Hampton	9/19/93, vs. Rams
38	Joe Montgomery	12/5/99, vs. Jets
38	Harry Newman	11/11/34, vs. Green Bay

Most Yards Gained

6,927	Tiki Barber	1997–2004
6,897	Rodney Hampton	1990–1997
5,296	Joe Morris	1982–1989

Most Yards Gained, Season

1,518	Tiki Barber	2004
1,516	Joe Morris	1986
1,387	Tiki Barber	2002

Most Yards Gained, Game

218	Gene Roberts	11/12/50, vs. Chicago Cardinals
203	Tiki Barber	12/28/2002, vs. Philadelphia
202	Joe Morris	12/21/85, vs. Pittsburgh

Most Games, 100+ Yards

22	Tiki Barber	1997–2004
19	Joe Morris	1982–1989
17	Rodney Hampton	1990–1997

Most Games, 100+ Yards, Season

9	Tiki Barber	2004
8	Joe Morris	1986
6	Gary Brown	1998
6	Joe Morris	1985

Highest Average Gain (500 Attempts)

4.50	Tiki Barber	1997–2004
4.30	Frank Gifford	1952–1960, 1962–1964
4.14	Mel Triplett	1955–1960

Highest Average Gain, Season

5.58	Eddie Price	1950
5.21	Tiki Barber	2001
5.15	Frank Gifford	1956

Highest Average Gain, Game (10 Attempts)

13.30	Frank Reagan	12/1/46, vs. Rams
12.23	Alphonse "Tuffy" Leemans	11/20/38, vs. Green Bay
11.43	Ernie Koy	10/1/67, vs. Washington

Most Rushing Touchdowns

49	Rodney Hampton	1990–1997
48	Joe Morris	1982–1989
41	Tiki Barber	1997–2004

Most Rushing Touchdowns, Season

21	Joe Morris	1985
14	Rodney Hampton	1992
14	Ottis Anderson	1989

Most Rushing Touchdowns, Game

4	Rodney Hampton	9/24/95, vs. New Orleans
3	many players	

Most Consecutive Games, Rushing Touchdowns

7	Bill Paschal	1944
6	Joe Morris	1985–1986
5	many players	

Passing

Most Attempted

4,647	Phil Simms	1979–1993
2,833	Charlie Conerly	1948–1961
2,473	Kerry Collins	1999–2003

Most Attempts, Season

568	Kerry Collins	2001
545	Kerry Collins	2002
533	Phil Simms	1984

Most Attempts, Game

62	Phil Simms	10/13/85, vs. Cincinnati
59	Kerry Collins	10/12/2003, vs. New England
59	Kerry Collins	1/6/2002, vs. Green Bay

Most Completions

2,576	Phil Simms	1979–1993
1,447	Kerry Collins	1999–2003
1,418	Charlie Conerly	1948–1961

Most Completions, Season

335	Kerry Collins	2002
327	Kerry Collins	2001
311	Kerry Collins	2000

Most Completions, Game

40	Phil Simms	10/13/85, vs. Cincinnati
36	Kerry Collins	1/6/2002, vs. Green Bay
36	Charlie Conerly	12/5/48, vs. Pittsburgh

Most Consecutive Completions

13	Kerry Collins	9/10-9/17/00 vs. Eagles-Bears
13	Phil Simms	10/13/85, vs. Cincinnati
12	Y. A. Tittle	10/28/62, vs. Washington

Highest Completion Percentage (1,000 Attempts)
58.51	Kerry Collins	1999–2003, 1,447 of 2,473
55.89	Y. A. Tittle	1961–1964, 731 of 1,308
55.43	Phil Simms	1979–1993, 2,576 of 4,647

Highest Completion Percentage, Season
62.81	Jeff Hostetler	1991, 179 of 285
61.75	Phil Simms	1993, 247 of 400
61.46	Kerry Collins	2003, 335 of 545

Highest Completion Percentage, Game (20 Attempts)
84.61	Kerry Collins vs. St. Louis	9/15/2002, 22 of 26
82.35	Jeff Hostetler vs. Dallas	9/29/91, 28 of 34
80.95	Phil Simms vs. Indianapolis	11/5/90, 17 of 21
80.95	Phil Simms vs. St. Louis	10/25/87, 17 of 21

Most Yards Passing
33,462	Phil Simms	1979–1993
19,488	Charlie Conerly	1948–1961
16,875	Kerry Collins	1999–2003

Most Yards Passing, Season
4,073	Kerry Collins	2002
4,044	Phil Simms	1984
3,829	Phil Simms	1985

Most Yards Passing, Game
513	Phil Simms	10/13/85, vs. Cincinnati
505	Y. A. Tittle	10/28/62, vs. Washington
432	Phil Simms	10/6/85, vs. Dallas

Most Games, 300 + Yards Passing
21	Phil Simms	1979–1993
17	Kerry Collins	1999–2003
9	Y. A. Tittle	1961–1964

Most Games, 300 + Yards Passing, Season
5	Kerry Collins	2001
4	many players	

Longest Pass Completion
98	Earl Morrall to Homer Jones, 9/11/66, vs. Pittsburgh
94	Norm Snead to Rich Houston, 9/24/72, vs. Dallas
89	Earl Morrall to Homer Jones, 10/17/65, vs. Philadelphia

Most Touchdown Passes
199	Phil Simms	1979–1993
173	Charlie Conerly	1948–1961
103	Fran Tarkenton	1967–1971

Most Touchdown Passes, Season
36	Y. A. Tittle	1963
33	Y. A. Tittle	1962
29	Fran Tarkenton	1967

Most Touchdown Passes, Game
7	Y. A. Tittle	10/28/62, vs. Washington
6	Y. A. Tittle	12/16/62, vs. Dallas
5	Phil Simms	9/7/80, vs. St. Louis
5	Fran Tarkenton	10/25/70, vs. St. Louis

Most Consecutive Games Touchdown Passes
15	Y. A. Tittle	1962–1964
10	Phil Simms	1988–1989
10	Phil Simms	1986–1987
10	Charlie Conerly	1948–1949

Most Passes Intercepted

167	Charlie Conerly	1949–1961
157	Phil Simms	1979–1993
72	Fran Tarkenton	1967–1971

Most Passes Intercepted, Season

25	Charlie Conerly	1953
25	Frank Filchock	1946
23	Joe Pisarcik	1978

Most Passes Intercepted, Game

5	many players	

Pass Receptions

Most Receptions

474	Tiki Barber	1997–2004
469	Amani Toomer	1996–2004
395	Joe Morrison	1959–1972

Most Receptions, Season

82	Amani Toomer	2002
79	Amani Toomer	1999
78	Amani Toomer	2000
78	Earnest Gray	1983

Most Receptions, Game

13	Tiki Barber	1/2/2000, vs. Dallas
12	Mark Bavaro	10/13/85, vs. Cincinnati
11	many players	

Most Consecutive Games, Reception

83	Amani Toomer	1998–2003
68	Ike Hilliard	1997–2002
47	Chris Calloway	1996–1998

Most Yards Gained, Receptions

7,113	Amani Toomer	1998–2004
5,434	Frank Gifford	1952–1960, 1962–1964
4,993	Joe Morrison	1959–1972

Most Yards, Season, Receptions

1,343	Amani Toomer	2002
1,209	Homer Jones	1967
1,181	Del Shofner	1963

Most Yards, Game, Receptions

269	Del Shofner	10/28/62, vs. Washington
212	Gene Roberts	10/23/49, vs. Green Bay
204	Amani Toomer	12/22/02, vs. Indianapolis

Highest Average Gain (200 Minimum)

22.6	Homer Jones	1964–1969, 214 for 4,845
18.1	Del Shofner	1961–1967, 239 for 4,315
17.2	Aaron Thomas	1962–1970, 247 for 4,253

Highest Average Gain, Season

24.7	Homer Jones	1967, 49 for 1,209
23.5	Homer Jones	1968, 45 for 1,057
21.8	Homer Jones	1966, 48 for 1,044

Highest Average Gain, Game (4 Minimum)

50.3	Homer Jones vs. Bears	10/23/49, 4 for 201
49.0	Homer Jones vs. Washington	10/1/67, 4 for 196
37.5	Frank Liebel vs. Detroit	11/18/45, 4 for 150

Most Touchdown Receptions

48	Kyle Rote	1951–1961
47	Joe Morrison	1959–1971
43	Frank Gifford	1952–1960, 1962–1964

Most Touchdown Receptions, Season

13	Homer Jones	1967
12	Del Shofner	1962
11	Del Shofner	1961

Most Touchdown Receptions, Game

4	Earnest Gray	9/7/80, vs. St. Louis
3	many players	

Kickoff Returns

Most Kickoff Returns

146	David Meggett	1989–1994
126	Clarence Childs	1964–1967
84	David Patten	1997–1999

Most Kickoff Returns, Season

55	Brian Mitchell	2003
43	David Patten	1998
41	Herschel Walker	1995

Most Kickoff Returns, Game

8	Brian Mitchell	9/15/2003, vs. Dallas
7	many players	

Most Kickoff Return Yardage

3,163	Clarence Childs	1964–1967
2,989	David Meggett	1989–1994
1,768	Symonds "Rocky" Thompson	1971–1973

Most Kickoff Return Yardage, Season

1,117	Brian Mitchell	2003
987	Clarence Childs	1964
947	Symonds "Rocky" Thompson	1971

Most Kickoff Return Yardage, Game

207	Joe Scott	11/14/48, vs. Rams
198	Symonds "Rocky" Thompson	9/17/72, vs. Detroit
194	Brian Mitchell	9/15/2003, vs. Dallas

Longest Kickoff Return

100	Clarence Childs	12/6/64, vs. Minnesota
100	Emlen Tunnell	11/4/51, vs. N.Y. Yanks
99	Joe Scott	11/14/48, vs. Rams

Most Kickoff Return Touchdowns

2	Symonds "Rocky" Thompson	1971–1973
2	Clarence Childs	1964–1967

Most Kickoff Return Touchdowns, Season

1	many players

Punt Returns

Most Punt Returns

261	Emlen Tunnell	1948–1958
213	Phil McConkey	1984–1988
202	David Meggett	1989–1994

Most Punt Returns, Season

53	Phil McConkey	1985
52	Leon Bright	1981
47	Amani Toomer	1997

Most Punt Returns, Game

9	Phil McConkey	12/6/87, vs. Philadelphia
9	Pete Shaw	11/20/83, vs. Philadelphia
9	Leon Bright	12/11/82, vs. Philadelphia

Most Punt-Return Yardage

2,230	David Meggett	1989–1994
2,214	Emlen Tunnell	1948–1958
1,708	Phil McConkey	1984–1988

Most Punt-Return Yardage, Season

582	David Meggett	1989
506	Tiki Barber	1999
489	Emlen Tunnell	1951

Most Punt-Return Yardage, Game

147	Emlen Tunnell	10/14/51, vs. Chicago Cardinals
143	Leon Bright	12/11/82, vs. Philadelphia
123	Tiki Barber	10/18/99, vs. Dallas

Longest Punt Return

87	Amani Toomer	9/1/96, vs. Buffalo
85	Tiki Barber	10/18/99, vs. Dallas
83	Eddie Dove	9/29/63, vs. Philadelphia

Most Punt-Return Touchdowns

6	David Meggett	1989–1994
5	Emlen Tunnell	1948–1958
3	Amani Toomer	1996–2001

Most Punt-Return Touchdowns, Season

3	Emlen Tunnell	1951
2	Amani Toomer	1996
2	David Meggett	1994

Most Punt-Return Touchdowns, Game

1	many players

Interceptions

Most Interceptions

74	Emlen Tunnell	1948–1958
52	Jimmy Patton	1955–1966
41	Carl Lockhart	1965–1975

Most Interceptions, Season

11	Jimmy Patton	1958
11	Otto Schnellbacher	1951
10	many players	

Most Interceptions, Game

3	many players

Most Consecutive Games, Interception

7	Tom Landry	1950–1951
6	Willie Williams	1968
5	Carl Lockhart	1969–1970
5	Emlen Tunnell	1954–1955

Most Yardage, Interceptions

1,240	Emlen Tunnell	1948–1958
712	Jimmy Patton	1955–1966
574	Terry Kinard	1983–1989

Most Yardage, Season, Interceptions

251	Dick Lynch	1963
251	Emlen Tunnell	1949
203	Frank Reagan	1947

Most Yardage, Game, Interceptions

109	Ward Cuff	9/13/41, vs. Philadelphia
104	George Cheverko	10/3/48, vs. Washington
102	Erich Barnes	10/15/61, vs. Dallas

Longest Interception Return

102	Erich Barnes	10/15/61, vs. Dallas
101	Henry Carr	11/13/66, vs. Rams
97	Lawrence Taylor	11/25/82, vs. Detroit

Most Interception Touchdowns

4	Jason Sehorn	1994–2002
4	Dick Lynch	1959–1966
4	Emlen Tunnell	1948–1958

Most Interception Touchdowns, Season

3	Dick Lynch	1963
2	many players	

Most Interception Touchdowns, Game

1	many players

Sacks

Most Sacks

132½	Lawrence Taylor	1981–1993
118	Michael Strahan	1993–2004
79½	Leonard Marshall	1983–1992

Most Sacks, Season

22½	Michael Strahan	2001
20½	Lawrence Taylor	1986
18½	Michael Strahan	2003

Most Sacks, Game

4¹/₂	Pepper Johnson	11/24/91, vs. Tampa Bay
4	Michael Strahan	10/14/01, vs. St. Louis
4	Lawrence Taylor	10/12/86, vs. Philadelphia
4	Lawrence Taylor	9/23/84, vs. Tampa Bay

Fumble Recoveries

Most Recoveries

19	Jim Katcavage	1956–1968
15	George Martin	1975–1988
14	Harry Carson	1976–1988

Most Recoveries, Season

5	Ernie Jones	1978
5	Ray Poole	1950
4	many players	

Most Recoveries, Game

| 2 | many players | |

Longest Recovery Return

87	Keith Hamilton	9/10/95, vs. Kansas City
81	Andy Headen	9/9/84, vs. Dallas
72	Wendell Harris	9/11/66, vs. Pittsburgh

Punting

Most Punts

931	Dave Jennings	1974–1984
526	Sean Landeta	1985–1993
525	Don Chandler	1956–1964

Most Punts, Season

111	Brad Maynard	1997
104	Dave Jennings	1979
102	Mike Horan	1996

Most Punts, Game

14	Carl Kinscherf	11/7/43, vs. Detroit
13	Brad Maynard	11/23/97, vs. Washington
12	Brad Maynard	9/12/99, vs. Tampa Bay

Most Punting Yardage

38,792	Dave Jennings	1974–1984
23,019	Don Chandler	1956–1964
22,806	Sean Landeta	1985–1993

Most Punting Yardage, Season

4,566	Brad Maynard	1998
4,531	Brad Maynard	1997
4,445	Dave Jennings	1979

Most Punting Yardage, Game

583	Carl Kinscherf	11/7/43, vs. Detroit
537	Brad Maynard	11/23/97, vs. Washington
526	Brad Maynard	9/12/99, vs. Tampa Bay

Longest Punt

90	Rodney Williams	9/10/01, vs. Denver
74	Don Chandler	10/11/64, vs. Dallas
74	Len Younce	11/14/43, vs. Bears

Highest Punting Average (150 Minimum)

43.8	Don Chandler	525, 1956–1964
43.4	Sean Landeta	526, 1985–1993
42.1	Mike Horan	303, 1993–1996

Highest Punting Average, Season (35 Minimum)

46.6	Don Chandler	55, 1959
45.6	Don Chandler	73, 1964
45.2	Brad Maynard	101, 1998

Highest Punting Average, Game (4 Minimum)

55.4	Brad Maynard	5, 10/1/00
55.3	Dave Jennings	4, 12/5/82
55.1	Rodney Williams	8, 9/10/01

Fumbles

Most Fumbles

93	Phil Simms	1979–1993
61	Kerry Collins	1999–2003
54	Charlie Conerly	1948–1961

Most Fumbles, Season

23	Kerry Collins	2001
16	Phil Simms	1985
11	many players	

Most Fumbles, Game

5	Charlie Conerly	12/1/57, vs. San Francisco
4	Y. A. Tittle	9/13/64, vs. Philadelphia
3	many players	

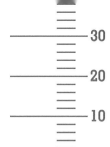

INDEX